Frederic P. Miller, Agnes F. Vandome,
John McBrewster (Ed.)

Copywriting

**Person, Business, Opinion, Idea, Copy
(written), Advertising, Television, Radio,
Mass media, Marketing, Promotion
(marketing), Persuasion, Product
(business), Perspective (cognitive)**

Alphascript Publishing

Imprint

Permission is granted to copy, distribute and/or modify this document under the terms of the GNU Free Documentation License, Version 1.2 or any later version published by the Free Software Foundation; with no Invariant Sections, with the Front-Cover Texts, and with the Back-Cover Texts. A copy of the license is included in the section entitled "GNU Free Documentation License".

All parts of this book are extracted from Wikipedia, the free encyclopedia (www.wikipedia.org).

You can get detailed informations about the authors of this collection of articles at the end of this book. The editors (Ed.) of this book are no authors. They have not modified or extended the original texts.

Pictures published in this book can be under different licences than the GNU Free Documentation License. You can get detailed informations about the authors and licences of pictures at the end of this book.

The content of this book was generated collaboratively by volunteers. Please be advised that nothing found here has necessarily been reviewed by people with the expertise required to provide you with complete, accurate or reliable information. Some information in this book maybe misleading or wrong. The Publisher does not guarantee the validity of the information found here. If you need specific advice (f.e. in fields of medical, legal, financial, or risk management questions) please contact a professional who is licensed or knowledgeable in that area.

Any brand names and product names mentioned in this book are subject to trademark, brand or patent protection and are trademarks or registered trademarks of their respective holders. The use of brand names, product names, common names, trade names, product descriptions etc. even without a particular marking in this works is in no way to be construed to mean that such names may be regarded as unrestricted in respect of trademark and brand protection legislation and could thus be used by anyone.

Cover image: www.PureStockX.com
Concerning the licence of the cover image please contact PureStockX.

Publisher:
Alphascript Publishing is a trademark of
VDM Publishing House Ltd.,17 Rue Meldrum, Beau Bassin,1713-01 Mauritius
Email: info@vdm-publishing-house.com
Website: www.vdm-publishing-house.com

Published in 2010

Printed in: U.S.A., U.K., Germany. This book was not produced in Mauritius.

ISBN: 978-613-0-70973-0

Contents

Articles

References

Copywriting

Copywriting is the use of words to promote a → person, → business, → opinion or → idea. Although the word → *copy* may be applied to any content intended for printing (as in the body of a newspaper article or book), the term *copywriter* is generally limited to such promotional situations, regardless of media (as advertisements for print, → television, → radio or other → media). The author of newspaper or magazine copy, for example, is generally called a reporter or writer or a copywriter.

(Although the word *copywriting* is regularly used as a noun or gerund, and *copywrite* is sometimes used as a verb by professionals.)

Thus, the purpose of → marketing copy, or → promotional text, is to → persuade the reader, listener or viewer to act — for example, to buy a → product or subscribe to a certain → viewpoint. Alternatively, copy might also be intended to dissuade a reader.

Copywriting can appear in direct mail pieces, taglines, → jingle → lyrics, → web page content (although if the purpose is not ultimately promotional, its author might prefer to be called a *content writer*), online ads, → e-mail and other → Internet content, → television or → radio commercial → scripts, → press releases, white papers, → catalogs, billboards, brochures, postcards, sales letters, and other → marketing communications media.

Content writing on → websites is also referred to as copywriting, and may include among its objectives the achievement of higher → rankings in search engines. Known as "organic" → *search engine optimization* (SEO), this practice involves the → strategic placement and repetition of keywords and keyword phrases on web pages, writing in a manner that human readers would consider normal.

Copywriters

Most copywriters are employees within organizations such as advertising agencies, public relations firms, web developers, company advertising departments, large stores, marketing firms, broadcasters and cable providers, newspapers, book publishers and magazines. Copywriters can also be independent contractors freelancing for a variety of clients, at the clients' offices or working from their own, or partners or employees in specialized copywriting agencies.

A copywriter usually works as part of a creative team. Agencies and advertising departments partner copywriters with art directors. The copywriter has ultimate responsibility for the advertisement's verbal or textual content, which often includes receiving the copy information from the client. (Where this formally extends into the role of account executive, the job may be described as "copy/contact.") The art director has ultimate responsibility for visual communication and, particularly in the case of print work, may oversee production. Either person may come up with the overall idea for the advertisement or commercial (typically referred to as the concept or "big idea"), and the process of collaboration often improves the work.

Copywriters are similar to technical writers and the careers may overlap. Broadly speaking, however, technical writing is dedicated to informing readers rather than persuading them. For example, a copywriter writes an ad to sell a car, while a technical writer writes the operator's manual explaining how to use it.

Because the words sound alike, copywriters are sometimes confused with people who work in copyright law. These careers are unrelated.

Famous copywriters include David Ogilvy, William Bernbach and Leo Burnett. Many creative artists spent some of their career as copywriters before becoming famous for other things, including Peter Carey, Dorothy L. Sayers, Viktor Pelevin, Eric Ambler, Joseph Heller, Terry Gilliam, William S. Burroughs, Salman Rushdie, Don DeLillo, Lawrence Kasdan, Fay Weldon, Philip Kerr and Shigesato Itoi. (Herschell Gordon Lewis, on the other hand, became famous for directing violent exploitation films, then became a very successful copywriter.)

The Internet has expanded the range of copywriting opportunities to include web content, ads, commercial emails and other online media. It has also brought new opportunities for copywriters to learn their craft, conduct research and view others' work. And the Internet has made it easier for employers, copywriters and art directors to find each other.

As a result of these factors, along with increased use of independent contractors and virtual commuting generally, freelancing has become a more viable job option, particularly in certain copywriting specialties and markets. A generation ago, professional freelance copywriters (except those between full-time jobs) were rare.

While schooling may be a good start or supplement in a budding copywriter's professional education, working as part of an advertising team arguably remains the best way for novices to gain the experience and business sense required by many employers, and expands the range of career opportunities.

See also

- List of copywriters
- List of former copywriters
- → Copy (written)
- SEO Copywriting
- → Advertising
- White papers
- Swipe file
- → Search engine optimization
- Communication design

Person

A **person** is a legal concept both permitting rights to and imposing duties on one by law. In the fields of law, philosophy, medicine, and others, the term has specialised context-specific meanings.

In many jurisdictions, for example, a corporation is considered a legal person with standing to sue or be sued in court. In philosophy and medicine, *person* may mean only humans who are capable of certain kinds of thought.[1] [2] This could also extend to late fetuses and neonates, dependent on what level of thought is required.

Scientific approach

As an application of Social psychology and other disciplines, phenomena such as the *perception* and *attribution* of personhood have been scientifically studied.[3] [4] Typical questions addressed in social psychology are the accuracy of attribution, processes of perception and the formation of bias. Various other scientific/medical disciplines address the myriad of issues in the development of personality.

Individual rights and responsibility

Closely related to the debate on the definition of personhood is the relationship between persons, individual rights, and ethical responsibility. Many philosophers would agree that all and only people are expected to be ethically responsible, and that all people deserve a varying degree of individual rights. There is less consensus on whether only people deserve individual rights and whether people deserve greater individual rights than non-people. The rights of animals are an example of contention on this issue.

Who is a person?

- Persons - In contemporary global thought, once humans are born, personhood is considered automatic via Legal fiction created by a Birth certificate.
- Animals - Some philosophers and those involved in animal welfare, ethology, animal rights and related subjects, consider that certain animals should also be granted personhood. Commonly named species in this context include the Great Apes and possibly cetaceans or elephants, due to the acknowledged intelligence and intricate societies of such species. In animistic religion, animals, plants, and other entities may be persons or deities.
- Certain societal constructs - certain social entities, are considered legally as persons, for example some corporations and other legal entities. This is known as legal, or corporate, personhood.

In addition speculatively, there are several other likely categories of beings where personhood might be at issue:

- Unknown intelligent life-forms - for example, should alien life be found to exist, under what circumstances would they be counted as 'persons'?
- Artificially created life - at what point might human-created biological life be considered to have achieved personhood?
- Artificial intelligence - assuming the eventual creation of an intelligent and self-aware system of hardware and software, what criteria would be used to confer or withhold the status of person?
- Modified living humans, cyborgs - for example, how much of a human can be replaced by artificial parts before personhood is lost, if ever?
  - Further, if the brain is the reason people are considered persons, then if the human brain and all its thought patterns, memories and other attributes could also in future be transposed faithfully into some form of artificial device (for example to avoid illness such as brain cancer) would the patient still be considered a 'person' after the operation?
  - If the person (or "individual") could go back in time and relate to his/her earlier self. Would it then be two persons yet the same being. Or one person in two bodies?
  - Are the surgical separations of conjoined twins cases more complicated, challenging and controversial than abortion?
- Do we have to consider any "willing and communicative (capable to register its own will) autonomous body" in the universe, no matter the species, an individual (a person)? Do they deserve equal rights with the human race?

Such questions are used by philosophers to clarify thinking concerning what it means to be human, or living, or a person, or an individual.

Implications of the person/non-person debate

The personhood theory has become a pivotal issue in the interdisciplinary field of bioethics. While historically most humans did not enjoy full legal protection as persons (women, children, non-landowners, minorities, slaves, etc.), from the late 18th through the late 20th century, being born as a member of the human species gradually became secular grounds for the basic rights of liberty, freedom from persecution, and humanitarian care.

Since modern movements emerged to oppose animal cruelty (and advocate vegan philosophy) and theorists like Turing have recognized the possibility of artificial minds with human-level competence, the identification of personhood protections exclusively with human species membership has been challenged. On the other hand, some proponents of human exceptionalism (also referred to by its critics as speciesism) have countered that we must institute a strict demarcation of personhood based on species membership in order to avoid the horrors of genocide (based on propaganda dehumanizing one or more ethnicities) or the injustices of forced sterilization (as occurred in many countries to people with low I.Q. scores and prisoners).

While the former advocates tend to be comfortable constraining personhood status within the human species based on basic capacities (e.g. excluding human stem cells, fetuses, and bodies that cannot recover awareness), the latter often wish to include all these forms of human bodies even if they have never had awareness (which some would call *pre-people*) or had awareness, but could never have awareness again due to massive and irrecoverable brain damage (some would call these *post-people*). The Vatican has recently been advancing a human exceptionalist understanding of personhood theory, while other communities, such as Christian Evangelicals in the U.S. have sometimes rejected the personhood theory as biased against human exceptionalism. Of course, many religious communities (of many traditions) view the other versions of the personhood theory perfectly compatible with their faith, as do the majority of modern Humanists.

The theoretical landscape of the personhood theory has been altered recently by controversy in the bioethics community concerning an emerging community of scholars, researchers, and activists identifying with an explicitly Transhumanist position, which supports morphological freedom, even if a person changed so much as to no longer be considered a member of the human species (by whatever standard is used to determine that).

Nonhuman sentient beings as persons

The idea of extending personhood to all animals has the support of legal scholars such as Alan Dershowitz[5] and Laurence Tribe of Harvard Law School,[6] and animal law courses are now taught in 92 out of 180 law schools in the United States.[7] On May 9, 2008, Columbia University Press published Animals as Persons: Essays on the Abolition of Animal Exploitation [8] by Professor Gary L. Francione of Rutgers University School of Law, a collection of writings that summarizes his work to date and makes the case for non-human animals as persons.

There are also hypothetical persons, sentient non-human persons such as sentient extraterrestrial life and self aware machines. The novel and animated series Ghost in the Shell touch on the potential of inorganic sentience, while classical works of fiction and fantasy regarding extraterrestrials have challenged people to reconsider long held traditional definitions.

See also

- Legal fiction
- Surety
- Anthropocentrism
- Anthropology
- Beginning of human personhood
- Being
- Consciousness
- Corporate Personhood Debate
- Great Ape personhood
- Juridical person
- Juristic person
- Kant
- Nonperson
- People
- People (disambiguation)
- Personoid
- Phenomenology
- Subject (philosophy)
- Theory of mind
- Citizenship

References

- *The category of the person. Anthropology, philosophy, history* Edited by M. Carruthers, S. Collins, and L. Steven. Cambridge: Cambridge University Press 1985
- Cornelia J.de Vogel *The concept of personality in Greek and Christian thought*. In Studies in philosophy and the history of philosophy. Vol. 2. Edited by J. K. Ryan, Washington: Catholic University of America Press 1963. pp. 20-60

External links

- *Stanford Encyclopedia of Philosophy*
- *The Internet Encyclopedia of Philosophy* [9]
- Carsten Korfmacher, 'Personal Identity' [10], in the IEP
- "Person" [11]. *Catholic Encyclopedia*. New York: Robert Appleton Company. 1913.

References

[1] Strawson, P.F. 1959. *Individuals*. London: Methuen: 104.

[2] Locke, John. 1961. *Essay Concerning Human Understanding*. London:Dent: 280.

[3] Person Perception. Second Edition. Schneider, Hastdorf, and Ellsworth. 1979, Addison Wesley ISBN 0-201-06768-4

[4] Second-Language Fluency and Person Perception in China and the United States (http://jls.sagepub.com/cgi/content/abstract/10/2/99)

[5] Dershowitz, Alan. *Rights from Wrongs: A Secular Theory of the Origins of Rights*, 2004, pp. 198–99, and "Darwin, Meet Dershowitz," *The Animals' Advocate*, Winter 2002, volume 21.

[6] "'Personhood' Redefined: Animal Rights Strategy Gets at the Essence of Being Human" (http://www.aamc.org/newsroom/reporter/oct03/animalrights.htm), Association of American Medical Colleges, retrieved July 12, 2006.

[7] "Animal law courses" (http://www.aldf.org/content/index.php?pid=83), Animal Legal Defense Fund.

[8] http://www.columbia.edu/cu/cup/catalog/data/978023113/9780231139502.HTM

[9] http://www.iep.utm.edu/

[10] http://www.iep.utm.edu/p/person-i.htm

[11] http://en.wikipedia.org/wiki/Wikisource%3Acatholic_encyclopedia_%281913%29%2Fperson

Business

A **business** (also called a **company, enterprise** or **firm**) is a legally recognized organization designed to provide goods and/or services to consumers.[1] Businesses are predominant in capitalist economies, most being privately owned and formed to earn profit that will increase the wealth of its owners and grow the business itself. The owners and operators of a business have as one of their main objectives *the receipt or generation of a financial return* in exchange for work and acceptance of risk. Notable exceptions include cooperative enterprises and state-owned enterprises. Businesses can also be formed not-for-profit or be state-owned.

The etymology of "business" relates to the state of being busy either as an individual or society as a whole, doing commercially viable and profitable work. The term "business" has at least three usages, depending on the scope — the singular usage (above) to mean a particular company or corporation, the generalized usage to refer to a particular market sector, such as "the music business" and compound forms such as agribusiness, or the broadest meaning to include all activity by the community of suppliers of goods and services. However, the exact definition of business, like much else in the philosophy of business, is a matter of debate and complexity of meanings

Basic forms of ownership

Although forms of business ownership vary by jurisdiction, there are several common forms:

- **Sole proprietorship:** A sole proprietorship is a business owned by one person. The owner may operate on his or her own or may employ others. The owner of the business has personal liability of the debts incurred by the business.
- **Partnership:** A partnership is a form of business in which two or more people operate for the common goal which is often making profit. In most forms of partnerships, each partner has personal liability of the debts incurred by the business. There are three typical classifications of partnerships: general partnerships, limited partnerships, and limited liability partnerships.
- **Corporation:** A corporation is either a limited or unlimited liability entity that has a separate legal personality from its members. A corporation can be organized for-profit or not-for-profit. A corporation is owned by multiple shareholders and is overseen by a board of directors, which hires the business's managerial staff. In addition to privately-owned corporate models, there are state-owned corporate models.
- **Cooperative:** Often referred to as a "co-op", a cooperative is a limited liability entity that can organize for-profit or not-for-profit. A cooperative differs from a corporation in that it has members, as opposed to shareholders, who share decision-making authority. Cooperatives are typically classified as either consumer cooperatives or worker cooperatives. Cooperatives are fundamental to the ideology of economic democracy.

For a country-by-country listing of legally recognized business forms, see Types of business entity.

Classifications

There are many types of businesses, and because of this, businesses are classified in many ways. One of the most common focuses on the primary profit-generating activities of a business:

Wall Street, Manhattan is the location of the New York Stock Exchange and is often used as a symbol for the world of business.

- Agriculture and mining businesses are concerned with the production of raw material, such as plants or minerals.
- Financial businesses include banks and other companies that generate profit through investment and management of capital.
- Information businesses generate profits primarily from the resale of intellectual property and include movie studios, publishers and packaged software companies.
- Manufacturers produce → products, from raw materials or component parts, which they then sell at a profit. Companies that make physical goods, such as cars or pipes, are considered manufacturers.
- Real estate businesses generate profit from the selling, renting, and development of properties, homes, and buildings.
- Retailers and Distributors act as middle-men in getting goods produced by manufacturers to the intended consumer, generating a profit as a result of providing sales or distribution services. Most consumer-oriented stores and catalogue companies are distributors or retailers. *See also:* Franchising
- Service businesses offer intangible goods or services and typically generate a profit by charging for labor or other services provided to government, other businesses or consumers. Organizations ranging from house decorators to consulting firms to restaurants and even to entertainers are types of service businesses.
- Transportation businesses deliver goods and individuals from location to location, generating a profit on the transportation costs
- Utilities produce public services, such as heat, electricity, or sewage treatment, and are usually government chartered.

There are many other divisions and subdivisions of businesses. The authoritative list of business types for North America is generally considered to be the North American Industry Classification System, or NAICS. The equivalent European Union list is the NACE.

Management

The efficient and effective operation of a business, and study of this subject, is called management. The main branches of management are financial management, → marketing management, human resource management, strategic management, production management, service management, information technology management, and business intelligence.

Reforming State Enterprises

In recent decades, assets and enterprises that were run by various states have been modeled after business enterprises. In 2003, the People's Republic of China reformed 80% of its state-owned enterprises and modeled them on a company-type management system.[2] Many state institutions and enterprises in China and Russia have been transformed into joint-stock companies, with part of their shares being listed on public stock markets.

Government regulation

Most legal jurisdictions specify the forms of ownership that a business can take, creating a body of commercial law for each type.

Organizing

The major factors affecting how a business is organized are usually:

The Bank of England in Threadneedle Street, London, England.

- **The size and scope of the business**, and its anticipated management and ownership. Generally a smaller business is more flexible, while larger businesses, or those with wider ownership or more formal structures, will usually tend to be organized as partnerships or (more commonly) corporations. In addition a business which wishes to raise money on a stock market or to be owned by a wide range of people will often be required to adopt a specific legal form to do so.
- **The sector and country.** Private profit making businesses are different from government owned bodies. In some countries, certain businesses are legally obliged to be organized certain ways.
- **Limited liability.** Corporations, limited liability partnerships, and other specific types of business organizations protect their owners or shareholders from business failure by doing business under a separate legal entity with certain legal protections. In contrast, unincorporated businesses or persons working on their own are usually not so protected.
- **Tax advantages.** Different structures are treated differently in tax law, and may have advantages for this reason.
- **Disclosure and compliance requirements**. Different business structures may be required to make more or less information public (or reported to relevant authorities), and may be bound to comply with different rules and regulations.

Many businesses are operated through a separate entity such as a corporation or a partnership (either formed with or without limited liability). Most legal jurisdictions allow people to organize such an entity by filing certain charter documents with the relevant Secretary of State or equivalent and complying with certain other ongoing obligations. The relationships and legal rights of shareholders, limited partners, or members are governed partly by the charter documents and partly by the law of the jurisdiction where the entity is organized. Generally speaking, shareholders in a corporation, limited partners in a limited partnership, and members in a limited liability company are shielded from personal liability for the debts and obligations of the entity, which is legally treated as a separate "person." This means that unless there is misconduct, the owner's own possessions are strongly protected in law, if the business does not succeed.

Where two or more individuals own a business together but have failed to organize a more specialized form of vehicle, they will be treated as a general partnership. The terms of a partnership are partly governed by a partnership agreement if one is created, and partly by the law of the jurisdiction where the partnership is located. No paperwork or filing is necessary to create a partnership, and without an agreement, the relationships and legal rights of the partners will be entirely governed by the law of the jurisdiction where the partnership is located.

A single person who owns and runs a business is commonly known as a *sole proprietor*, whether he or she owns it directly or through a formally organized entity.

A few relevant factors to consider in deciding how to operate a business include:

1. General partners in a partnership (other than a limited liability partnership), plus anyone who personally owns and operates a business without creating a separate legal entity, are personally liable for the debts and obligations of the business.
2. Generally, corporations are required to pay tax just like "real" people. In some tax systems, this can give rise to so-called double taxation, because first the corporation pays tax on the profit, and then when the corporation distributes its profits to its owners, individuals have to include dividends in their income when they complete their personal tax returns, at which point a second layer of income tax is imposed.
3. In most countries, there are laws which treat small corporations differently than large ones. They may be exempt from certain legal filing requirements or labor laws, have simplified procedures in specialized areas, and have simplified, advantageous, or slightly different tax treatment.
4. To "go public" (sometimes called IPO) -- which basically means to allow a part of the business to be owned by a wider range of investors or the public in general—you must organize a separate entity, which is usually required to comply with a tighter set of laws and procedures. Most public entities are corporations that have sold shares, but increasingly there are also public LLCs that sell units (sometimes also called shares), and other more exotic entities as well (for example, REITs in the USA, Unit Trusts in the UK). However, you cannot take a general partnership "public."

Commercial law

Most commercial transactions are governed by a very detailed and well-established body of rules that have evolved over a very long period of time, it being the case that governing trade and commerce was a strong driving force in the creation of law and courts in Western civilization.

As for other laws that regulate or impact businesses, in many countries it is all but impossible to chronicle them all in a single reference source. There are laws governing treatment of labor and generally relations with employees, safety and protection issues (OSHA or Health and Safety), anti-discrimination laws (age, gender, disabilities, race, and in some jurisdictions, sexual orientation), minimum wage laws, union laws, workers compensation laws, and annual vacation or working hours time.

In some specialized businesses, there may also be licenses required, either due to special laws that govern entry into certain trades, occupations or professions, which may require special education, or by local governments. Professions that require special licenses range from law and medicine to flying airplanes to selling liquor to radio broadcasting to selling investment securities to selling used cars to roofing. Local jurisdictions may also require special licenses and taxes just to operate a business without regard to the type of business involved.

Some businesses are subject to ongoing special regulation. These industries include, for example, public utilities, investment securities, banking, insurance, broadcasting, aviation, and health care providers. Environmental regulations are also very complex and can impact many kinds of businesses in unexpected ways.

Capital

When businesses need to raise money (called 'capital'), more laws come into play. A highly complex set of laws and regulations govern the offer and sale of investment securities (the means of raising money) in most Western countries. These regulations can require disclosure of a lot of specific financial and other information about the business and give buyers certain remedies. Because "securities" is a very broad term, most investment transactions will be potentially subject to these laws, unless a special exemption is available.

Capital may be raised through private means, by public offer (IPO) on a stock exchange, or in many other ways. Major stock exchanges include the Shanghai Stock Exchange, Singapore Exchange, Hong Kong Stock Exchange, New York Stock Exchange and Nasdaq (USA), the London Stock Exchange (UK), the Tokyo Stock Exchange (Japan), and so on. Most countries with capital markets have at least one.

Business that have gone "public" are subject to extremely detailed and complicated regulation about their internal governance (such as how executive officers' compensation is determined) and when and how information is disclosed to the public and their shareholders. In the United States, these regulations are primarily implemented and enforced by the United States Securities and Exchange Commission (SEC). Other Western nations have comparable regulatory bodies. The regulations are implemented and enforced by the China Securities Regulation Commission (CSRC), in China. In Singapore, the regulation authority is Monetary Authority of Singapore (MAS), and in Hong Kong, it is Securities and Futures Commission (SFC).

As noted at the beginning, it is impossible to enumerate all of the types of laws and regulations that impact on business today. In fact, these laws have become so numerous and complex, that no business lawyer can learn them all, forcing increasing specialization among corporate attorneys. It is not unheard of for teams of 5 to 10 attorneys to be required to handle certain kinds of corporate transactions, due to the sprawling nature of modern regulation. Commercial law spans general corporate law, employment and labor law, healthcare law, securities law, M&A law (who specialize in acquisitions), tax law, ERISA law (ERISA in the United States governs employee benefit plans), food and drug regulatory law, intellectual property law (specializing in copyrights, patents, trademarks and such), telecommunications law, and more.

In Thailand, for example, it is necessary to *register* a particular amount of capital for each employee, and pay a fee to the government for the amount of capital registered. There is no legal requirement to prove that this capital actually exists, the only requirement is to pay the fee. Overall, processes like this are detrimental to the development and GDP of a country, but often exist in "feudal" developing countries.

Intellectual property

Businesses often have important "intellectual property" that needs protection from competitors for the company to stay profitable. This could require patents or copyrights or preservation of trade secrets. Most businesses have names, logos and similar branding techniques that could benefit from trademarking. Patents and copyrights in the United States are largely governed by federal law, while trade secrets and trademarking are mostly a matter of state law. Because of the nature of intellectual property, a business needs protection in every jurisdiction in which they are concerned about competitors. Many countries are signatories to international treaties concerning intellectual property, and thus companies registered in these countries are subject to national laws bound by these treaties.

Exit plans

Businesses can be bought and sold. Business owners often refer to their plan of disposing of the business as an "exit plan." Common exit plans include IPOs, MBOs and mergers with other businesses. Businesses are rarely liquidated, as it is often very unprofitable to do so.

See also

- Accounting
  - List of accounting topics
- → Advertising
- Banking

- Big business
- Business acumen
- Business broker
- Business ethics
  - List of business ethics, political economy, and philosophy of business topics
  - Social responsibility
- Business hours

- Business mediator
- Business schools
- Business trip

- Capitalism

- Change management analyst

- Commerce

- Commercial law
  - List of business law topics
- Company
- Cooperative
- Corporate law
- Corporation

- Cost overrun
- Economics
  - Economic democracy
  - Financial economics
  - List of economics topics
- Electronic commerce
  - E-business
- Entrepreneurship
- Finance
  - List of finance topics

- Franchising

- Government ownership
- Human Resources
  - List of human resource management topics
- Industry
- Insurance
- Intellectual property
- Interim Management

- International trade
  - List of international trade topics
- Investment
- Limited liability
- Management
  - List of management topics
- Management information systems
  - List of information technology management topics
- Manufacturing
  - List of production topics
- → Marketing
  - List of marketing topics
- Money

- Organizational studies
- Partnership
- Real Estate
- Renewable Energy
  - List of real estate topics
- Revenue shortfall
- Small business

- Sole proprietorship

- Strategic Management
- Strategic Planning

- Types of business entity

- List of oldest companies

External links

- Better Business Bureau [3] US & Canada
- Business Current Events [4] Open Directory
- Doing Business project - World Bank/IFC [5]
- OECD Business Demography Statistics [6]
- Business.gov - Small Business Resources from the US Small Business Administration [7]

References

[1] Sullivan, arthur; Steven M. Sheffrin (2003). *Economics: Principles in action* (http://www.pearsonschool.com/index.
     cfm?locator=PSZ3R9&PMDbSiteId=2781&PMDbSolutionId=6724&PMDbCategoryId=&PMDbProgramId=12881&level=4). Upper
     Saddle River, New Jersey 07458: Pearson Prentice Hall. pp. 29. ISBN 0-13-063085-3. .
[2] http://english.people.com.cn/data/China_in_brief/Economy/Major%20Industries.html
[3] http://www.bbb.org/
[4] http://www.dmoz.org/News/Current_Events/Business_and_Economy/
[5] http://www.doingbusiness.org/
[6] http://stats.oecd.org/Index.aspx?DataSetCode=SDBS_BDI
[7] http://business.gov/

Opinion

An **opinion** is a subjective statement or thought about an issue or topic, and may be the result of emotion or interpretation of facts. An opinion may be supported by an argument, although people may draw opposing opinions from the same set of facts. Opinions rarely change without new arguments being presented. However, it can be reasoned that one opinion is better supported by the facts than another by analysing the supporting aguments. [1]

An opinion may be the result of a person's → perspective, understanding, particular feelings, beliefs, and desires. In casual use, the term *opinion* may refer to unsubstantiated information, in contrast to knowledge and fact-based beliefs.

Epistemology

In economics, other social sciences and philosophy, analysis based on opinion is referred to as normative analysis (what *ought* to be), as opposed to positive analysis, which is based on scientific observation (what materially *is* or is experimentally demonstrable).

Historically, the distinction of demonstrated knowledge and opinion was articulated by Ancient Greek philosophers. Today Plato's analogy of the divided line is a well-known illustration of the distinction between knowledge and opinion, or knowledge and belief, in customary terminology of contemporary philosophy. Opinions can be persuasive, but only the assertions they are based on can be said to be true or false.

Collective and Professional Opinions

The public opinion is the aggregate of individual attitudes or beliefs held by the population. Public opinion can also be defined as the complex collection of opinions of many different people and the sum of all their views.

A 'Scientific opinion' is any opinion formed via the scientific method, and so is necessarily evidence backed. A scientific opinion which represents the formally-agreed consensus of a scientific body or establishment, often takes the form of a published position paper citing the research producing the Scientific evidence upon which the opinion is based. 'The Scientific Opinion' can be compared to 'the public opinion' and means the complex collection of the opinions of many different scientific organizations and entities, and also the opinions of scientists undertaking scientific research in the relevant field.

A Legal opinion or Closing Opinion is a type of professional opinion, usually contained in a formal legal opinion letter, given by an attorney to a client or a third party. Most legal opinions are given in connection with business transactions. The opinion expresses the attorney's professional judgment regarding the legal matters addressed. A legal opinion is not a guaranty that a court will reach any particular result.[2] However, a mistaken or incomplete legal opinion may be grounds for a professional malpractice claim against the attorney, pursuant to which the attorney may be required to pay the claimant damages incurred as a result of relying on the faulty opinion.

A Judicial opinion or Opinion of the Court is an opinion of a judge or group of judges that accompanies and explains an order or ruling in a controversy before the court, laying out the rationale and legal principles the court relied on in reaching its decision.[3] Judges in United States are usually required to provide a well-reasoned basis for their decisions and the contents of their judicial opinions may contain the grounds for appealing and reversing of their decision by a higher court.

An editorial opinion is the stated opinion of a newspaper or it's publisher, as conveyed on the editorial page.

See also

- Doxa
- → Perspective (cognitive)
- Epistemology
- Editorial

External links

- What is the Difference Between Fact and Opinion? [4]
- I'm entitled to an opinion. [5]

References

[1] Damer, T. Edward (2008). *Attacking Faulty Reasoning: A Practical Guide to Fallacy-free Arguments* (http://books.google.com/ books?id=-qZabUx0FmkC&pg=PA15&dq="just+an+opinion"&lr=&ei=zkUxS4TZNZDskwSCkICpAQ&cd=7#v=snippet& q="Distinguishing argument from opinion"&f=false). Cengage Learning. pp. 14-15. ISBN 978-0495095064. .

[2] American Bar Association Committee on Legal Opinions, Legal Opinion Principles, 53 Bus. Law. 831 (1998). (http://www.abanet.org/ buslaw/tribar/materials/20050120000000.pdf)

[3] O.S. Kerr, How to Read a Judicial Opinion: A Guide for New Law Students. (http://euro.ecom.cmu.edu/program/law/08-732/Courts/ howtoreadv2.pdf)

[4] http://www.wisegeek.com/what-is-the-difference-between-fact-and-opinion.htm

[5] http://www.skeptics.org.uk/article.php?dir=articles&article=I_am_entitled_to_an_opinion.php

Idea

In the most narrow sense, an **idea** is just whatever is before the mind when one thinks. Very often, ideas are construed as representational images; i.e. images of some object. In other contexts, ideas are taken to be concepts, although abstract concepts do not necessarily appear as images.[1] Many philosophers consider ideas to be a fundamental ontological category of being.

The capacity to create and understand the meaning of ideas is considered to be an essential and defining feature of human beings.

In a popular sense, an idea arises in a reflex, spontaneous manner, even without thinking or serious reflection, for example, when we talk about the *idea* of a person or a place.

Innate and adventitious ideas

One view on the nature of ideas is that there exist some ideas (called *innate ideas*) which are so general and abstract, that they could not have arisen as a representation of any object of our perception, but rather were, in some sense, always in the mind before we could learn them. These are distinguished from *adventitious ideas* which are images or concepts which are accompanied by the judgment that they are caused by some object outside of the mind.[2]

Another view holds that we only discover ideas in the same way that we discover the real world, from personal experiences. The view that humans acquire all or almost all their behavioral traits from nurture (life experiences) is known as tabula rasa ("blank slate"). Most of the confusions in the way of ideas arise at least in part from the use of the term "idea" to cover both the representation percept and the object of conceptual thought. This can be illustrated in terms of the doctrines of innate ideas, "concrete ideas versus abstract ideas", as well as "simple ideas versus complex ideas". [3]

Philosophy

Plato

Plato was one of the earliest philosopher to provide a detailed discussion of ideas. He considered the concept of idea in the realm of metaphysics and its implications for epistemology. He asserted that there is realm of Forms or Ideas, which exist independently of anyone who may have thought of these ideas. Material things are then imperfect and transient reflections or instantiations of the perfect and unchanging ideas. From this it follows that these Ideas are the principal reality (see also idealism). In contrast to the individual objects of sense experience, which undergo constant change and flux, Plato held that ideas are perfect, eternal, and immutable. Consequently, Plato considered that knowledge of material things is not really knowledge; real knowledge can only be had of unchanging ideas.

René Descartes

Descartes often wrote of the meaning of *idea* as an image or representation, often but not necessarily "in the mind", which was well known in the vernacular. In spite of the fact that Descartes is usually credited with the invention of the non-Platonic use of the term, we find him at first following this vernacular use.[b] In his Meditations on First Philosophy he says, "Some of my thoughts are like images of things, and it is to these alone that the name 'idea' properly belongs." He sometimes maintained that ideas were innate [4] and uses of the term *idea* diverge from the original primary scholastic use. He provides multiple non-equivalent definitions of the term, uses it to refer to as many as six distinct kinds of entities, and divides *ideas* inconsistently into various genetic categories. [5] For him knowledge took the form of ideas and philosophical investigation is the deep consideration of these ideas. Many times however his thoughts of knowledge and ideas were like those of Plotinus and Neoplatonism. In Neoplatonism the Intelligence (*Nous*) is the true first principle -- the determinate, referential 'foundation' (*arkhe*) -- of all existents; for it is not a self-sufficient entity like the One, but rather possesses the ability or capacity to contemplate both the One, as its prior, as well as its own thoughts, which Plotinus identifies with the Platonic Ideas or Forms (*eide*)[6]. A non-philosophical definition of *Nous* is **good sense** (a.k.a. "common sense"). Descartes is quoted as saying, "Of all things, **good sense** is the most fairly distributed: everyone thinks he is so well supplied with it that even those who are the hardest to satisfy in every other respect never desire more of it than they already have."[7]

John Locke

In striking contrast to Plato's use of idea [8] is that of John Locke in his masterpiece An Essay Concerning Human Understanding in the Introduction where he defines **idea** as "It being that term which, I think, serves best to stand for whatsoever is the object of the understanding when a man thinks, I have used it to express whatever is meant by phantasm, notion, species, or whatever it is which the mind can be employed about in thinking ; and I could not avoid frequently using it." He said he regarded the book necessary to examine our own abilities and see what objects our understandings were, or were not, fitted to deal with. In his philosophy other outstanding figures followed in his footsteps - Hume and Kant in the 18th century, Arthur Schopenhauer in the 19th century, and Bertrand Russell, Ludwig Wittgenstein, and Karl Popper in the 20th century. Locke always believed in **good sense** - not pushing things to extremes and on taking fully into account the plain facts of the matter. He considered his common sense ideas "good-tempered, moderate, and down-to-earth." ᶜ

David Hume

Hume differs from Locke by limiting "idea" to the more or less vague mental reconstructions of perceptions, the perceptual process being described as an "impression."[9] Hume shared with Locke the basic empiricist premise that it is only from life experiences (whether their own or others') that humans' knowledge of the existence of anything outside of themselves can be ultimately derived, that they shall carry on doing what they are prompted to do by their emotional drives of varying kinds. In choosing the means to those ends, they shall follow their accustomed associations of ideas.ᵈ Hume has contended and defended the notion that "reason alone is merely the 'slave of the passions'"[10] [11]

"Modern Book Printing" from the
Walk of Ideas

Immanuel Kant

Immanuel Kant defines an "idea" as opposed to a "concept". "Regulator ideas" are ideals that one must tend towards, but by definition may not be completely realized. Liberty, according to Kant, is an idea. The autonomy of the rational and universal subject is opposed to the determinism of the empirical subject.[12] Kant felt that it is precisely in knowing its limits that philosophy exists. The business of philosophy he thought was not to give rules, but to analyze the private judgements of good common sense.ᵉ

Rudolf Steiner

Whereas Kant declares limits to knowledge ("we can never know the thing in itself"), in his epistemological work, Rudolf Steiner sees *ideas* as "objects of experience" which the mind apprehends, much as the eye apprehends light. In *Goethean Science* (1883), he declares, "Thinking... is no more and no less an organ of perception than the eye or ear. Just as the eye perceives colors and the ear sounds, so thinking perceives ideas." He holds this to be the premise upon which Goethe made his natural-scientific observations.

Wilhelm Wundt

Wundt widens the term from Kant's usage to include *conscious representation of some object or process of the external world*. In so doing, he includes not only ideas of memory and imagination, but also perceptual processes, whereas other psychologists confine the term to the first two groups. One of Wundt's main concerns was to investigate conscious processes in their own context by experiment and introspection. He regarded both of these as *exact methods*, interrelated in that experimentation created optimal conditions for introspection. Where the experimental method failed, he turned to other *objectively valuable aids*, specifically to *those products of cultural communal life which lead one to infer particular mental motives. Outstanding among these are speech, myth, and social custom.* Wundt designed the basic mental activity apperception - a unifying function which should be understood as an activity of the will. Many aspects of his empirical physiological psychology are used today. One is his principles of mutually enhanced contrasts and of assimilation and dissimilation (i.e. in color and form perception and his advocacy of *objective* methods of expression and of recording results, especially in language. Another is the principle of heterogony of ends - that multiply motivated acts lead to unintended side effects which in turn become motives for new actions.[13]

Charles Sanders Peirce

C. S. Peirce published the first full statement of pragmatism in his important works "How to Make Our Ideas Clear" (1878) and "The Fixation of Belief" (1877) [14] . In "How to Make Our Ideas Clear" he proposed that a *clear idea* (in his study he uses concept and *idea* as synonymic) is defined as one, when it is apprehended such as it will be recognized wherever it is met, and no other will be mistaken for it. If it fails of this clearness, it is said to be obscure. He argued that to understand an idea clearly we should ask ourselves what difference its application would make to our evaluation of a proposed solution to the problem at hand. Pragmatism (a term he appropriated for use in this context), he defended, was a method for ascertaining the meaning of terms (as a theory of meaning). The originality of his ideas is in their rejection of what was accepted as a view and understanding of knowledge by scientists for some 250 years, i.e. that, he pointed, knowledge was an impersonal fact. Peirce contended that we acquire knowledge as *participants*, not as *spectators*. He felt "the real" is which, sooner or later, information acquired through ideas and knowledge with the application of logical reasoning would finally result in. He also published many papers on logic in relation to *ideas*.

G. F. Stout and J. M. Baldwin

G. F. Stout and J. M. Baldwin, in the *Dictionary of Philosophy and Psychology* [15], define "idea" as "the reproduction with a more or less adequate image, of an object not actually present to the senses." They point out that an idea and a perception are by various authorities contrasted in various ways. "Difference in degree of intensity", "comparative absence of bodily movement on the part of the subject", "comparative dependence on mental activity", are suggested by psychologists as characteristic of an idea as compared with a perception.

It should be observed that an idea, in the narrower and generally accepted sense of a mental reproduction, is frequently composite. That is, as in the example given above of the idea of chair, a great many objects, differing materially in detail, all call a single idea. When a man, for example, has obtained an idea of chairs in general by comparison with which he can say "This is a chair, that is a stool", he has what is known as an "abstract idea" distinct from the reproduction in his mind of any particular chair (see abstraction). Furthermore a complex idea may not have any corresponding physical object, though it particular constituent elements may severally be the reproductions of actual perceptions. Thus the idea of a centaur is a complex mental picture composed of the ideas of man and horse, that of a mermaid of a woman and a fish.

In anthropology and the social sciences

Diffusion studies explore the spread of ideas from culture to culture. Some anthropological theories hold that all cultures imitate ideas from one or a few original cultures, the Adam of the Bible or several cultural circles that overlap. Evolutionary diffusion theory holds that cultures are influenced by one another, but that similar ideas can be developed in isolation.

In mid-20th century, social scientists began to study how and why ideas spread from one person or culture to another. Everett Rogers pioneered diffusion of innovations studies, using research to prove factors in adoption and profiles of adopters of ideas. In 1976, in his book *The Selfish Gene, Richard Dawkins suggested applying biological evolutionary theories to spread of ideas. He coined the term 'meme' to describe an abstract unit of selection, equivalent to the gene in evolutionary biology.*

Semantics

Dr. Samuel Johnson

James Boswell recorded Dr.Samuel Johnson' s opinion about ideas. Johnson claimed that they are mental images or internal visual pictures. As such, they have no relation to words or the concepts which are designated by verbal names.

> He was particularly indignant against the almost universal use of the word *idea* in the sense of *notion* or *opinion*, when it is clear that *idea* can only signify something of which an image can be formed in the mind. We may have an *idea* or *image* of a mountain, a tree, a building; but we cannot surely have an *idea* or *image* of an *argument* or *proposition*. Yet we hear the sages of the law 'delivering their *ideas* upon the question under consideration;' and the first speakers in parliament 'entirely coinciding in the *idea* which has been ably stated by an honourable member;' — or 'reprobating an *idea* unconstitutional, and fraught with the most dangerous consequences to a great and free country.' Johnson called this 'modern cant.'
>
> – *Boswell's Life of Johnson, Tuesday, 23 September 1777*

Validity of ideas

In the objective worth of our *ideas* there remains the problem of the validity. As all cognition is by *ideas*, it is obvious that the question of the validity of *our ideas* in this broad sense is that of the truth of our knowledge as a whole. Otherwise to dispute this is to take up the position of skepticism. This has often been pointed out as a means intellectual suicide. Any chain of reasoning (common sense) by which it is attempted to demonstrate the falsity of our *ideas* has to employ the very concept of *ideas* itself. Then insofar as it demands assent to the conclusion, it implies belief in the validity of all the *ideas* employed in the premises of the argument.

To assent the fundamental mathematical and logical axioms, including that of the principle of contradiction, implies admission of the truth of the *ideas* expressed in these principles. With respect to the objective worth of ideas, as involved in perception generally, the question raised is that of the existence of an independent material world comprising other human beings. The idealism of David Hume and John Stuart Mill would lead logically to solipsism (the denial of any others besides ourselves). The main foundation of all idealism and skepticism is the assumption (explicit or implicit), that the mind can never know what is outside of itself. This is to say that an *idea* as a cognition can never go outside of itself. This can be further expressed as we can never reach to and mentally apprehend anything outside of anything of what is actually a present state of our own consciousness.

- First, this is based on a prior assumption for which no real proof is or can be given
- Second, it is not only not self-evident, but directly contrary to what our mind affirms to be our direct intellectual experience.

What is possible for a human mind to apprehend cannot be laid down beforehand. It must be ascertained by careful observations and by study of the process of cognition. This postulates that the mind cannot apprehend or cognize any reality existing outside of itself and is not only a self-evident proposition, it is directly contrary to what such observation and the testimony of mankind affirms to be our actual intellectual experience.

John Stuart Mill and most extreme idealists have to admit the validity of memory and expectation. This is to say that in every act of memory or expectation which refers to any experience outside the present instant, our cognition is transcending the present modifications of the mind and judging about reality beyond and distinct from the present states of consciousness. Considering the question as specially concerned with universal concepts, only the theory of moderate realism adopted by Aristotle and Saint Thomas can claim to guarantee objective value to our ideas. According to the nominalist and conceptualist theories there is no true correlate in *rerum naturâ* corresponding to the universal term.

Mathematics, astronomy, physics, chemistry, and the rest claim that their universal propositions are true and deal with realities. It is involved in the very notion of science that the physical laws formulated by the mind do mirror the working of agents in the external universe. The general terms of these sciences and *the ideas* which they signify have objective correlatives in the common natures and essences of the objects with which these sciences deal. Otherwise these general statements are unreal and each science is nothing more than a consistently arranged system of barren propositions deduced from empty arbitrary definitions. These postulates then have no more genuine objective value than any other coherently devised scheme of artificial symbols standing for imaginary beings. However the fruitfulness of science and the constant verifications of its predictions are incompatible with such a hypothesis.[16]

Relationship of ideas to modern legal time- and scope-limited monopolies

Relationship between ideas and patents

On Susceptibility to Exclusive Property

Thomas Jefferson, letter to Isaac McPherson, 13 August 1813 [17]

"It has been pretended by some, (and in England especially,) that inventors have a natural and exclusive right to their inventions, and not merely for their own lives, but inheritable to their heirs. But while it is a moot question whether the origin of any kind of property is derived from nature at all, it would be singular to admit a natural and even an hereditary right to inventors. It is agreed by those who have seriously considered the subject, that no individual has, of natural right, a separate property in an acre of land, for instance.

By a universal law, indeed, whatever, whether fixed or movable, belongs to all men equally and in common, is the property for the moment of him who occupies it, but when he relinquishes the occupation, the property goes with it. Stable ownership is the gift of social law, and is given late in the progress of society. It would be curious then, if an idea, the fugitive fermentation of an individual brain, could, of natural right, be claimed in exclusive and stable property.

If nature has made any one thing less susceptible than all others of exclusive property, it is the action of the thinking power called an idea, which an individual may exclusively possess as long as he keeps it to himself; but the moment it is divulged, it forces itself into the possession of every one, and the receiver cannot dispossess himself of it. Its peculiar character, too, is that no one possesses the less, because every other possesses the whole of it. He who receives an idea from me, receives instruction himself without lessening mine; as he who lights his taper at mine, receives light without darkening me.

That ideas should freely spread from one to another over the globe, for the moral and mutual instruction of man, and improvement of his condition, seems to have been peculiarly and benevolently designed by nature, when she made them, like fire, expansible over all space, without lessening their density in any point, and like the air in which we breathe, move, and have our physical being, incapable of confinement or exclusive appropriation. Inventions then cannot, in nature, be a subject of property.

Society may give an exclusive right to the profits arising from them, as an encouragement to men to pursue ideas which may produce utility, but this may or may not be done, according to the will and convenience of the society, without claim or complaint from anybody. Accordingly, it is a fact, as far as I am informed, that England was, until we copied her, the only country on earth which ever, by a general law, gave a legal right to the exclusive use of an idea. In some other countries it is sometimes done, in a great case, and by a special and personal act, but, generally speaking, other nations have thought that these monopolies produce more embarrassment than advantage to society; and it may be observed that the nations which refuse monopolies of invention, are as fruitful as England in new and useful devices."

To protect the cause of invention and innovation, the legal constructions of Copyrights and Patents was established. Patent law regulates various aspects related to the functional manifestation of inventions based on new ideas or an incremental improvements to existing ones. Thus, patents have a direct relationship to ideas.

Relationship between ideas and copyrights

In some cases, authors can be granted limited legal monopolies on the manner in which certain works are expressed. This is known colloquially as copyright, although the term intellectual property is used mistakenly in place of *copyright*. Copyright law regulating the aforementioned monopolies generally does not cover the actual ideas. The law does not bestow the legal status of property upon ideas per se. Instead, laws purport to regulate events related to the usage, copying, production, sale and other forms of exploitation of the fundamental expression of a work, that may or may not carry ideas. Copyright law is fundamentally different to patent law in this respect: patents do grant monopolies on ideas (more on this below).

A copyright is meant to regulate some aspects of the usage of expressions of a work, **not** an idea. Thus, copyrights have a negative relationship to ideas.

Work means a tangible medium of expression. It may be an original or derivative work of art, be it literary, dramatic, musical recitation, artistic, related to sound recording, etc. In (at least) countries adhering to the Berne Convention, copyright automatically starts covering the work upon the original creation and fixation thereof, without any extra steps. While creation usually involves an idea, the idea in itself does not suffice for the purposes of claiming copyright.

Relationship of ideas to confidentiality agreements

Confidentiality and nondisclosure agreements are legal instruments that assist corporations and individuals in keeping ideas from escaping to the general public. Generally, these instruments are covered by contract law.

See also

- Form
- Meme
- → Opinion
- Ideology
- Think tank
- Mental image
- Brainstorming
- Portal: thinking
- Object of the mind
- Perception related
- Notion (philosophy)

- Thought experiment
- Creativity techniques
- Diffusion of innovations
- Universal (metaphysics)
- Introspection and Extrospection
- Mind map
- Freemind
- Global Ideas Bank
- Opencourseware
- TED (conference)

Bibliography

- Paul Natorp, *Platons Ideenlehre (Leipzig 1930)*
- W. D. Ross, *Plato's Theory of Ideas* (Oxford 1951)
- M. H. Carre, *Realists and Nominalists* (Oxford 1946)
- Lawrence Lessig, *The Future of Ideas* (New York 2001)
- J. W. Yolton, *John Lock and the Way of Ideas* (Oxford 1956)
- Eugenio Garin, *La Theorie de l'idee suivant l'ecole thomiste (Paris 1932)*
- Peter Watson, *Ideas: A History from Fire to Freud*, Weidenfeld & Nicolson (London 2005).
- A. G. Balz, *Idea and Essence in the Philosophy of Hobbes and Spinoza* (New York 1918)
- William Rose Benet, The Reader's Encyclopedia 1965, Library of Congress Card No. 65-12510
- Melchert, Norman (2002). *The Great Conversation: A Historical Introduction to Philosophy*. McGraw Hill. ISBN 0-19-517510-7.

References

- *The Encyclopedia of Philosophy*, MacMillian Publishing Company, New York, 1973 ISBN 0028949501 ISBN 978-0028949505
- Dictionary of the History of Ideas [18] Charles Scribner's Sons, New York 1973-74, Library of Congress Catalog Card Number 72-7943 SBN 684-16425-6
    - Nous [19]
    [1] Volume IV 1a, 3a
    [2] Volume IV 4a, 5a
    [3] Volume IV 32 - 37
    - Ideas [20]
    Idealogy [21]
    Authority [22]
    Education [23]
    Liberalism [24]
    Idea of God [25]
    Pragmatism [26]
    Chain of Being [27]
- *The Story of Thought*, DK Publishing, Bryan Magee, London, 1998, ISBN 0-7894-4455-0
    aka *The Story of Philosophy*, Dorling Kindersley Publishing, 2001, ISBN 0-7894-7994-X

(subtitled on cover: *The Essential Guide to the History of Western Philosophy*)

[a] Plato, pages 11 - 17, 24 - 31, 42, 50, 59, 77, 142, 144, 150

[b] Descartes, pages 78, 84 - 89, 91, 95, 102, 136 - 137, 190, 191

[c] Locke, pages 59 - 61, 102 - 109, 122 - 124, 142, 185

[d] Hume, pages 61, 103, 112 - 117, 142 - 143, 155, 185

[e] Kant, pages 9, 38, 57, 87, 103, 119, 131 - 137, 149, 182

[f] Pierce, pages 61, *How to Make Our Ideas Clear* 186 - 187 and 189

[g] Saint Augustine, pages 30, 144; *City of God* 51, 52, 53 and *The Confessions* 50, 51, 52

- additional in the Dictionary of the History of Ideas for Saint Augustine and Neo-Platonism [28]

[h] Stoics, pages 22, 40, 44; The governing philosophy of the Roman Empire on pages 46 - 47.

- additional in Dictionary of the History of Ideas for Stoics [29], also here [30], and here [30], and here [31]

- *The Reader's Encyclopedia*, 2nd Edition 1965, Thomas Y. Crowell Company, Library of Congress No. 65-12510

  An Encyclopedia of World Literature

  [1a] page 774 Plato (c.427-348 BC)

  [2a] page 779 Francesco Petrarca

  [3a] page 770 Charles Sanders Peirce

  [1b] page 849 the Renaissance

- This article incorporates text from the old Catholic Encyclopedia of 1914, a publication now in the public domain.
- This article incorporates text from the Schaff-Herzog Encyclopedia of Religious Knowledge, a publication now in the public domain.

References

[1] Cambridge Dictionary of Philosophy

[2] Cambridge Dictionary of Philosophy

[3] *The Encyclopedia of Philosophy*, MacMillian Publishing Company, New York, 1973 ISBN 0028949501 ISBN 978-0028949505 Vol 4: 120 - 121

[4] Vol 4: 196 - 198

[5] http://plato.stanford.edu/entries/descartes-ideas

[6] http://www.iep.utm.edu/p/plotinus.htm

[7] http://en.wikiquote.org/wiki/Ren%C3%A9_Descartes

[8] Vol 4: 487 - 503

[9] Vol 4: 74 - 90

[10] http://plato.stanford.edu/entries/hume-moral/#inmo

[11] Hume, David: A Treatise of Human Nature: Being an Attempt to introduce the experimental Method of Reasoning into Moral Subjects. (1739–40)

[12] Vol 4: 305 - 324

[13] Vol 8: 349 -351

[14] Pierce's pragmatism

[15] http://psychclassics.yorku.ca/Baldwin/Dictionary

[16] http://www.newadvent.org/cathen/07630a.htm

[17] http://press-pubs.uchicago.edu/founders/documents/a1_8_8s12.html

[18] http://etext.virginia.edu/cgi-local/DHI/dhi.cgi?id=dv1-45

[19] http://etext.virginia.edu/cgi-local/DHI/ot2www-dhi?specfile=%2Ftexts%2Fenglish%2Fdhi%2Fdhi.o2w&query=nous&docs=div1& title=&sample=1-100&grouping=work

[20] http://etext.virginia.edu/cgi-local/DHI/ot2www-dhi?specfile=%2Ftexts%2Fenglish%2Fdhi%2Fdhi.o2w&query=Idea&docs=div1& title=&sample=1-100&grouping=work

[21] http://etext.virginia.edu/cgi-local/DHI/ot2www-dhi?specfile=/texts/english/dhi/dhi.o2w&act=text&offset=9030627&query=Idea& tag=IDEOLOGY

[22] http://etext.virginia.edu/cgi-local/DHI/ot2www-dhi?specfile=/texts/english/dhi/dhi.o2w&act=text&offset=1129686&query=Idea&tag=AUTHORITY

[23] http://etext.virginia.edu/cgi-local/DHI/ot2www-dhi?specfile=/texts/english/dhi/dhi.o2w&act=text&offset=5531029&query=Idea&tag=EDUCATION

[24] http://etext.virginia.edu/cgi-local/DHI/ot2www-dhi?specfile=/texts/english/dhi/dhi.o2w&act=text&offset=10374338&query=Idea&tag=LIBERALISM

[25] http://etext.virginia.edu/cgi-local/DHI/ot2www-dhi?specfile=/texts/english/dhi/dhi.o2w&act=text&offset=7593812&query=Idea&tag=IDEA+OF+GOD+SINCE+1800

[26] http://etext.virginia.edu/cgi-local/DHI/ot2www-dhi?specfile=/texts/english/dhi/dhi.o2w&act=text&offset=14090262&query=Idea&tag=PRAGMATISM

[27] http://etext.virginia.edu/cgi-local/DHI/ot2www-dhi?specfile=/texts/english/dhi/dhi.o2w&act=text&offset=2479574&query=Idea&tag=CHAIN+OF+BEING

[28] http://etext.virginia.edu/cgi-local/DHI/dhi.cgi?id=dv3-64

[29] http://etext.virginia.edu/cgi-local/DHI/ot2www-dhi?specfile=/texts/english/dhi/dhi.o2w&act=text&offset=15375238&query=stoics&tag=RATIONALITY+AMONG+THE+GREEKS+AND+ROMANS

[30] http://etext.virginia.edu/cgi-local/DHI/ot2www-dhi?specfile=/texts/english/dhi/dhi.o2w&act=text&offset=11461153&query=stoics&tag=CHANGING+CONCEPTS+OF+MATTER+FROM+ANTIQUITY+TO+NEWTON

[31] http://etext.virginia.edu/cgi-local/DHI/ot2www-dhi?specfile=/texts/english/dhi/dhi.o2w&act=text&offset=17347564&query=stoics&tag=ETHICS+OF+STOICISM

Copy (written)

Copy refers to written material, in contrast to photographs or other elements of layout, in a large number of contexts, including magazines, advertising, and book publishing.

In → advertising, web marketing and similar fields, *copy* refers to the output of → copywriters, who are employed to write material which encourages consumers to buy goods or services.

In publishing more generally, the term *copy* refers to the text in books, magazines, and newspapers. In books it means the text as written by the author, which the copy editor then prepares for typesetting and printing. In newspapers and magazines it means the "body copy", the main article or text that writers are responsible for, as opposed to the accompanying material such as headlines, which are written by copy editors or sub-editors.

See also

- → Copywriting
- Copy editing
- Publishing

Advertising

A Coca-Cola ad from the 1890s

→ **Marketing**
Key concepts
Product • Pricing • → Promotion Distribution • Service • Retail Brand management Account-based marketing Marketing ethics Marketing effectiveness Market research Market segmentation Marketing strategy Marketing management Market dominance
Promotional content
→ Advertising • Branding • Underwriting Direct marketing • Personal Sales Product placement • Publicity Sales promotion • Sex in advertising
Promotional media

Printing • Publication • Broadcasting
Out-of-home • Internet marketing
Point of sale • Promotional items
Digital marketing • In-game
In-store demonstration • Word of mouth

Advertising is a form of communication intended to persuade its viewers, readers or listeners to take some action. It usually includes the name of a product or service and how that product or service could benefit the consumer, to persuade potential customers to purchase or to consume that particular brand. Modern advertising developed with the rise of mass production in the late 19th and early 20th centuries.[1]

Commercial advertisers often seek to generate increased consumption of their products or services through branding, which involves the repetition of an image or product name in an effort to associate related qualities with the brand in the minds of consumers. Different types of media can be used to deliver these messages, including traditional media such as newspapers, magazines, television, radio, billboards or direct mail. Advertising may be placed by an advertising agency on behalf of a company or other organization.

Organizations that spend money on advertising promoting items other than a consumer product or service include political parties, interest groups, religious organizations and governmental agencies. Non-profit organizations may rely on free modes of persuasion, such as a public service announcement.

Money spent on advertising has declined in recent years. In 2007, spending on advertising was estimated at more than $150 billion in the United States[2] and $385 billion worldwide,[3] and the latter to exceed $450 billion by 2010.

History

Egyptians used papyrus to make sales messages and wall posters. Commercial messages and political campaign displays have been found in the ruins of Pompeii and ancient Arabia. Lost and found advertising on papyrus was common in Ancient Greece and Ancient Rome. Wall or rock painting for commercial advertising is another manifestation of an ancient advertising form, which is present to this day in many parts of Asia, Africa, and South America. The tradition of wall painting can be traced back to Indian rock art paintings that date back to 4000 BC.[4] History tells us that Out-of-home advertising and Billboards are the oldest forms of advertising.

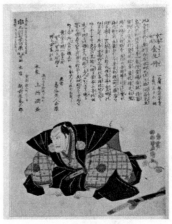
Edo period advertising flyer from 1806 for a traditional medicine called *Kinseitan*

As the towns and cities of the Middle Ages began to grow, and the general populace was unable to read, signs that today would say cobbler, miller, tailor or blacksmith would use an image associated with their trade such as a boot, a suit, a hat, a clock, a diamond, a horse shoe, a candle or even a bag of flour. Fruits and vegetables were sold in the city square from the backs of carts and wagons and their proprietors used street callers (town criers) to announce their whereabouts for the convenience of the customers.

As education became an apparent need and reading, as well as printing, developed advertising expanded to include handbills. In the 17th century advertisements started to appear in weekly newspapers in England. These early print advertisements were used mainly to promote books and newspapers, which became increasingly affordable with advances in the printing press; and medicines, which were increasingly sought after as disease ravaged Europe. However, false advertising and so-called "quack" advertisements became a problem, which ushered in the regulation of advertising content.

As the economy expanded during the 19th century, advertising grew alongside. In the United States, the success of this advertising format eventually led to the growth of mail-order advertising.

In June 1836, French newspaper *La Presse* was the first to include paid advertising in its pages, allowing it to lower its price, extend its readership and increase its profitability and the formula was soon copied by all titles. Around 1840, Volney Palmer established a predecessor to advertising agencies in Boston.[5] Around the same time, in France, Charles-Louis Havas extended the services of his news agency, Havas to include advertisement brokerage, making it the first French group to organize. At first, agencies were brokers for advertisement space in newspapers. N. W. Ayer & Son was the first full-service agency to assume responsibility for advertising content. N.W. Ayer opened in 1869, and was located in Philadelphia.[5]

At the turn of the century, there were few career choices for women in business; however, advertising was one of the few. Since women were responsible for most of the purchasing done in their household, advertisers and agencies recognized the value of women's insight during the creative process. In fact, the first American advertising to use a sexual sell was created by a woman – for a soap product. Although tame by today's standards, the advertisement featured a couple with the message "The skin you love to touch".[6]

In the early 1920s, the first radio stations were established by radio equipment manufacturers and retailers who offered programs in order to sell more radios to consumers. As time passed, many non-profit organizations followed suit in setting up their own radio stations, and included: schools, clubs and civic groups.[7] When the practice of sponsoring programs was popularised, each individual radio program was usually sponsored by a single business in exchange for a brief mention of the business' name at the beginning and end of the sponsored shows. However, radio station owners soon realised they could earn more money by selling sponsorship rights in small time allocations to multiple businesses throughout their radio station's broadcasts, rather than selling the sponsorship rights to single businesses per show.

An 1895 advertisement for a weight gain product.

WHEN IN DOUBT—"LOOK IT UP" IN
The
Encyclopaedia Britannica

The Sum of Human
Knowledge

*29 volumes, 28,150 pages,
44,000,000 words of text.
Printed on thin, but strong
opaque India paper, each
volume but one inch in
thickness.*

New U.S. Edition issued 1910-11 by the
CAMBRIDGE UNIVERSITY PRESS (England)

THE BOOK TO ASK QUESTIONS OF | FOR READING OR FOR STUDY

A print advertisement for the 1913 issue of the
Encyclopædia Britannica

This practice was carried over to television in the late 1940s and early 1950s. A fierce battle was fought between those seeking to commercialise the radio and people who argued that the radio spectrum should be considered a part of the commons — to be used only non-commercially and for the public good. The United Kingdom pursued a public funding model for the BBC, originally a private company, the British Broadcasting Company, but incorporated as a public body by Royal Charter in 1927. In Canada, advocates like Graham Spry were likewise able to persuade the federal government to adopt a public funding model, creating the Canadian Broadcasting Corporation. However, in the United States, the capitalist model prevailed with the passage of the Communications Act of 1934 which created the Federal Communications Commission.[7] To placate the socialists, the U.S. Congress did require commercial broadcasters to operate in the "public interest, convenience, and necessity".[8] Public broadcasting now exists in the United States due to the 1967 Public Broadcasting Act which led to the Public Broadcasting Service and National Public Radio.

In the early 1950s, the DuMont Television Network began the modern trend of selling advertisement time to multiple sponsors. Previously, DuMont had trouble finding sponsors for many of their programs and compensated by selling smaller blocks of advertising time to several businesses. This eventually became the standard for the commercial television industry in the United States. However, it was still a common practice to have single sponsor shows, such as The United States Steel Hour. In some instances the sponsors exercised great control over the content of the show - up to and including having one's advertising agency actually writing the show. The single sponsor model is much less prevalent now, a notable exception being the Hallmark Hall of Fame.

The 1960s saw advertising transform into a modern approach in which creativity was allowed to shine, producing unexpected messages that made advertisements more tempting to consumers' eyes. The Volkswagen ad campaign—featuring such headlines as "Think Small" and "Lemon" (which were used to describe the appearance of the car)—ushered in the era of modern advertising by promoting a "position" or "unique selling proposition" designed to associate each brand with a specific idea in the reader or viewer's mind. This period of American advertising is called the Creative Revolution and its archetype was William Bernbach who helped create the revolutionary Volkswagen ads among others. Some of the most creative and long-standing American advertising dates to this period.

The late 1980s and early 1990s saw the introduction of cable television and particularly MTV. Pioneering the concept of the music video, MTV ushered in a new type of advertising: the consumer tunes in *for* the advertising message, rather than it being a by-product or afterthought. As cable and satellite television became increasingly prevalent, specialty channels emerged, including channels entirely devoted to advertising, such as QVC, Home Shopping Network, and ShopTV Canada.

Marketing through the → Internet opened new frontiers for advertisers and contributed to the "dot-com" boom of the 1990s. Entire corporations operated solely on advertising revenue, offering everything from coupons to free Internet access. At the turn of the 21st century, a number of websites including the → search engine Google, started a change in online advertising by emphasizing contextually relevant, unobtrusive ads intended to help, rather than inundate, users. This has led to a plethora of similar efforts and an increasing trend of interactive advertising.

The share of advertising spending relative to GDP has changed little across large changes in → media. For example, in the U.S. in 1925, the main advertising media were newspapers, magazines, signs on streetcars, and outdoor posters. Advertising spending as a share of GDP was about 2.9 percent. By 1998, television and radio had become major advertising media. Nonetheless, advertising spending as a share of GDP was slightly lower—about 2.4 percent.[9]

A recent advertising innovation is "guerrilla marketing", which involve unusual approaches such as staged encounters in public places, giveaways of products such as cars that are covered with brand messages, and interactive advertising where the viewer can respond to become part of the advertising message. Guerrilla advertising is becoming increasing more popular with a lot of companies. This type of advertising is unpredictable and innovative, which causes consumers to buy the product or idea. This reflects an increasing trend of interactive and "embedded" ads, such as via product placement, having consumers vote through text messages, and various innovations utilizing social network services such as MySpace.

Public service advertising

The same advertising techniques used to promote commercial goods and services can be used to inform, educate and motivate the public about non-commercial issues, such as HIV/AIDS, political ideology, energy conservation and deforestation.

Advertising, in its non-commercial guise, is a powerful educational tool capable of reaching and motivating large audiences. "Advertising justifies its existence when used in the public interest - it is much too powerful a tool to use solely for commercial purposes." - Attributed to Howard Gossage by David Ogilvy.

Public service advertising, non-commercial advertising, public interest advertising, cause marketing, and social marketing are different terms for (or aspects of) the use of sophisticated advertising and marketing communications techniques (generally associated with commercial enterprise) on behalf of non-commercial, public interest issues and initiatives.

In the United States, the granting of television and radio licenses by the FCC is contingent upon the station broadcasting a certain amount of public service advertising. To meet these requirements, many broadcast stations in America air the bulk of their required public service announcements during the late night or early morning when the smallest percentage of viewers are watching, leaving more day and prime time commercial slots available for high-paying advertisers.

Public service advertising reached its height during World Wars I and II under the direction of several governments.

A common advert is Esure who stars michael winner(see link->0 [[10]]

Types of advertising

Virtually any medium can be used for advertising. Commercial advertising media can include wall paintings, billboards, street furniture components, printed flyers and rack cards, radio, cinema and television adverts, web banners, mobile telephone screens, shopping carts, web popups, skywriting, bus stop benches, human billboards, magazines, newspapers, town criers, sides of buses, banners attached to or sides of airplanes ("logojets"), in-flight advertisements on seatback tray tables or overhead storage bins, taxicab doors, roof mounts and passenger screens, musical stage shows, subway platforms and trains, elastic bands on disposable diapers,doors of bathroom stalls,stickers on apples in supermarkets, shopping cart handles (grabertising), the opening section of streaming audio and video, posters, and the backs of

Paying people to hold signs is one of the oldest forms of advertising, as with this Human directional pictured above

event tickets and supermarket receipts. Any place an "identified" sponsor pays to deliver their message through a medium is advertising.

Television

The TV commercial is generally considered the most effective mass-market advertising format, as is reflected by the high prices TV networks charge for commercial airtime during popular TV events. The annual Super Bowl football game in the United States is known as the most prominent advertising event on television. The average cost of a single thirty-second TV spot during this game has reached US$3 million (as of 2009).

The majority of television commercials feature a song or → jingle that listeners soon relate to the product.

A bus with an advertisement for GAP in Singapore. Buses and other vehicles are popular mediums for advertisers.

Virtual advertisements may be inserted into regular television programming through computer graphics. It is typically inserted into otherwise blank backdrops[11] or used to replace local billboards that are not relevant to the remote broadcast audience.[12] More controversially, virtual billboards may be inserted into the background[13] where none exist in real-life. Virtual product placement is also possible.[14] [15]

Infomercials

An infomercial is a long-format television commercial, typically five minutes or longer. The word "infomercial" is a portmanteau of the words "information" and "commercial". The main objective in

A DBAG Class 101 with UNICEF ads at Ingolstadt main railway station

an infomercial is to create an impulse purchase, so that the consumer sees the presentation and then immediately buys the product through the advertised toll-free telephone number or → website. Infomercials describe, display, and often demonstrate products and their features, and commonly have testimonials from consumers and industry professionals.

Radio advertising

Radio advertising is a form of advertising via the medium of → radio.

Radio advertisements are broadcasted as radio waves to the air from a transmitter to an antenna and a thus to a receiving device. Airtime is purchased from a station or network in exchange for airing the commercials. While radio has the obvious limitation of being restricted to sound, proponents of radio advertising often cite this as an advantage.

Print advertising

Print advertising describes advertising in a printed medium such as a newspaper, magazine, or trade journal. This encompasses everything from media with a very broad readership base, such as a major national newspaper or magazine, to more narrowly targeted media such as local newspapers and trade journals on very specialized topics. A form of print advertising is classified advertising, which allows private individuals or companies to purchase a small, narrowly targeted ad for a low fee advertising a product or service.

Online advertising

Online advertising is a form of → promotion that uses the → Internet and → World Wide Web for the expressed purpose of delivering → marketing messages to attract customers. Examples of online advertising include contextual ads that appear on search engine results pages, banner ads, in text ads, Rich Media Ads, Social network advertising, online classified advertising, advertising networks and e-mail marketing, including e-mail spam.

Billboard advertising

→ Billboards are large structures located in public places which display advertisements to passing pedestrians and motorists. Most often, they are located on main roads with a large amount of passing motor and pedestrian traffic; however, they can be placed in any location with large amounts of viewers, such as on mass transit vehicles and in stations, in shopping malls or office buildings, and in stadiums.

Mobile billboard advertising

Mobile billboards are truck- or blimp-mounted → billboards or digital screens. These can be dedicated vehicles built solely for carrying advertisements along routes preselected by clients, or they can be specially-equipped cargo trucks. The billboards are often lighted; some being backlit, and others employing spotlights. Some billboard displays are static, while others change; for example, continuously or periodically rotating among a set of advertisements.

Mobile displays are used for various situations in metropolitan areas throughout the world, including:

* Target advertising
* One-day, and long-term campaigns
* Conventions
* Sporting events
* Store openings and similar promotional events
* Big advertisements from smaller companies
* Others

The *RedEye* newspaper advertised to its target market at North Avenue Beach with a sailboat billboard on Lake Michigan.

In-store advertising

In-store advertising is any advertisement placed in a retail store. It includes placement of a product in visible locations in a store, such as at eye level, at the ends of aisles and near checkout counters, eye-catching displays promoting a specific product, and advertisements in such places as shopping carts and in-store video displays.

Covert advertising

Covert advertising, also known as guerrilla advertising, is when a product or brand is embedded in entertainment and media. For example, in a film, the main character can use an item or other of a definite brand, as in the movie *Minority Report*, where Tom Cruise's character John Anderton owns a phone with the *Nokia* logo clearly written in the top corner, or his watch engraved with the *Bulgari* logo. Another example of advertising in film is in *I, Robot*, where main character played by Will Smith mentions his *Converse* shoes several times, calling them "classics," because the film is set far in the future. *I, Robot* and *Spaceballs* also showcase futuristic cars with the *Audi* and *Mercedes-Benz* logos clearly displayed on the front of the vehicles. Cadillac chose to advertise in the movie *The Matrix Reloaded*, which as a result contained many scenes in which Cadillac cars were used. Similarly, product placement for Omega Watches, Ford, VAIO, BMW and Aston Martin cars are featured in recent James Bond films, most notably *Casino Royale*. In "Fantastic Four 2: Rise of the Silver Surfer", the main transport vehicle shows a large Dodge logo on the front. *Blade Runner* includes some of the most obvious product placement; the whole film stops to show a Coca-Cola billboard.

Celebrities

This type of advertising focuses upon using celebrity power, fame, money, popularity to gain recognition for their products and promote specific stores or products. Advertisers often advertise their products, for example, when celebrities share their favorite products or wear clothes by specific brands or designers. Celebrities are often involved in advertising campaigns such as television or print adverts to advertise specific or general products.

The use of celebrities to endorse a brand can have its downsides, however. One mistake by a celebrity can be detrimental to the public relations of a brand. For example, following his performance of eight gold medals at the 2008 Olympic Games in Beijing, China, swimmer Michael Phelps' contract with Kellogg's was terminated, as Kellogg's did not want to associate with him after he was photographed smoking marijuana.

Media and advertising approaches

Increasingly, other media are overtaking many of the "traditional" media such as television, radio and newspaper because of a shift toward consumer's usage of the Internet for news and music as well as devices like digital video recorders (DVR's) such as TiVo.

Advertising on the → World Wide Web is a recent phenomenon. Prices of Web-based advertising space are dependent on the "relevance" of the surrounding web content and the traffic that the website receives.

Digital signage is poised to become a major mass media because of its ability to reach larger audiences for less money. Digital signage also offer the unique ability to see the target audience where they are reached by the medium. Technology advances has also made it possible to control the message on digital signage with much precision, enabling the messages to be relevant to the target audience at any given time and location which in turn, gets more response from the advertising. Digital signage is being successfully employed in supermarkets.[16] Another successful use of digital signage is in hospitality locations such as restaurants.[17] and malls.[18]

E-mail advertising is another recent phenomenon. Unsolicited bulk E-mail advertising is known as "e-mail spam". Spam has been a problem for email users for many years. But more efficient filters are now available making it relatively easy to control what email you get.

Some companies have proposed placing messages or corporate logos on the side of booster rockets and the International Space Station. Controversy exists on the effectiveness of subliminal advertising (see mind control), and the pervasiveness of mass messages (see propaganda).

Unpaid advertising (also called "publicity advertising"), can provide good exposure at minimal cost. Personal recommendations ("bring a friend", "sell it"), spreading buzz, or achieving the feat of equating a brand with a common noun (in the United States, "Xerox" = "photocopier", "Kleenex" = tissue, "Vaseline" = petroleum jelly, "Hoover" = vacuum cleaner, "Nintendo" (often used by those exposed to many video games) = video games, and "Band-Aid" = adhesive bandage) — these can be seen as the pinnacle of any advertising campaign. However, some companies oppose the use of their brand name to label an object. Equating a brand with a common noun also risks turning that brand into a genericized trademark - turning it into a generic term which means that its legal protection as a trademark is lost.

As the mobile phone became a new mass media in 1998 when the first paid downloadable content appeared on mobile phones in Finland, it was only a matter of time until mobile advertising followed, also first launched in Finland in 2000. By 2007 the value of mobile advertising had reached $2.2 billion and providers such as Admob delivered billions of mobile ads.

More advanced mobile ads include banner ads, coupons, Multimedia Messaging Service picture and video messages, advergames and various engagement marketing campaigns. A particular feature driving mobile ads is the 2D Barcode, which replaces the need to do any typing of web addresses, and uses the camera feature of modern phones to gain immediate access to web content. 83 percent of Japanese mobile phone users already are active users of 2D barcodes.

A new form of advertising that is growing rapidly is social network advertising. It is online advertising with a focus on social networking sites. This is a relatively immature market, but it has shown a lot of promise as advertisers are able to take advantage of the demographic information the user has provided to the social networking site. Friendertising is a more precise advertising term in which people are able to direct advertisements toward others directly using social network service.

From time to time, The CW Television Network airs short programming breaks called "Content Wraps," to advertise one company's product during an entire commercial break. The CW pioneered "content wraps" and some products featured were Herbal Essences, Crest, Guitar Hero II, CoverGirl, and recently Toyota.

Recently, there appeared a new promotion concept, "ARvertising", advertising on Augmented Reality technology.

Criticism of advertising

While advertising can be seen as necessary for economic growth, it is not without social costs. Unsolicited Commercial Email and other forms of spam have become so prevalent as to have become a major nuisance to users of these services, as well as being a financial burden on internet service providers.[19] Advertising is increasingly invading public spaces, such as schools, which some critics argue is a form of child exploitation.[20] In addition, advertising frequently uses psychological pressure (for example, appealing to feelings of inadequacy) on the intended consumer, which may be harmful.

Hyper-commercialism and the commercial tidal wave

Criticism of advertising is closely linked with criticism of media and often interchangeable. They can refer to its audio-visual aspects (e. g. cluttering of public spaces and airwaves), environmental aspects (e. g. pollution, oversize packaging, increasing consumption), political aspects (e. g. media dependency, free speech, censorship), financial aspects (costs), ethical/moral/social aspects (e. g. sub-conscious influencing, invasion of privacy, increasing consumption and waste, target groups, certain products, honesty) and, of course, a mix thereof. Some aspects can be subdivided further and some can cover more than one category.

As advertising has become increasingly prevalent in modern Western societies, it is also increasingly being criticized. A person can hardly move in the public sphere or use a medium without being subject to advertising. Advertising occupies public space and more and more invades the private sphere of people, many of which consider it a nuisance. "It is becoming harder to escape from advertising and the media. ... Public space is increasingly turning into a gigantic billboard for products of all kind. The aesthetical and political consequences cannot yet be foreseen."[21] Hanno Rauterberg in the German newspaper 'Die Zeit' calls advertising a new kind of dictatorship that cannot be escaped.[22]

Ad creep: "There are ads in schools, airport lounges, doctors offices, movie theaters, hospitals, gas stations, elevators, convenience stores, on the Internet, on fruit, on ATMs, on garbage cans and countless other places. There are ads on beach sand and restroom walls."[23] "One of the ironies of advertising in our times is that as commercialism increases, it makes it that much more difficult for any particular advertiser to succeed, hence pushing the advertiser to even greater efforts."[24] Within a decade advertising in radios climbed to nearly 18 or 19 minutes per hour; on prime-time television the standard until 1982 was no more than 9.5 minutes of advertising per hour, today it's between 14 and 17 minutes. With the introduction of the shorter 15-second-spot the total amount of ads increased even more dramatically. Ads are not only placed in breaks but e. g. also into baseball telecasts during the game itself. They flood the internet, a market growing in leaps and bounds.

Other growing markets are "product placements" in entertainment programming and in movies where it has become standard practice and "virtual advertising" where products get placed retroactively into rerun shows. Product billboards are virtually inserted into Major League Baseball broadcasts and in the same manner, virtual street banners or logos are projected on an entry canopy or sidewalks, for example during the arrival of celebrities at the 2001 Grammy Awards. Advertising precedes the showing of films at cinemas including lavish 'film shorts' produced by companies such as Microsoft or DaimlerChrysler. "The largest advertising agencies have begun working aggressively to co-produce programming in conjunction with the largest media firms"[25] creating Infomercials resembling entertainment programming.

Opponents equate the growing amount of advertising with a "tidal wave" and restrictions with "damming" the flood. Kalle Lasn, one of the most outspoken critics of advertising on the international stage, considers advertising "the most prevalent and toxic of the mental pollutants. From the moment your radio alarm sounds in the morning to the wee hours of late-night TV microjolts of commercial pollution flood into your brain at the rate of around 3,000 marketing messages per day. Every day an estimated twelve billion display ads, 3 million radio commercials and more than 200,000 television commercials are dumped into North America's collective unconscious".[26] In the course of his life the average American watches three years of advertising on television.[27]

More recent developments are video games incorporating products into their content, special commercial patient channels in hospitals and public figures sporting temporary tattoos. A method unrecognisable as advertising is so-called "guerrilla marketing" which is spreading 'buzz' about a new product in target audiences. Cash-strapped U.S. cities do not shrink back from offering police cars for advertising.[28] A trend, especially in Germany, is companies buying the names of sports stadiums. The Hamburg soccer Volkspark stadium first became the AOL Arena and then the HSH Nordbank Arena. The Stuttgart Neckarstadion became the Mercedes-Benz Arena, the Dortmund Westfalenstadion now is the Signal Iduna Park. The former SkyDome in Toronto was renamed Rogers Centre. Other recent developments are, for example, that whole subway stations in Berlin are redesigned into product halls and exclusively leased to a company. Düsseldorf even has 'multi-sensorial' adventure transit stops equipped with loudspeakers and systems that spread the smell of a detergent. Swatch used beamers to project messages on the Berlin TV-tower and Victory column, which was fined because it was done without a permit. The illegality was part of the scheme and added promotion.[22]

It's standard business management knowledge that advertising is a pillar, if not "the" pillar of the growth-orientated free capitalist economy. "Advertising is part of the bone marrow of corporate capitalism."[29] "Contemporary capitalism could not function and global production networks could not exist as they do without advertising."[1]

For communication scientist and media economist Manfred Knoche at the University of Salzburg, Austria, advertising isn't just simply a 'necessary evil' but a 'necessary elixir of life' for the media business, the economy and capitalism as a whole. Advertising and mass media economic interests create ideology. Knoche describes advertising for products and brands as 'the producer's weapons in the competition for customers' and trade advertising, e. g. by the automotive industry, as a means to collectively represent their interests against other groups, such as the train companies. In his view editorial articles and programmes in the media, promoting consumption in general, provide a 'cost free' service to producers and sponsoring for a 'much used means of payment' in advertising.[30] Christopher Lasch argues that advertising leads to an overall increase in consumption in society; "Advertising serves not so much to advertise products as to promote consumption as a way of life."[31]

Advertising and constitutional rights

Advertising is equated with constitutionally guaranteed freedom of opinion and speech.[32] Therefore criticizing advertising or any attempt to restrict or ban advertising is almost always considered to be an attack on fundamental rights (First Amendment in the USA) and meets the combined and concentrated resistance of the business and especially the advertising community. "Currently or in the near future, any number of cases are and will be working their way through the court system that would seek to prohibit any government regulation of ... commercial speech (e. g. advertising or food labelling) on the grounds that such regulation would violate citizens' and corporations' First Amendment rights to free speech or free press."[33] An example for this debate is advertising for tobacco or alcohol but also advertising by mail or fliers (clogged mail boxes), advertising on the phone, in the internet and advertising for children. Various legal restrictions concerning spamming, advertising on mobile phones, addressing children, tobacco, alcohol have been introduced by the US, the EU and various other countries. Not only the business community resists restrictions of advertising. Advertising as a means of free expression has firmly established itself in western society. McChesney argues, that the government deserves constant vigilance when it comes to such regulations, but that it is certainly not "the only antidemocratic force in our society. ...corporations and the wealthy enjoy a power every bit as immense as that enjoyed by the lords and royalty of feudal times" and "markets are not value-free or neutral; they not only tend to work to the advantage of those with the most money, but they also by their very nature emphasize profit over all else....Hence, today the debate is over whether advertising or food labelling, or campaign contributions are speech...if the rights to be protected by the First Amendment can only be effectively employed by a fraction of the citizenry, and their exercise of these rights gives them undue political power and undermines the ability of the balance of the citizenry to exercise the same rights and/or constitutional rights, then it is not necessarily legitimately protected by the First Amendment." In addition, "those with the capacity to engage in free press are in a position to determine who can speak to the great mass of citizens and who cannot".[34] Critics in turn argue, that advertising invades privacy which is a constitutional right. For, on the one hand, advertising physically invades privacy, on the other, it increasingly uses relevant, information-based communication with private data assembled without the knowledge or consent of consumers or target groups.

For Georg Franck at Vienna University of Technology advertising is part of what he calls "mental capitalism",[35] [36] taking up a term (mental) which has been used by groups concerned with the mental environment, such as Adbusters. Franck blends the "Economy of Attention" with Christopher Lasch's culture of narcism into the mental capitalism:[37] In his essay „Advertising at the Edge of the Apocalypse", Sut Jhally writes: "20. century advertising is the most powerful and sustained system of propaganda in human history and its cumulative cultural effects, unless quickly checked, will be responsible for destroying the world as we know it.[38]

The price of attention and hidden costs

Advertising has developed into a billion-dollar business on which many depend. In 2006 391 billion US dollars were spent worldwide for advertising. In Germany, for example, the advertising industry contributes 1.5% of the gross national income; the figures for other developed countries are similar. Thus, advertising and growth are directly and causally linked. As far as a growth based economy can be blamed for the harmful human lifestyle (affluent society) advertising has to be considered in this aspect concerning its negative impact, because its main purpose is to raise consumption. "The industry is accused of being one of the engines powering a convoluted economic mass production system which promotes consumption."[39]

Attention and attentiveness have become a new commodity for which a market developed. "The amount of attention that is absorbed by the media and redistributed in the competition for quotas and reach is not identical with the amount of attention, that is available in society. The total amount circulating in society is made up of the attention exchanged among the people themselves and the attention given to media information. Only the latter is homogenised by quantitative measuring and only the latter takes on the character of an anonymous currency."[35] [36] According to Franck, any surface of presentation that can guarantee a certain degree of attentiveness works as magnet for attention, e. g. media which are actually meant for information and entertainment, culture and the arts, public space etc. It is this attraction which is sold to the advertising business. The German Advertising Association stated that in 2007 30.78 billion Euros were spent on advertising in Germany,[40] 26% in newspapers, 21% on television, 15% by mail and 15% in magazines. In 2002 there were 360.000 people employed in the advertising business. The internet revenues for advertising doubled to almost 1 billion Euros from 2006 to 2007, giving it the highest growth rates.

Spiegel-Online reported that in the USA in 2008 for the first time more money was spent for advertising on internet (105.3 billion US dollars) than on television (98.5 billion US dollars). The largest amount in 2008 was still spent in the print media (147 billion US dollars).[41] For that same year, Welt-Online reported that the US pharmaceutical industry spent almost double the amount on advertising (57.7 billion dollars) than it did on research (31.5 billion dollars). But Marc-André Gagnon und Joel Lexchin of York University, Toronto, estimate that the actual expenses for advertising are higher yet, because not all entries are recorded by the research institutions.[42] Not included are indirect advertising campaigns such as sales, rebates and price reductions. Few consumers are aware of the fact that they are the ones paying for every cent spent for public relations, advertisements, rebates, packaging etc. since they ordinarily get included in the price calculation.

Influencing and conditioning

The most important element of advertising is not information but suggestion more or less making use of associations, emotions (appeal to emotion) and drives dormant in the sub-conscience of people, such as sex drive, herd instinct, of desires, such as happiness, health, fitness, appearance, self-esteem, reputation, belonging, social status, identity, adventure, distraction, reward, of fears (appeal to fear), such as illness, weaknesses, loneliness, need, uncertainty, security or of prejudices, learned opinions and comforts. "All human needs, relationships, and fears – the deepest recesses of the human psyche – become mere means for the expansion of the commodity universe under the force of modern marketing. With the rise to prominence of modern marketing, commercialism – the translation of human relations into commodity relations – although a phenomenon intrinsic to capitalism, has expanded exponentially."[43] 'Cause-related marketing' in which advertisers link their product to some worthy social cause has boomed over the past decade.

Advertising for McDonald's on the Via di Propaganda, Rome, Italy

Advertising exploits the model role of celebrities or popular figures and makes deliberate use of humour as well as of associations with colour, tunes, certain names and terms. Altogether, these are factors of how one perceives himself and one's self-worth. In his description of 'mental capitalism' Franck says, "the promise of consumption making someone irresistible is the ideal way of objects and symbols into a person's subjective experience. Evidently, in a society in which revenue of attention moves to the fore, consumption is drawn by one's self-esteem. As a result, consumption becomes 'work' on a person's attraction. From the subjective point of view, this 'work' opens fields of unexpected dimensions for advertising. Advertising takes on the role of a life councillor in matters of attraction. (...) The cult around one's own attraction is what Christopher Lasch described as 'Culture of Narcissism'."[36] [37]

For advertising critics another serious problem is that "the long standing notion of separation between advertising and editorial/creative sides of media is rapidly crumbling" and advertising is increasingly hard to tell apart from news, information or entertainment. The boundaries between advertising and programming are becoming blurred. According to the media firms all this commercial involvement has no influence over actual media content, but, as

McChesney puts it, "this claim fails to pass even the most basic giggle test, it is so preposterous."[44]

Advertising draws "heavily on psychological theories about how to create subjects, enabling advertising and marketing to take on a 'more clearly psychological tinge' (Miller and Rose, 1997, cited in Thrift, 1999, p. 67). Increasingly, the emphasis in advertising has switched from providing 'factual' information to the symbolic connotations of commodities, since the crucial cultural premise of advertising is that the material object being sold is never in itself enough. Even those commodities providing for the most mundane necessities of daily life must be imbued with symbolic qualities and culturally endowed meanings via the 'magic system (Williams, 1980) of advertising. In this way and by altering the context in which advertisements appear, things 'can be made to mean "just about anything"' (McFall, 2002, p. 162) and the 'same' things can be endowed with different intended meanings for different individuals and groups of people, thereby offering mass produced visions of individualism."[1]

Before advertising is done, market research institutions need to know and describe the target group to exactly plan and implement the advertising campaign and to achieve the best possible results. A whole array of sciences directly deal with advertising and marketing or is used to improve its effects. Focus groups, psychologists and cultural anthropologists are "'de rigueur'" in marketing research".[45] Vast amounts of data on persons and their shopping habits are collected, accumulated, aggregated and analysed with the aid of credit cards, bonus cards, raffles and internet surveying. With increasing accuracy this supplies a picture of behaviour, wishes and weaknesses of certain sections of a population with which advertisement can be employed more selectively and effectively. The efficiency of advertising is improved through advertising research. Universities, of course supported by business and in co-operation with other disciplines (s. above), mainly Psychiatry, Anthropology, Neurology and behavioural sciences, are constantly in search for ever more refined, sophisticated, subtle and crafty methods to make advertising more effective. "Neuromarketing is a controversial new field of marketing which uses medical technologies such as functional Magnetic Resonance Imaging (fMRI) -- not to heal, but to sell products. Advertising and marketing firms have long used the insights and research methods of psychology in order to sell products, of course. But today these practices are reaching epidemic levels, and with a complicity on the part of the psychological profession that exceeds that of the past. The result is an enormous advertising and marketing onslaught that comprises, arguably, the largest single psychological project ever undertaken. Yet, this great undertaking remains largely ignored by the American Psychological Association."[46] Robert McChesney calls it "the greatest concerted attempt at psychological manipulation in all of human history."[47]

Dependency of the media and corporate censorship

Almost all mass media are advertising media and many of them are exclusively advertising media and, with the exception of public service broadcasting are privately owned. Their income is predominantly generated through advertising; in the case of newspapers and magazines from 50 to 80%. Public service broadcasting in some countries can also heavily depend on advertising as a source of income (up to 40%).[48] In the view of critics no media that spreads advertisements can be independent and the higher the proportion of advertising, the higher the dependency. This dependency has "distinct implications for the nature of media content.... In the business press, the media are often referred to in exactly the way they present themselves in their candid moments: as a branch of the advertising industry."[49]

In addition, the private media are increasingly subject to mergers and concentration with property situations often becoming entangled and opaque. This development, which Henry A. Giroux calls an "ongoing threat to democratic culture",[50] by itself should suffice to sound all alarms in a democracy. Five or six advertising agencies dominate this 400 billion U.S. dollar global industry.

"Journalists have long faced pressure to shape stories to suit advertisers and owners .... the vast majority of TV station executives found their news departments 'cooperative' in shaping the news to assist in 'non-traditional revenue development."[51] Negative and undesired reporting can be prevented or influenced when advertisers threaten to cancel orders or simply when there is a danger of such a cancellation. Media dependency and such a threat becomes very real when there is only one dominant or very few large advertisers. The influence of advertisers is not only in regard to news or information on their own products or services but expands to articles or shows not directly linked to them. In order to secure their advertising revenues the media has to create the best possible 'advertising environment'. Another problem considered censorship by critics is the refusal of media to accept advertisements that are not in their interest. A striking example of this is the refusal of TV stations to broadcast ads by Adbusters. Groups try to place advertisements and are refused by networks.[52]

It is principally the viewing rates which decide upon the programme in the private radio and television business. "Their business is to absorb as much attention as possible. The viewing rate measures the attention the media trades for the information offered. The service of this attraction is sold to the advertising business"[36] and the viewing rates determine the price that can be demanded for advertising.

"Advertising companies determining the contents of shows has been part of daily life in the USA since 1933. Procter & Gamble (P&G) .... offered a radio station a history-making trade (today know as "bartering"): the company would produce an own show for "free" and save the radio station the high expenses for producing contents. Therefore the company would want its commercials spread and, of course, its products placed in the show. Thus, the series 'Ma Perkins' was created, which P&G skilfully used to promote Oxydol, the leading detergent brand in those years and the Soap opera was born ..."[53]

While critics basically worry about the subtle influence of the economy on the media, there are also examples of blunt exertion of influence. The US company Chrysler, before it merged with Daimler Benz had its agency, PentaCom, send out a letter to numerous magazines, demanding them to send, an overview of all the topics before the next issue is published to "avoid potential conflict". Chrysler most of all wanted to know, if there would be articles with "sexual, political or social" content or which could be seen as "provocative or offensive". PentaCom executive David Martin said: "Our reasoning is, that anyone looking at a 22.000 $ product would want it surrounded by positive things. There is nothing positive about an article on child pornography."[53] In another example, the „USA Network held top-level ‚off-the-record' meetings with advertisers in 2000 to let them tell the network what type of programming content they wanted in order for USA to get their advertising."[54] Television shows are created to accommodate the needs for advertising, e. g. splitting them up in suitable sections. Their dramaturgy is typically designed to end in suspense or leave an unanswered question in order to keep the viewer attached.

The movie system, at one time outside the direct influence of the broader marketing system, is now fully integrated into it through the strategies of licensing, tie-ins and product placements. The prime function of many Hollywood films today is to aid in the selling of the immense collection of commodities.[55] The press called the 2002 Bond film 'Die Another Day' featuring 24 major promotional partners an 'ad-venture' and noted that James Bond "now has been 'licensed to sell'" As it has become standard practise to place products in motion pictures, it "has self-evident implications for what types of films will attract product placements and what types of films will therefore be more likely to get made".[56]

Advertising and information are increasingly hard to distinguish from each other. "The borders between advertising and media .... become more and more blurred.... What August Fischer, chairman of the board of Axel Springer publishing company considers to be a 'proven partnership between the media and advertising business' critics regard as nothing but the infiltration of journalistic duties and freedoms". According to RTL-executive Helmut Thoma "private stations shall not and cannot serve any mission but only the goal of the company which is the 'acceptance by the advertising business and the viewer'. The setting of priorities in this order actually says everything about the 'design of the programmes' by private television."[53] Patrick Le Lay, former managing director of TF1, a private French television channel with a market share of 25 to 35%, said: "There are many ways to talk about television. But from the business point of view, let's be realistic: basically, the job of TF1 is, e. g. to help Coca Cola sell its product. (...) For an advertising message to be perceived the brain of the viewer must be at our disposal. The job of our programmes is to make it available, that is to say, to distract it, to relax it and get it ready between two messages. It is disposable human brain time that we sell to Coca Cola."[57]

Because of these dependencies a widespread and fundamental public debate about advertising and its influence on information and freedom of speech is difficult to obtain, at least through the usual media channels; otherwise these would saw off the branch they are sitting on. "The notion that the commercial basis of media, journalism, and communication could have troubling implications for democracy is excluded from the range of legitimate debate" just as "capitalism is off-limits as a topic of legitimate debate in U.S. political culture".[58]

An early critic of the structural basis of U.S. journalism was Upton Sinclair with his novel The Brass Check in which he stresses the influence of owners, advertisers, public relations, and economic interests on the media. In his book "Our Master's Voice – Advertising" the social ecologist James Rorty (1890–1973) wrote: "The gargoyle's mouth is a loudspeaker, powered by the vested interest of a two-billion dollar industry, and back of that the vested interests of business as a whole, of industry, of finance. It is never silent, it drowns out all other voices, and it suffers no rebuke, for it is not the voice of America? That is its claim and to some extent it is a just claim..."[59]

It has taught us how to live, what to be afraid of, what to be proud of, how to be beautiful, how to be loved, how to be envied, how to be successful.. Is it any wonder that the American population tends increasingly to speak, think, feel in terms of this jabberwocky? That the stimuli of art, science, religion are progressively expelled to the periphery of American life to become marginal values, cultivated by marginal people on marginal time?"[60]

The commercialisation of culture and sports

Performances, exhibitions, shows, concerts, conventions and most other events can hardly take place without sponsoring. The increasing lack arts and culture they buy the service of attraction. Artists are graded and paid according to their art's value for commercial purposes. Corporations promote renown artists, therefore getting exclusive rights in global advertising campaigns. Broadway shows, like 'La Bohème' featured commercial props in its set.[61]

Advertising itself is extensively considered to be a contribution to culture. Advertising is integrated into fashion. On many pieces of clothing the company logo is the only design or is an important part of it. There is only little room left outside the consumption economy, in which culture and art can develop independently and where alternative values can be expressed. A last important sphere, the universities, is under strong pressure to open up for business and its interests.[62]

Competitive sports have become unthinkable without sponsoring and there is a mutual dependency. High income with advertising is only possible with a comparable number of spectators or viewers. On the other hand, the poor performance of a team or a sportsman results in less advertising revenues. Jürgen Hüther and Hans-Jörg Stiehler talk about a 'Sports/Media Complex which is a complicated mix of media, agencies, managers, sports promoters, advertising etc. with partially common and partially diverging interests but in any case with common commercial interests. The media presumably is at centre stage because it can supply the other parties involved with a rare commodity, namely

Inflatable billboard in front of a sports stadium

(potential) public attention. In sports "the media are able to generate enormous sales in both circulation and advertising."[63]

"Sports sponsorship is acknowledged by the tobacco industry to be valuable advertising. A Tobacco Industry journal in 1994 described the Formula One car as 'The most powerful advertising space in the world'. .... In a cohort study carried out in 22 secondary schools in England in 1994 and 1995 boys whose favourite television sport was motor racing had a 12.8% risk of becoming regular smokers compared to 7.0% of boys who did not follow motor racing."[64]

Not the sale of tickets but transmission rights, sponsoring and merchandising in the meantime make up the largest part of sports association's and sports club's revenues with the IOC (International Olympic Committee) taking the lead. The influence of the media brought many changes in sports including the admittance of new 'trend sports' into the Olympic Games, the alteration of competition distances, changes of rules, animation of spectators, changes of sports facilities, the cult of sports heroes who quickly establish themselves in the advertising and entertaining business because of their media value[65] and last but not least, the naming and renaming of sport stadiums after big companies. "In sports adjustment into the logic of the media can contribute to the erosion of values such as equal chances or fairness, to excessive demands on athletes through public pressure and multiple exploitation or to deceit (doping, manipulation of results …). It is in the very interest of the media and sports to counter this danger because media sports can only work as long as sport exists.[65]

Occupation and commercialisation of public space

Every visually perceptible place has potential for advertising. Especially urban areas with their structures but also landscapes in sight of through fares are more and more turning into media for advertisements. Signs, posters, billboards, flags have become decisive factors in the urban appearance and their numbers are still on the increase. "Outdoor advertising has become unavoidable. Traditional billboards and transit shelters have cleared the way for more pervasive methods such as wrapped vehicles, sides of buildings, electronic signs, kiosks, taxis, posters, sides of buses, and more. Digital technologies are used on buildings to sport 'urban wall displays'. In urban areas commercial content is placed in our sight and into our consciousness every moment we are in public space. The German Newspaper 'Zeit' called it a new kind of 'dictatorship that one cannot escape'.[22] Over time, this domination of the surroundings has become the "natural" state. Through long-term commercial saturation, it has become implicitly understood by the public that advertising has the right to own, occupy and control every inch of available space. The steady normalization of invasive advertising dulls the public's perception of their surroundings, re-enforcing a general attitude of powerlessness toward creativity and change, thus a cycle develops enabling advertisers to slowly and consistently increase the saturation of advertising with little or no public outcry."[66]

The massive optical orientation toward advertising changes the function of public spaces which are utilised by brands. Urban landmarks are turned into trademarks. The highest pressure is exerted on renown and highly frequented public spaces which are also important for the identity of a city (e. g. Piccadilly Circus, Times Square, Alexanderplatz). Urban spaces are public commodities and in this capacity they are subject to "aesthetical environment protection", mainly through building regulations, heritage protection and landscape protection. "It is in this capacity that these spaces are now being privatised. They are peppered with billboards and signs, they are remodelled into media for advertising."[35] [36]

Socio-cultural aspects: sexism, discrimination and stereotyping

"Advertising has an "agenda setting function" which is the ability, with huge sums of money, to put consumption as the only item on the agenda. In the battle for a share of the public conscience this amounts to non-treatment (ignorance) of whatever is not commercial and whatever is not advertised for. Advertising should be reflection of society norms and give clear picture of target market. Spheres without commerce and advertising serving the muses and relaxation remain without respect. With increasing force advertising makes itself comfortable in the private sphere so that the voice of commerce becomes the dominant way of expression in society."[67] Advertising critics see advertising as the leading light in our culture. Sut Jhally and James Twitchell go beyond considering advertising as kind of religion and that advertising even replaces religion as a key institution.[68] "Corporate advertising (or is it commercial media?) is the largest single psychological project ever undertaken by the human race. Yet for all of that, its impact on us remains unknown and largely ignored. When I think of the media's influence over years, over decades, I think of those brainwashing experiments conducted by Dr. Ewen Cameron in a Montreal psychiatric hospital in the 1950s (see MKULTRA). The idea of the CIA-sponsored "depatterning" experiments was to outfit conscious, unconscious or semiconscious subjects with headphones, and flood their brains with thousands of repetitive "driving" messages that would alter their behaviour over time....Advertising aims to do the same thing."[26] Advertising is especially aimed at young people and children and it increasingly reduces young people to consumers.[50] For Sut Jhally it is not "surprising that something this central and with so much being expended on it should become an important presence in social life. Indeed, commercial interests intent on maximizing the consumption of the immense collection of commodities have colonized more and more of the spaces of our culture. For instance, almost the entire media system (television and print) has been developed as a delivery system for marketers its prime function is to produce audiences for sale to advertisers. Both the advertisements it carries, as well as the editorial matter that acts as a support for it, celebrate the consumer society. The movie system, at one time outside the direct influence of the broader marketing system, is now fully integrated into it through the strategies of licensing, tie-ins and product placements. The prime function of many Hollywood films today is to aid in the selling of the immense collection of commodities. As public funds are drained from the non-commercial cultural sector, art galleries, museums and symphonies bid for corporate sponsorship."[55] In the same way effected is the education system and advertising is increasingly penetrating schools and universities. Cities, such as New York, accept sponsors for public playgrounds. "Even the pope has been commercialized ... The pope's 4-day visit to Mexico in ...1999 was sponsored by Frito-Lay and PepsiCo.[69] The industry is accused of being one of the engines powering a convoluted economic mass production system which promotes consumption. As far as social effects are concerned it does not matter whether advertising fuels consumption but which values, patterns of behaviour and assignments of meaning it propagates. Advertising is accused of hijacking the language and means of pop culture, of protest movements and even of subversive criticism and does not shy away from scandalizing and breaking taboos (e. g. Benneton). This in turn incites counter action, what Kalle Lasn in 2001 called "Jamming the Jam of the Jammers". Anything goes. "It is a central social-scientific question what people can be made to do by suitable design of conditions and of great practical importance. For example, from a great number of experimental psychological experiments it can be assumed, that people can be made to do anything they are capable of, when the according social condition can be created."[70]

Advertising often uses stereotype gender specific roles of men and women reinforcing existing clichés and it has been criticized as "inadvertently or even intentionally promoting sexism, racism, and ageism... At very least, advertising often reinforces stereotypes by drawing on recognizable "types" in order to tell stories in a single image or 30 second time frame."[39] Activities are depicted as typical male or female (stereotyping). In addition people are reduced to their sexuality or equated with commodities and gender specific qualities are exaggerated. Sexualized female bodies, but increasingly also males, serve as eye-catchers. In advertising it is usually a woman being depicted as

- servants of men and children that react to the demands and complaints of their loved ones with a bad conscience and the promise for immediate improvement (wash, food)
- a sexual or emotional play toy for the self-affirmation of men
- a technically totally clueless being that can only manage a childproof operation
- female expert, but stereotype from the fields of fashion, cosmetics, food or at the most, medicine
- as ultra thin, slim, and very skinny.
- doing ground-work for others, e. g. serving coffee while a journalist interviews a politician[71]

A large portion of advertising deals with promotion of products that pertain to the "ideal body image." This is mainly targeted toward women, and, in the past, this type of advertising was aimed nearly exclusively at women. Women in advertisements are generally portrayed as good-looking women who are in good health. This, however, is not the case of the average woman. Consequently, they give a negative message of body image to the average woman. Because of the media, girls and women who are overweight, and otherwise "normal" feel almost obligated to take care of themselves and stay fit. They feel under high pressure to maintain an acceptable bodyweight and take care of their health. Consequences of this are low self-esteem,eating disorders, self mutilations, and beauty operations for those women that just cannot bring themselves eat right or get the motivation to go to the gym. The EU parliament passed a resolution in 2008 that advertising may not be discriminating and degrading. This shows that politicians are increasingly concerned about the negative impacts of advertising. However, the benefits of promoting overall health and fitness are often overlooked.

Children and adolescents as target groups

The children's market, where resistance to advertising is weakest, is the "pioneer for ad creep".[72] "Kids are among the most sophisticated observers of ads. They can sing the jingles and identify the logos, and they often have strong feelings about products. What they generally don't understand, however, are the issues that underlie how advertising works. Mass media are used not only to sell goods but also ideas: how we should behave, what rules are important, who we should respect and what we should value."[73] Youth is increasingly reduced to the role of a consumer. Not only the makers of toys, sweets, ice cream, breakfast food and sport articles prefer to aim their promotion at children and adolescents. For example, an ad for a breakfast cereal on a channel aimed at adults will have music that is a soft ballad, whereas on a channel aimed at children, the same ad will use a catchy rock jingle of the same song to aim at kids. Advertising for other products preferably uses media with which they can also reach the next generation of consumers.[74] "Key advertising messages exploit the emerging independence of young people". Cigarettes, for example, "are used as a fashion accessory and appeal to young women. Other influences on young people include the linking of sporting heroes and smoking through sports sponsorship, the use of cigarettes by popular characters in television programmes and cigarette promotions. Research suggests that young people are aware of the most heavily advertised cigarette brands."[64]

"Product placements show up everywhere, and children aren't exempt. Far from it. The animated film, Foodfight, had 'thousands of products and character icons from the familiar (items) in a grocery store.' Children's books also feature branded items and characters, and millions of them have snack foods as lead characters."[75] Business is interested in children and adolescents because of their buying power and because of their influence on the shopping habits of their parents. As they are easier to influence they are especially targeted by the advertising business. "The marketing industry is facing increased pressure over claimed links between exposure to food advertising and a range of social problems, especially growing obesity levels."[76] In 2001, children's programming accounted for over 20% of all U.S. television watching. The global market for children's licensed products was some 132 billion U.S. dollars in 2002.[45] Advertisers target children because, e. g. in Canada, they "represent three distinct markets:

1. Primary Purchasers ($2.9 billion annually)
2. Future Consumers (Brand-loyal adults)
3. Purchase Influencers ($20 billion annually)

Kids will carry forward brand expectations, whether positive, negative, or indifferent. Kids are already accustomed to being catered to as consumers. The long term prize: Loyalty of the kid translates into a brand loyal adult customer"[77]

The average Canadian child sees 350,000 TV commercials before graduating from high school, spends nearly as much time watching TV as attending classes. In 1980 the Canadian province of Québec banned advertising for children under age 13.[78] "In upholding the consititutional validity of the Quebec Consumer Protection Act restrictions on advertising to children under age 13 (in the case of a challenge by a toy company) the Court held: '...advertising directed at young children is per se manipulative. Such advertising aims to promote products by convincing those who will always believe.'"[79] Norway (ads directed at children under age 12), and Sweden (television ads aimed at children under age 12) also have legislated broad bans on advertising to children, during child programmes any kind of advertising is forbidden in Sweden, Denmark, Austria and Flemish Belgium. In Greece there is no advertising for kids products from 7 to 22 h. An attempt to restrict advertising directed at children in the USA failed with reference to the First Amendment. In Spain bans are also considered undemocratic.[80] [81]

Opposition and campaigns against advertising

According to critics, the total commercialization of all fields of society, the privatization of public space, the acceleration of consumption and waste of resources including the negative influence on lifestyles and on the environment has not been noticed to the necessary extent. The "hyper-commercialization of the culture is recognized and roundly detested by the citizenry, although the topic scarcely receives a whiff of attention in the media or political culture".[82] "The greatest damage done by advertising is precisely that it incessantly demonstrates the prostitution of men and women who lend their intellects, their voices, their artistic skills to purposes in which they themselves do not believe, and .... that it helps to shatter and ultimately destroy our most precious non-material possessions: the confidence in the existence of meaningful purposes of human activity and respect for the integrity of man."[83] "The struggle against advertising is therefore essential if we are to overcome the pervasive alienation from all genuine human needs that currently plays such a corrosive role in our society. But in resisting this type of hyper-commercialism we should not be under any illusions.

Billboard in Lund, Sweden, saying "One Night Stand?" (2005)

Advertising may seem at times to be an almost trivial of omnipresent aspect of our economic system. Yet, as economist A. C. Pigou pointed out, it could only be 'removed altogether' if 'conditions of monopolistic competition' inherent to corporate capitalism were removed. To resist it is to resist the inner logic of capitalism itself, of which it is the pure expression."[84]

"Visual pollution, much of it in the form of advertising, is an issue in all the world's large cities. But what is pollution to some is a vibrant part of a city's fabric to others. New York City without Times Square's huge digital billboards or Tokyo without the Ginza's commercial panorama is unthinkable. Piccadilly Circus would be just a London roundabout without its signage. Still, other cities, like Moscow, have reached their limit and have begun to crack down on over-the-top outdoor advertising."[85] "Many communities have chosen to regulate billboards to protect and enhance their scenic character. The following is by no means a complete list of such communities, but it does give a good idea of the geographic diversity of cities, counties and states that prohibit new construction of billboards. Scenic America estimates the nationwide total of cities and communities prohibiting the construction of new billboards to be at least 1500. A number of States in the USA prohibit all billboards:

- Vermont - Removed all billboards in 1970s
- Hawaii - Removed all billboards in 1920s
- Maine - Removed all billboards in 1970s and early 80s
- Alaska - State referendum passed in 1998 prohibits billboards[86]
- Almost two years ago the city of São Paulo, Brazil, ordered the downsizing or removal of all billboards and most other forms of commercial advertising in the city."[87]

Technical appliances, such as Spam filters, TV-Zappers, Ad-Blockers for TV's and stickers on mail boxes: "No Advertising" and an increasing number of court cases indicate a growing interest of people to restrict or rid themselves of unwelcome advertising.

Consumer protection associations, environment protection groups, globalization opponents, consumption critics, sociologists, media critics, scientists and many others deal with the negative aspects of advertising. "Antipub" in France, "subverting", culture jamming and adbusting have become established terms in the anti-advertising community. On the international level globalization critics such as Naomi Klein and Noam Chomsky are also renown media and advertising critics. These groups criticize the complete occupation of public spaces, surfaces, the airwaves, the media, schools etc. and the constant exposure of almost all senses to advertising messages, the invasion of privacy, and that only few consumers are aware that they themselves are bearing the costs for this to the very last penny. Some of these groups, such as the 'The Billboard Liberation Front Creative Group' in San Francisco or Adbusters in Vancouver, Canada, have manifestos.[88] Grassroots organizations campaign against advertising or certain aspects of it in various forms and strategies and quite often have different roots. Adbusters, for example contests and challenges the intended meanings of advertising by subverting them and creating unintended meanings instead. Other groups, like 'Illegal Signs Canada' try to stem the flood of billboards by detecting and reporting ones that have been put up without permit.[89] Examples for various groups and organizations in different countries are 'L'association Résistance à l'Agression Publicitaire'[90] in France, where also media critic Jean Baudrillard is a renown author. [91] The 'Anti Advertising Agency' works with parody and humour to raise awareness about advertising.[92] and 'Commercial Alert' campaigns for the protection of children, family values, community, environmental integrity and democracy.[93] Media literacy organisations aim at training people, especially children in the workings of the media and advertising in their programmes. In the U. S., for example, the 'Media Education Foundation' produces and distributes documentary films and other educational resources.[94] 'MediaWatch', a Canadian non-profit women's organization works to educate consumers about how they can register their concerns with advertisers and regulators.[95] The Canadian 'Media Awareness Network/Réseau éducation médias' offers one of the world's most comprehensive collections of media education and Internet literacy resources. Its member organizations represent the public, non-profit but also private sectors. Although it stresses its independence it accepts financial support from Bell Canada, CTVGlobeMedia, CanWest, TELUS and S-VOX.[96]

To counter the increasing criticism of advertising aiming at children media literacy organizations are also initiated and funded by corporations and the advertising business themselves. In the U. S. 'The Advertising Educational Foundation' was created in 1983 supported by ad agencies, advertisers and media companies. It is the "advertising industry's provider and distributor of educational content to enrich the understanding of advertising and its role in culture, society and the economy"[97] sponsored for example by American Airlines, Anheuser-Busch, Campbell Soup, Coca-Cola, Colgate-Palmolive, Walt Disney, Ford, General Foods, General Mills, Gillette, Heinz, Johnson & Johnson, Kellogg, Kraft, Nestle, Philip Morris, Quaker Oats, Nabisco, Schering, Sterling, Unilever, Warner Lambert, advertising agencies like Saatchi & Saatchi Compton and media companies like American Broadcasting Companies, CBS, Capital Cities Communications, Cox Enterprises, Forbes, Hearst, Meredith, The New York Times, RCA/NBC, Reader's Digest, Time, Washington Post, just to mention a few. Canadian businesses established 'Concerned Children's Advertisers' in 1990 "to instill confidence in all relevant publics by actively demonstrating our commitment, concern, responsibility and respect for children".[98] Members are CanWest, Corus, CTV, General Mills, Hasbro, Hershey's, Kellogg's, Loblaw, Kraft, Mattel, McDonald's, Nestle, Pepsi, Walt Disney, Weston as well as almost 50 private broadcast partners and others.[99] Concerned Children's Advertisers was example for similar organizations in other countries like 'Media smart' in the United Kingdom with offspring in Germany, France, the Netherlands and Sweden. New Zealand has a similar business-funded programme called 'Willie Munchright'. "While such interventions are claimed to be designed to encourage children to be critical of commercial messages in general, critics of the marketing industry suggest that the motivation is simply to be seen to address a problem created by the industry itself, that is, the negative social impacts to which marketing activity has contributed.... By contributing media literacy education resources, the marketing industry is positioning itself as being part of the solution to these problems, thereby seeking to avoid wide restrictions or outright bans on marketing communication, particularly for food products deemed to have little nutritional value directed at children.... The need to be seen to be taking positive action primarily to avert potential restrictions on advertising is openly acknowledged by some sectors of the industry itself.... Furthermore, Hobbs (1998) suggests that such programs are also in the interest of media organizations that support the interventions to reduce criticism of the potential negative effects of the media themselves."[76]

Taxation as revenue and control

Public interest groups suggest that "access to the mental space targeted by advertisers should be taxed, in that at the present moment that space is being freely taken advantage of by advertisers with no compensation paid to the members of the public who are thus being intruded upon. This kind of tax would be a Pigovian tax in that it would act to reduce what is now increasingly seen as a public nuisance. Efforts to that end are gathering more momentum, with Arkansas and Maine considering bills to implement such a taxation. Florida enacted such a tax in 1987 but was forced to repeal it after six months, as a result of a concerted effort by national commercial interests, which withdrew planned conventions, causing major losses to the tourism industry, and cancelled advertising, causing a loss of 12 million dollars to the broadcast industry alone".[39]

In the U. S., for example, advertising is tax deductible and suggestions for possible limits to the advertising tax deduction are met with fierce opposition from the business sector, not to mention suggestions for a special taxation. In other countries, advertising at least is taxed in the same manner services are taxed and in some advertising is subject to special taxation although on a very low level. In many cases the taxation refers especially to media with advertising (e. g. Austria, Italy, Greece, Netherlands, Turkey, Estonia). Tax on advertising in European countries:[100]

- Belgium: Advertising or billboard tax (taxe d'affichage or aanplakkingstaks) on public posters depending on size and kind of paper as well as on neon signs
- France: Tax on television commercials (taxe sur la publicité télévisée) based on the cost of the advertising unit
- Italy: Municipal tax on acoustic and visual kinds of advertisements within the municipality (imposta communale sulla publicità) and municipal tax on signs, posters and other kinds of advertisements (diritti sulle pubbliche offisioni), the tariffs of which are under the jurisdiction of the municipalities
- Netherlands: Advertising tax (reclamebelastingen) with varying tariffs on certain advertising measures (excluding ads in newspapers and magazines) which can be levied by municipalities depending on the kind of advertising (billboards, neon signs etc.)
- Austria: Municipal announcement levies on advertising through writing, pictures or lights in public areas or publicly accessible areas with varying tariffs depending on the fee, the surface or the duration of the advertising measure as well as advertising tariffs on paid ads in printed media of usually 10% of the fee.
- Sweden: Advertising tax (reklamskatt) on ads and other kinds of advertising (billboards, film, television, advertising at fairs and exhibitions, flyers) in the range of 4% for ads in newspapers and 11% in all other cases. In the case of flyers the tariffs are based on the production costs, else on the fee
- Spain: Municipalities can tax advertising measures in their territory with a rather unimportant taxes and fees of various kinds.

In his book "When Corporations Rule the World" U.S. author and globalization critic David Korten even advocates a 50% tax on advertising to counterattack what he calls "an active propaganda machinery controlled by the world's largest corporations" which "constantly reassures us that consumerism is the path to happiness, governmental restraint of market excess is the cause of our distress, and economic globalization is both a historical inevitability and a boon to the human species."[101]

Regulation

In the US many communities believe that many forms of outdoor advertising blight the public realm.[102] As long ago as the 1960s in the US there were attempts to ban billboard advertising in the open countryside.[103] Cities such as São Paulo have introduced an outright ban[104] with London also having specific legislation to control unlawful displays.

There have been increasing efforts to protect the public interest by regulating the content and the influence of advertising. Some examples are: the ban on television tobacco advertising imposed in many countries, and the total ban of advertising to children under 12 imposed by the Swedish government in 1991. Though that regulation continues in effect for broadcasts originating within the country, it has been weakened by the European Court of Justice, which had found that Sweden was obliged to accept foreign programming, including those from neighboring countries or via satellite.

In Europe and elsewhere, there is a vigorous debate on whether (or how much) advertising to children should be regulated. This debate was exacerbated by a report released by the Kaiser Family Foundation in February 2004 which suggested fast food advertising that targets children was an important factor in the epidemic of childhood obesity in the United States.

In New Zealand, South Africa, Canada, and many European countries, the advertising industry operates a system of self-regulation. Advertisers, advertising agencies and the media agree on a code of advertising standards that they attempt to uphold. The general aim of such codes is to ensure that any advertising is 'legal, decent, honest and truthful'. Some self-regulatory organizations are funded by the industry, but remain independent, with the intent of upholding the standards or codes like the Advertising Standards Authority in the UK.

In the UK most forms of outdoor advertising such as the display of billboards is regulated by the UK Town and County Planning system. Currently the display of an advertisement without consent from the Planning Authority is a criminal offense liable to a fine of £2,500 per offence. All of the major outdoor billboard companies in the UK have convictions of this nature.

Naturally, many advertisers view governmental regulation or even self-regulation as intrusion of their freedom of speech or a necessary evil. Therefore, they employ a wide-variety of linguistic devices to bypass regulatory laws (e.g. printing English words in bold and French translations in fine print to deal with the Article 120 of the 1994 Toubon Law limiting the use of English in French advertising).[105] The advertisement of controversial products such as cigarettes and condoms are subject to government regulation in many countries. For instance, the tobacco industry is required by law in most countries to display warnings cautioning consumers about the health hazards of their products. Linguistic variation is often used by advertisers as a creative device to reduce the impact of such requirements.

Future

Global advertising

Advertising has gone through five major stages of development: domestic, export, international, multi-national, and global. For global advertisers, there are four, potentially competing, business objectives that must be balanced when developing worldwide advertising: building a brand while speaking with one voice, developing economies of scale in the creative process, maximising local effectiveness of ads, and increasing the company's speed of implementation. Born from the evolutionary stages of global marketing are the three primary and fundamentally different approaches to the development of global advertising executions: exporting executions, producing local executions, and importing ideas that travel.[106]

Advertising research is key to determining the success of an ad in any country or region. The ability to identify which elements and/or moments of an ad that contributes to its success is how economies of scale are maximised.

Once one knows what works in an ad, that idea or ideas can be imported by any other market. Market research measures, such as Flow of Attention, Flow of Emotion and branding moments provide insight into what is working in an ad in any country or region because the measures are based on the visual, not verbal, elements of the ad.[107]

Trends

With the dawn of the Internet came many new advertising opportunities. Popup, Flash, banner, Popunder, advergaming, and email advertisements (the last often being a form of spam) are now commonplace.

In the last three quarters of 2009 mobile and internet advertising grew by 18.1% and 9.2% respectively. Older media advertising saw declines: -10.1% (TV), -11.7% (radio), -14.8% (magazines) and -18.7% (newspapers).

The ability to record shows on digital video recorders (such as TiVo) allow users to record the programs for later viewing, enabling them to fast forward through commercials. Additionally, as more seasons of pre-recorded box sets are offered for sale of television programs; fewer people watch the shows on TV. However, the fact that these sets are **sold**, means the company will receive additional profits from the sales of these sets. To counter this effect, many advertisers have opted for product placement on TV shows like Survivor.

Particularly since the rise of "entertaining" advertising, some people may like an advertisement enough to wish to watch it later or show a friend. In general, the advertising community has not yet made this easy, although some have used the Internet to widely distribute their ads to anyone willing to see or hear them.

Another significant trend regarding future of advertising is the growing importance of the niche market using niche or targeted ads. Also brought about by the Internet and the theory of The Long Tail, advertisers will have an increasing ability to reach specific audiences. In the past, the most efficient way to deliver a message was to blanket the largest mass market audience possible. However, usage tracking, customer profiles and the growing popularity of niche content brought about by everything from blogs to social networking sites, provide advertisers with audiences that are smaller but much better defined, leading to ads that are more relevant to viewers and more effective for companies' marketing products. Among others, Comcast Spotlight is one such advertiser employing this method in their video on demand menus. These advertisements are targeted to a specific group and can be viewed by anyone wishing to find out more about a particular business or practice at any time, right from their home. This causes the viewer to become proactive and actually choose what advertisements they want to view.[108]

In the realm of advertising agencies, continued industry diversification has seen observers note that "big global clients don't need big global agencies any more".[109] This trend is reflected by the growth of non-traditional agencies in various global markets, such as Canadian business TAXI and SMART in Australia and has been referred to as "a revolution in the ad world".[110]

In freelance advertising, companies hold public competitions to create ads for their product, the best one of which is chosen for widespread distribution with a prize given to the winner(s). During the 2007 Super Bowl, PepsiCo held such a contest for the creation of a 30-second television ad for the Doritos brand of chips, offering a cash prize to the winner. Chevrolet held a similar competition for their Tahoe line of SUVs. This type of advertising, however, is still in its infancy. It may ultimately decrease the importance of advertising agencies by creating a niche for independent freelancers.

Advertising education has become widely popular with bachelor, master and doctorate degrees becoming available in the emphasis. A surge in advertising interest is typically attributed to the strong relationship advertising plays in cultural and technological changes, such as the advance of online social networking. A unique model for teaching advertising is the student-run advertising agency, where advertising students create campaigns for real companies.[111] Organizations such as American Advertising Federation and AdU Network partner established companies with students to create these campaigns.

Advertising research

Advertising research is a specialized form of research that works to improve the effectiveness and efficiency of advertising. It entails numerous forms of research which employ different methodologies. Advertising research includes pre-testing (also known as copy testing) and post-testing of ads and/or campaigns—pre-testing is done before an ad airs to gauge how well it will perform and post-testing is done after an ad airs to determine the in-market impact of the ad or campaign on the consumer. Continuous ad tracking and the Communicus System are competing examples of post-testing advertising research types.

See also

- Advertising Adstock
- Advertising to children
- American Advertising Federation Hall of Fame
- Branded content
- Classified advertising
- Communication design
- Conquesting
- Coolhunting
- Copy testing
- → Copywriting
- Graphic design

- Integrated Marketing Communications

- Informative advertising
- Senior media creative
- Local advertising
- Market overhang
- Meta-advertising
- Mobile Marketing
- Performance-based advertising
- Pseudo-event
- Psychological manipulation
- Public relations
- Reality marketing

- SEO Copywriting
- Sex in advertising
- Shock advertising
- Shockvertising
- Tobacco advertising
- Video commerce
- Video news release
- Viral marketing
- Visual communication
- Web analytics
- World Federation of Advertisers

Bibliography

General

- Bhatia, Tej K. 2000. *Advertising in Rural India: Language, Marketing Communication, and Consumerism.* Institute for the Study of Languages and Cultures of Asia and Africa. Tokyo University of Foreign Studies. Tokyo Press: Japan. ISBN 4-87297-782-3
- Arthur Richards, Kent USA (2008) Teacher, Pirate, renaissance man
- Clark, Eric, "The Want Makers", Viking, 1988. ISBN 0340320281
- Cook, Guy (2001 2nd edition) "The Discourse of Advertising", London: Routledge, ISBN 0-415-23455-7
- Graydon, Shari (2003) "Made You Look - How Advertising Works and Why You Should Know", Toronto: Annick Press, ISBN 1-55037-814-7
- Johnson, J. Douglas, "Advertising Today", Chicago: Science Research Associates, 1978. ISBN 0-574-19355-3
- Klein, Naomi (2000) *No Logo* . Harper-Collins, ISBN 0-00-653040-0
- Kleppner, Otto, "Advertising Procedure", Englewood Cliffs, N.J., Prentice-Hall, 1966.
- Kotabe, Masaki and Kristiaan Helsen, *Global Marketing Management, 3rd Edition*, John Wiley & Sopns, Inc, publishers, Copyright 2004, ISBN 0-471-23062-6
- Laermer, Richard; Simmons, Mark, *Punk Marketing*, New York : Harper Collins, 2007. ISBN 978-0-06-115110-1 (Review of the book by Marilyn Scrizzi, in *Journal of Consumer Marketing* 24(7), 2007)
- Lears, Jackson, *Fables of Abundance: A Cultural History of Advertising in America*, Basic Books, 1995, ISBN 0465090753
- Leon, Jose Luis (1996) "Los effectos de la publicidad". Barcelona: Ariel, ISBN 84-344-1266-7
- Leon, Jose Luis (2001) "Mitoanálisis de la publicidad". Barcelona. Ariel, ISBN 84-344-1285-3

- McFall, Liz, *Advertising: A Cultural Economy*, Thousand Oaks, CA: Sage Publications Inc., 2004. ISBN 0-7619-4255-6
- Mulvihill, Donald F., "Marketing Research for the Small Company" [112], Journal of Marketing, Vol. 16, No. 2, Oct., 1951, pp. 179–183.
- Packard, Vance, *The Hidden Persuaders*, New York, D. McKay Co., 1957.
- Petley, Julian (2002) "Advertising". North Mankato, Minnesota: Smart Apple Media., ISBN 1-58340-255-1
- Young, Charles E., *The Advertising Handbook*, Ideas in Flight, Seattle, WA April 2005, ISBN 0-9765574-0-1
- Wernick, Andrew (1991) "Promotional Culture: Advertising, Ideology and Symbolic Expression (Theory, Culture & Society S.)", London: Sage Publications Ltd, ISBN 0-8039-8390-5

Advertising critics

- Achbar, Mark (editor), *Manufacturing consent : Noam Chomsky and the media : the companion book to the award-winning film by Peter Wintonick and Mark Achbar*, Montréal ; New York : Black Rose Books, 1994. ISBN 1551640031
- Baines, Paul. (2001) "A Pie in the Face" in Alternatives Journal, Spring 2001 v27 i2 p14. Retrieved: InfoTrac Web: Expanded Academic ASAP plus. (24/07/2002).
- Blisset, Luther: *Handbuch der Kommunikationsguerilla*. Assoziation a, August 2001, ISBN 978-3-922611-64-6.
- Boiler, David in: Silent Theft. The Private Plunder of Our Common Wealth, Routledge, New York, February 2003, ISBN 9780415944823, ISBN 0415944821
- Chomsky, Noam, (edited by Peter R. Mitchell and John Schoeffel) *Understanding Power: The Indispensable Chomsky*, New York: The New Press, 2002. Cf. "An Exchange on Manufacturing Consent"
- De Certeau, Michel. (1984) The Practice of Everyday Life. Berkley, London: University of California Press.
- Franck, Georg: *Mentaler Kapitalismus. Eine politische Ökonomie des Geistes.* 1. Edition. Carl Hanser, August 2005, ISBN 978-3-446-20687-8
- Franck, Georg: *Ökonomie der Aufmerksamkeit. Ein Entwurf.* 1. Edition. Carl Hanser, März 1998, ISBN 978-3-446-19348-2.
- Fraser, Nancy. (2000) "Rethinking the Public Sphere: A contribution to the critique of actually existing democracy" in S. During (ed), The Cultural Studies Reader. London and New York: Routledge.
- Goldman, Debra. (1999) "Consumer Republic" in Adweek.Com , Nov22, 1999 v36 i47 p13. Retrieved: www.adweek.com (8/08/2002).
- Habermas, Jürgen. (c1989) The Structural Transformation of the Public Sphere: an Inquiry into a Category of Bourgeois Society. Cambridge, Mass.: MIT Press.
- Harkin, James. (1996) "The Logos Fight Back" in New Statesman, June 18, 20001 v130 i4542 p25. Retrieved: InfoTrac Web: Expanded Academic ASAP plus. (8/08/2002).
- Hoepfner, Friedrich Georg (1976). Verbraucherverhalten. Stuttgart: Kohlhammer (Urban TB).
- Hoffmann, Hans-Joachim (). Werbepsychologie. Berlin DeGruyter (Sammlung Göschen 5009).
- Hodge, R. and Kress, G. (1988) Social Semiotics. Cambridge: Polity Press.
- Holt, D. (2002) "Why Brands Cause Trouble? A dialectical theory of Consumer Culture and Branding" in Journal of Consumer Research, June 2002 v29 i1 p70(21). Retrieved: InfoTrac Web: Expanded Academic ASAP plus. (29/07/2002).
- Horkheimer, Max and Adorno, Theodor W. (1973) Dialectic of Enlightenment. London: Allen Lane.
- Irle, Martin & Bussmann, Wolfs (1983, Hrsg.). Marktpsychologie. Handbuch der Psychologie, Vol. 12., 2. Halbbände. 1. Halbband: Marktpsychologie als Sozialwissenschaft. 2. Halbband: Methoden und Anwendungen in der Marktpsychologie. Göttingen: Hogrefe
- Jhully, Sut. (2006) The Spectacle of Accumulation. Essays in Media. Culture & Politics, Peter Lang Publishing (June 24, 2006), ISBN 0820479047, ISBN 978-0820479040

- Jhully, Sut (1990) The Codes of Advertising: Fetishism and the political Economy of Meaning, Routledge; 1 edition (December 12, 1990), ISBN 041590353X, ISBN 978-0415903530
- Jhully, Sut, Leiss, William, Kline, Stephen, Botterill, Jacqueline (2005): Social Communication in Advertising: Consumption in the Mediated Marketplace, Routledge; 3 edition (September 28, 2005), ISBN 0415966760, ISBN 978-0415966764
- Kaiser, Andreas (1980, Hrsg.). Werbung. Theorie und Praxis werblicher Beeinflussung. München: Vahlen.
- Kilbourne, Jean: Can't Buy My Love: How Advertising Changes the Way We Think and Feel, Free Press; 1 edition (November 2, 2000), ISBN 0684866005
- Klein, Naomi. (2000) No Logo: Taking Aim at the Brand Bullies. New York: Picador.
- Korten, David. (1995) When Corporations Rule the World. 2. Edition 2001: Berrett-Koehler, San Francisco, California, ISBN 1-887208-04-6
- Lasch, Christopher: *Zeitalter des Narzissmus*. 1. Edition. Hoffmann und Campe, Hamburg 1995.
- Lasch, Christopher. The Culture of Narcissism: American Life in an Age of Diminishing Expectations, Norton, New York, ISBN 978-0393307382
- Lasn, Kalle. (2000) Culture Jam: how to reverse America's suicidal consumer binge - and why we must, Harper Paperbacks (November 7, 2000), ISBN 0688178057. ISBN 978-0688178055
- Lasn, Kalle. (1999) Culture Jam: The Uncooling of America, William Morrow & Company; 1st edition (November 1999), ISBN 0688156568
- Lees, Loretta, (1998) "Urban Renaissance and the Street" in Nicholas R. Fyfe (ed) Images of the Street: Planning, Identity and Control in Public Space. London; New York: Routledge.
- Leiss, William: (1990) Social Communication in Advertising, Routledge; 2 edition (July 27, 1990), ISBN 0415903548, ISBN 978-0415903547
- Lemke, Jay L. (1995) Textual Politics: Discourse and Social Dynamics. London: Taylor & Francis.
- Livingston, Sonia and Lunt, Peter. (1994) Talk on Television: Audience Participation and Public Debate. London & New York: Routledge.
- Louw, Eric. (2001) The Media and Cultural Production. London: Sage Publications.
- McChesney, Robert W., Stolzfus, Duane C. S. and Nerone, John C, (2007) Freedom from Advertising: E. W. Scripps's Chicago Experiment (History of Communication), Univ of Illinois Pr (30 March 2007)
- McChesney, Robert W. "The Political Economy of Media: Enduring Issues, Emerging Dilemmas". Monthly Review Press, New York, (May 1, 2008), ISBN 978-1583671610
- Prothers, Lisa (1998) "Culture Jamming: An Interview with Pedro Carvajal" [113], in *Bad Subjects: Political Education for Everyday Life, Issue #37, March 1998.*
- Quart, Alissa: *Branded. Wie wir gekauft und verkauft werden.* Riemann, März 2003, ISBN 978-3-570-50029-3.
- Richter, Hans-Jürgen (1977). Einführung in das Image-Marketing. Feldtheoretische Forschung. Stuttgart: Kohlhammer (Urban TB).
- Rorty, James: "Our Master's Voice: Advertising" Ayer Co Pub, 1976, ISBN 978-0405080449
- Schmölders, Günter (1978). Verhaltensforschung im Wirtschaftsleben. Reinbek: Rowohlt.
- Schmidt, S. J. & Spieß, B. (1994). Die Geburt der schönen Builder (1994)
- Schmidt, S. J. & Spieß, B. (1995). Werbung, Medien und Kultur, Westdeutscher Verlag,1995,Opladen
- Sinclair, Upton (1919): The Brass Check
- Stuart, Ewen. Captains of Consciousness: Advertising and the Social Roots of the Consumer Culture, Basic Books, ISBN 9780465021550, ISBN 0465021557
- Williamson, Judith (1994): Decoding Advertisements (Ideas in Progress), Marion Boyars Publishers Ltd (March 1, 1994),ISBN 0714526150, ISBN 978-0714526157

External links

- Advertising Educational Foundation [114], archived advertising exhibits and classroom resources
- A collection of over 100,000 print ads from the past decades [115]
- Duke University Libraries Digital Collections:
  - Ad*Access [116], over 7,000 U.S. and Canadian advertisements, dated 1911-1955, includes World War II propaganda.
  - Emergence of Advertising in America [117], 9,000 advertising items and publications dating from 1850 to 1920, illustrating the rise of consumer culture and the birth of a professionalized advertising industry in the United States.
  - AdViews [118], vintage television commercials
- On-Line exhibits [119] at William F. Eisner Museum of Advertising & Design

References

[1] "JEG - Sign In Page" (http://joeg.oxfordjournals.org/cgi/content/full/8/3/421). Joeg.oxfordjournals.org. . Retrieved 2009-04-20.

[2] "TNS Media Intelligence" (http://www.tns-mi.com/news/01082007.htm). Tns-mi.com. 2007-01-08. . Retrieved 2009-04-20.

[3] "Global Entertainment and Media Outlook: 2006–2010, a report issued by global accounting firm PricewaterhouseCoopers" (http://www.pwc.com/extweb/pwcpublications.nsf/docid/5AC172F2C9DED8F5852570210044EEA7?opendocument&vendor=none). Pwc.com. . Retrieved 2009-04-20.

[4] Bhatia (2000). Advertising in Rural India: Language, Marketing Communication, and Consumerism, 62+68

[5] Eskilson, Stephen J. (2007). Graphic Design: A New History. New Haven, Connecticut: Yale University Press. p. 58. ISBN 978-0-300-12011-0.

[6] Advertising Slogans (http://www.tvacres.com/adslogans_w.htm), Woodbury Soap Company, "The skin you love to touch", J. Walter Thompson Co., 1911

[7] McChesney, Robert, Educators and the Battle for Control of U.S. Broadcasting, 1928-35, Rich Media, Poor Democracy, ISBN 0-252-02448-6 (1999)

[8] "Public Interest, Convenience and Necessity" (http://www.museum.tv/archives/etv/P/htmlP/publicintere/publicintere.htm). Museum.tv. . Retrieved 2009-04-20.

[9] "Annual U.S. Advertising Expenditure Since 1919" (http://www.galbithink.org/ad-spending.htm). Galbithink.org. 2008-09-14. . Retrieved 2009-04-20.

[10] http://en.wikipedia.org/wiki/Michael_Winner

[11] McCarthy, Michael (2002-10-17). "Digitally inserted ads pop up more in sports" (http://www.usatoday.com/money/advertising/2002-10-17-fake-ads_x.htm). Usatoday.Com. . Retrieved 2009-04-20.

[12] Keith Mcarthur. "Business" (http://www.theglobeandmail.com/servlet/story/LAC.20060315.RVIRTUAL15/TPStory/Business). globeandmail.com. . Retrieved 2009-04-20.

[13] http://www.canwestmediaworks.com/television/nontraditional/opportunities/virtual_advertising/

[14] Advertising's Twilight Zone: That Signpost Up Ahead May Be a Virtual Product - New York Times (http://www.nytimes.com/glogin?URI=http://www.nytimes.com/2006/01/02/business/media/02digital.html&OQ=_rQ3D1&OP=295c0536Q2FQ5B6ZQ3DQ5BamQ2BpemmbtQ5BtQ3FQ3FQ3AQ5BQ3FqQ5BQ3FtQ5BQ3DQ24p.Q5DZppQ5BIZa.Q2FQ5BQ3Fta.d.bQ2FyPibIy)

[15] "Welcome to E-Commerce Times" (http://www.ecommercetimes.com/story/48956.html). Ecommercetimes.com. . Retrieved 2009-04-20.

[16] http://www.aimdigitalvisions.com/content/weis-markets

[17] http://www.aimdigitalvisions.com/content/shady-maple

[18] http://www.aimdigitalvisions.com/content/strawberry-square

[19] "Slashdot | ISP Operator Barry Shein Answers Spam Questions" (http://interviews.slashdot.org/article.pl?sid=03/03/03/1528247&tid=111). Interviews.slashdot.org. 2003-03-03. . Retrieved 20x09-04-20.

[20] "How Marketers Target Kids" (http://www.media-awareness.ca/english/parents/marketing/marketers_target_kids.cfm). Media-awareness.ca. 2009-02-13. . Retrieved 2009-04-20.

[21] Franck, Georg: Ökonomie der Aufmerksamkeit. Ein Entwurf. 1. Edition, Carl Hanser, March 1998, ISBN 3-446-19348-0, ISBN 978-3-446-19348-2

[22] Die Zeit, Hamburg, Germany (2008-11-13). "Öffentlichkeit: Werbekampagnen vereinnahmen den öffentlichen Raum | Kultur | Nachrichten auf ZEIT ONLINE" (http://www.zeit.de/2008/47/Vermuellung) (in **German**). Zeit.de. . Retrieved 2009-04-20.

[23] "Ad Creep — Commercial Alert" (http://www.commercialalert.org/issues/culture/ad-creep). Commercialalert.org. . Retrieved 2009-04-20.

[24] McChesney, Robert W. "The Political Economy of Media: Enduring Issues, Emerging Dilemmas". Monthly Review Press, New York, (May 1, 2008), p. 266, ISBN 978-158367161-0

[25] McChesney, Robert W. "The Political Economy of Media: Enduring Issues, Emerging Dilemmas". Monthly Review Press, New York, (May 1, 2008), p. 272, ISBN 978-158367161-0

[26] Lasn, Kalle in: Culture Jam: The Uncooling of America, William Morrow & Company; 1st edition (November 1999),ISBN 0688156568, ISBN 978-0688156565

[27] Kilbourne, Jean: Can't Buy My Love: How Advertising Changes the Way We Think and Feel, Touchstone, 2000, ISBN 978-0684866000

[28] McChesney, Robert W. "The Political Economy of Media: Enduring Issues, Emerging Dilemmas". Monthly Review Press, New York, (May 1, 2008), ISBN 978-158367161-0

[29] McChesney, Robert W. "The Political Economy of Media: Enduring Issues, Emerging Dilemmas". Monthly Review Press, New York, (May 1, 2008), p. 265, ISBN 978-158367161-0

[30] Knoche, Manfred (2005): Werbung - ein notwendiges "Lebenselixier" für den Kapitalismus: Zur Kritik der politischen Ökonomie der Werbung, in: Seufert, Wolfgang/Müller-Lietzkow, Jörg (Hrsg.): Theorie und Praxis der Werbung in den Massenmedien. Baden-Baden: Nomos, p. 239-255.

[31] Lasch, Christopher. The Culture of Narcissism: American Life in an Age of Diminishing Expectations, Norton, New York, ISBN 978-0393307382

[32] http://www.csupomona.edu/~jkirkpatrick/Papers/EthicsAdvtTaxation.pdf

[33] McChesney, Robert W. "The Political Economy of Media: Enduring Issues, Emerging Dilemmas". Monthly Review Press, New York, (May 1, 2008), pp. 132, 249, ISBN 978-158367161-0

[34] McChesney, Robert W. "The Political Economy of Media: Enduring Issues, Emerging Dilemmas". Monthly Review Press, New York, (May 1, 2008), p. 252, 249, 254, 256, ISBN 978-158367161-0

[35] Franck, Georg: Ökonomie der Aufmerksamkeit. Ein Entwurf. (Economy of Attention), 1. Edition. Carl Hanser, March 1998, ISBN 3-446-19348-0, ISBN 978-3-446-19348-2.

[36] Lecture held at Philosophicum Lech (Austria) 2002, published in Konrad Paul Liessmann (Hrg.), Die Kanäle der Macht. Herrschaft und Freiheit im Medienzeitalter, Philosophicum Lech Vol. 6, Vienna: Zsolnay, 2003, p. 36-60; preprint in Merkur No. 645, January 2003, S. 1-15

[37] Lasch, Christopher: Das Zeitalter des Narzissmus. (The Culture of Narcissism), 1. Edition. Hoffmann und Campe, Hamburg 1995.

[38] "Sut Jhally Website - Advertising at the Edge of the Apocalypse" (http://www.sutjhally.com/articles/advertisingattheed/). Sutjhally.com. . Retrieved 2009-04-20.

[39] "Advertising - Social impact" (http://www.spiritus-temporis.com/advertising/social-impact.html). Spiritus-temporis.com. . Retrieved 2009-04-20.

[40] "ZAW - Zentralverband der deutschen Werbewirtschaft e.V" (http://www.zaw.de). Zaw.de. . Retrieved 2009-04-20.

[41] "US-Werbeausgaben: Internet überflügelt erstmals TV - SPIEGEL ONLINE - Nachrichten - Wirtschaft" (http://www.spiegel.de/wirtschaft/0,1518,566081,00.html). Spiegel.de. 2008-07-15. . Retrieved 2009-04-20.

[42] "Pharmaindustrie: Mehr Geld für Werbung als für Forschung - Nachrichten Wissenschaft - WELT ONLINE" (http://www.welt.de/wissenschaft/article1510150/Mehr_Geld_fuer_Werbung_als_fuer_Forschung.html) (in (German)). Welt.de. 2008-01-04. . Retrieved 2009-04-20.

[43] McChesney, Robert W. "The Political Economy of Media: Enduring Issues, Emerging Dilemmas". Monthly Review Press, New York, (May 1, 2008), p.265, ISBN 978-1583671610

[44] McChesney, Robert W. "The Political Economy of Media: Enduring Issues, Emerging Dilemmas". Monthly Review Press, New York, (May 1, 2008), p. 270, 272, ISBN 978-158367161-0

[45] McChesney, Robert W. "The Political Economy of Media: Enduring Issues, Emerging Dilemmas". Monthly Review Press, New York, (May 1, 2008), p.277, ISBN 978-1583671610

[46] "Psychology — Commercial Alert" (http://www.commercialalert.org/issues/culture/psychology). Commercialalert.org. 1999-10-31. . Retrieved 2009-04-20.

[47] McChesney, Robert W. "The Political Economy of Media: Enduring Issues, Emerging Dilemmas". Monthly Review Press, New York, (May 1, 2008), p. 277, ISBN 978-1583671610

[48] Siegert, Gabriele, Brecheis Dieter in: Werbung in der Medien- und Informationsgesellschaft, Verlag für Sozialwissenschaften, 2005, ISBN 3531138936

[49] McChesney, Robert W. "The Political Economy of Media: Enduring Issues, Emerging Dilemmas". Monthly Review Press, New York, (May 1, 2008), p. 256, ISBN 978-158367161-0

[50] Giroux, Henry A., McMaster University, Hamilton, Canada, in the foreword for: The Spectacle of Accumulation by Sut Jhally, http://www.sutjhally.com/biography

[51] McChesney, Robert W. "The Political Economy of Media: Enduring Issues, Emerging Dilemmas". Monthly Review Press, New York, (May 1, 2008), p. 43, ISBN 978-158367161-0

[52] "Adbusters' Ads Busted" (http://www.inthesetimes.com/article/3581/adbusters_ads_busted/). In These Times. . Retrieved 2009-04-20.

[53] "Seminar: Werbewelten - Werbung und Medien" (http://viadrina.euv-ffo.de/~sk/SS99/werbung99/medien.html) (in (German)). Viadrina.euv-ffo.de. . Retrieved 2009-04-20.

[54] McChesney, Robert W. "The Political Economy of Media: Enduring Issues, Emerging Dilemmas". Monthly Review Press, New York, (May 1, 2008), p. 271, ISBN 978-158367161-0

[55] Jhally, Sut. Advertising at the edge of the apocalypse: http://www.sutjhally.com/articles/advertisingattheed/

[56] McChesney, Robert W. "The Political Economy of Media: Enduring Issues, Emerging Dilemmas". Monthly Review Press, New York, (May 1, 2008), pp. 269,270, ISBN 978-158367161-0

[57] "Selon Le Lay, TF1 a une mission : fournir du "temps de cerveau humain disponible" - [Observatoire français des médias] (http://www. observatoire-medias.info/article.php3?id_article=225). Observatoire-medias.info. . Retrieved 2009-04-20.

[58] McChesney, Robert W. "The Political Economy of Media: Enduring Issues, Emerging Dilemmas". Monthly Review Press, New York, (May 1, 2008), pp. 235, 237, ISBN 978-158367161-0

[59] Rorty, James: "Our Master's Voice: Advertising" Ayer Co Pub, 1976, ISBN 0405080441, ISBN 9780405080449

[60] Rorty, James: (1934) "Our Master's Voice – Advertising", Mcmaster Press (June 30, 2008), ISBN 1409769739, ISBN 978-1409769736

[61] McChesney, Robert W. "The Political Economy of Media: Enduring Issues, Emerging Dilemmas". Monthly Review Press, New York, (May 1, 2008), p. 276, ISBN 978-158367161-0

[62] Jhally, Sut in: Stay Free Nr. 16, 1999

[63] McChesney, Robert W. "The Political Economy of Media: Enduring Issues, Emerging Dilemmas". Monthly Review Press, New York, (May 1, 2008), p. 213, ISBN 978-158367161-0

[64] Report of the Scientific Committee on Tobacco and Health, Prepared 20 March 1998 in: http://www.archive.official-documents.co.uk/ document/doh/tobacco/part-4.htm

[65] Hüther, Jürgen and Stiehler, Hans-Jörg in: Merz, Zeitschrift für Medien und Erziehung, Vol. 2006/6: merzWissenschaft - Sport und Medien, http://www.jff.de/merz/list.php?katid=3&heft_id=80

[66] "Our Mission" (http://antiadvertisingagency.com/our-mission). The Anti-Advertising Agency. . Retrieved 2009-04-20.

[67] Eicke, Ulrich in: Die Werbelawine. Angriff auf unser Bewußtsein. München, 1991

[68] Stay Free Nr. 16, On Advertising, Summer 1999

[69] Mularz, Stephen: The Negative Effects of Advertising, http://www.mularzart.com/writings/ THE%20NEGATIVE%20EFFECTS%20OF%20ADVERTISING.pdf

[70] Richter, Hans Jürgen. Einführung in das Image-Marketing. Feldtheoretische Forschung. Stuttgart: Kohlhammer (Urban TB, 1977). Hieraus: Aufgabe der Werbung S. 12

[71] "Humanistische Union: Aktuelles" (http://www.humanistische-union.de). Humanistische-union.de. . Retrieved 2009-04-20.

[72] McChesney, Robert W. "The Political Economy of Media: Enduring Issues, Emerging Dilemmas". Monthly Review Press, New York, (May 1, 2008), p. 269, ISBN 978-158367161-0

[73] Schechter, Danny (2009-04-16). "Home" (http://www.mediachannel.org). Media Channel. . Retrieved 2009-04-20.

[74] Eicke Ulrich u. Wolfram in: Medienkinder : Vom richtigen Umgang mit der Vielfalt, Knesebeck München, 1994, ISBN 3-926901-67-5

[75] McChesney, Robert W. "The Political Economy of Media: Enduring Issues, Emerging Dilemmas". Monthly Review Press (May 1, 2008), ISBN 978-1583671610

[76] "Commercial media literacy: what does it do, to whom-and does it matter? (22-JUN-07) Journal of Advertising" (http://www. accessmylibrary.com/coms2/summary_0286-31767632_ITM). Accessmylibrary.com. 2007-06-22. . Retrieved 2009-04-20.

[77] YTV's 2007 Tween Report in: http://ontariondp.com/ban-advertising-aimed-children-under-13

[78] Consumer Protection Act, R.S.Q., c. P-40.1, ss. 248-9 (see also: ss. 87-91 of the Consumer Protection Regulations, R.R.Q., 1981, c. P-40.1; and Application Guide for Sections 248 and 249 of the Québec Consumer Protection Act (Advertising Intended for Children Under 13 Years of Age).

[79] Redirection (http://www.lexum.umontreal.ca/csc-scc/en/pub/1989/vol1/html/1989scr1_0927.html)

[80] Melanie Rother (2008-05-31). "Leichtes Spiel für die Werbeindustrie : Textarchiv : Berliner Zeitung Archiv" (https://www.berlinonline. de/berliner-zeitung/archiv/.bin/dump.fcgi/2001/0203/none/0086/index.html). Berlinonline.de. . Retrieved 2009-04-20.

[81] Corinna Hawkes, Marketing Food to Children: The Global Regulatory Environment, (Geneva: World Health Organization, 2004) at http:// whqlibdoc.who.int/publications/2004/9241591579.pdf

[82] McChesney, Robert W. "The Political Economy of Media: Enduring Issues, Emerging Dilemmas". Monthly Review Press, New York, (May 1, 2008), p. 279, ISBN 978-1583671610

[83] Baran, Paul and Sweezy, Paul (1964) "Monopoly Capital" in: McChesney, Robert W. "The Political Economy of Media: Enduring Issues, Emerging Dilemmas". Monthly Review Press, New York, (May 1, 2008), p. 52, ISBN 978-1583671610

[84] McChesney, Robert W. "The Political Economy of Media: Enduring Issues, Emerging Dilemmas". Monthly Review Press, New York, (May 1, 2008), p. 281, ISBN 978-1583671610

[85] Downie, Andrew. "São Paulo Sells Itself - Inner Workings of the World's Megacities" (http://www.time.com/time/specials/2007/article/ 0,28804,1709961_1711305_1860002,00.html). TIME. . Retrieved 2009-04-20.

[86] "Scenic America :: Communities Prohibiting Billboard Construction" (http://www.scenic.org/billboards/background/communities). Scenic.org. 2008-08-01. . Retrieved 2009-04-20.

[87] Plummer, Robert (2006-09-19). "Brazil's ad men face billboard ban, BBC News, 19 September 2006" (http://news.bbc.co.uk/2/hi/ business/5355692.stm). BBC News. . Retrieved 2009-04-20.

[88] "Billboard Liberation Front Creative Group" (http://www.billboardliberation.com/manifesto.html). Billboardliberation.com. . Retrieved 2009-04-20.

[89] ::: illegalsigns.ca (http://illegalsigns.ca/)

[90] "Résistance À l'Agression Publicitaire" (http://www.antipub.org/). Antipub.org. . Retrieved 2009-04-20.

[91] "Media Education Foundation" (http://www.mediaed.org). Mediaed.org. . Retrieved 2009-04-20.

[92] "The Anti-Advertising Agency" (http://antiadvertisingagency.com/). The Anti-Advertising Agency. . Retrieved 2009-04-20.

[93] "Commercial Alert — Protecting communities from commercialism" (http://www.commercialalert.org/). Commercialalert.org. .
      Retrieved 2009-04-20.

[94] "Media Education Foundation" (http://www.mediaed.org/). Mediaed.org. . Retrieved 2009-04-20.

[95] http://www.mediawatch.ca

[96] Media Awareness Network | Réseau éducation médias (http://www.media-awareness.ca/)

[97] Advertising Educational Foundation (2008-05-20). "Advertising Educational Foundation - Educational Advertising Content" (http://www.
      aef.com/index.html). AEF. . Retrieved 2009-04-20.

[98] "Mission and Mandate" (http://www.cca-kids.ca/about_cca/mission_mandate.html). Cca-kids.ca. . Retrieved 2009-04-20.

[99] "Concerned Children's Advertisers" (http://www.cca-kids.ca/). Cca-kids.ca. . Retrieved 2009-04-20.

[100] http://dip21.bundestag.de/dip21/btd/13/082/1308226.asc

[101] Korten, David. (1995) When Corporations Rule the World. 2. Edition 2001: Berrett-Koehler, San Francisco, California, ISBN
       1-887208-04-6

[102] "Welcome to SCRUB" (http://www.urbanblight.org/). Urbanblight.org. . Retrieved 2009-04-20.

[103] "How the Highway Beautification Act Became a Law" (http://www.fhwa.dot.gov/infrastructure/beauty.htm). Fhwa.dot.gov. .
       Retrieved 2009-04-20.

[104] "Billboard ban in São Paulo angers advertisers - Americas - International Herald Tribune" (http://www.iht.com/articles/2006/12/12/
       news/brazil.php). International Herald Tribune. 2009-03-29. . Retrieved 2009-04-20.

[105] Bhatia and Ritchie 2006:542

[106] Global marketing Management, 2004, pg 13-18

[107] Young, p.131

[108] "Interactive - VOD" (http://www.comcastspotlight.com/sites/Default.aspx?pageid=7608&siteid=62&subnav=3) "Comcast Spotlight
       website". Retrieved October 5, 2006.

[109] Howard, Theresa (2005-10-10). "USA Today, October 9, 2005" (http://www.usatoday.com/money/companies/management/
       2005-10-09-goodson-profile_x.htm). Usatoday.com. . Retrieved 2009-04-20.

[110] Leonard, Devin (2005-12-12). "Madison Ave. Lights Up" (http://money.cnn.com/magazines/fortune/fortune_archive/2005/12/12/
       8363132/index.htm) (in en). Fortune. .

[111] Avery, James (1992-08-00). "Student-Run Advertising Agency: A Showcase for Student Work." (http://www.eric.ed.gov/
       ERICWebPortal/custom/portlets/recordDetails/detailmini.jsp?_nfpb=true&_&ERICExtSearch_SearchValue_0=ED351711&
       ERICExtSearch_SearchType_0=no&accno=ED351711) (in en). .

[112] http://links.jstor.org/sici?sici=0022-2429%28195110%2916%3A2%3C179%3AMRFTSC%3E2.0.CO%3B2-I

[113] http://bad.eserver.org/issues/1998/37/prothers.html

[114] http://www.aef.com/index.html

[115] http://www.vintageadbrowser.com

[116] http://library.duke.edu/digitalcollections/adaccess/

[117] http://library.duke.edu/digitalcollections/eaa/

[118] http://library.duke.edu/digitalcollections/adviews/

[119] http://www.eisnermuseum.org/exhibits/online.shtm

Television

Television (TV) is a widely used telecommunication medium for transmitting and receiving moving images, either monochromatic ("black and white") or color, usually accompanied by sound. "Television" may also refer specifically to a television set, television programming or television transmission. The word is derived from mixed Latin and Greek roots, meaning "far sight": Greek *tele* (τῆλε), far, and Latin *visio*, sight (from *video, vis-* to see, or to view in the first person).

Commercially available since the late 1930s, the television set has become a common communications receiver in homes, businesses and institutions, particularly as a source of entertainment and news. Since the 1970s the availability of video cassettes, laserdiscs, DVDs and now Blu-ray Discs, have resulted in the television set frequently being used for viewing recorded as well as broadcast material.

Braun HF 1, Germany, 1958

Although other forms such as closed-circuit television (CCTV) are in use, the most common usage of the medium is for broadcast television, which was modeled on the existing radio broadcasting systems developed in the 1920s, and uses high-powered radio-frequency transmitters to broadcast the television signal to individual TV receivers.

Broadcast TV is typically disseminated via → radio transmissions on designated channels in the 54–890 megahertz frequency band[1] . Signals are now often transmitted with stereo and/or surround sound in many countries. Until the 2000s broadcast TV programs were generally recorded and transmitted as an analog signal, but in recent years public and commercial broadcasters have been progressively introducing digital television broadcasting technology.

A standard television set comprises multiple internal electronic circuits, including those for receiving and decoding broadcast signals. A visual display device which lacks a tuner is properly called a monitor, rather than a television. A television system may use different technical standards such as digital television (DTV) and high-definition television (HDTV). Television systems are also used for surveillance, industrial process control, and guiding of weapons, in places where direct observation is difficult or dangerous.

Amateur television (*ham TV* or *ATV*) is also used for experimentation, pleasure and public service events by amateur radio operators. Ham TV stations were on the air in many cities before commercial TV stations came on the air.[2]

History

In its early stages of development, television employed a combination of optical, mechanical and electronic technologies to capture, transmit and display a visual image. By the late 1920s, however, those employing only optical and electronic technologies were being explored. All modern television systems rely on the latter, although the knowledge gained from the work on mechanical-dependent systems was crucial in the development of fully electronic television.

The first time images were transmitted electrically were via early mechanical fax machines, including the pantelegraph, developed in the late 1800s. The concept of electrically-powered transmission of television images in motion, was first sketched in 1878 as the telephonoscope, shortly after the invention of the telephone. At the time, it was imagined by early science fiction authors, that someday that light could be transmitted over wires, as sounds were.

The idea of using scanning to transmit images was put to actual practical use in 1881 in the pantelegraph, through the use of a pendulum-based scanning mechanism. From this period forward, scanning in one form or another, has been used in nearly every image transmission technology to date, including television. This is the

American family watching TV, 1958

concept of "rasterization", the process of converting a visual image into a stream of electrical pulses.

In 1884 Paul Gottlieb Nipkow, a 20-year old university student in Germany, patented the first electromechanical television system which employed a scanning disk, a spinning disk with a series of holes spiraling toward the center, for rasterization. The holes were spaced at equal angular intervals such that in a single rotation the disk would allow light to pass through each hole and onto a light-sensitive selenium sensor which produced the electrical pulses. As an image was focused on the rotating disk, each hole captured a horizontal "slice" of the whole image.

Nipkow's design would not be practical until advances in amplifier tube technology became available. The device was only useful for transmitting still "halftone" images — represented by equally spaced dots of varying size — over telegraph or telephone lines. Later designs would use a rotating mirror-drum scanner to capture the image and a cathode ray tube (CRT) as a display device, but moving images were still not possible, due to the poor sensitivity of the selenium sensors. In 1907 Russian scientist Boris Rosing became the first inventor to use a CRT in the receiver of an experimental television system. He used mirror-drum scanning to transmit simple geometric shapes to the CRT.[3]

Scottish inventor John Logie Baird demonstrated the transmission of moving silhouette images in London in 1925, and of moving, monochromatic images in 1926. Baird's scanning disk produced an image of 30 lines resolution, just enough to discern a human face, from a double spiral of lenses.. Remarkably, in 1927 Baird also invented the world's first video recording system, "Phonovision" — by modulating the output signal of his TV camera down to the audio range he was able to capture the signal on a 10-inch wax audio disc using conventional audio recording technology. A handful of Baird's 'Phonovision' recordings survive and these were finally decoded and rendered into viewable images in the 1990s using modern digital signal-processing technology[4] .

In 1926, Hungarian engineer Kálmán Tihanyi designed a television system utilizing fully electronic scanning and display elements, and employing the principle of "charge storage" within the scanning (or "camera") tube.[5] [6] [7] [8]

By 1927, Russian inventor Léon Theremin developed a mirror drum-based television system which used interlacing to achieve an image resolution of 100 lines.

Also in 1927, Herbert E. Ives of Bell Labs transmitted moving images from a 50-aperture disk producing 16 frames per minute over a cable from Washington, DC to New York City, and via → radio from Whippany, New Jersey. Ives used viewing screens as large as 24 by 30 inches (60 by 75 centimeters). His subjects included Secretary of Commerce Herbert Hoover.

In 1927, Philo Farnsworth made the world's first working television system with electronic scanning of both the pickup and display devices,[9] which he first demonstrated to the press on 1 September 1928.[9] [10]

The first practical use of television was in Germany. Regular television broadcasts began in Germany in 1929 and in 1936 the Olympic Games in Berlin were broadcast to television stations in Berlin and Leipzig where the public could view the games live.[11]

In 1936, Kálmán Tihanyi described the principle of plasma television, the first flat panel system.[12] [13]

Geographical usage

* Timeline of the introduction of television in countries

Content

Programming

Getting TV programming shown to the public can happen in many different ways. After production the next step is to market and deliver the product to whatever markets are open to using it. This typically happens on two levels:

Television introduction by country   1930 to 1939   1940 to 1949   1950 to 1959   1960 to 1969   1970 to 1979   1980 to 1989   1990 to 1999   No data

1. **Original Run** or **First Run**: a producer creates a program of one or multiple episodes and shows it on a station or network which has either paid for the production itself or to which a license has been granted by the producers to do the same.
2. **Broadcast syndication**: this is the terminology rather broadly used to describe secondary programming usages (beyond original run). It includes secondary runs in the country of first issue, but also international usage which may or may not be managed by the originating producer. In many cases other companies, TV stations or individuals are engaged to do the syndication work, in other words to sell the product into the markets they are allowed to sell into by contract from the copyright holders, in most cases the producers.

First run programming is increasing on subscription services outside the U.S., but few domestically produced programs are syndicated on domestic free-to-air (FTA) elsewhere. This practice is increasing however, generally on digital-only FTA channels, or with subscriber-only first-run material appearing on FTA.

Unlike the U.S., repeat FTA screenings of a FTA network program almost only occur on that network. Also, affiliates rarely buy or produce non-network programming that is not centred around local events.

Funding

Around the globe, broadcast television is financed by either government, advertising, licensing (a form of tax), subscription or any combination of these. To protect revenues, subscription TV channels are usually encrypted to ensure that only subscription payers receive the decryption codes to see the signal. Non-encrypted channels are known as **free to air** or **FTA**.

Television sets per 1000 people of the world   1000+   500–1000   300–500   200–300   100–200   50–100   0–50   No data

Advertising

Television's broad reach makes it a powerful and attractive medium for advertisers. Many television networks and stations sell blocks of broadcast time to advertisers ("sponsors") in order to fund their programming.

United States

Since inception in the U.S. in 1940, TV commercials have become one of the most effective, persuasive, and popular method of selling products of many sorts, especially consumer goods. U.S. → advertising rates are determined primarily by Nielsen Ratings. The time of the day and popularity of the channel determine how much a television commercial can cost. For example, the highly popular American Idol can cost approximately $750,000 for a thirty second block of commercial time; while the same amount of time for the World Cup and the Super Bowl can cost several million dollars.

In recent years, the paid program or infomercial has become common, usually in lengths of 30 minutes or one hour. Some drug companies and other businesses have even created "news" items for broadcast, known in the industry as video news releases, paying program directors to use them.[14]

Some TV programs also weave advertisements into their shows, a practice begun in film and known as product placement. For example, a character could be drinking a certain kind of soda, going to a particular chain restaurant, or driving a certain make of car. (This is sometimes very subtle, where shows have vehicles provided by manufacturers for low cost, rather than wrangling them.) Sometimes a specific brand or trade mark, or music from a certain artist or group, is used. (This excludes guest appearances by artists, who perform on the show.)

United Kingdom

The TV regulator oversees TV advertising in the United Kingdom. Its restrictions have applied since the early days of commercially funded TV. Despite this, an early TV mogul, Lew Grade, likened the broadcasting licence as being a "licence to print money". Restrictions mean that the big three national commercial TV channels: ITV, Channel 4, and Five can show an average of only seven minutes of advertising per hour (eight minutes in the peak period). Other broadcasters must average no more than nine minutes (twelve in the peak). This means that many imported TV shows from the US have unnatural breaks where the UK company has edited out the breaks intended for US advertising. Advertisements must not be inserted in the course of certain specific proscribed types of programs which last less than half an hour in scheduled duration, this list includes any news or current affairs program, documentaries, and programs for children. Nor may advertisements be carried in a program designed and broadcast for reception in schools or in any religious service or other devotional program, or during a formal Royal ceremony or occasion. There also must be clear demarcations in time between the programs and the advertisements.

The BBC, being strictly non-commercial is not allowed to show advertisements on television in the UK, although it has many advertising-funded channels abroad. The majority of its budget comes from TV licencing (see below) and the sale of content to other broadcasters.

Republic of Ireland

The Broadcasting Commission of Ireland (**BCI**) (Irish: *Coimisiún Craolacháin na hÉireann*)[15] oversees advertising on television and radio within the Republic of Ireland on both private and state owned broadcasters. Similar to other European countries, advertising is found on both private and state owned broadcasters. There are some restrictions based on advertising, especially in relation to the advertising of alcohol. Such advertisements are prohibited until after 7pm. Broadcasters in the Republic of Ireland adhere to broadcasting legislation implemented by the Broadcasting Commission of Ireland and the European Union. Sponsorship of current affairs programming is prohibited at all times.

As of October 1, 2009 the responsibilities held by the BCI are gradually being transferred to the Broadcasting Authority of Ireland.

Taxation or license

Television services in some countries may be funded by a television licence, a form of taxation which means advertising plays a lesser role or no role at all. For example, some channels may carry no advertising at all and some very little, including:

- Australia (ABC)
- Norway (NRK)
- Sweden (SVT)
- United Kingdom (BBC)

The BBC carries no advertising on its UK channels and is funded by an annual licence paid by all households owning a television. This licence fee is set by government, but the BBC is not answerable to or controlled by government and is therefore genuinely independent.

The two main BBC TV channels are watched by almost 90 percent of the population each week and overall have 27 per cent share of total viewing.[16] This in spite of the fact that 85% of homes are multichannel, with 42% of these having access to 200 free to air channels via satellite and another 43% having access to 30 or more channels via Freeview.[17] The licence that funds the seven advertising-free BBC TV channels currently costs £139.50 a year (about US$215) irrespective of the number of TV sets owned. When the same sporting event has been presented on both BBC and commercial channels, the BBC always attracts the lion's share of the audience, indicating viewers prefer to watch TV uninterrupted by advertising.

The Australian Broadcasting Corporation (ABC) carries no advertising (except for internal promotional material) as it is banned under the ABC Act 1983 [18]. The ABC receives its funding from the Australian Government every three years. In the 2008/09 Federal Budget the ABC received A$1.13 Billion [19]. The funds assist in providing the ABC's Television, Radio, Online and International outputs. The ABC also receives funds from its many ABC Shops across Australia. However funded by the Australian Government the editorial independence of the ABC is ensured through law.

In France and the Republic of Ireland government-funded channels carry advertisements yet those who own television sets have to pay an annual tax ("la redevance audiovisuelle").[20]

Subscription

Some TV channels are partly funded from subscriptions and therefore the signals are encrypted during broadcast to ensure that only paying subscribers have access to the decryption codes. Most subscription services are also funded by advertising.

Genres

Television genres include a broad range of programming types that entertain, inform, and educate viewers. The most expensive entertainment genres to produce are usually drama and dramatic miniseries. However, other genres, such as historical Western genres, may also have high production costs.

Popular entertainment genres include action-oriented shows such as police, crime, detective dramas, horror, or thriller shows. As well, there are also other variants of the drama genre, such as medical dramas and daytime soap operas. Science fiction shows can fall into either the drama or action category, depending on whether they emphasize philosophical questions or high adventure. Comedy is a popular genre which includes situation comedy (sitcom) and animated shows for the adult demographic such as *Family Guy*.

The least expensive forms of entertainment programming are game shows, talk shows, variety shows, and reality TV. Game shows show contestants answering questions and solving puzzles to win prizes. Talk shows feature interviews with film, television and music celebrities and public figures. Variety shows feature a range of musical performers and other entertainers such as comedians and magicians introduced by a host or Master of Ceremonies.

There is some crossover between some talk shows and variety shows, because leading talk shows often feature performances by bands, singers, comedians, and other performers in between the interview segments. *Reality TV* shows "regular" people (*i.e.*, not actors) who are facing unusual challenges or experiences, ranging from arrest by police officers (*COPS*) to weight loss (*The Biggest Loser*). A variant version of reality shows depicts celebrities doing mundane activities such as going about their everyday life (*Snoop Dogg's Father Hood*) or doing manual labour (*Simple Life*).

Social aspects

Television has played a pivotal role in the socialization of the 20th and 21st centuries. There are many aspects of television that can be addressed, including media violence research.

Environmental aspects

With high lead content in CRTs, and the rapid diffusion of new, flat-panel display technologies, some of which (LCDs) use lamps containing mercury, there is growing concern about electronic waste from discarded televisions. Related occupational health concerns exist, as well, for disassemblers removing copper wiring and other materials from CRTs. Further environmental concerns related to television design and use relate to the devices' increasing electrical energy requirements.[21]

The 50 years of Television commemorative coin

In numismatics

Television has had such an impact in today's life, that it has been the main motif for numerous collectors' coins and medals. One of the most recent ones is the Euro gold and silver commemorative coins (Austria) minted in March 9, 2005. The obverse of the coin shows a "test pattern", while the reverse shows several milestones in the history of television.

See also

- Broadcast-safe
- Handheld television
- How television works
- Satellite television
- Information-action ratio
- Internet television
- List of countries by number of television broadcast stations
- List of television manufacturers
- List of years in television
- Media psychology
- Sign language on television
- Technology of television

Further reading

- Albert Abramson, *The History of Television, 1942 to 2000*, Jefferson, NC, and London, McFarland, 2003, ISBN 0786412208.
- Pierre Bourdieu, *On Television*, The New Press, 2001.
- Tim Brooks and Earle March, *The Complete Guide to Prime Time Network and Cable TV Shows*, 8th ed., Ballantine, 2002.
- Jacques Derrida and Bernard Stiegler, *Echographies of Television*, Polity Press, 2002.
- David E. Fisher and Marshall J. Fisher, *Tube: the Invention of Television*, Counterpoint, Washington, DC, 1996, ISBN 1887178171.
- Steven Johnson, *Everything Bad is Good for You: How Today's Popular Culture Is Actually Making Us Smarter*, New York, Riverhead (Penguin), 2005, 2006, ISBN 1594481946.
- Jerry Mander, *Four Arguments for the Elimination of Television*, Perennial, 1978.
- Jerry Mander, *In the Absence of the Sacred*, Sierra Club Books, 1992, ISBN 0871565099.
- Neil Postman, *Amusing Ourselves to Death: Public Discourse in the Age of Show Business*, New York, Penguin US, 1985, ISBN 0670804541.
- Evan I. Schwartz, *The Last Lone Inventor: A Tale of Genius, Deceit, and the Birth of Television*, New York, Harper Paperbacks, 2003, ISBN 0060935596.
- Beretta E. Smith-Shomade, *Shaded Lives: African-American Women and Television*, Rutgers University Press, 2002.
- Alan Taylor, *We, the Media: Pedagogic Intrusions into US Mainstream Film and Television News Broadcasting Rhetoric*, Peter Lang, 2005, ISBN 3631518528.

External links

- A History of Television [22] at the Canada Science and Technology Museum
- The Encyclopedia of Television [23] at the Museum of Broadcast Communications
- The Evolution of TV, A Brief History of TV Technology in Japan [24] NHK
- Television's History — The First 75 Years [25]
- Worldwide Television Standards [26]

References

[1] *Television Frequency Table* (http://www.csgnetwork.com/tvfreqtable.html), CSGNetwork.com., a Division of Computer Support Group.

[2] Kowalewski, Anthony, "An Amateur's Television Transmitter" (http://www.earlytelevision.org/1940_home_camera.html), *Radio News*, April 1938. Early Television Museum and Foundation Website, retrieved 2009-07-19.

[3] "History of the Cathode Ray Tube" (http://inventors.about.com/od/cstartinventions/a/CathodeRayTube.htm). *About.com*. . Retrieved 2009-10-04.

[4] World's First TV Recordings (http://www.tvdawn.com/)

[5] "Hungary - [[Kálmán TihanyiIKálmán Tihanyi's (http://portal.unesco.org/ci/en/ev.php-URL_ID=23240&URL_DO=DO_TOPIC& URL_SECTION=201.html)] 1926 Patent Application 'Radioskop'". *Memory of the World*. United Nations Educational, Scientific and Cultural Organization (UNESCO). . Retrieved 2008-02-22.

[6] United States Patent Office, Patent No. 2,133,123, Oct. 11, 1938.

[7] United States Patent Office, Patent No. 2,158,259, May 16, 1939

[8] "Vladimir Kosma Zworykin, 1889-1982" (http://www.bairdtelevision.com/zworykin.html). Bairdtelevision.com. . Retrieved 2009-04-17.

[9] "Philo Taylor Farnsworth (1906-1971)" (http://www.sfmuseum.org/hist10/philo.html), *The Virtual Museum of the City of San Francisco*

[10] Farnsworth, Elma G., *Distant Vision: Romance and Discovery on an Invisible Frontier*, Salt Lake City, PemberlyKent, 1989, p. 108.

[11] "TV History" (http://www.tvhistory.tv). Gadgetrepublic. 2009-05-01. . Retrieved 2009-05-01.

[12] http://ewh.ieee.org/r2/johnstown/downloads/20090217_IEEE_JST_Trivia_Answers.pdf

[13] http://www.scitech.mtesz.hu/52tihanyi/flat-panel_tv_en.pdf

[14] Jon Stewart of "The Daily Show" was mock-outraged at this, saying, "That's what we do!", and calling it a new form of television, "infoganda".

[15] http://www.bci.ie/

[16] "viewing statistics in UK" (http://www.barb.co.uk/viewingsummary/weekreports.cfm?report=multichannel&requesttimeout=500& flag=viewingsummary). Barb.co.uk. . Retrieved 2009-04-17.
[17] OFCOM quarterly survey (http://www.ofcom.org.uk/research/tv/reports/dtv/dtv_2007_q3/dtvq307.pdf)
[18] http://www.comlaw.gov.au/ComLaw/Legislation/ActCompilation1.nsf/all/search/8B104AA963F8AB9FCA25718D002260DC
[19] http://www.abc.net.au/corp/pubs/documents/budget2008-09.pdf
[20] Ministry of Finance (http://www.minefi.gouv.fr/paca/minefi_relais_sociaux/impots/fiche21.html)
[21] "The Rise of the Machines: A Review of Energy Using Products in the Home from the 1970s to Today" (http://www.energysavingtrust. org.uk/uploads/documents/aboutest/Riseofthemachines.pdf) (PDF). Energy Saving Trust. July 3, 2006. . Retrieved 2007-08-31.
[22] http://www.sciencetech.technomuses.ca/english/collection/television.cfm
[23] http://www.museum.tv/archives/etv/index.html
[24] http://www.nhk.or.jp/strl/aboutstrl/evolution-of-tv-en/index-e.html
[25] http://www.tvhistory.tv/
[26] http://radiostationworld.com/directory/television_standards/default.asp

Radio

Radio is the transmission of signals by modulation of electromagnetic waves with frequencies below those of visible light.[1] Electromagnetic radiation travels by means of oscillating electromagnetic fields that pass through the air and the vacuum of space. Information is carried by systematically changing (modulating) some property of the radiated waves, such as amplitude, frequency, phase, or pulse width. When radio waves pass an electrical conductor, the oscillating fields induce an alternating current in the conductor. This can be detected and transformed into sound or other signals that carry information.

Classic radio receiver dial

Etymology

Originally, radio or radiotelegraphy was called "wireless telegraphy", which was shortened to "wireless" by the British. The prefix radio- in the sense of wireless transmission, was first recorded in the word radioconductor, coined by the French physicist Édouard Branly in 1897 and based on the verb to radiate (in Latin "radius" means "spoke of a wheel, beam of light, ray"). "Radio" as a noun is said to have been coined by the advertising expert Waldo Warren (White 1944). This word also appears in a 1907 article by Lee De Forest, was adopted by the United States Navy in 1912 and became common by the time of the first commercial broadcasts in the United States in the 1920s. (The noun "broadcasting" itself came from an agricultural term, meaning "scattering seeds widely".) The term was then adopted by other languages in Europe and Asia. British Commonwealth countries continued to mainly use the term "wireless" until the mid-20th century, though the magazine of the BBC in the UK has been called Radio Times ever since it was first published in the early 1920s.

In recent years the term "wireless" has gained renewed popularity through the rapid growth of short-range computer networking, e.g., Wireless Local Area Network (WLAN), WiFi, and Bluetooth, as well as mobile telephony, e.g., GSM and UMTS. Today, the term "radio" often refers to the actual transceiver device or chip, whereas "wireless" refers to the system and/or method used for radio communication, hence one talks about radio transceivers and Radio Frequency Identification (RFID), but about wireless devices and wireless sensor networks.

Processes

Radio systems used for communications will have the following elements. With more than 100 years of development, each process is implemented by a wide range of methods, specialized for different communications purposes.

Each system contains a transmitter. This consists of a source of electrical energy, producing alternating current of a desired frequency of oscillation. The transmitter contains a system to modulate (change) some property of the energy produced to impress a signal on it. This modulation might be as simple as turning the energy on and off, or altering more subtle properties such as amplitude, frequency, phase, or combinations of these properties. The transmitter sends the modulated electrical energy to a tuned resonant antenna; this structure converts the rapidly-changing alternating current into an electromagnetic wave that can move through free space (sometimes with a particular polarization (waves)).

Electromagnetic waves travel through space either directly, or have their path altered by reflection, refraction or diffraction. The intensity of the waves diminishes due to geometric dispersion (the inverse-square law); some energy may also be absorbed by the intervening medium in some cases. Noise will generally alter the desired signal; this electromagnetic interference comes from natural sources, as well as from artificial sources such as other transmitters and accidental radiators. Noise is also produced at every step due to the inherent properties of the devices used. If the magnitude of the noise is large enough, the desired signal will no longer be discernible; this is the fundamental limit to the range of radio communications.

The electromagnetic wave is intercepted by a tuned receiving antenna; this structure captures some of the energy of the wave and returns it to the form of oscillating electrical currents. At the receiver, these currents are demodulated, which is conversion to a usable signal form by a detector sub-system. The receiver is "tuned" to respond preferentially to the desired signals, and reject undesired signals.

Early radio systems relied entirely on the energy collected by an antenna to produce signals for the operator. Radio became more useful after the invention of electronic devices such as the vacuum tube and later the transistor, which made it possible to amplify weak signals. Today radio systems are used for applications from walkie-talkie children's toys to the control of space vehicles, as well as for broadcasting, and many other applications.

Electromagnetic spectrum

Radio frequencies occupy the range from a few tens of hertz to three hundred gigahertz, although commercially important uses of radio use only a small part of this spectrum.[2] Other types of electromagnetic radiation, with frequencies above the RF range, are microwave, infrared, visible light, ultraviolet, X-rays and gamma rays. Since the energy of an individual photon of radio frequency is too low to remove an electron from an atom, radio waves are classified as non-ionizing radiation.

History

Invention

The meaning and usage of the word "radio" has developed in parallel with developments within the field and can be seen to have three distinct phases: electromagnetic waves and experimentation; wireless communication and technical development; and radio broadcasting and commercialization. Many individuals -- inventors, engineers, developers, businessmen - contributed to produce the modern idea of radio and thus the origins and 'invention' are multiple and controversial. Early radio could not transmit sound or speech and was called the "wireless telegraph".

Development from a laboratory demonstration to a commercial entity spanned several decades and required the efforts of many practitioners. In 1878, David E. Hughes noticed that sparks could be heard in a telephone receiver when experimenting with his carbon microphone. He developed this carbon-based detector further and eventually could detect signals over a few hundred yards. He demonstrated his discovery to the Royal Society in 1880, but was told it was merely induction, and therefore abandoned further research.

Experiments, later patented, were undertaken by Thomas Edison and his employees of Menlo Park.[3] Edison applied in 1885 to the U.S. Patent Office for his patent on an electrostatic coupling system between elevated terminals. The patent was granted as U.S. Patent 465971 [4] on December 29, 1891. The Marconi Company would later purchase rights to the Edison patent to protect them legally from lawsuits.[5]

In 1893, in St. Louis, Missouri, Nikola Tesla made devices for his experiments with electricity. Addressing the *Franklin Institute* in Philadelphia and the *National Electric Light Association*, he described and demonstrated the principles of his wireless work.[6] The descriptions contained all the [[#Processes|elements that were later incorporated into radio systems]] before the development of the vacuum tube. He initially experimented with magnetic receivers, unlike the coherers (detecting devices consisting of tubes filled with iron filings which had been invented by Temistocle Calzecchi-Onesti at Fermo in Italy in 1884) used by Guglielmo Marconi and other early experimenters.[7]

Tesla demonstrating wireless transmissions during his high frequency and potential lecture of 1891. After continued research, Tesla presented the fundamentals of radio in 1893.

A demonstration of wireless telegraphy took place in the lecture theater of the Oxford University Museum of Natural History on August 14, 1894, carried out by Professor Oliver Lodge and Alexander Muirhead. During the demonstration a radio signal was sent from the neighboring Clarendon laboratory building, and received by apparatus in the lecture theater.

In 1895 Alexander Stepanovich Popov built his first radio receiver, which contained a coherer. Further refined as a lightning detector, it was presented to the Russian Physical and Chemical Society on May 7, 1895. A depiction of Popov's lightning detector was printed in the Journal of the Russian Physical and Chemical Society the same year. Popov's receiver was created on the improved basis of Lodge's receiver, and originally intended for reproduction of its experiments.

Commercialization

In 1896, Marconi was awarded the British patent 12039, *Improvements in transmitting electrical impulses and signals and in apparatus there-for*, for radio. In 1897 he established a radio station on the Isle of Wight, England. Marconi opened his "wireless" factory in Hall Street, Chelmsford, England in 1898, employing around 50 people.

Although Marconi has long been credited with inventing the radio, in 1943, maybe for political reasons related to Marconi suing the U.S. over Patent infringement during WWI, the U.S. Supreme Court upheld Tesla's radio patent number 645,576. It's interesting to note that Marconi's first successful test was using a Tesla coil.

Telephone Herald in Budapest, Hungary (1901).

The next advancement was the vacuum tube detector, invented by Westinghouse engineers. On Christmas Eve, 1906, Reginald Fessenden used a synchronous rotary-spark transmitter for the first radio program broadcast, from Ocean Bluff-Brant Rock, Massachusetts. Ships at sea heard a broadcast that included Fessenden playing *O Holy Night* on the violin and reading a passage from the Bible. This was, for all intents and purposes, the first transmission of what is now known as amplitude modulation or AM radio. The first radio news program was broadcast August 31, 1920 by station 8MK in Detroit, Michigan, which survives today as all-news format station WWJ under ownership of the CBS network. The first college radio station began broadcasting on October 14, 1920, from Union College, Schenectady, New York under the personal call letters of Wendell King, an African-American student at the school.[8] That month 2ADD, later renamed WRUC in 1940, aired what is believed to be the first public entertainment broadcast in the United States, a series of Thursday night concerts initially heard within a 100-mile (160 km) radius and later for a 1000-mile (1600 km) radius. In November 1920, it aired the first broadcast of a sporting event.[8] [9] At 9 pm on August 27, 1920, Sociedad Radio Argentina aired a live performance of Richard Wagner's Parsifal opera from the Coliseo Theater in downtown Buenos Aires. Only about twenty homes in the city had receivers to tune in this radio program. Meanwhile, regular entertainment broadcasts commenced in 1922 from the Marconi Research Centre at Writtle, England.

One of the first developments in the early 20th century (1900-1959) was that aircraft used commercial AM radio stations for navigation. This continued until the early 1960s when VOR systems finally became widespread (though AM stations are still marked on U.S. aviation charts). In the early 1930s, single sideband and frequency modulation were invented by amateur radio operators. By the end of the decade, they were established commercial modes. Radio was used to transmit pictures visible as → television as early as the 1920s. Commercial television transmissions started in North America and Europe in the 1940s. In 1954, the Regency company introduced a pocket transistor radio, the TR-1, powered by a "standard 22.5 V Battery".

American girl listens to radio during the Great Depression.

In 1960, the Sony company introduced its first transistorized radio. It was small enough to fit in a vest pocket, and able to be powered by a small battery. It was durable, because it had no vacuum tubes to burn out. Over the next 20 years, transistors replaced tubes almost completely except for very high-power transmitter uses. By 1963, color television was being regularly broadcast commercially (though not all broadcasts or programs were in color), and the first (radio) communication satellite, *Telstar*, was launched. In the late 1960s, the U.S. long-distance telephone network began to convert to a digital network, employing digital radios for many of its links. In the 1970s, LORAN became the premier radio navigation system. Soon, the U.S. Navy experimented with satellite navigation, culminating in the invention and launch of the GPS constellation in 1987. In the early 1990s, amateur radio experimenters began to use personal computers with audio cards to process radio signals. In 1994, the U.S. Army and DARPA launched an aggressive, successful project to construct a software-defined radio that can be programmed to be virtually any radio by changing its software program. Digital transmissions began to be applied to broadcasting in the late 1990s.

Uses of radio

Early uses were maritime, for sending telegraphic messages using Morse code between ships and land. The earliest users included the Japanese Navy scouting the Russian fleet during the Battle of Tsushima in 1905. One of the most memorable uses of marine telegraphy was during the sinking of the RMS *Titanic* in 1912, including communications between operators on the sinking ship and nearby vessels, and communications to shore stations listing the survivors.

Radio was used to pass on orders and communications between armies and navies on both sides in World War I; Germany used radio communications for diplomatic messages once it discovered that its submarine cables had been tapped by the British. The United States passed on President Woodrow Wilson's Fourteen Points to Germany via radio during the war. Broadcasting began from San Jose, California in 1909,[10] and became feasible in the 1920s, with the widespread introduction of radio receivers, particularly in Europe and the United States. Besides broadcasting, point-to-point broadcasting, including telephone messages and relays of radio programs, became widespread in the 1920s and 1930s. Another use of radio in the pre-war years was the development of detection and locating of aircraft and ships by the use of radar (*RA*dio *D*etection *A*nd *R*anging).

Today, radio takes many forms, including wireless networks and mobile communications of all types, as well as radio broadcasting. Before the advent of → television, commercial radio broadcasts included not only news and music, but dramas, comedies, variety shows, and many other forms of entertainment. Radio was unique among methods of dramatic presentation in that it used only sound. For more, see radio programming.

Audio

AM radio uses amplitude modulation, in which the amplitude of the transmitted signal is made proportional to the sound amplitude captured (transduced) by the microphone, while the transmitted frequency remains unchanged. Transmissions are affected by static and interference because lightning and other sources of radio emissions on the same frequency add their amplitudes to the original transmitted amplitude. In the early part of the 20th century, American AM radio stations broadcast with powers as high as 500 kW, and some could be heard worldwide; these stations' transmitters were commandeered for military use by the US Government during World War II. Currently,

A Fisher 500 AM/FM hi-fi receiver from 1959.

the maximum broadcast power for a civilian AM radio station in the United States and Canada is 50 kW, and the majority of stations that emit signals this powerful were grandfathered in (see List of 50kw AM radio stations in the USA). In 1986 KTNN received the last granted 50,000 watt license. These 50 kW stations are generally called "clear channel" stations (not to be confused with Clear Channel Communications), because within North America each of these stations has exclusive use of its broadcast frequency throughout part or all of the broadcast day.

FM broadcast radio sends music and voice with higher fidelity than AM radio. In frequency modulation, amplitude variation at the microphone causes the transmitter frequency to fluctuate. Because the audio signal modulates the frequency and not the amplitude, an FM signal is not subject to static and interference in the same way as AM signals. Due to its need for a wider bandwidth, FM is transmitted in the Very High Frequency (VHF, 30 MHz to 300 MHz) radio spectrum. VHF radio waves act more like light, traveling in straight lines; hence the reception range is generally limited to about 50-100 miles. During unusual upper atmospheric conditions, FM signals are occasionally reflected back towards the Earth by the ionosphere, resulting in long distance FM reception. FM receivers are subject to the capture effect, which causes the radio to only receive the strongest signal when multiple signals appear on the same frequency. FM receivers are relatively immune to lightning and spark interference.

Bush House, home of the BBC World Service.

High power is useful in penetrating buildings, diffracting around hills, and refracting in the dense atmosphere near the horizon for some distance beyond the horizon. Consequently, 100,000 watt FM stations can regularly be heard up to 100 miles (160 km) away, and farther (e.g., 150 miles, 240 km) if there are no competing signals. A few old, "grandfathered" stations do not conform to these power rules. WBCT-FM (93.7) in Grand Rapids, Michigan, USA, runs 320,000 watts ERP, and can increase to 500,000 watts ERP by the terms of its original license. Such a huge power level does not usually help to increase range as much as one might expect, because VHF frequencies travel in nearly straight lines over the horizon and off into space. Nevertheless, when there were fewer FM stations competing, this station could be heard near Bloomington, Illinois, USA, almost 300 miles (500 km) away.

FM subcarrier services are secondary signals transmitted in a "piggyback" fashion along with the main program. Special receivers are required to utilize these services. Analog channels may contain alternative programming, such as reading services for the blind, background music or stereo sound signals. In some extremely crowded metropolitan areas, the sub-channel program might be an alternate foreign language radio program for various ethnic groups. Sub-carriers can also transmit digital data, such as station identification, the current song's name, web addresses, or stock quotes. In some countries, FM radios automatically re-tune themselves to the same channel in a different district by using sub-bands.

Aviation voice radios use VHF AM. AM is used so that multiple stations on the same channel can be received. (Use of FM would result in stronger stations blocking out reception of weaker stations due to FM's capture effect). Aircraft fly high enough that their transmitters can be received hundreds of miles (or kilometres) away, even though they are using VHF.

Marine voice radios can use single sideband voice (SSB) in the shortwave High Frequency (HF—3 MHz to 30 MHz) radio spectrum for very long ranges or narrowband FM in the VHF spectrum for much shorter ranges. Narrowband FM sacrifices fidelity to make more channels available within the radio spectrum, by using a smaller range of radio frequencies, usually with five kHz of deviation, versus the 75 kHz used by commercial FM broadcasts, and 25 kHz used for TV sound.

Government, police, fire and commercial voice services also use narrowband FM on special frequencies. Early police radios used AM receivers to receive one-way dispatches.

Civil and military HF (high frequency) voice services use shortwave radio to contact ships at sea, aircraft and isolated settlements. Most use single sideband voice (SSB), which uses less bandwidth than AM. On an AM radio SSB sounds like ducks quacking, or the adults in a Charlie Brown cartoon. Viewed as a graph of frequency versus power, an AM signal shows power where the frequencies of the voice add and subtract with the main radio frequency. SSB cuts the bandwidth in half by suppressing the carrier and (usually) lower sideband. This also makes the transmitter about three times more powerful, because it doesn't need to transmit the unused carrier and sideband.

TETRA, Terrestrial Trunked Radio is a digital cell phone system for military, police and ambulances. Commercial services such as XM, WorldSpace and Sirius offer encrypted digital Satellite radio.

Telephony

Mobile phones transmit to a local cell site (transmitter/receiver) that ultimately connects to the public switched telephone network (PSTN) through an optic fiber or microwave radio and other network elements. When the mobile phone nears the edge of the cell site's radio coverage area, the central computer switches the phone to a new cell. Cell phones originally used FM, but now most use various digital modulation schemes. Recent developments in Sweden (such as DROPme) allow for the instant downloading of digital material from a radio broadcast (such as a song) to a mobile phone.

Satellite phones use satellites rather than cell towers to communicate.

Video

→ Television sends the picture as AM and the sound as AM or FM, with the sound carrier a fixed frequency (4.5 MHz in the NTSC system) away from the video carrier. Analog television also uses a vestigial sideband on the video carrier to reduce the bandwidth required.

Digital television uses 8VSB modulation in North America (under the ATSC digital television standard), and COFDM modulation elsewhere in the world (using the DVB-T standard). A Reed–Solomon error correction code adds redundant correction codes and allows reliable reception during moderate data loss. Although many current and future codecs can be sent in the MPEG transport stream container format, as of 2006 most systems use a standard-definition format almost identical to DVD: MPEG-2 video in Anamorphic widescreen and MPEG layer 2 (*MP2*) audio. High-definition television is possible simply by using a higher-resolution picture, but H.264/AVC is being considered as a replacement video codec in some regions for its improved compression. With the compression and improved modulation involved, a single "channel" can contain a high-definition program and several standard-definition programs.

Navigation

All satellite navigation systems use satellites with precision clocks. The satellite transmits its position, and the time of the transmission. The receiver listens to four satellites, and can figure its position as being on a line that is tangent to a spherical shell around each satellite, determined by the time-of-flight of the radio signals from the satellite. A computer in the receiver does the math.

Radio direction-finding is the oldest form of radio navigation. Before 1960 navigators used movable loop antennas to locate commercial AM stations near cities. In some cases they used marine radiolocation beacons, which share a range of frequencies just above AM radio with amateur radio operators. LORAN systems also used time-of-flight radio signals, but from radio stations on the ground. VOR (Very High Frequency Omnidirectional Range), systems (used by aircraft), have an antenna array that transmits two signals simultaneously. A directional signal rotates like a lighthouse at a fixed rate. When the directional signal is facing north, an omnidirectional signal pulses. By measuring the difference in phase of these two signals, an aircraft can determine its bearing or radial from the station, thus establishing a line of position. An aircraft can get readings from two VORs and locate its position at the intersection of the two radials, known as a "fix." When the VOR station is collocated with DME (Distance Measuring Equipment), the aircraft can determine its bearing and range from the station, thus providing a fix from only one ground station. Such stations are called VOR/DMEs. The military operates a similar system of navaids, called TACANs, which are often built into VOR stations. Such stations are called VORTACs. Because TACANs include distance measuring equipment, VOR/DME and VORTAC stations are identical in navigation potential to civil aircraft.

Radar

Radar (Radio Detection And Ranging) detects objects at a distance by bouncing radio waves off them. The delay caused by the echo measures the distance. The direction of the beam determines the direction of the reflection. The polarization and frequency of the return can sense the type of surface. Navigational radars scan a wide area two to four times per minute. They use very short waves that reflect from earth and stone. They are common on commercial ships and long-distance commercial aircraft.

General purpose radars generally use navigational radar frequencies, but modulate and polarize the pulse so the receiver can determine the type of surface of the reflector. The best general-purpose radars distinguish the rain of heavy storms, as well as land and vehicles. Some can superimpose sonar data and map data from GPS position.

Search radars scan a wide area with pulses of short radio waves. They usually scan the area two to four times a minute. Sometimes search radars use the Doppler effect to separate moving vehicles from clutter. Targeting radars use the same principle as search radar but scan a much smaller area far more often, usually several times a second or more. Weather radars resemble search radars, but use radio waves with circular polarization and a wavelength to reflect from water droplets. Some weather radar use the Doppler effect to measure wind speeds.

Data (digital radio)

Most new radio systems are digital, see also: Digital TV, Satellite Radio, Digital Audio Broadcasting. The oldest form of digital broadcast was spark gap telegraphy, used by pioneers such as Marconi. By pressing the key, the operator could send messages in Morse code by energizing a rotating commutating spark gap. The rotating commutator produced a tone in the receiver, where a simple spark gap would produce a hiss, indistinguishable from static. Spark gap transmitters are now illegal, because their transmissions span several hundred megahertz. This is very wasteful of both radio frequencies and power.

2008 Pure One Classic digital radio

The next advance was continuous wave telegraphy, or CW (Continuous Wave), in which a pure radio frequency, produced by a vacuum tube electronic oscillator was switched on and off by a key. A receiver with a local oscillator would "heterodyne" with the pure radio frequency, creating a whistle-like audio tone. CW uses less than 100 Hz of bandwidth. CW is still used, these days primarily by amateur radio operators (hams). Strictly, on-off keying of a carrier should be known as "Interrupted Continuous Wave" or ICW or on-off keying (OOK).

Radio teletypes usually operate on short-wave (HF) and are much loved by the military because they create written information without a skilled operator. They send a bit as one of two tones. Groups of five or seven bits become a character printed by a teletype. From about 1925 to 1975, radio teletype was how most commercial messages were sent to less developed countries. These are still used by the military and weather services.

Aircraft use a 1200 Baud radioteletype service over VHF to send their ID, altitude and position, and get gate and connecting-flight data. Microwave dishes on satellites, telephone exchanges and TV stations usually use quadrature amplitude modulation (QAM). QAM sends data by changing both the phase and the amplitude of the radio signal. Engineers like QAM because it packs the most bits into a radio signal when given an exclusive (non-shared) fixed narrowband frequency range. Usually the bits are sent in "frames" that repeat. A special bit pattern is used to locate the beginning of a frame.

Communication systems that limit themselves to a fixed narrowband frequency range are vulnerable to jamming. A variety of jamming-resistant spread spectrum techniques were initially developed for military use, most famously for Global Positioning System satellite transmissions. Commercial use of spread spectrum began in the 1980s. Bluetooth, most cell phones, and the 802.11b version of Wi-Fi each use various forms of spread spectrum.

Modern GPS receivers.

Systems that need reliability, or that share their frequency with other services, may use "coded orthogonal frequency-division multiplexing" or COFDM. COFDM breaks a digital signal into as many as several hundred slower subchannels. The digital signal is often sent as QAM on the subchannels. Modern COFDM systems use a small computer to make and decode the signal with digital signal processing, which is more flexible and far less expensive than older systems that implemented separate electronic channels. COFDM resists fading and ghosting because the narrow-channel QAM signals can be sent slowly. An adaptive system, or one that sends error-correction codes can also resist interference, because most interference can affect only a few of the QAM channels. COFDM is used for Wi-Fi, some cell phones, Digital Radio Mondiale, Eureka 147, and many other local area network, digital TV and radio standards.

Heating

Radio-frequency energy generated for heating of objects is generally not intended to radiate outside of the generating equipment, to prevent interference with other radio signals. Microwave ovens use intense radio waves to heat food. Diathermy equipment is used in surgery for sealing of blood vessels. Induction furnaces are used for melting metal for casting, and induction hobs for cooking.

Amateur radio service

Amateur radio, also known as "ham radio", is a hobby in which enthusiasts are licensed to communicate on a number of bands in the radio frequency spectrum non-commercially and for their own enjoyment. They may also provide emergency and public service assistance. This has been very beneficial in emergencies, saving lives in many instances.[11] Radio amateurs use a variety of modes, including nostalgic ones like Morse code and experimental ones like Low-Frequency Experimental Radio. Several forms of radio were pioneered by radio amateurs and later became commercially important including FM, single-sideband (SSB), AM, digital packet radio and satellite repeaters. Some amateur frequencies may be disrupted by power-line internet service.

Amateur radio station with multiple receivers and transceivers

Unlicensed radio services

Unlicensed, government-authorized personal radio services such as Citizens' band radio in Australia, the USA, and Europe, and Family Radio Service and Multi-Use Radio Service in North America exist to provide simple, (usually) short range communication for individuals and small groups, without the overhead of licensing. Similar services exist in other parts of the world. These radio services involve the use of handheld units.

Free radio stations, sometimes called pirate radio or "clandestine" stations, are unauthorized, unlicensed, illegal broadcasting stations. These are often low power transmitters operated on sporadic schedules by hobbyists, community activists, or political and cultural dissidents. Some pirate stations operating offshore in parts of Europe and the United Kingdom more closely resembled legal stations, maintaining regular schedules, using high power, and selling commercial advertising time.[12] [13]

Radio control (R C)

Radio remote controls use radio waves to transmit control data to a remote object as in some early forms of guided missile, some early TV remotes and a range of model boats, cars and airplanes. Large industrial remote-controlled equipment such as cranes and switching locomotives now usually use digital radio techniques to ensure safety and reliability.

In Madison Square Garden, at the Electrical Exhibition of 1898, Nikola Tesla successfully demonstrated a radio-controlled boat.[14] He was awarded U.S. patent No. 613,809 for a "Method of and Apparatus for Controlling Mechanism of Moving Vessels or Vehicles."[15]

See also

- Amateur radio
- Antique radio
- Batteryless radio
- Carrier current
- Crystal radio
- Digital radio
- Hertz
- Longwave
- Medium wave
- Old-time radio
- Pirate radio
- Power line communication
- Radio astronomy
- Radio documentary
- History of radio
- Radio direction finder
- Direction finding
- Radio navigation
- Radio programming
- Radio propagation and ionosphere
- Radio software
- Receiver (radio)
- Satellite radio
- Shortwave
- Software-defined radio
- Superheterodyne_receiver
- Outline of radio
- Timeline of radio
- Transistor radio
- Tuner (radio)
- Types of radio emissions
- Wireless energy transfer

References

General information

- *A História da Rádio em Datas (1819-1997)* (in Portuguese) - notes on etymology [16]
- Leigh White, *Buck Fuller and the Dymaxion World* (refers to Waldo Warren as the inventor of the word *radio*), in: The Saturday Evening Post, 14 October 1944, cited in: Joachim Krausse and Claude Lichtenstein (eds.), *Your Private Sky*, Lars Müller Publishers, Baden/Switzerland, 1999, page 132. ISBN 3-907044-88-6
- L. de Forest, article in Electrical World 22 June 1270/1 (1907), early use of word "radio".
- http://web.mit.edu/varun_ag/www/bose.html - It contains a proof that Sir Jagadish Chandra Bose invented the Mercury Coherer which was later used by Guglielmo Marconi and along with other patents.
- Cheney, Margaret (1981). *Tesla - Man Out of Time*. New York: Simon & Schuster. ISBN 978-0743215367.

Footnotes

[1] Dictionary of Electronics By Rudolf F. Graf (1974). Page 467.

[2] *The Electromagnetic Spectrum*, University of Tennessee, Dept. of Physics and Astronomy

[3] Many of Edison's patents were actually made by his employees - Edison patented their work and did not share the credit of the innovation. During the timeframe that the patentable work was undertaken, Nikola Tesla worked for Edison in America (beginning in 1884).

[4] http://www.google.com/patents?vid=465971

[5] Edison, his life and inventions (http://books.google.com/books?id=GuA3AAAAMAAJ) By Frank Lewis Dyer, Thomas Commerford Martin. Page 830 (http://books.google.com/books?id=GuA3AAAAMAAJ&pg=PA830).

[6] IEEEVM: Nikola Tesla (http://www.ieee-virtual-museum.org/collection/people.php?taid=&id=1234597&lid=1)

[7] K. Corum; J. Corum. "Tesla's Colorado Springs Receivers" (http://www.teslasociety.com/teslarec.pdf) (PDF). . Retrieved 2009-07-22.

[8] "Radio Broadcasting" (http://w2uc.union.edu/RADIO_web.htm). W2uc.union.edu. . Retrieved 2009-07-22.

[9] "Union College Magazine" (http://2000.union.edu/N/DS/edition_display.php?e=677&s=2700). 2000.union.edu. . Retrieved 2009-07-22.

[10] "The History Of KQW Radio - KCBS" (http://www.bayarearadio.org/schneider/kqw.shtml). Bayarearadio.org. . Retrieved 2009-07-22.

[11] ""Amateur Radio "Saved Lives" in South Asia"" (http://www.arrl.org/news/stories/2004/12/29/100/?nc=1). Arrl.org. 2004-12-29. . Retrieved 2009-07-22.

[12] *Free radio: electronic civil disobedience* by Lawrence C. Soley. Published by Westview Press, 1998. ISBN 0813390648, 9780813390642

[13] *Rebel Radio: The Full Story of British Pirate Radio* by John Hind, Stephen Mosco. Published by Pluto Press, 1985. ISBN 0745300553, 9780745300559

[14] "Tesla - Master of Lightning: Remote Control" (http://www.pbs.org/tesla/ins/lab_remotec.html). PBS. . Retrieved 2009-07-22.

[15] "Tesla - Master of Lightning: Selected Tesla Patents" (http://www.pbs.org/tesla/res/613809.html). PBS. . Retrieved 2009-07-22.

[16] http://pagina.vizzavi.pt/~nc22723a/radio.htm

Further reading

- Aitkin Hugh G. J. *The Continuous Wave: Technology and the American Radio, 1900-1932* (Princeton University Press, 1985).
- Briggs Asa. *The History of Broadcasting in the United Kingdom* (Oxford University Press, 1961).
- De Forest, Lee. *Father of Radio: The Autobiography of Lee de Forest* (1950).
- Ewbank Henry and Lawton Sherman P. *Broadcasting: Radio and Television* (Harper & Brothers, 1952).
- Fisher, Marc *Something In The Air: Radio, Rock, and the Revolution That Shaped A Generation* (Random House, 2007).
- Leland I. Anderson (ed.), " John Stone Stone, Nikola Tesla's Priority in Radio and Continuous-Wave Radiofrequency Apparatus (http://www.tfcbooks.com/mall/more/436ntpr.htm)". The Antique Wireless Review, Vol. 1. 1986. 24 pages, illustrated.
- Maclaurin W. Rupert. *Invention and Innovation in the Radio Industry* (The Macmillan Company, 1949).
- Ray William B. *FCC: The Ups and Downs of Radio-TV Regulation* (Iowa State University Press, 1990).
- Scannell, Paddy, and Cardiff, David. *A Social History of British Broadcasting, Volume One, 1922-1939* (Basil Blackwell, 1991).
- Schwoch James. *The American Radio Industry and Its Latin American Activities, 1900-1939* (University of Illinois Press, 1990).
- Sterling Christopher H. *Electronic Media, A Guide to Trends in Broadcasting and Newer Technologies 1920-1983* (Praeger, 1984).
- White Llewellyn. *The American Radio* (University of Chicago Press, 1947).
- Ulrich L. Rohde, Jerry Whitaker "Communications Receivers, Third Edition ", McGraw Hill, New York, NY, 2001, ISBN 0-07-136121-9.

External links

General

- Radio (http://www.dmoz.org/Arts/Radio/) at the Open Directory Project
- "It's Radi-O! (http://www.theatlantic.com/issues/98jan/radio.htm) Essay by Richard Rubin, The Atlantic Monthly, January 1998.

History

- U.S. Supreme Court, " *Marconi Wireless Telegraph co. of America v. United States* (http://caselaw.lp.findlaw. com/scripts/getcase.pl?court=us&vol=320&invol=1)". 320 U.S. 1. Nos. 369, 373. Argued 9 April-12, 1943. Decided 21 June 1943.
- Horzepa, Stan, " *Surfin': Who Invented Radio* (http://www.arrl.org/news/features/2003/10/10/1/)?" Arrl.org. 10 October 2003.
- Steven Schoenherr's History of Radio (http://history.sandiego.edu/gen/recording/radio.html)
- The Broadcast Archive - Radio History on the Web! (http://www.oldradio.com)
- Canadian Communications Foundation - The History on Canadian Broadcasting (http://www. broadcasting-history.ca).
- United States Early Radio History (http://earlyradiohistory.us)
- Historic Radios from Around the World at Kurrajong Radio Museum, Australia (http://www.vk2bv.org/ museum)
- Early Canadian Radio Station Lists (http://members.aol.com/jeff560/canada.html)
- United States Early Radio History (http://earlyradiohistory.us)

Antiques

- George H. Clark Radioana Collection, ca. 1880 - 1950 (http://invention.smithsonian.org/resources/ fa_clark_index.aspx) - Archives Center, National Museum of American History, Smithsonian Institution
- A gallery of Antiques from the 1920s to the 1960s (http://members.aol.com/djadamson/arp.html)

Technical

- Radio Frequency Chart (http://www.commandline.net/Radio Frequency Chart1.htm) commandline.net.
- IAteacher: Interactive Explanation of Radio Receiver Construction (http://www.iateacher.com/Lesson 6/ L6P1-Title.htm)
- How Stuff Works - Radio (http://electronics.howstuffworks.com/radio.htm)
- VOR Basic Information (http://www.allstar.fiu.edu/aero/VOR.htm)
- Dr. Phil's Receiver Designs (http://home.comcast.net/~phils_radio_designs/) Single-Triode and Single-Transistor Regenerative Radio Designs

DX

- The British DX Club (http://www.bdxc.org.uk)
- www.worldofradio.com (http://www.worldofradio.com/) Glenn Hauser's internationally-known DX radio show

Mass media

Mass media denotes a section of the media specifically designed to reach a very large audience such as the population of a nation state. The term was coined in the 1920s with the advent of nationwide radio networks, mass-circulation newspapers and magazines. However, some forms of mass media such as books and manuscripts had already been in use centuries. The term **public media** has a similar meaning: it is the sum of the public mass distributors of news and entertainment across media such as newspapers, → television, → radio, broadcasting, which may require union membership in some large markets such as Newspaper Guild, AFTRA, and text publishers.

Mass media includes Internet media (like blogs, message boards, podcasts, and video sharing) because individuals now have a means to exposure that is comparable in scale to that previously restricted to a select group of mass media producers. The communications audience has been viewed by some commentators as forming a mass society with special characteristics, notably atomization or lack of social connections, which render it especially susceptible to the influence of modern mass-media techniques such as → advertising and propaganda. The term "MSM" or "mainstream media" has been widely used in the blogosphere in discussion of the mass media and media bias.

History

Types of drama in numerous cultures were probably the first mass-media, going back into the Ancient World. The first dated printed book known is the "Diamond Sutra", printed in China in 868 AD, although it is clear that books were printed earlier. Movable clay type was invented in 1041 in China. However, due to the slow spread of literacy to the masses in China, and the relatively high cost of paper there, the earliest printed mass-medium was probably European popular prints from about 1400. Although these were produced in huge numbers, very few early examples survive, and even most known to be printed before about 1600 have not survived. Johannes Gutenberg printed the first book on a printing press with movable type in 1453. This invention transformed the way the world received printed materials, although books remained too expensive really to be called a mass-medium for at least a century after that.

Newspapers developed around from 1612, with the first example in English in 1620 [1] ; but they took until the nineteenth century to reach a mass-audience directly.

During the 20th century, the growth of mass media was driven by technology that allowed the massive duplication of material. Physical duplication technologies such as printing, record pressing and film duplication allowed the duplication of books, newspapers and movies at low prices to huge audiences. → Radio and → television allowed the electronic duplication of information for the first time.

Mass media had the economics of linear replication: a single work could make money An example of Riel and Neil's theory. proportional to the number of copies sold, and as volumes went up, unit costs went down, increasing profit margins further. Vast fortunes were to be made in mass media. In a democratic society, independent media serve electorate about issues regarding government and corporate entities (see Media influence). Some consider the concentration of media ownership to be a grave threat to democracy.

Purposes

Mass media can be used for various purposes:

- Advocacy, both for business and social concerns. This can include → advertising, → marketing, propaganda, public relations, and political communication.
- Entertainment, traditionally through performances of acting, music, and sports, along with light reading; since the late 20th century also through video and computer games.
- Public service announcements.

Negative characteristics of mass media

Another description of Mass Media is central media which implies:

- An inability to transmit tacit knowledge (or perhaps it can only transfer bad tacit).
- The manipulation of large groups of people through media outlets, for the benefit of a particular political party and/or group of people.
- Marshall McLuhan, one of the biggest critics in media's history, brought up the idea that "the medium is the message."
- Bias, political or otherwise, towards favoring a certain individual, outcome or resolution of an event.
- "The corporate media is not a watchdog protecting us from the powerful, it is a lapdog begging for scraps."[2]

This view of central media can be contrasted with lateral media, such as email networks, where messages are all slightly different and spread by a process of lateral diffusion.

Journalism

Journalism is the discipline of collecting, analyzing, verifying and presenting information regarding current events, trends, issues and people. Those who practice journalism are known as journalists.

News-oriented journalism is sometimes described as the "first rough draft of history" (attributed to Phil Graham), because journalists often record important events, producing news articles on short deadlines. While under pressure to be first with their stories, news media organizations usually edit and proofread their reports prior to publication, adhering to each organization's standards of accuracy, quality and style. Many news organizations claim proud traditions of holding government officials and institutions accountable to the public, while media critics have raised questions about holding the press itself accountable.

Public relations

Public relations is the art and science of managing communication between an organization and its key publics to build, manage and sustain its positive image. Examples include:

- Corporations use marketing public relations (MPR) to convey information about the products they manufacture or services they provide to potential customers to support their direct sales efforts. Typically, they support sales in the short and long term, establishing and burnishing the corporation's branding for a strong, ongoing market.
- Corporations also use public-relations as a vehicle to reach legislators and other politicians, seeking favorable tax, regulatory, and other treatment, and they may use public relations to portray themselves as enlightened employers, in support of human-resources recruiting programs.
- Non-profit organizations, including schools and universities, hospitals, and human and social service agencies, use public relations in support of awareness programs, fund-raising programs, staff recruiting, and to increase patronage of their services.
- Politicians use public relations to attract votes and raise money, and, when successful at the ballot box, to promote and defend their service in office, with an eye to the next election or, at career's end, to their legacy.

Forms

Electronic media and print media include:

- Broadcasting, in the narrow sense, for → radio and → television.
- Various types of discs or tapes. In the 20th century, these were mainly used for music. Video and computer uses followed.
- Film, most often used for entertainment, but also for documentaries.
- → Internet, which has many uses and presents both opportunities and challenges. Blogs and podcasts (such as news, music, pre-recorded speech, and video)
- Mobile phones, often called the 7th Mass Media, used for rapid breaking news, short clips of entertainment like jokes, horoscopes, alerts, games, music, and advertising
- Publishing, including electronic publishing
- Video games, which have developed into a mass form of media since cutting-edge devices such as the PlayStation 3, XBox 360, and Wii broadened their use.

Audio recording and reproduction

Sound recording and reproduction is the electrical or mechanical re-creation and/or amplification of sound, often as music. This involves the use of audio equipment such as microphones, recording devices and loudspeakers. From early beginnings with the invention of the phonograph using purely mechanical techniques, the field has advanced with the invention of electrical recording, the mass production of the 78 record, the magnetic wire recorder followed by the tape recorder, the vinyl LP record. The invention of the compact cassette in the 1960s, followed by Sony's Walkman, gave a major boost to the mass distribution of music recordings, and the invention of digital recording and the compact disc in 1983 brought massive improvements in ruggedness and quality. The most recent developments have been in digital audio players.

An album is a collection of related audio recordings, released together to the public, usually commercially.

The term record album originated from the fact that 78 RPM Phonograph disc records were kept together in a book resembling a photo album. The first collection of records to be called an "album" was Tchaikovsky's *Nutcracker Suite*, release in April 1909 as a four-disc set by Odeon records.[3] [4] It retailed for 16 shillings — about £15 in modern currency.

A music video (also promo) is a short film or video that accompanies a complete piece of music, most commonly a song. Modern music videos were primarily made and used as a marketing device intended to promote the sale of music recordings. Although the origins of music videos go back much further, they came into their own in the 1980s, when Music Television's format was based around them. In the 1980s, the term "rock video" was often used to describe this form of entertainment, although the term has fallen into disuse.

Music videos can accommodate all styles of filmmaking, including animation, live action films, documentaries, and non-narrative, abstract film.

The sequencing of content in a broadcast is called a schedule. With all technological endeavours a number of technical terms and slang are developed please see the list of broadcasting terms for a glossary of terms used.

→ Television and → radio programs are distributed through radio broadcasting over frequency bands that are highly regulated by the Federal Communications Commission. Such regulation includes determination of the width of the bands, range, licencing, types of receivers and transmitters used, and acceptable content.

Cable programs are often broadcast simultaneously with radio and television programs, but have a more limited audience. By coding signals and having decoding equipment in homes, cable also enables subscription-based channels and pay-per-view services.

A broadcasting organisation may broadcast several programs at the same time, through several channels (frequencies), for example BBC One and Two. On the other hand, two or more organisations may share a channel and each use it during a fixed part of the day. Digital radio and digital television may also transmit multiplexed programming, with several channels compressed into one ensemble.

When broadcasting is done via the Internet the term webcasting is often used. In 2004 a new phenomenon occurred when a number of technologies combined to produce podcasting. Podcasting is an asynchronous broadcast/narrowcast medium, with one of the main proponents being Adam Curry and his associates the Podshow.

Film

'Film' encompasses motion pictures as individual projects, as well as the field in general. The name comes from the photographic film (also called filmstock), historically the primary medium for recording and displaying motion pictures. Many other terms exist — *motion pictures* (or just *pictures* and "picture"), *the silver screen, photoplays, the cinema, picture shows, flicks* — and commonly *movies*.

Films are produced by recording people and objects with cameras, or by creating them using animation techniques and/or special effects. They comprise a series of individual frames, but when these images are shown rapidly in succession, the illusion of motion is given to the viewer. Flickering between frames is not seen due to an effect known as persistence of vision — whereby the eye retains a visual image for a fraction of a second after the source has been removed. Also of relevance is what causes the perception of motion; a psychological effect identified as beta movement.

Film is considered by many to be an important art form; films entertain, educate, enlighten and inspire audiences. Any film can become a worldwide attraction, especially with the addition of dubbing or subtitles that translate the film message. Films are also artifacts created by specific cultures, which reflect those cultures, and, in turn, affect them.

Internet

The → Internet (also known simply as "the Net" or "the Web") is a more interactive medium of mass media, and can be briefly described as "a network of networks". Specifically, it is the worldwide, publicly accessible network of interconnected computer networks that transmit data by packet switching using the standard Internet Protocol (IP). It consists of millions of smaller domestic, academic, business, and governmental networks, which together carry various information and services, such as electronic mail, online chat, file transfer, and the interlinked → Web pages and other documents of the → World Wide Web.

Contrary to some common usage, the Internet and the → World Wide Web are not synonymous: the Internet is the system of interconnected *computer networks*, linked by copper wires, fiber-optic cables, wireless connections etc.; the Web is the contents, or the interconnected *documents*, linked by hyperlinks and URLs. The World Wide Web is accessible through the Internet, along with many other services including → e-mail, file sharing and others described below.

Toward the end of the 20th century, the advent of the → World Wide Web marked the first era in which any individual could have a means of exposure on a scale comparable to that of mass media. For the first time, anyone with a web site can address a global audience, although serving to high levels of web traffic is still relatively expensive. It is possible that the rise of peer-to-peer technologies may have begun the process of making the cost of bandwidth manageable. Although a vast amount of information, imagery, and commentary (i.e. "content") has been made available, it is often difficult to determine the authenticity and reliability of information contained in web pages (in many cases, self-published). The invention of the Internet has also allowed breaking news stories to reach around the globe within minutes. This rapid growth of instantaneous, decentralized communication is often deemed likely to change mass media and its relationship to society.

"Cross-media" means the idea of distributing the same message through different media channels. A similar idea is expressed in the news industry as "convergence". Many authors understand cross-media publishing to be the ability to publish in both print and on the → web without manual conversion effort. An increasing number of wireless devices with mutually incompatible data and screen formats make it even more difficult to achieve the objective "create once, publish many".

The internet is quickly becoming the center of mass media. Everything is becoming accessible via the internet. Instead of picking up a newspaper, or watching the 10 o'clock news, people will log onto the internet to get the news they want, when they want it. Many workers listen to the radio through the internet while sitting at their desk. Games are played through the internet. The Internet and Education: Findings of the Pew Internet & American Life Project [5] Even the education system relies on the internet.Teachers can contact the entire class by sending one e-mail. They have web pages where students can get another copy of the class outline or assignments. Some classes even have class blogs where students must post weekly, and are graded on their contributions. The internet thus far has become an extremely dominant form of media.

Blogs (Web Logs)

Blogging has become a huge form of media, popular through the internet. A blog is a website, usually maintained by an individual, with regular entries of commentary, descriptions of events, or other material such as graphics or video. Entries are commonly displayed in reverse chronological order. Many blogs provide commentary or news on a particular subject; others function as more personal online diaries. A typical blog combines text, images, and links to other blogs, web pages, and other media related to its topic. The ability for readers to leave comments in an interactive format is an important part of many blogs. Most blogs are primarily textual, although some focus on art (artlog), photographs (photoblog), sketchblog, videos (vlog), music (MP3 blog), audio (podcasting) are part of a wider network of social media. Micro-blogging is another type of blogging which consists of blogs with very short posts.

RSS feeds

RSS is a format for syndicating news and the content of news-like sites, including major news sites like Wired, news-oriented community sites like Slashdot, and personal blogs. It is a family of Web feed formats used to publish frequently updated content such as blog entries, news headlines, and podcasts. An RSS document (which is called a "feed" or "web feed" or "channel") contains either a summary of content from an associated web site or the full text. RSS makes it possible for people to keep up with web sites in an automated manner that can be piped into special programs or filtered displays.

Podcast

A podcast is a series of digital-media files which are distributed over the Internet using syndication feeds for playback on portable media players and computers. The term podcast, like broadcast, can refer either to the series of content itself or to the method by which it is syndicated; the latter is also called podcasting. The host or author of a podcast is often called a podcaster.

Mobile

Mobile phones were introduced in Japan in 1979 but became a mass media only in 1998 when the first downloadable ringing tones were introduced in Finland. Soon most forms of media content were introduced on mobile phones, and today the total value of media consumed on mobile towers over that of internet content, and was worth over 31 billion dollars in 2007 (source Informa). The mobile media content includes over 8 billion dollars worth of mobile music (ringing tones, ringback tones, truetones, MP3 files, karaoke, music videos, music streaming services etc); over 5 billion dollars worth of mobile gaming; and various news, entertainment and advertising services. In Japan mobile phone books are so popular that five of the ten best-selling printed books were originally released as mobile phone books.

Similar to the internet, mobile is also an interactive media, but has far wider reach, with 3.3 billion mobile phone users at the end of 2007 to 1.3 billion internet users (source ITU). Like email on the internet, the top application on mobile is also a personal messaging service, but SMS text messaging is used by over 2.4 billion people. Practically all internet services and applications exist or have similar cousins on mobile, from search to multiplayer games to virtual worlds to blogs. Mobile has several unique benefits which many mobile media pundits claim make mobile a more powerful media than either TV or the internet, starting with mobile being permanently carried and always connected. Mobile has the best audience accuracy and is the only mass media with a built-in payment channel available to every user without any credit cards or paypal accounts or even an age limit. Mobile is often called the 7th Mass Medium and either the fourth screen (if counting cinema, TV and PC screens) or the third screen (counting only TV and PC).

Publishing

Publishing is the industry concerned with the production of literature or information − the activity of making information available for public view. In some cases, authors may be their own publishers.

Traditionally, the term refers to the distribution of printed works such as books and newspapers. With the advent of digital information systems and the → Internet, the scope of publishing has expanded to include → websites, blogs, and the like.

As a → business, publishing includes the development, → marketing, production, and distribution of newspapers, magazines, books, literary works, musical works, software, other works dealing with information.

Publication is also important as a legal concept; (1) as the process of giving formal notice to the world of a significant intention, for example, to marry or enter bankruptcy, and; (2) as the essential precondition of being able to claim defamation; that is, the alleged libel must have been published.

Book

A book is a collection of sheets of paper, parchment or other material with a piece of text written on them, bound together along one edge within covers. A book is also a literary work or a main division of such a work. A book produced in electronic format is known as an e-book.

Magazine

A magazine is a periodical publication containing a variety of articles, generally financed by → advertising and/or purchase by readers.

Brockhaus Konversations-Lexikon, 1902.

Magazines are typically published weekly, biweekly, monthly, bimonthly or quarterly, with a date on the cover that is in advance of the date it is actually published. They are often printed in color on coated paper, and are bound with a soft cover.

Magazines fall into two broad categories: consumer magazines and business magazines. In practice, magazines are a subset of periodicals, distinct from those periodicals produced by scientific, artistic, academic or special interest publishers which are subscription-only, more expensive, narrowly limited in circulation, and often have little or no advertising.

Magazines can be classified as:

- General interest magazines (e.g. Frontline, India Today, The Week,The Sunday Indian etc)
- Special interest magazines (women's, sports, business, scuba diving, etc)

Newspaper

A newspaper is a publication containing news and information and advertising, usually printed on low-cost paper called newsprint. It may be general or special interest, most often published daily or weekly. The first printed newspaper was published in 1605, and the form has thrived even in the face of competition from technologies such as radio and television. Recent developments on the Internet are posing major threats to its business model, however. Paid circulation is declining in most countries, and advertising revenue, which makes up the bulk of a newspaper's income, is shifting from print to online; some commentators, nevertheless, point out that historically new media such as radio and television did not entirely supplant existing.

Software publishing

A software publisher is a publishing company in the software industry between the developer and the distributor. In some companies, two or all three of these roles may be combined (and indeed, may reside in a single person, especially in the case of shareware).

Software publishers often license software from developers with specific limitations, such as a time limit or geographical region. The terms of licensing vary enormously, and are typically secret.

Developers may use publishers to reach larger or foreign markets, or to avoid focussing on marketing. Or publishers may use developers to create software to meet a market need that the publisher has identified.

Mass wire media

Mass wire media is a new frontier of news reporting in the high-tech age. A few decades ago news reporting was through newspapers and → radio and → television. The radio broadcasts that were made famous by Franklin D. Roosevelt during World War II changed the way radio was looked at. These fireside chats made the radio news and news radio. Things are different now as we are witnessing a revolution of people-oriented reporting in real time and other times. This element of intimate knowledge of the event or story being reported has dramatically changed the way we all view news stories.

This is called by some the Social Media Revolution. This revolution has intrinsically altered the way news is reported almost the way it happens. The trend of people-oriented reporting is only on the rise as reporting news becomes more personal and more accurate - although also more subjective.

Video games

A video game is a computer-controlled game where a video display such as a monitor or → television is the primary feedback device. The term "computer game" also includes games which display only text (and which can therefore theoretically be played on a teletypewriter) or which use other methods, such as sound or vibration, as their primary feedback device, but there are very few new games in these categories. There always must also be some sort of input device, usually in the form of button/joystick combinations (on arcade games), a keyboard & mouse/trackball combination (computer games), or a controller (console games), or a combination of any of the above. Also, more esoteric devices have been used for input. Usually there are rules and goals, but in more open-ended games the player may be free to do whatever they like within the confines of the virtual universe.

In common usage, a "computer game" or a "PC game" refers to a game that is played on a personal computer. "Console game" refers to one that is played on a device specifically designed for the use of such, while interfacing with a standard → television set. "Arcade game" refers to a game designed to be played in an establishment in which patrons pay to play on a per-use basis. "Video game" (or "videogame") has evolved into a catchall phrase that encompasses the aforementioned along with any game made for any other device, including, but not limited to, mobile phones, PDAs, advanced calculators, etc.

Personal media

Non-mass or "personal" media (point-to-point and person-to-person communication) include:

- Gestures
- Interactive
- → Internet
- Mail
- Speech
- Telephony

See also

- Concentration of media ownership
- Media bias
- Media echo chamber
- Media-system dependency
- Mediatization (media)
- Narcotizing Dysfunction
- *The Problem of the Media: U.S. Communication Politics in the 21st Century* (book)
- Propaganda
- Paparazzi
- Sign language media
- State media

Further reading

- Understanding Media: The Extensions of Man (1st Ed. McGraw Hill, NY; reissued MIT Press, 1994, with introduction by Lewis H. Lapham; reissued by Gingko Press, 2003 ISBN 1-58423-073-8)

External links

- C. Wright Mills, The Mass Society, Chapter in the Power Elite,1956 [6]
- The Media: Carriers of Contagious Information [7]

References

[1] (http://www.bl.uk/collections/britnews.html)
[2] "The Future of Media Doesn't Belong to Murdoch; It Belongs to Us" (http://freepress.net/node/41272). Free Press. 2008-06-06. . Retrieved 2010-01-15.
[3] "Recording Technology History" (http://history.sandiego.edu/gen/recording/notes.html). .
[4] "Chronomedia" (http://www.terramedia.co.uk/Chronomedia/years/1909.htm). .
[5] http://www.pewinternet.org
[6] http://www.thirdworldtraveler.com/Book_Excerpts/MassSociety_PE.html
[7] http://www.in-mind.org/issue-4/the-media-carriers-of-contagious-information.html

Marketing

→ Marketing
Key concepts
Product • Pricing • → Promotion Distribution • Service • Retail Brand management Account-based marketing Marketing ethics Marketing effectiveness Market research Market segmentation Marketing strategy Marketing management Market dominance
Promotional content
→ Advertising • Branding • Underwriting Direct marketing • Personal Sales Product placement • Publicity Sales promotion • Sex in advertising
Promotional media
Printing • Publication • Broadcasting Out-of-home • Internet marketing Point of sale • Promotional items Digital marketing • In-game In-store demonstration • Word of mouth

Marketing is the process associated with promotion for sale goods or services. It is considered a "social and managerial process by which individuals and groups obtain what they need and want through creating and exchanging products and values with others."[1] It is an integrated process through which companies create value for customers and build strong customer relationships in order to capture value from customers in return.[1]

Marketing is used to create the customer, to keep the customer and to satisfy the customer. With the customer as the focus of its activities, it can be concluded that *marketing management* is one of the major components of business management. The evolution of marketing was caused due to mature markets and overcapacities in the last decades. Companies then shifted the focus from production to the customer in order to stay profitable.

The term *marketing concept* holds that achieving organizational goals depends on knowing the needs and wants of target markets and delivering the desired satisfactions.[2] It proposes that in order to satisfy its organizational objectives, an organization should anticipate the needs and wants of consumers and satisfy these more effectively than competitors.[2]

Further definitions

Marketing is defined by the American Marketing Association [AMA] as *"the activity, set of institutions, and processes for creating, communicating, delivering, and exchanging offerings that have value for customers, clients, partners, and society at large."*[3] The term developed from the original meaning which referred literally to going to a market to buy or sell goods or services. Seen from a systems point of view, sales process engineering views marketing as *"a set of processes that are interconnected and interdependent with other functions,*[4] *whose methods can be improved using a variety of relatively new approaches."*

The Chartered Institute of Marketing defines marketing as *"the management process responsible for identifying, anticipating and satisfying customer requirements profitably."*[5] A different concept is the *value-based marketing* which states the role of marketing to contribute to increasing shareholder value.[6] In this context, marketing is defined as *"the management process that seeks to maximise returns to shareholders by developing relationships with valued customers and creating a competitive advantage."*[6]

Marketing practice tended to be seen as a creative industry in the past, which included → advertising, distribution and selling. However, because the academic study of marketing makes extensive use of social sciences, psychology, sociology, mathematics, economics, anthropology and neuroscience, the profession is now widely recognized as a science, allowing numerous universities to offer Master-of-Science (MSc) programmes. The overall process starts with marketing research and goes through market segmentation, business planning and execution, ending with pre and post-sales promotional activities. It is also related to many of the creative arts. The marketing literature is also adept at re-inventing itself and its vocabulary according to the times and the culture.

Marketing orientations

An orientation, in the marketing context, relates to a perception or attitude a firm holds towards its product or service, essentially concerning consumers and end-users.

Earlier approaches

The marketing orientation evolved from earlier orientations namely the production orientation, the product orientation and the selling orientation.[7]

Orientation	Profit driver	Western European timeframe	Description
Production[7]	Production methods	until the 1950s	A firm focusing on a production orientation specializes in producing as much as possible of a given product or service. Thus, this signifies a firm exploiting economies of scale, until the minimum efficient scale is reached. A production orientation may be deployed when a high demand for a product or service exists, coupled with a good certainty that consumer tastes do not rapidly alter (similar to the sales orientation).
→ Product[7]	Quality of the product	until the 1960s	A firm employing a product orientation is chiefly concerned with the quality of its own product. A firm would also assume that as long as its product was of a high standard, people would buy and consume the product.
Selling[7]	Selling methods	1950s and 1960s	A firm using a sales orientation focuses primarily on the selling/promotion of a particular product, and not determining new consumer desires as such. Consequently, this entails simply selling an already existing product, and using promotion techniques to attain the highest sales possible. Such an orientation may suit scenarios in which a firm holds dead stock, or otherwise sells a product that is in high demand, with little likelihood of changes in consumer tastes diminishing demand.
Marketing[7]	Needs and wants of customers	1970 to present day	The *marketing orientation* is perhaps the most common orientation used in contemporary marketing. It involves a firm essentially basing its marketing plans around the marketing concept, and thus supplying products to suit new consumer tastes. As an example, a firm would employ market research to gauge consumer desires, use R&D to develop a product attuned to the revealed information, and then utilize promotion techniques to ensure persons know the product exists.

Product Innovation

In a product innovation approach, the company pursues product innovation, then tries to develop a market for the product. Product innovation drives the process and marketing research is conducted primarily to ensure that profitable market segment(s) exist for the innovation. The rationale is that customers may not know what options will be available to them in the future so we should not expect them to tell us what they will buy in the future. However, marketers can aggressively over-pursue product innovation and try to overcapitalize on a niche. When pursuing a product innovation approach, marketers must ensure that they have a varied and multi-tiered approach to product innovation. It is claimed that if Thomas Edison depended on marketing research he would have produced larger candles rather than inventing light bulbs. Many firms, such as research and development focused companies, successfully focus on product innovation. Many purists doubt whether this is really a form of marketing orientation at all, because of the ex post status of consumer research. Some even question whether it is marketing.

Contemporary approaches

Recent approaches in marketing is the *relationship marketing* with focus on the customer, the *business marketing* or *industrial marketing* with focus on an organization or institution and the *social marketing* with focus on benefits to the society.[8] New forms of marketing also uses the → internet and are therefore called *internet marketing* or more generally *e-marketing*, *online marketing*, *desktop advertising* or *affiliate marketing*. It tries to perfect the segmentation strategy used in traditional marketing. It targets its audience more precisely, and is sometimes called personalized marketing or one-to-one marketing.

Orientation	Profit driver	Western European timeframe	Description
Relationship marketing / Relationship management[8]	Building and keeping good customer relations	1960s to present day	Emphasis is placed on the whole relationship between suppliers and customers. The aim is to give the best possible attention, customer services and therefore build customer loyalty.
Business marketing / Industrial marketing	Building and keeping relationships between organizations	1980s to present day	In this context marketing takes place between → businesses or organizations. The product focus lies on industrial goods or capital goods than consumer products or end products. A different form of marketing activities like promotion, advertising and communication to the customer is used.
Social marketing[8]	Benefit to society	1990s to present day	Similar characteristics as marketing orientation but with the added proviso that there will be a curtailment on any harmful activities to society, in either product, production, or selling methods.

Customer orientation

A firm in the market economy survives by producing goods that persons are willing and able to buy. Consequently, ascertaining consumer demand is vital for a firm's future viability and even existence as a going concern. Many companies today have a customer focus (or market orientation). This implies that the company focuses its activities and products on consumer demands. Generally there are three ways of doing this: the customer-driven approach, the sense of identifying market changes and the product innovation approach.

In the consumer-driven approach, consumer wants are the drivers of all strategic marketing decisions. No strategy is pursued until it passes the test of consumer research. Every aspect of a market offering, including the nature of the product itself, is driven by the needs of potential consumers. The starting point is always the consumer. The rationale for this approach is that there is no point spending R&D funds developing products that people will not buy. History attests to many products that were commercial failures in spite of being technological breakthroughs.[9]

A formal approach to this customer-focused marketing is known as *SIVA*[10] (Solution, Information, Value, Access). This system is basically the four Ps renamed and reworded to provide a customer focus. The SIVA Model provides a demand/customer centric version alternative to the well-known 4Ps supply side model (product, price, place, promotion) of marketing management.

Product	→	Solution
Promotion	→	Information
Price	→	Value
Placement	→	Access

Organizational orientation

In this sense, a firm's marketing department is often seen as of prime importance within the functional level of an organization. Information from an organization's marketing department would be used to guide the actions of other departments within the firm. As an example, a marketing department could ascertain (via marketing research) that consumers desired a new type of product, or a new usage for an existing product. With this in mind, the marketing department would inform the R&D department to create a prototype of a product/service based on consumers' new desires.

The production department would then start to manufacture the product, while the marketing department would focus on the promotion, distribution, pricing, etc. of the product. Additionally, a firm's finance department would be consulted, with respect to securing appropriate funding for the development, production and promotion of the product. Inter-departmental conflicts may occur, should a firm adhere to the marketing orientation. Production may oppose the installation, support and servicing of new capital stock, which may be needed to manufacture a new product. Finance may oppose the required capital expenditure, since it could undermine a healthy cash flow for the organization.

Mutually beneficial exchange

A further marketing orientation is the focus on a *mutually beneficial exchange*. In a transaction in the market economy, a firm gains revenue, which thus leads to more profits/market share/sales. A consumer on the other hand gains the satisfaction of a need/want, utility, reliability and value for money from the purchase of a product or service. As no one has to buy goods from any one supplier in the market economy, firms must entice consumers to buy goods with contemporary marketing ideals.

Herd behavior

Herd behavior in marketing is used to explain the dependencies of customers' mutual behavior. *The Economist* reported a recent conference in Rome on the subject of the simulation of adaptive human behavior.[11] It shared mechanisms to increase impulse buying and get people "to buy more by playing on the herd instinct." The basic idea is that people will buy more of products that are seen to be popular, and several feedback mechanisms to get product popularity information to consumers are mentioned, including smart card technology and the use of Radio Frequency Identification Tag technology. A "swarm-moves" model was introduced by a Florida Institute of Technology researcher, which is appealing to supermarkets because it can "increase sales without the need to give people discounts."

Other recent studies on the "power of social influence" include an "artificial music market in which some 14,000 people downloaded previously unknown songs" (Columbia University, New York); a Japanese chain of convenience stores which orders its products based on "sales data from department stores and research companies;" a Massachusetts company exploiting knowledge of social networking to improve sales; and online retailers who are increasingly informing consumers about "which products are popular with like-minded consumers" (e.g., Amazon, eBay).

Further orientations

- An emerging area of study and practice concerns *internal marketing*, or how employees are trained and managed to deliver the brand in a way that positively impacts the acquisition and retention of customers, see also *employer branding*.
- *Diffusion of innovations* research explores how and why people adopt new products, services and ideas.
- With consumers' eroding attention span and willingness to give time to advertising messages, marketers are turning to forms of *permission marketing* such as *branded content, custom media* and *reality marketing*.

Marketing research

Marketing research involves conducting research to support marketing activities, and the statistical interpretation of data into information. This information is then used by managers to plan marketing activities, gauge the nature of a firm's marketing environment and attain information from suppliers. Marketing researchers use statistical methods such as quantitative research, qualitative research, hypothesis tests, Chi-squared tests, linear regression, correlations, frequency distributions, poisson distributions, binomial distributions, etc. to interpret their findings and convert data into information. The marketing research process spans a number of stages including the definition of a problem, development of a research plan, collecting and interpretation of data and disseminating information formally in form of a report. The task of marketing research is to provide management with relevant, accurate, reliable, valid, and current information.

A distinction should be made between **marketing research** and **market research**. Market research pertains to research in a given market. As an example, a firm may conduct research in a target market, after selecting a suitable market segment. In contrast, marketing research relates to all research conducted within marketing. Thus, market research is a subset of marketing research.

Marketing environment

The term *marketing environment* relates to all of the factors (whether internal, external, direct or indirect) that affect a firm's marketing decision-making or planning and is subject of the marketing research. A firm's marketing environment consists of two main areas, which are:

Macro environment

On the macro environment a firm holds only little control. It consists of a variety of external factors that manifest on a large (or macro) scale. These are typically economic, social, political or technological phenomena. A common method of assessing a firm's macro-environment is via a PESTLE (Political, Economic, Social, Technological, Legal, Ecological) analysis. Within a PESTLE analysis, a firm would analyze national political issues, culture and climate, key macroeconomic conditions, health and indicators (such as economic growth, inflation, unemployment, etc.), social trends/attitudes, and the nature of technology's impact on its society and the business processes within the society.

Micro environment

A firm holds a greater amount (though not necessarily total) control of the micro environment. It comprises factors pertinent to the firm itself, or stakeholders closely connected with the firm or company. A firm's micro environment typically spans:

- Customers/consumers
- Employees
- Suppliers
- The Media

By contrast to the macro environment, an organization holds a greater degree of control over these factors.

Market segmentation

Market segmentation pertains to the division of a market of consumers into persons with similar needs and wants. As an example, if using Kellogg's cereals in this instance, Frosties are marketed to children. Crunchy Nut Cornflakes are marketed to adults. Both goods aforementioned denote two products which are marketed to two distinct groups of persons, both with like needs, traits, and wants.

The purpose for market segmentation is conducted for two main issues. First, a segmentation allows a better allocation of a firm's finite resources. A firm only possesses a certain amount of resources. Accordingly, it must make choices (and appreciate the related costs) in servicing specific groups of consumers. Furthermore the diversified tastes of the contemporary Western consumers can be served better. With more diversity in the tastes of modern consumers, firms are taking noting the benefit of servicing a multiplicity of new markets.

Market segmentation can be defined in terms of the *STP* acronym, meaning *Segment*, *Target* and *Position*.

Segment

Segmentation involves the initial splitting up of consumers into persons of like needs/wants/tastes. Four commonly used criteria are used for segmentation, which include:

- **Geographical** (e.g. country, region, city, town, etc.)
- **Psychographic** (i.e. personality traits or character traits which influence consumer behaviour)
- **Demographic** (e.g. age, gender, socio-economic class, etc.)
- **Behavioural** (e.g. brand loyalty, usage rate, etc.)

Target

Once a segment has been identified, a firm must ascertain whether the segment is beneficial for them to service. The *DAMP* acronym, meaning *Discernible*, *Accessible*, *Measurable* and *Profitable*, are used as criteria to gauge the viability of a target market. DAMP is explained in further detail below:

- **Discernable** - How a segment can be differentiated from other segments.
- **Accessible** - How a segment can be accessed via Marketing Communications produced by a firm.
- **Measurable** - Can the segment be quantified and its size determined?
- **Profitable** - Can a sufficient return on investment be attained from a segment's servicing?

The next step in the targeting process is the level of differentiation involved in a segment serving. Three modes of differentiation exist, which are commonly applied by firms. These are:

- **Undifferentiated** - Where a company produces a like product for all of a market segment.
- **Differentiated** - In which a firm produced slight modifications of a product within a segment.
- **Niche** - In which an organisation forges a product to satisfy a specialised target market.

Position

Positioning concerns how to position a product in the minds of consumers. A firm often performs this by producing a perceptual map, which denotes products produced in its industry according to how consumers perceive their price and quality. From a product's placing on the map, a firm would tailor its marketing communications to suit meld with the product's perception among consumers.

Marketing information system

A *marketing information system (MKIS)* is an information system that is commonly used by marketing management to analyse and view information pertaining to marketing activities. As the label suggests, an MKIS is a computer-based information system therefore used to input, store, process and output marketing information.[12] An MKIS spans four subset components, which are detailed below:

Marketing intelligence system

This sub-system stores information gathered from a firm's marketing intelligence activities. Marketing intelligence consists of actions a firm would undertake within its own market or industry, geared towards information existing within its markets. This can be obtained via communication with suppliers, consumers or other bodies within a market.

Internal processes system

The internal processes system catalogues all internal marketing processes within a firm.

Marketing research system

This section of the overall system contains data from a firm's marketing research activities.

Analytical system

The analytical system is the only sub-system which does not store data or information. It's function is to analyse and process data from the other three systems, into reliable, timely and relevant information for the perusal and use of marketing management.

Types of marketing research

Marketing research, as a sub-set aspect of marketing activities, can be divided into the following parts:

- Primary research (also known as field research), which involves the conduction and compilation of research for the purpose it was intended.
- Secondary research (also referred to as desk research), is initially conducted for one purpose, but often used to support another purpose or end goal.

By these definitions, an example of primary research would be market research conducted into health foods, which is used *solely* to ascertain the needs/wants of the target market for health foods. Secondary research, again according to the above definition, would be research pertaining to health foods, but used by a firm wishing to develop an unrelated product.

Primary research is often expensive to prepare, collect and interpret from data to information. Nonetheless, while secondary research is relatively inexpensive, it often can become outdated and outmoded, given it is used for a purpose other than for which is was intended. Primary research can also be broken down into quantitative research and qualitative research, which as the labels suggest, pertain to numerical and non-numerical research methods, techniques. The appropriateness of each mode of research depends on whether data can be quantified (quantitative research), or whether subjective, non-numeric or abstract concepts are required to be studied (qualitative research).

There also exists additional modes of marketing research, which are:

- Exploratory research, pertaining to research that investigates an assumption.
- Descriptive research, which as the label suggests, describes "what is".
- Predictive research, meaning research conducted to predict a future occurrence.
- Conclusive research, for the purpose of deriving a conclusion via a research process.

Marketing planning

The area of *marketing planning* involves forging a plan for a firm's marketing activities. A marketing plan can also pertain to a specific product, as well as to an organisation's overall marketing strategy. Generally speaking, an organisation's marketing planning process is derived from its overall business strategy. Thus, when top management are devising the firm's strategic direction or mission, the intended marketing activities are incorporated into this plan. Within the overall strategic marketing plan, the marketing planning process contains the following stages:

- Mission statement
- Corporate objectives - These are the broad-based objectives resulting from the firm's mission statement.
- Marketing audit - a marketing audit is an audit of all marketing processes within a firm. It's purpose is to highlight which areas require improvement, and which ones require modification, prior to the establishment of the marketing plan.
- SWOT analysis
- Assumptions arising from the marketing audit and SWOT analysis
- Marketing objectives derived from the assumptions
- An estimation of the expected results of the objectives
- Identification of alternative plans or mixes
- Budgeting for the marketing plan
- A first-year implementation program

There are several levels of marketing objectives within an organization. As stated previously, the senior management of a firm would formulate a general business strategy for a firm. However, this general business strategy would be interpreted and implemented in different contexts throughout the firm.

Corporate

Corporate marketing objectives are typically broad-based in nature, and pertain to the general vision of the firm in the short, medium or long-term. As an example, if one pictures a group of companies (or a conglomerate), top management may state that sales for the group should increase by 25% over a ten year period.

Strategic business unit

An SBU is an autonomous entity within a firm, which produces a unique product/service. It could be a single product, a product line, or a subsidiary of a larger group of companies. The SBU would embrace the corporate strategy, and attune it to its own particular industry. For instance, an SBU may partake in the sports goods industry. It thus would ascertain how it would attain additional sales of sports goods, in order to satisfy the overall business strategy.

Functional

The functional level relates to departments within the SBUs, such as marketing, finance, HR, production, etc. The functional level would adopt the SBU's strategy and determine how to accomplish the SBU's own objectives in its market. To use the example of the sports goods industry again, the marketing department would draw up marketing plans, strategies and communications to help the SBU achieve its marketing aims.

New Product Development (NPD)

NPD relates to, as the label denotes, the development of a new to market product. The stages of the process are so:

- Idea Generation
- Idea Screening
- Business Analysis
- Product Development
- Product Testing
- Test Marketing
- Commercialisation

Given the resources placed in the development of a product, a firm must gauge the economic viability of a good, coupled with the viability of the notion of the good, prior to releasing it onto the market.new

Product Life Cycle

The **Product Life Cycle** or *PLC* is a tool used by marketing managers to gauge the progress of a product, especially relating to sales or revenue accrued over time. The PLC is based on a few key assumptions, including that a given product would possess an *introduction, growth, maturity* and *decline* stage. Furthermore it is assumed that no product lasts perpetually on the market. Last but not least a firm must employ differing strategies, according to where a product is on the PLC.

Introduction

In this stage, a product is launched onto the market. To stimulate growth of sales/revenue, use of advertising may be high, in order to heighten awareness of the product in question.

Growth

The product's sales/revenue is increasing, which may stimulate more marketing communications to sustain sales. More entrants enter into the market, to reap the apparent high profits that the industry is producing.

Maturity

A product's sales start to level off, and an increasing number of entrants to a market produce price falls for the product. Firms may utilise sales promotions to raise sales.

Decline

Demand for a good begins to taper off, and the firm may opt to discontinue manufacture of the product. This is so, if revenue for the product comes from efficiency savings in production, over actual sales of a good/service. However, if a product services a niche market, or is complementary to another product, it may continue manufacture of the product, despite a low level of sales/revenue being accrued.

Marketing strategy

The field of marketing strategy encompasses the strategy involved in the management of a given product.

A given firm may hold numerous products in the marketplace, spanning numerous and sometimes wholly unrelated industries. Accordingly, a plan is required in order to manage effectively such products. Such decisions consist of the following decisions:

- Should we (,i.e. the firm) enter a market/industry?
- Should we increase funding for our product(s)?
- Should we maintain funding for our product(s)?
- Should we divest or cease production of our product(s)?

Evidently, a company needs to weigh up and ascertain how to utilise effectively its finite resources. As an example, a start-up car manufacturing firm would face little success, should it attempt to rival immediately Toyota, Ford, Nissan or any other large global car maker. Moreover, a product may be reaching the end of its life-cycle. Thus, the issue of divest, or a ceasing of production may be made. With regard to the aforesaid questions, each scenario requires a unique marketing strategy to be employed. Below are listed some prominent marketing strategy models, which seek to propose means to answer the preceding questions.

Ansoff Matrix

The Ansoff Matrix was devised by Igor Ansoff, a Russian-born American pioneer of strategic planning

Ansoff proposed his Matrix, as a means of identifying how a firm should market its product in differing scenarios. The labels are listed below:

- X-axis
- Existing markets
- Existing products
- Y-axis
- New markets
- New products

Four quadrants can then be determined, which are:

- Market penetration
- Diversification
- Market development
- Product Development

Each aforesaid category provides a unique marketing scenario, in which Ansoff denoted a given strategy.

Marketing mix

In the early 1960s, Professor Neil Borden at Harvard Business School identified a number of company performance actions that can influence the consumer decision to purchase goods or services. Borden suggested that all those actions of the company represented a "Marketing Mix". Professor E. Jerome McCarthy, at the Michigan State University in the early 1960s, suggested that the Marketing Mix contained 4 elements product, price, place and promotion.

→ **Product**

> The product aspects of marketing deal with the specifications of the actual goods or services, and how it relates to the end-user's needs and wants. The scope of a product generally includes supporting elements such as warranties, guarantees, and support.

Pricing

> This refers to the process of setting a price for a product, including discounts. The price need not be monetary; it can simply be what is exchanged for the product or services, e.g. time, energy, or attention. Methods of setting prices optimally are in the domain of pricing science. A number of modes of pricing techniques exist, which span:

- Elasticities (whether Price Elasticity of Demand, Cross Elasticity of Demand, or Income Elasticity of Demand)
- Market skimming pricing
- Market penetration pricing

Elasticities are a microeconomic concept, which gauges how elastic demand is for a given good/service. In a marketing context, its usefulness relates to the suitable level at which a product can be priced, in accordance with price, a product's complements and substitutes, and the level of income a consumer possesses.

Market skimming pertains to firm releasing a good in a "first to market" scenario. As an example, picture a company which releases a new type of personal media playing system. It may set the good at an initially high level, but reduce it over time, once the level of demand gradually rises. Market skimming is best operable within a first to market scenario, since there would be few competitors within the company's industry. This pricing strategy is also best implemented within a market of high entry barriers (such as a monopoly or an oligopoly). This is so since the high barriers to entry discourage competitors into the industry for the product.

Market penetration concerns pricing policies for late entrants to a market. As another example, a company could release a product into a market years after it is initially introduced, but at an artificially low price in order to stimulate demand. The result of such a pricing strategy would be to draw consumers from competitors and into purchasing its own product. Market penetration, in contrast to market skimming, best functions within a market form with low barriers to entry (such as perfect competition or monopolistic competition). Low barriers to entry facilitates a company's ability to sell goods at a price lower than its market clearing point.

Placement (or distribution)

> This refers to how the product gets to the customer; for example, point-of-sale placement or retailing. This third P has also sometimes been called *Place*, referring to the channel by which a product or service is sold (e.g. online vs. retail), which geographic region or industry, to which segment (young adults, families, business people), etc. also referring to how the environment in which the product is sold in can affect sales.

→ Promotion

> This includes → advertising, sales promotion, including promotional education, publicity, and personal selling. Branding refers to the various methods of promoting the product, brand, or company.

These four elements are often referred to as the marketing mix,[13] which a marketer can use to craft a marketing plan. The four Ps model is most useful when marketing low value consumer products. Industrial products, services, high value consumer products require adjustments to this model. Services marketing must account for the unique nature of services.

Industrial or B2B marketing must account for the long term contractual agreements that are typical in supply chain transactions. Relationship marketing attempts to do this by looking at marketing from a long term relationship perspective rather than individual transactions. As a counter to this, Morgan, in *Riding the Waves of Change* (Jossey-Bass, 1988), suggests that one of the greatest limitations of the 4 Ps approach "is that it unconsciously emphasizes the inside–out view (looking from the company outwards), whereas the essence of marketing should be the outside–in approach".

In order to recognize the different aspects of selling **services**, as opposed to **Products**, a further three Ps were added to make a range of *Seven Ps* for service industries:

- **Process** - the way in which orders are handled, customers are satisfied and the service is delivered.
- **Physical Evidence** - is tangible evidence of the service customers will receive (for example a holiday brochure).
- **People** - the people meeting and dealing with the customers.

As markets have become more satisfied, the 7 Ps have become relevant to those companies selling products, as well as those solely involved with services: customers now differentiate between sellers of goods by the service they receive in the process from the people involved. Some authors cite a further P - **Packaging** - this is thought by many to be part of **Product**, but in certain markets (Japan, China for example) and with certain products (perfume, cosmetics) the packaging of a product has a greater importance - maybe even than the product itself.

Marketing communications

Marketing communications is defined by actions a firm takes to communicate with end-users, consumers and external parties. A simple definition of marketing communication is *"the means by which a supplier of goods, services, values and/or ideas represent themselves to their target audience with the goal of stimulating dialog leading to better commercial or other relationships"*.[14] Marcoms is a frequently used short-form for marketing communications.[14] Marketing communications can be seen as a part of the promotional mix, as the exact nature of how to apply marketing communications depends on the nature of the product in question. Accordingly, a given product would require a unique communications mix, in order to convey successfully information to consumers. Some products may require a stronger emphasis on personal sales, while others may need more focus on advertising.

The process in which the differing modes of marketing communications are complemented and synthesised is called *integrated marketing communications (IMC)*. It is used in order to create a single and coherent marketing communications process. As an example, a firm can advertise the existence of a sales promotion, via a newspaper, magazine, TV, radio, etc. The same promotion can also be communicated via direct marketing, or personal selling. The aim of IMC is to lessen confusion among a product's target market, and to lessen cost for the firm. Several different subsets of marketing communications can be distinguished.

Personal selling

Oral presentation given by a salesperson who approaches individuals or a group of potential customers. Personal selling is often used in business to business (,i.e. "B2B") settings, in addition to business to consumer (,i.e. "B2C") scenarios in which a personal and face to face medium is required for the communication of the product. In B2B situations, personal selling is preferred if the product is technical in nature. Personal selling can compose of the use of presentations, in order to convey the benefits of a firm's good/service. In B2C settings, personal selling is utilised if the product requires to be tailored to the unique needs of an individual. Examples of this include car (and other vehicle) sales, financial services (such as insurance or investment), etc. Personal selling involves the following points:

- Live, interactive relationship
- Personal interest
- Attention and response
- Interesting presentation
- Clear and thorough.

Sales promotion

Short-term incentives to encourage buying of products.

- Instant appeal
- Anxiety to sell

An example is coupons or a sale. People are given an incentive to buy, but this does not build customer loyalty or encourage future repeat buys. A major drawback of sales promotion is that it is easily copied by competition. It cannot be used as a sustainable source of differentiation. Sales promotions are typically used to heighten sales/revenue, especially if a firm holds dead/excess stock, or if the market for a product has matured.

Public relations

Public Relations (or PR, as an acronym) is the use of media tools by a firm in order to promote goodwill from an organization to a target market segment, or other consumers of a firm's good/service. PR stems from the fact that a firm cannot seek to antagonize or inflame its market base, due to incurring a lessened demand for its good/service. Organizations undertake PR in order to assure consumers, and to forestall negative perceptions towards it. PR can span:

- Interviews
- Speeches/Presentations

- Corporate literature, such as financial statements, brochures, etc.

Publicity

Publicity involves attaining space in media, without having to pay directly for such coverage. As an example, an organization may have the launch of a new product covered by a newspaper or TV news segment. This benefits the firm in question since it is making consumers aware of its product, without necessarily paying a newspaper or television station to cover the event.

→ Advertising

Advertising occurs when a firm directly pays a media channel to publicize its product. Common examples of this include TV and radio adverts, billboards, branding, sponsorship, etc.

Direct marketing

Direct marketing is a process where a firm uses communication channels to attain and retain consumers for its product. It is a comparatively new mode of marketing communications (when compared with forms such as advertising, sales promotions, personal selling, etc.) Direct marketing involves carefully seeking out persons within a target market, and communicating to them about the nature of a product. This process is signified by brochures sent via the mail, e-mails from companies, etc. It can also constitute the use of telemarketing, in order to communicate with a target market.

Marketing specializations

International marketing

With the rapidly emerging force of globalization, the distinction between marketing within a firm's home country and marketing within external markets is disappearing very quickly. With this occurrence in mind, firms need to reorient their marketing strategies to meet the challenges of the global marketplace, in addition to sustaining their competitiveness within home markets. [15]

International marketing can be defined as the application of marketing strategies, planning and activities to external or foreign markets. International marketing is of consequence to firms which operate in countries and territories other than their home country, or the country in which they are registered in and have their head office. The factors influencing international marketing are culture, political and legal factors, a country's level of economic development, and the mode of involvement in foreign markets. The reasons why a firm would engage in international markets are numerous, including the maturity within domestic markets or increasing general market share, sales or revenue.

Culture

Social norms, attitudes towards buying foreign goods, and the working practices of foreign markets are all cultural factors when opting to invest in foreign markets. Social norms affect business practices, since social norms are one factor in the demand for a product. In the tobacco industry, for example, adolescents in developing countries are often the focus for the marketing and advertisement campaigns due to their vulnerability. Tobacco companies will often use symbols and fabrications in western society associated with smoking as a means of attracting these prospective consumers.[16] A company marketing pork would experience less sales in an Islamic country, than it would in China (which is the world's largest consumer of pork). In Western societies, sexuality and sexual topics are often used in marketing communications (such as advertising, for instance). However, in a comparatively more conservative society (such as India for instance) social attitudes may shun the use of sexual topics to advertise products.

Political and legal factors

The following political/legal factors are of bearing in international marketing:

- Government attitude to business
- The level of governmental regulations, red-tape and bureaucracy
- Monetary regulations
- Political stability

Not all governments are as open to foreign investment as others, nor are all governments equally favourable to business. Typically, a firm may opt to invest in an economy in which the government is more inclined to support business activity in a country. In other words, the "business-friendliness" of a foreign government is paramount in this instance.

Additionally, some economies are more "liberal" and less regulated, by comparison to other economies. Excessive regulations can be a hindrance on a firm, since they contribute to additional costs to a firm. Conversely, regulations can aid in assisting firms, by easing the path of doing business. A firm seeking to invest in foreign markets must gauge the regulatory arrangement of the economy it is looking to invest in. Monetary regulations, akin to the above points, can hinder the ability to do business. A high level of monetary regulations can hamper foreign investment within an economy.

Lastly, the political stability of a country is also a key factor in foreign investment decisions. Nation-states experiencing continual coup-d'etat can appear unattractive to invest in, since the continual changes in political system can compound the inherent risk in investing. Typically, a firm would opt to invest in a country which had a stable mode of government, and in which handovers of power were peaceful and non-violent. Even if a country is not a liberal democracy, a firm may often opt to invest in such an economy, if the country in question demonstrated a stable political system. The key factor in noting a nation-state's political stability is to avert excessive costs from dimished production, coupled with the loss of current and non-current assets.

Level of economic development

The level of economic development of an economy can affect foreign investment decisions. Within the field of developmental economics, differing modes of economic development can be identified. These are:

- Developing economy
- Newly-Industrialised country
- Industrialised country (also known as a developed country, advanced economy or first world economy)

A developing economy has a comparatively low general living standard (as defined by material lifestyle/level of material possession). Moreover, a developing economy may also be at subsistence level, or possess a large share of its Gross Domestic Product in primary industries. Accordingly, a developing country would not be a profitable market for high-end consumer goods, or fast-moving consumer goods commonly found in developed/advanced economies. Exports of machinery (related to the extraction and processing of raw materials) may be viable for a developing economy, due to primary industries possessing a large share of national income.

A newly-industrialised economy is an economy which has experienced high recent economic growth, and thus has experienced a rise in general living standards. Coupled with the rapid economic growth, the emergence of a middle class leads to the development of a consumerist culture in the society. A newly-industrialised economy would consequently possess a small general demand for high-end consumer goods, but not to the extent of an advanced economy. A newly-industralised economy may export manufactured goods to other countries, and often possess secondary sector industries as a high percentage of its economic output.

An industrialised economy is typically identified via a high Gross Domestic Product per capita, a high United Nations Human Development Index rating and a high level of tertiary/quaternary/quinary sector industries in the context of its national income. Thus, the high general living standard denotes the highest generalised demand for goods and services within all modes of economic development. Commonly, developed/advanced economies are high exporters of high-tech manufactured goods, as well as service sector products (such as financial services, for instance).

Globalisation

The greater economic ties/links between economies has presented a prime opportunity for firms trading internationally. The advantages to an international marketing firm are that regulations and costs are lower, which can promote the use of outsourcing to foreign economies. The disadvantages to a firm in a globalised economy include negative public relations resulting from the exploitation of low cost labour, concerns surrounding environmental degradation, etc.

Regional trading blocks

Within the past few decades, numerous regional trading blocks have emerged, as a means of encouraging and easing closer economic ties between neighbouring countries. Common examples of such blocks include the European Union, the North American Free Trade Agreement (NAFTA) and the Association of South East Asian Nations (ASEAN). Other examples are:

- CARICOM (the Caribbean Community)
- EFTA (European Free Trade Association)
- ECOWAS (Economic Community of West African States)

Regional economic blocks often permit free (and thus less inhibited/restricted) trade between member nation-states. As such, a British firm would find trading in Germany less problematic (and vice versa, as both the United Kingdom and Germany are both EU member states), by comparison with a British firm trading with Mexico or Thailand.

Such trading blocks can also, conversely, place restrictions/regulations on trade. To use the earlier example of the EU again, the EU may place regulations on the packaging, labelling and distribution of a product. Consequently, a UK firm trading in Germany would have to adhere to the European Union regulations, in order to trade legitimately within the European Union.

Green marketing

Green marketing can be defined as the marketing of products which are environmentally sound. The notion of green marketing is a comparatively new one within general marketing thought, as it has chiefly grown in acceptance since the 1990s. Nonetheless, as a contemporary branch of marketing thought, it can be seen as one of the fastest growing areas of marketing principles.

The rationale for the devising and emergence of green marketing is thus:

- A higher quantity of persons willing and able to buy green products.
- Heightened awareness among consumers, concerning the potentially negative aspects of global climate change.

Green marketers thus target persons who are more environmentally conscious. The segmentation and market research processes of numerous firms denote that the target market for green products has grown widely in numerous years. Accordingly, green marketers are willing to supply what persons are willing and able to buy.

It can also be stated that green products are often more expensive than "non-green" products, due perhaps to higher production costs. Nevertheless, green consumers are typically willing to pay higher prices, as a means of doing their part to safeguard the environment of the planet Earth.

Some drawbacks of green marketing are thus:

- The perception of "green washing"
- Disputes and contention surrounding the exact meaning of a green product

Green washing pertains to when a firm misleadingly produces a product, with ostensible green characteristics, which is not actually environmentally sound. In addition to evident ethical issues concerning deceit, such conduct can undermine an organisation's drive to be deemed a "green" company. Accordingly, a firm must be sincere in its efforts to be environmentally sound, regarding its environmental practices and policies.

Moreover, the extent and nature of a green product can be a moot point. To some, a product must be wholly green to be viewed as green. To others, a product may only possess a reduction in environmentally harmful inputs to be worthy of being labelled green. Nonetheless, a firm can enhance its green marketing efforts if it persuades consumers that the purchase of green products can enhance environmental protection.

Buying behaviour

A marketing firm, in the course of its operations, must ascertain the nature of buying behaviour, if it is to market properly its product. In order to entice and persuade a consumer to buy a product, the psychological/behavioural process of how a given product is purchased.

Buying behaviour consists of two prime strands, namely being consumer (B2C) behaviour and organisational/industrial behavior(B2B).

B2C buying behaviour

This mode of behaviour concerns consumers, in the purchase of a given product. The B2C buying process is as thus:

- Need/want recognition
- Information search
- Search for alternatives (to satisfy need/want)
- Purchase decision
- Post-purchase evaluation

As an example, if one pictures a pair of sneakers, the desire for a pair of sneakers would be followed by an information search on available types/brands. This may include perusing media outlets, but most commonly consists of information gathered from family and friends.

If the information search is insufficient, the consumer may search for alternative means to satisfy the need/want. In this case, this may be buying leather shoes, sandals, etc. The purchase decision is then made, in which the consumer actually buys the product.

Following this stage, a post-purchase evaluation is often conducted, comprising an appraisal of the value/utility brought by the purchase of the sneakers. If the value/utility is high, then a repeat purchase may be bought. This could then develop into consumer loyalty, for the firm producing the pair of sneakers.

B2B buying behaviour

B2B buying behaviour relates to organisational/industrial buying behaviour[17] . B2C and B2B behaviour are not exact, as similarities and differences exist. Some of the key differences are listed below:

- **Consumer behaviour**
- Low in monetary value
- Low in volume/mass
- Swift purchase
- Transaction marketing-based
- Single buying instances
- Number of consumer is higher
- Individual/market-based demand

- **Organisational behaviour**

- High in monetary value
- High in volume/mass
- Lengthy purchase process
- Relationship marketing-based
- Multiple buying instances
- Number of consumers is lesser
- Demand is consumer derived (in that firms purchase goods to ultimately meet consumer demand)

The organisational buying process is thus:

- Problem recognition
- Need description
- Product specification
- Supplier search
- Proposal solicitation
- Supplier selection
- Order routine specification
- Supplier performance review

In a straight rebuy, the fourth, fifth and sixth stages are omitted. In a modified rebuy scenario, the fifth and sixth stages are precluded. In a new buy, all aforementioned stages are conducted.

The Decision Making Unit (DMU)

The DMU, in other terms, can be labelled as the Purchasing or Procurement departments of an organisation[18] Accordingly, it is responsible for the purchasing of organisational items and assets. The persons comprising a DMU are as thus:

- Gatekeepers
- Users
- Buyers
- Decision Makers
- Influencers
- Initiators

Use of technologies

Marketing management can also note the importance of technology, within the scope of its marketing efforts. Computer-based information systems can be employed, aiding in a better processing and storage of data. Marketing researchers can use such systems to devise better methods of converting data into information, and for the creation of enhanced data gathering methods. Information technology can aid in improving an MKIS' software and hardware components, to improve a company's marketing decision-making process.

In recent years, the netbook personal computer has gained significant market share among laptops, largely due to its more user-friendly size and portability. Information technology typically progress at a fast rate, leading to marketing managers being cognizant of the latest technological developments. Moreover, the launch of smartphones into the cellphone market is commonly derived from a demand among consumers for more technologically advanced products. A firm can lose out to competitors, should it refrain from noting the latest technological occurrences in its industry.

Technological advancements can facilitate lesser barriers between countries and regions. Via using the World Wide Web, firms can quickly dispatch information from one country to another, without much restriction. Prior to the mass usage of the Internet, such transfers of information would have taken longer to send, especially if via snail mail, telex, etc.

Areas of marketing specialization

- Agricultural marketing
- Article marketing
- Cause marketing
- Communal marketing
- Business marketing
- Database marketing
- Digital marketing
- Direct marketing
- Engagement marketing
- Ethical marketing
- Evangelism marketing
- Experiential marketing
- Global marketing
- Green marketing
- Guerrilla marketing
- Integrated marketing
- International marketing
- Internet marketing
- Industrial marketing
- Macromarketing
- Mobile marketing
- Multichannel marketing
- Permission marketing
- Political marketing
- Product marketing
- Proximity marketing
- Public marketing
- Reality marketing
- Referral marketing
- Relationship marketing
- Reverse marketing
- Search engine marketing
- Shopper marketing
- Social media marketing
- Technical marketing
- Trade marketing
- Value-based marketing
- Wholesale marketing

See also

- → Advertising
- Advertising research
- AIDA
- Borderless selling
- Brand orientation
- Branded content
- Branding
- Business communication
- → Copywriting
- Customer relationship management (CRM)
- Demand generation
- Early adopter
- Event management
- Fear, uncertainty and doubt
- Market research
- Market segment
- Marketeer
- Marketing collateral
- Marketing co-operation
- → Marketing communications
- Marketing effectiveness
- Marketing mix
- Marketing plan
- Marketing strategy
- Merchandising
- Predictive analytics
- Professional selling
- Retailing
- Return on marketing investment
- Segmentation
- Selling technique
- Search engine optimization copywriting
- Sex in advertising
- Senior media creative
- Sponsorship
- Sponsor (commercial)
- Strategic management
- Tertiary sector of the economy
- Visual brand language

Related lists and outlines

See outline of marketing for an extensive list of the marketing articles.

- Accounting
- Business ethics, political economy, and philosophy of business
- Business law
- Business theorists
- Economics
- Finance
- Human resource management
- Information technology management
- International trade
- Management
- Production

Marketing acronyms

Acronym	Meaning
AIDA(S)	*Attention, Interest, Desire, Action (Satisfaction)*
B2B	*Business-to-Business*
B2C	*Business-to-Consumer*
B2G	*Business-to-Government*
CLV	*Customer Lifetime Value*
CRM	*Cause-Related Marketing*
CRM	*Customer Relationship Management*
DAMP	*Discernible, Accessible, Measurable, Profitable*
DMU	*Decision Making Unit*
IMC	*Integrated Marketing Communications*
IMC	*Internet Marketing Conference*
LCV	*Lifetime Customer Value*
LTV	*Lifetime Value*
MKIS	*Marketing Information System*
PLC	*Product Life Cycle*
PLCM	*Product Lifecycle Management*
SIVA	*Solution, Information, Value, Access*
STP	*Segment, Target, Position*

References

[1] Kotler, Philip; Gary Armstrong, Veronica Wong, John Saunders (2008). "Marketing defined" (http://books.google.com/books?id=6T2R0_ESU5AC&lpg=PP1&pg=PA7#v=onepage&q=&f=true). *Principles of marketing* (5th ed.). p. 7. . Retrieved 2009-10-23.

[2] Kotler, Philip; Gary Armstrong, Veronica Wong, John Saunders (2008). "Marketing defined" (http://books.google.com/books?id=6T2R0_ESU5AC&lpg=PP1&pg=PA7#v=onepage&q=&f=true). *Principles of marketing* (5th ed.). p. 17. . Retrieved 2009-10-23.

[3] "Definition of Marketing" (http://www.marketingpower.com/AboutAMA/Pages/DefinitionofMarketing.aspx). American Marketing Association. . Retrieved 2009-10-30.

[4] Paul H. Selden (1997). *Sales Process Engineering: A Personal Workshop*. Milwaukee, WI: ASQ Quality Press. p. 23.

[5] "Definition of marketing" (http://www.cim.co.uk/resources/understandingmarket/definitionmkting.aspx). Chartered Institute of Marketing. . Retrieved 2009-10-30.

[6] Paliwoda, Stanley J.; John K. Ryans (2008). "Back to first principles" (http://books.google.com/books?id=dwZz2eHBCjUC&lpg=PP1&pg=PA25#v=onepage&q=&f=false). *International Marketing: Modern and Classic Papers* (1st ed.). p. 25. . Retrieved 2009-10-15.

[7] Adcock, Dennis; Al Halborg, Caroline Ross (2001). "Introduction" (http://books.google.com/books?id=hQ8XfLd1cGwC&lpg=PP1&pg=PA15#v=onepage&q=&f=true). *Marketing: principles and practice* (4th ed.). p. 15. . Retrieved 2009-10-23.

[8] Adcock, Dennis; Al Halborg, Caroline Ross (2001). "Introduction" (http://books.google.com/books?id=hQ8XfLd1cGwC&lpg=PP1&pg=PA16#v=onepage&q=&f=true). *Marketing: principles and practice* (4th ed.). p. 16. . Retrieved 2009-10-23.

[9] "Marketing Management: Strategies and Programs", Guiltinan et al., McGraw Hill/Irwin, 1996

[10] Dev, Chekitan S.; Don E. Schultz (January/February 2005). "In the Mix: A Customer-Focused Approach Can Bring the Current Marketing Mix into the 21st Century". *Marketing Management* 14 (1).

[11] "Swarming the shelves: How shops can exploit people's herd mentality to increase sales?". The Economist. 2006-11-11. p. 90.

[12] Robert R. Harmon. "Marketing Information Systems" (http://www.cpd.ogi.edu/MST/CapstoneSPR2005/MKIS.pdf). Portland State University. . Retrieved 2009-10-25.

[13] "The Concept of the Marketing Mix". *Journal of Advertising Research*: 2-7. June 1964.

[14] Egan, John (2007). "Introduction" (http://books.google.com/books?id=jEIy-XfNHpMC&lpg=PP1&pg=PA1#v=onepage&q=&f=true). *Marketing communications*. p. 1. . Retrieved 2009-10-24.

[15] Joshi, Rakesh Mohan, (2005) International Marketing, Oxford University Press, New Delhi and New York ISBN 0195671236

[16] Nichter M, Cartwright EL (September 1991). "Saving the Children for the Tobacco Industry". *Medical Anthropology Quarterly* 5 (3): 236-256.

[17] http://www-rohan.sdsu.edu/~renglish/370/notes/chapt06/index.htm

[18] http://www.internet-marketing-consultancy.com/decision_making_unit.html

Promotion (marketing)

→ **Marketing**
Key concepts
Product • Pricing • → Promotion Distribution • Service • Retail Brand management Account-based marketing Marketing ethics Marketing effectiveness Market research Market segmentation Marketing strategy Marketing management Market dominance
Promotional content
→ Advertising • Branding • Underwriting Direct marketing • Personal Sales Product placement • Publicity Sales promotion • Sex in advertising
Promotional media
Printing • Publication • Broadcasting Out-of-home • Internet marketing Point of sale • Promotional items Digital marketing • In-game In-store demonstration • Word of mouth

Promotion involves disseminating information about a → product, product line, brand, or company. It is one of the four key aspects of the marketing mix. (The other three elements are product marketing, pricing, place.)

Promotion is generally sub-divided into two parts:

- Above the line promotion: Promotion in the → media (e.g. TV, → radio, newspapers, → Internet, Mobile Phones, and, historically, illustrated songs) in which the advertiser pays an advertising agency to place the ad
- Below the line promotion: All other promotion. Much of this is intended to be subtle enough for the consumer to be unaware that promotion is taking place. E.g. sponsorship, product placement, endorsements, sales promotion, merchandising, direct mail, personal selling, public relations, trade shows

The specification of these four variables creates a promotional mix or promotional plan. A promotional mix specifies how much attention to pay to each of the four subcategories, and how much money to budget for each. A promotional plan can have a wide range of objectives, including: sales increases, new product acceptance, creation of brand equity, positioning, competitive retaliations, or creation of a corporate image.

The term "promotion" is usually an "in" expression used internally by the marketing company, but not normally to the public or the market - phrases like "special offer" are more common. An example of a fully integrated, long-term, large-scale promotion are My Coke Rewards and Pepsi Stuff.

See also

- Promotional mix
- Marketing mix
- Marketing management
- List of marketing topics
- Spin (public relations)

Persuasion

Persuasion is a form of social influence. It is the process of guiding people and oneself toward the adoption of an idea, attitude, or action by rational and symbolic (though not always logical) means.

Methods

Persuasion methods are also sometimes referred to as *persuasion tactics* or *persuasion strategies*.

Weapons of influence

According to Robert Cialdini in his book on persuasion, he defined six "weapons of influence":[1]

- **Reciprocity** - People tend to return a favor. Thus, the pervasiveness of free samples in marketing and advertising. In his conferences, he often uses the example of Ethiopia providing thousands of dollars in humanitarian aid to Mexico just after the 1985 earthquake, despite Ethiopia suffering from a crippling famine and civil war at the time. Ethiopia had been reciprocating for the diplomatic support Mexico provided when Italy invaded Ethiopia in 1937.

- **Commitment and Consistency** - Once people commit to what they think is right, orally or in writing, they are more likely to honor that commitment, even if the original incentive or motivation is subsequently removed. For example, in car sales, suddenly raising the price at the last moment works because the buyer has already decided to buy.

- **Social Proof** - People will do things that they see other people are doing. For example, in one experiment, one or more confederates would look up into the sky; bystanders would then look up into the sky to see what they were seeing. At one point this experiment aborted, as so many people were looking up that they stopped traffic. See conformity, and the Asch conformity experiments.

- **Authority** - People will tend to obey authority figures, even if they are asked to perform objectionable acts. Cialdini cites incidents, such as the Milgram experiments in the early 1960s and the My Lai massacre.

- **Liking** - People are easily persuaded by other people whom they like. Cialdini cites the marketing of Tupperware in what might now be called viral marketing. People were more likely to buy if they liked the person selling it to them. Some of the many biases favoring more attractive people are discussed, but generally more aesthetically pleasing people tend to use this influence excellently over others. See physical attractiveness stereotype.

- **Scarcity** - Perceived scarcity will generate demand. For example, saying offers are available for a "limited time only" encourages sales.

Relationship based persuasion

In their book "The Art of Woo" G. Richard Shell and Mario Moussa describe a four step approach to strategic persuasion[2] . They explain that persuasion means to win others over, not to defeat them. Thus it is very important to be able to see the topic from different angles in order to anticipate the reaction of others to a proposal.

Step 1: *Survey your situation*

This step includes an analysis of the situation of the persuader, his goals and the challenges he faces in his organization.

Step 2: *Confront the five barriers*

There are five obstacles that pose the greatest risks to a successful influence encounter: relationships, credibility, communication mismatches, belief systems, interest and needs.

Step 3: *Make your pitch*

People need solid reason to justify a decision, yet at the same time many decisions are taken on the basis of intuition. This step also deals with presentation skills.

Step 4: *Secure your commitments*

In order to safeguard the longtime success it is vital to deal with politics at the individual and organizational level.

Propaganda

Propaganda is also closely related to Persuasion. It's a concerted set of messages aimed at influencing the opinions or behavior of large numbers of people. Instead of impartially providing information, propaganda in its most basic sense presents information in order to influence its audience. The most effective propaganda is often completely truthful, but some propaganda presents facts selectively to encourage a particular synthesis, or gives loaded messages in order to produce an emotional rather than rational response to the information presented. The desired result is a change of the cognitive narrative of the subject in the target audience. The term 'propaganda' first appeared in 1622 when Pope Gregory XV established the Sacred Congregation for Propagating the Faith. Propaganda was then as now about convincing large numbers of people about the veracity of a given set of ideas. Propaganda is as old as people, politics and religion.

List of methods

By appeal to reason:

- Logical argument
- Logic
- Rhetoric
- Scientific method
- Proof

By appeal to emotion:

- → Advertising
- Faith
- Presentation and Imagination
- Propaganda
- Seduction
- Tradition
- Pity

Aids to persuasion:

- Body language

- Communication skill or Rhetoric
- Sales techniques
- Personality tests and conflict style inventory help devise strategy based on an individual's preferred style of interaction

Other techniques:

- Deception
- Hypnosis
- Subliminal advertising
- Power (sociology)

Coercive techniques, some of which are highly controversial and/or not scientifically proven to be effective:

- Brainwashing
- Coercive persuasion
- Mind control
- Torture

Systems of persuasion for the purpose of seduction:

- Seduction
- Love System (formerly known as Mystery Method)
- Venusian Arts

See also

- Communication
- Regulatory Focus Theory
- Elaboration Likelihood Model
- Social psychology
- Inoculation theory
- Persuasion design
- Rafal Ohme
- The North Wind and the Sun
- → Advertising

External links

changing minds [3]

References

[1] Cialdini, R. B. (2001). *Influence: Science and practice* (4th ed.). Boston: Allyn & Bacon.
[2] The art of Woo by G. Richard Shell and Mario Moussa, New York 2007, ISBN 978-1-59184-176-0
[3] http://changingminds.org

Product (business)

The noun **product** is defined as a "thing produced by labor or effort"[1] or the "result of an act or a process"[2], and stems from the verb **produce**, from the Latin *prōdūce(re)* '(to) lead or bring forth'. Since 1575, the word "product" has referred to anything produced[3]. Since 1695, the word has referred to "thing or things produced". The economic or commercial meaning of product was first used by political economist Adam Smith[4]

In → marketing, a product is anything that can be offered to a market that might satisfy a want or need[5]. In retailing, products are called merchandise. In manufacturing, products are purchased as raw materials and sold as finished goods. Commodities are usually raw materials such as metals and agricultural products, but a commodity can also be anything widely available in the open market. In project management, products are the formal definition of the project deliverables that make up or contribute to delivering the objectives of the project.

In general usage, product may refer to a single item or unit, a group of equivalent products, a grouping of goods or services, or an industrial classification for the goods or services.

A related concept is subproduct, a secondary but useful result of a production process.

Product groups

Tangible and Intangible Products

Products can be classified as tangible or intangible. [6] A tangible product is any physical product like a computer, automobile, etc. An intangible product is a non-physical product like an insurance policy.

In its online product catalog, retailer Sears, Roebuck and Company divides its products into departments, then presents products to shoppers according to (1) function or (2) brand.[7] Each product has a Sears item number and a manufacturer's model number. The departments and product groupings that Sears uses are intended to help customers browse products by function or brand within a traditional department store structure.[8]

Sizes and colors

A catalog number, especially for clothing, may group sizes and colors. When ordering the product, the customer specifies size, color and other variables.[9] example: you walk into a store and see a group of shoes and in that group are sections of different colors of that type of shoe and sizes for that shoe to satisfy your need.

Product line

A product line is "a group of products that are closely related, either because they function in a similar manner, are sold to the same customer groups, are marketed through the same types of outlets, or fall within given price ranges."[10]

Many businesses offer a range of product lines which may be unique to a single organization or may be common across the business's industry. In 2002 the US Census compiled revenue figures for the finance and insurance industry by various product lines such as "accident, health and medical insurance premiums" and "income from secured consumer loans".[11] Within the insurance industry, product lines are indicated by the type of risk coverage, such as auto insurance, commercial insurance and life insurance.[12]

National and international product classifications

Various classification systems for products have been developed for economic statistical purposes. The North American Industry Classification System (NAICS) classifies companies by their primary product [this is not even close to true, NAICS is a production-oriented classification system, not a product-oriented classification system --- the NAFTA signatories are working on a system that classifies products called NAPCS as a companion to NAICS http://www.census.gov/eos/www/napcs/napcs.htm.]. The European Union uses a "Classification of Products by Activity" among other product classifications.[13] The United Nations also classifies products for international economic activity reporting.[14]

The **Aspinwall Classification System** (Leo Aspinwall, 1958) classifies and rates products based on five variables:

1. Replacement rate (How frequently is the product repurchased?)
2. Gross margin (How much profit is obtained from each product?)
3. Buyer goal adjustment (How flexible are the buyers' purchasing habits with regard to this product?)
4. Duration of product satisfaction (How long will the product produce benefits for the user?)
5. Duration of buyer search behavior (How long will consumers shop for the product?)

The National Institute of Governmental Purchasing (NIGP)[15] developed a commodity and services classification system for use by state and local governments, the NIGP Code. [16] The NIGP Code is used by 33 states within the United States as well as thousands of cities, counties and political subdivisions. The NIGP Code is a hierarchical schema consisting of a 3 digit class, 5 digit class-item, 7 digit class-item-group and an 11 digit class-item-group-detail. [17] Applications of the NIGP Code include vendor registration, inventory item identification, contract item management, spend analysis and strategic sourcing.

See also

• Product teardown

References

[1] Random House Dictionary, 1975
[2] *Glossary of the terms related to quality assurance* (http://www.unizg.hr/tempusprojects/glossary.htm) from the Tempus Joint European Project for the Development of Quality Assurance
[3] Etymology of *product* (http://www.etymonline.com/index.php?term=product), etymonline.com.
[4] Etymology of *produce* (http://www.etymonline.com/index.php?term=produce)
[5] Kotler, P., Armstrong, G., Brown, L., and Adam, S. (2006) *Marketing*, 7th Ed. Pearson Education Australia/Prentice Hall.
[6] upenn.edu (http://docs.google.com/gview?a=v&q=cache:ZbQD7QYmcrkJ:knowledge.wharton.upenn.edu/papers/840.pdf+tangible+ products&hl=en&gl=us,)
[7] Sears online (http://www.sears.com), sears.com.
[8] When an online Sears customer goes to the "Parts and accessories" section of the website to find parts for a particular Sears item, the "model number" field actually requires a Sears item number, not a manufacturer's model number. This is a typical problem with product codes or item codes that are internally assigned by a company but do not conform to an external standard.
[9] L.L. Beans webpage for ordering men's "Dress Chinos, Classic Fit Pleated", catalog number TA55203 (http://www.llbean.com/webapp/ wcs/stores/servlet/CategoryDisplay?page=dress-chinos&categoryId=35346&storeId=1&catalogId=1&langId=-1& parentCategory=3511&cat4=6352&shop_method=pp&feat=3511-tn). llbean.com. Accessed 2007-07-01.
[10] Kotler, Philip; Gary Armstrong (1989). *Principles of Marketing, fourth edition (Annotated Instructor's Edition)*. Prentice-Hall, Inc.. pp. 639 (glossary definition). ISBN 0137061293.
[11] "2002 Economic Census, Finance and Insurance" (http://www.census.gov/prod/ec02/ec0252slls.pdf) US Census Bureau, 2002, p.14.
[12] Insurance carrier product lines (http://www.dmoz.org/Business/Financial_Services/Insurance/Carriers/) at the Open Directory Project
[13] Eurostat classifications (http://ec.europa.eu/eurostat/ramon/nomenclatures/index.cfm?TargetUrl=LST_NOM& StrGroupCode=CLASSIFIC&StrLanguageCode=EN), ec.europa.eu.
[14] United Nations product classifications (http://unstats.un.org/unsd/cr/registry/regcst.asp?Cl=16), unstats.un.org.
[15] National Institute of Governmental Purchasing (http://www.nigp.org),nigp.org
[16] NIGP Code (http://www.nigp.com),nigp.com
[17] NIGP Code sample (http://www.nigp.com/nigp-code-sample-01.jsp),

Perspective (cognitive)

Perspective in theory of cognition is the choice of a context or a reference (or the result of this choice) from which to sense, categorize, measure or codify experience, cohesively forming a coherent belief, typically for comparing with another. One may further recognize a number of subtly distinctive meanings, close to those of paradigm, **point of view**, reality tunnel, umwelt, or weltanschauung.

To choose a perspective is to choose a value system and, unavoidably, an associated belief system. When we look at a *business perspective*, we are looking at a monetary base values system and beliefs. When we look at a *human perspective*, it is a more social value system and its associated beliefs.

Point of view

In social psychology one would talk in terms of the other person's point of view when soliciting or motivating the other person to do something for you. Being able to see the other person's point of view is one of Henry Ford's advice towards being successful in business. "If there is any one secret of success, it lies in the ability to get the other person's point of view and see things from that person's angle as well as from your own".

Perspection, a related concept, signifies the ability to auto-inspect one's perception, or perceiving an individual's inspection.

See also

- Perspective, a disambiguation page
- Point of view, a disambiguation page
- Point of view in literature

Advertising mail

Advertising mail, also known as **direct mail, junk mail**, or **admail**, is the delivery of → advertising material to recipients of postal mail.[1] [2] The delivery of advertising mail forms a large and growing service for many postal services, and direct-mail marketing forms a significant portion of the direct marketing industry. Some organizations attempt to help people opt out of receiving advertising mail, in many cases motivated by a concern over its negative environmental impact.

Typical advertising mail

Advertising mail includes advertising circulars, catalogs, CDs, "pre-approved" credit card applications, and other commercial merchandising materials delivered to both homes and businesses. It may be addressed to pre-selected individuals, or unaddressed and delivered on a neighbourhood-by-neighbourhood basis.[3] [4]

Postal services

Postal systems have enacted lower rates for buyers of bulk mail permits. In order to qualify for these rates, marketers must format and sort the mail in specific ways – which reduces the handling required by the postal service.[5]

Income from advertising mail represents a significant and growing portion of some postal services' budgets, and it is a service actively marketed by them.[6] In Canada, addressed and unaddressed advertising mail accounted for 20% of Canada Post's revenue in 2005,[7] and the share is increasing.[8] Postal services employ the terms *advertising mail, admail*, and *direct mail*, while avoiding and objecting to the pejorative term *junk mail*.[9] [10]

In many developed countries, advertising mail represents a significant and growing amount of the total volume of mail. In the United States, "Standard mail: advertising" comprised 29% of all mail in 1980 and 43% in 2003.[11]

1928 direct mail advertising letter offering mail delivery of fish and seafood

Direct-mail marketing

Design and format

Direct mail permits the marketer to design marketing pieces in many different formats. Indeed, there is an entire subsector of the industry that produces specialized papers, printing, envelopes, and other materials for direct-mail marketing. Some of the common formats include:

- Bookalogs: A promotion designed to look like a paperback book. Mailed in an envelope with an order form and cover letter.[12]
- Catalogs: Multi-page, bound promotions, usually featuring a selection of products for sale.
- Blind mailing: A mailer designed to look like personal mail.
- Self-mailers: Pieces usually created from a single sheet that has been printed and folded. For instance, a common practice is to print a page-length advertisement or promotion on one side of a sheet of paper. This is then folded in half or in thirds, with the promotional message to the inside. The two outside surfaces are then used for the address of the recipient and some "teaser" message designed to persuade the customer to open the piece.
- Clear bag packages: Large (often 9×12 or bigger) full-color packages sealed in a clear, plastic outer wrap. The contents show through the clear bag, giving the potential for maximum initial impact. Clear bag packages can be extremely effective and are very affordable based upon the campaign open-rate.
- Postcards: Simple, two-sided pieces, with a promotional message on one side and the customer's address on the other.
- Envelope mailers: Mailings in which the marketing material is placed inside an envelope. This permits the marketer to include more than one insert. When more than one advertiser is included, this is often called "marriage mail". Valpak is one of the largest examples of a marriage mail service.
- Snap Mailers: Mailers that fold and seal with pressure. The sides detach and the mailer is opened to reveal the message.
- Dimensional Mailers: Mailers that have some dimension to them, like a small box.
- Intelligent Documents: Programmable mail pieces built dynamically from database information, and printed digitally for faster production.

Advantages and disadvantages

Many people respond positively to direct mail advertising and find useful goods and services on offer. Traditionally, this was more true in rural areas where people had to travel many miles to do their shopping and direct mail and → mail order shopping was a major convenience. In current practice, people may opt in to direct mail lists in order to be alerted to a favorite vendor's sales or events. However, some people dislike it, in the same way as with telemarketers' calls and, as noted above, e-mail spam, and some jurisdictions like the US have laws requiring junk mailers to withhold their offerings from residents who opt out.

Advantages for marketers include the following:

- Targeting – Historically, the most important aspect of direct mail was its ability to precisely target previous customers. For many industries, including publishing and non-profit organizations, direct mail is the chief means of acquiring new customers, subscribers, or donors. The marketer rents or exchanges lists which most closely match the psychographic and demographic profiles of current best customers. These may be further qualified by past purchase of a similar product, financial data (e.g., income or past purchase amount), how recently the name was added to the mailing list, and how frequently the person purchases — factors referred to as RFM for "recency, frequency, monetary" qualification.
- Personalization - Direct mail can address the customers personally and be tailored to their needs based on previous transactions and gathered data. The evolution of variable data printing technology enables personalization of imagery as well as message and personal data (such as name or address). For example, all male recipients of an offer may receive a personalized package with a man's picture on the cover, while all female recipients receive a picture of a woman.

- Optimization - Because of its direct accountability, direct mail can be tested to find the best list; the best offer; the best creative treatment (writing or design); the best timing (and many other factors). Then the winning tests can be rolled out to a wider audience for optimal results.
- Analysis – The bulk mailing is large enough to allow statistical analyses. For example the results can be analysed to see in detail the performance of individual offers in say a squinch report which shows sales per square inch. With suitable media or source codes, the performance of lists can be captured. These enable better selection of offers and lists for future mailings.
- Accumulation - Responses (and non-responses) can be added to the database, allowing future mailings to be better targeted.
- Advocates make the following arguments:
  - Efficient use of advertising dollars
  - Highly selective, targeted and personalized
  - Flexible
  - High quality reproduction
  - Response easily measured
  - Return on investment (ROI) relatively predictable based on past performance
  - Can be designed with information or entertainment value to recipient, improving customer loyalty
    - 87% of consumers are either "very" or "quite" satisfied with the products they buy through direct mail
    - 56% of consumers said that value for money was the main benefit of buying through Direct Mail, whilst 63% said convenience.

Disadvantages include:

- Cost – The cost per thousand will be higher than almost any other form of mass promotion (although the wastage rate may be much lower). Also, development costs in database acquisition/development. It is however important to note that despite the production and development costs, direct mail can be very profitable, if executed correctly. Lastly, when comparing different media costs, return on investment is the best measure.
- Waste - Large quantities of paper and plastic are thrown away (see below).
- Alienation - Some recipients resent direct marketing being "forced" upon them, and boycott companies that do so. Moreover, they may obtain Prohibitory Orders against companies whose direct marketing mail they find offensive.

Targeting

Advertisers often call direct mail "targeted mailing", since mail is usually sent out following database analysis. For example a person who purchases golf supplies may receive direct mail for golf-related products or perhaps for goods and services that are appropriate for golfers. When direct mail uses database analysis, it is a type of database marketing.

Advances in computing and communications technology have significantly impacted the direct mailing industry in recent years. As computers become more powerful and databases become larger, new opportunities arise for direct mail companies to perform more in-depth processing of their mailing lists. Mailings can be targeted based on location and demographic data. This allows mailings to be targeted more specifically and potentially increases response rates. Web sites are appearing which allow clients to create their mailing lists interactively using map-based interfaces.

Personalized URLS

Personalized URLs, also known as PURLs, are personalized websites used in conjunction with direct mail that are designed to gather information about the person that visits it. Marketing companies find this useful when testing marketing methods and response rates.

Personalized URLs are generally printed on the direct mail piece in the format JohnSample.domain.com or domain.com/JohnSample. They recognize the individual who is visiting the site and can welcome them by name. They also have the ability to obtain and disperse detailed and specific information pertaining to the individual looking at the site.[13]

Personalized URLs are assigned to individual recipients based on the direct mail campaign database and are included either as the only variable or as one of several variable fields in the larger variable data printing communication. When recipients of the direct mail piece log onto their PURL, the information from the campaign database is used to tailor the web page experience to that specific recipient. They are referenced by name, and the graphics, text, offers, and other information on the page can also be tailored to them personally, based on the information in the marketer's database.Studies have shown that people prefer to get additional information online, so Personalized URLs create a seamless way to connect the printed piece to the Web.

Political use

Political campaigns make frequent use of direct mail, both to gain votes from the electorate as a whole, and to target certain groups of voters thought to be open to a candidate's message and to appeal for campaign funds.

Certain organizations and individuals have become known for their prowess in direct mail, including in the U.S. the Free Congress Foundation in the 1970s, Response Dynamics, Inc. in the 1980s, the National Congressional Club, and Richard Viguerie. With the advent of the Internet in political campaigns, direct mail became just one of many campaign management tools, but still played a significant role.

Political campaigns often use direct mail, such as these examples from Barack Obama's 2008 presidential campaign. Multiple mailings of the same item are common.

Business-to-Business mailings (B2B)

Business products and services have long used direct mail to promote themselves. Traditionally, this worked in one of two ways: as a direct sale, therefore precluding the use of a salesperson or a retail store, or as a method of generating leads for a salesforce. The former method was ideally used by products that were easy to sell, were familiar to the prospect and needed no demonstration. The latter method was used for large-ticket items or for those that needed demonstration for example.

One method of direct mailing used in B2B is known as "bill-me". In this direct-mail marketing offer, the buyer is shipped the product prior to payment and then is sent an invoice later.[14]

Opting out

Several organizations offer opt-out services to people who wish to reduce or eliminate the amount of addressed advertising mail they receive. In the United Kingdom, the Mailing Preference Service[15] allows people to register with them for removal from posted as opposed to hand-delivered mail. In the United States, several nonprofit organizations, such as 41pounds.org[16] , and DirectMail.com [17] , offer opt-out services. Some organizations are lobbying for a mandatory Do Not Mail registry in the U.S., similar to the United States National Do Not Call Registry.[18]

In response to a US Supreme Court ruling (Rowan v. Post Office Dept.[19]), the United States Postal Service enables an applicant to obtain a *Prohibitory Order*, which gives people the power to stop non-governmental organizations from sending them mail, and to demand such organizations remove the consumers' information from their mailing lists.

In Canada, the highly-publicized Red Dot Campaign[20] offers advice on reducing unaddressed advertising mail. The campaign focuses on advertising the Canada Post policy to respect "No Junkmail" signs, noting that this policy is not promoted by Canada Post itself. The name "red dot" refers to an internal marker used by Canada Post to indicate which households do not wish to receive

A "No Junkmail" sticker on a mailbox in Calgary, Canada

unaddressed admail.[8] [21] [22] The UK Royal Mail also offers an opt-out service, though it sparked public outrage by warning that unaddressed government mailings could not be separated from advertisements, and those who opted out of the latter would stop receiving the former as well.[23]

Several websites critical of junk mail have guides for people interested in reducing the amount of junk mail they get, such as the Center for a New American Dream[24]

Environmental impact

Several of the above organizations, as well as environmental groups, express concern about the environmental impact generated by junk mail.

In the US, the Environmental Protection Agency estimates that 44% of junk mail is discarded without being opened or read, equaling four million tons of waste paper per year,[25] with 32% recovered for recycling.[26] Further, the Ohio Office of Compliance Assistance and Pollution Prevention (OCAPP) estimates that 250,000 homes could be heated for a single day's junk mail.[27]

In the UK, the Minister of State responsible for the Department for Environment, Food and Rural Affairs estimated that "direct mail and promotions" accounted for between 500,000 and 600,000 tonnes of paper in 2002, with 13% being recycled.[28] The government and the Direct Marketing Association (UK) together agreed on recycling targets for the direct mail industry, including a goal of 55% by 2009, though the DMA's latest estimates are that the industry will fall well short of this mark.[29]

The CO_2 emissions from 41 pounds of advertising mail received annually by the average United States consumer is about 47.6 kilograms (105 pounds) according to one study.[30] The loss of natural habitat potential from the 41 pounds of advertising mail is estimated to be 36.6 square meters (396 square feet).[31]

In the United States many commercial envelope printing companies are moving towards water-based or vegetable-based ink and laminates, and have increased the use of recycled paper.[32]

See also

- Direct marketing
  - Direct mail fundraising
  - Direct response marketing
  - Direct Marketing Associations

External links

- DMOZ entry [33]
- Direct Marketing Quantified: The Knowledge is in the Numbers, Target Marketing Publishing [34], 2005 Gary Hennerberg [35]ISBN: 1-931068-22-4

References

[1] "Direct mail" (http://www.merriam-webster.com/dictionary/direct mail), *Merriam-Webster Online*, 2008,

[2] "Junk mail" (http://www.merriam-webster.com/dictionary/junk mail), *Merriam-Webster Online*, 2008,

[3] "Canada Post - Unaddressed Admail" (http://www.canadapost.ca/business/offerings/unaddressed_admail/can/default-e.asp). . Retrieved 2008-02-27.

[4] "India Post - Direct Post" (http://www.assampost.gov.in/DirectPost.htm). . Retrieved 2008-02-27.

[5] "United States Postal Service Tips for Using a Postage Meter for Bulk Mailings" (http://www.usps.com/businessmail101/postage/tipsPostageMeter.htm). 2008-02-27. .

[6] See e.g. "Royal Mail - Reach your customers with Direct Mail" (http://www.royalmail.com/portal/rm/jump2?catId=400054&mediaId=20900328). 2008-02-27. .

[7] "Canada Post chief seeks to boost profit" (http://www.cbc.ca/canada/manitoba/story/2006/06/13/mb-canada-post-20060613.html). *CBC* (CBC). 2006-06-13. . Retrieved 2008-02-28.

[8] "Website shows way to stop Canada Post junk mail" (http://www.ctv.ca/servlet/ArticleNews/story/CTVNews/20080211/post_mail_080211/20080211?hub=SciTech). *CTV.ca* (CTV). 2008-02-11. . Retrieved 2008-02-28.

[9] "USPS defends junk mail" (http://vitanuova.loyalty.org/weblog/nb.cgi/view/vitanuova/2005/09/05/0). 2008-02-27. .

[10] "Canada Post Letter to the Editor" (http://www.canadapost.ca/corporate/about/newsroom/letters_editor/letters-e.asp?l=brampton_admail). 2008-02-27. .

[11] Schmid, Greg (May 2003) (PDF). *Two Scenarios of Future Mail Volumes* (http://www.ustreas.gov/offices/domestic-finance/usps/pdf/mail-volume-scenarios-5-20.pdf). U.S. Department of the Treasury. . Retrieved 2008-02-27.

[12] FuelNet Glossary, http://www.fuelnet.com/category/glossary/

[13] "Purls of Wisdom" (http://www.sbtechnologymagazine.org/magazine/read/archives/articles/article.php?ProposalOnlineID=907). . Retrieved 2008-04-28.

[14] "Glossary" (http://www.fuelnet.com/category/glossary/#B). *Fuel Net*. . Retrieved 2009-07-14.

[15] "MPS online" (http://www.mpsonline.org.uk/mpsr/). . Retrieved 2008-02-27.

[16] See e.g. Green, Chuck (2006-09-25). "The direct mail stops here: New company 41pounds.org helps people halt the deluge". *Waste News*.

[17] https://www.directmail.com/directory/mail_preference/

[18] http://www.donotmail.org

[19] "Rowan v. United States Post Office" (http://www.law.cornell.edu/supct/html/historics/USSC_CR_0397_0728_ZO.html). .

[20] "Red Dot Campaign" (http://www.reddotcampaign.ca/). . Retrieved 2008-02-27.

[21] "Website promotes red dots to stop junk mail" (http://www.cbc.ca/canada/british-columbia/story/2008/01/31/bc-red-dot-campaign.html). *CBC.ca* (CBC). 2008-01-31. . Retrieved 2008-02-27.

[22] "Campaign seeks to save paper by refusing junk mail" (http://www.canada.com/topics/news/national/story.html?id=9b5386e8-cba4-4bdd-8d46-9d1b4aded077&k=88559). *canada.com* (CanWest). 2008-02-10. . Retrieved 2008-02-27.

[23] Barrow, Becky (2006-08-29). "Anger over Royal Mail's junk mail warning" (http://www.dailymail.co.uk/pages/live/articles/news/news.html?in_article_id=402781&in_page_id=1770). . Retrieved 2008-02-27.

[24] See e.g. Ryan, Terri Jo (2007-08-06). "You're pre-approved to dunk the junk!". *The Virginian-Pilot & The Ledger-Star.*, "How to Junk Junk Mail and Other Paper Clutter" (http://www.washingtonpost.com/wp-dyn/content/article/2008/01/17/AR2008011701793.html). *The Washington Post*. 2008-01-20. . Retrieved 2008-03-18.

[25] EPA Junk Mail Reduction (http://www.epa.gov/region7/waste/solidwaste/junkmail.htm)

[26] *Municipal Solid Waste Generation, Recycling, and Disposal in the United States: Facts and Figures for 2003* (http://www.epa.gov/msw/pubs/msw03rpt.pdf), EPA, 2005,

[27] Ohio OCAPP (http://www.epa.state.oh.us/opp/consumer/junkmail.html)

[28] "House of Commons Hansard Written Answers for 16 October 2003 (pt 4)" (http://www.publications.parliament.uk/pa/cm200203/
cmhansrd/vo031016/text/31016w04.htm#31016w04.html_spnew5). . Retrieved 2008-03-13.

[29] Hoffbrand, Jenny. "DMA: Recycling targets 'miles away'" (http://www.precisionmarketing.co.uk/Articles/256131/DMA+Recycling+
targets+âmiles+awayâ.html). *Precision Marketing*. .

[30] "Earth Day Rx:..." (http://www.41pounds.org/news/41pounds_press_release_04-13-2007_Earth_Day.pdf). 41pounds.org. . Retrieved
Mar 12, 2009.

[31] "environmental impact of junk mail" (http://ecofx.org/wiki/index.php?title=Junk_mail). ecofx.org. . Retrieved Mar 12, 2009.

[32] http://www.printingsmarter.com/2009/07/5-tips-to-reduce-environmental-impact.html

[33] http://www.dmoz.org/Business/Publishing_and_Printing/Printing/Products/Direct_Mail/

[34] http://bookstore.napco.com/TM/index.cfm?fua=shop&fa=bookDetail&wb=tm&l=b&id=18

[35] http://www.hennerberg.com

Jingle

A **jingle** is a memorable short tune with a lyric broadcast used in → radio and television commercials, which are usually intended to convey an advertising slogan. They are also utilised by pop music radio for disc jockey and station identification purposes.

History

The jingle had no definitive debut: its infiltration of the → radio was more of an evolutionary process than a sudden innovation. Product → advertisements with a musical tilt can be traced back to 1923[1] , around the same time commercial radio cbegan in the United States. If one entity has the best claim to the first jingle it is General Mills, who aired the world's first singing commercial. The seminal radio bite, entitled "Have You Tried Wheaties?", was first released on the Christmas Eve of 1926.[2] It featured four male singers, who were eventually christened "The Wheaties Quartet", singing the following lines:

> *Have you tried Wheaties?*
> *They're whole wheat with all of the bran.*
> *Won't you try Wheaties?*
> *For wheat is the best food of man.*
>
> *They're crispy and crunchy*
> *The whole year through,*
> *The kiddies never tire of them*
> *and neither will you.*
>
> *So just try Wheaties,*
> *The best breakfast food in the land.*

While the lyrics may appear corny to modern-day society, the advertisement was an absolute sensation to consumers at the time. In fact, it was such a success that it served to save the otherwise failing brand of cereal. In 1929, General Mills was seriously considering dropping Wheaties on the basis of poor sales. However, advertising manager Sam Gale pointed out that an astounding 30,000 of the 53,000 cases of cereal that General Mills sold were in the Minneapolis-St. Paul area, the only location where "Have You Tried Wheaties?" was being aired at the time.[2] Encouraged by the incredible results of this new method of advertising, General Mills changed tactics entirely. Instead of dropping the cereal, it purchased nationwide commercial time for the advertisement. The resultant climb in sales single-handedly saved the now incredibly popular cereal.

After the massive success that General Mills enjoyed, other companies began to investigate this new method of advertisement. The jingle movement was bursting. Ironically, part of the appeal of the jingle was that it circumvented broadcasting giant NBC's prohibition of direct advertising:[1] this new variety of advertisement could get a brand's name embedded in the heads of potential customers without trying to sell it. The art of the jingle reached its peak around the economic boom of the 1950s.

The jingle was used in the → advertising of branded products such as breakfast cereals, candy and snacks (including soda pop) and other processed foods, tobacco and alcoholic beverages, as well as various franchises and products that might reflect personal image such as automobiles, personal hygiene products (including deodorants, mouthwash, shampoo, and toothpaste) and household cleaning products, especially detergent.

Today, with the ever-increasing cost of licensing preexisting music, a growing number of businesses are rediscovering the custom jingle as a more affordable option for their advertising needs.

Parody

Jingles can also be used for parody purposes, popularized in Top 40/CHR radio formats primarily Hot30 Countdown, used primarily for branding reasons. Parody also allows radio networks to bypass copyright law through parody provisions. It brands the segment as both light-hearted and commercial, thus fulfilling its use as a branding component.

Examples

- Jinglestop Music Production http://www.jinglestop.com [3] For Jingle Examples
- Reklammuzik.com [4] For Commercial Jingles

References

[1] MWOTRC: Metro Washington Old Time Radio Club (http://www.mwotrc.com/rr2005_02/expert.htm)
[2] http://www.generalmills.com/corporate/company/hist_radio.pdf
[3] http://www.jinglestop.com
[4] http://www.reklammuzik.com

Lyrics

Lyrics (in singular form **Lyric**) are a set of words that make up a song. The writer of lyrics is a lyricist or lyrist. The meaning of lyrics can either be explicit or implicit. Some lyrics are abstract, almost unintelligible, and, in such cases, their explication emphasizes form, articulation, meter, and symmetry of expression. The lyricist of traditional musical forms such as Opera is known as a librettist.

Etymology and usage

Lyric derives from the Greek word *lyrikos*, meaning "singing to the lyre".[1] A lyric poem is one that expresses a subjective, personal point of view.

The word *lyric* came to be used for the "words of a song"; this meaning was recorded in 1876.[1] The common plural (perhaps because of the association between the plurals *lyrics* and *words*), predominates contemporary usage. Use of the singular form *lyric* remains grammatically acceptable, yet remains considered erroneous in referring to a singular song word as a *lyric*.

Copyright and royalties

See Royalties

Currently, there are many websites featuring song lyrics. This offering, however, is controversial, since some sites include copyrighted lyrics offered without the holder's permission. The U.S. Music Publishers' Association (MPA), which represents sheet music companies, launched a legal campaign against such websites in December 2005, the MPA's president, Lauren Keiser, said the free lyrics web sites are "completely illegal" and wanted some website operators jailed.[2]

Academic study

- Lyrics can be studied from an academic perspective. For example, some lyrics can be considered a form of social commentary. Lyrics often contain political, social and economic themes as well as aesthetic elements, and so can connote messages which are culturally significant. These messages can either be explicit or implied through metaphor or symbolism. Lyrics can also be analyzed with respect to the sense of unity (or lack of unity) it has with its supporting music. Analysis based on tonality and contrast are particular examples.
- Chinese lyrics (詞) are Chinese poems written in the set metrical and tonal pattern of a particular song.

Riskiest Search

McAfee claims searches for phrases containing "lyrics" and "free" are the most likely to have risky results. [3]

See also

- Lyricist, a lyrics writer
- Instrumental, music without voice
- Libretto, the name used for the text of traditional music forms like opera

References

[1] Online Etymology Dictionary. Retrieved 2008-08-23 (http://www.etymonline.com/index.php?term=lyric)
[2] "Song sites face legal crackdown" (http://news.bbc.co.uk/1/hi/entertainment/4508158.stm) BBC News, 12 December 2005. Site accessed 7 January 2007
[3] http://us.mcafee.com/en-us/local/docs/most_dangerous_searchterm_us.pdf

World Wide Web

The **World Wide Web**, abbreviated as **WWW** and **W3** and commonly known as **The Web**, is a system of interlinked hypertext documents contained on the → Internet. With a web browser, one can view → web pages that may contain text, images, videos, and other multimedia and navigate between them using hyperlinks. Using concepts from earlier hypertext systems, English engineer and computer scientist Sir Tim Berners-Lee, now the Director of the World Wide Web Consortium, wrote a proposal in March 1989 for what would eventually become the World Wide Web.[1] He was later joined by Belgian computer scientist Robert Cailliau while both were working at CERN in Geneva, Switzerland. In 1990, they proposed using "HyperText [...] to link and access information of various kinds as a web of nodes in which the user can browse at will",[2] and released that web in December.[3]

"The World-Wide Web (W3) was developed to be a pool of human knowledge, which would allow collaborators in remote sites to share their ideas and all aspects of a common project." [4] If two projects are independently created, rather than have a central figure make the changes, the two bodies of information could form into one cohesive piece of work.

History

In March 1989, Tim Berners-Lee wrote a proposal[5] that referenced ENQUIRE, a database and software project he had built in 1980, and described a more elaborate information management system.

With help from Robert Cailliau, he published a more formal proposal (on November 12, 1990) to build a "Hypertext project" called "WorldWideWeb" (one word, also "W3") as a "web" of "hypertext documents" to be viewed by "browsers", using a client-server architecture.[2] This proposal estimated that a read-only web would be developed within three months and that it would take six months to achieve, "the creation of new links and new material by readers, [so that] authorship becomes universal" as well as "the automatic notification of a reader when new material of interest to him/her has become available". See Web 2.0 and RSS/Atom, which have taken a little longer to mature.

The Web's historic logo designed by Robert Cailliau

The proposal had been modeled after the Dynatext SGML reader, by Electronic Book Technology, a spin-off from the Institute for Research in Information and Scholarship at Brown University. The Dynatext system, licensed by CERN, was technically advanced and was a key player in the extension of SGML ISO 8879:1986 to Hypermedia within HyTime, but it was considered too expensive and had an inappropriate licensing policy for use in the general high energy physics community, namely a fee for each document and each document alteration.

This NeXT Computer used by Sir Tim Berners-Lee at CERN became the first web server.

A NeXT Computer was used by Berners-Lee as the world's first web server and also to write the first web browser, WorldWideWeb, in 1990. By Christmas 1990, Berners-Lee had built all the tools necessary for a working Web:[6] the first web browser (which was a web editor as well), the first web server, and the first web pages[7] which described the project itself. On August 6, 1991, he posted a short summary of the World Wide Web project on the alt.hypertext newsgroup.[8] This date also marked the debut of the Web as a publicly available service on the Internet. The first server outside Europe was set up at SLAC in December 1991.[9] The crucial underlying concept of hypertext originated with older projects from the 1960s, such as the

Hypertext Editing System (HES) at Brown University--- among others Ted Nelson and Andries van Dam--- Ted Nelson's Project Xanadu and Douglas Engelbart's oN-Line System (NLS). Both Nelson and Engelbart were in turn inspired by Vannevar Bush's microfilm-based "memex," which was described in the 1945 essay "As We May Think".

Berners-Lee's breakthrough was to marry hypertext to the Internet. In his book *Weaving The Web*, he explains that he had repeatedly suggested that a marriage between the two technologies was possible to members of *both* technical communities, but when no one took up his invitation, he finally tackled the project himself. In the process, he developed a system of globally unique identifiers for resources on the Web and elsewhere: the Universal Document Identifier (UDI) later known as Uniform Resource Locator (URL) and Uniform Resource Identifier (URI); and the publishing language HyperText Markup Language (HTML); and the Hypertext Transfer Protocol (HTTP).[10]

The World Wide Web had a number of differences from other hypertext systems that were then available. The Web required only unidirectional links rather than bidirectional ones. This made it possible for someone to link to another resource without action by the owner of that resource. It also significantly reduced the difficulty of implementing web servers and browsers (in comparison to earlier systems), but in turn presented the chronic problem of link rot. Unlike predecessors such as HyperCard, the World Wide Web was non-proprietary, making it possible to develop servers and clients independently and to add extensions without licensing restrictions. On April 30, 1993, CERN announced[11] that the World Wide Web would be free to anyone, with no fees due. Coming two months after the announcement that the Gopher protocol was no longer free to use, this produced a rapid shift away from Gopher and towards the Web. An early popular web browser was ViolaWWW, which was based upon HyperCard.

Scholars generally agree that a turning point for the World Wide Web began with the introduction[12] of the Mosaic web browser[13] in 1993, a graphical browser developed by a team at the National Center for Supercomputing Applications at the University of Illinois at Urbana-Champaign (NCSA-UIUC), led by Marc Andreessen. Funding for Mosaic came from the U.S. *High-Performance Computing and Communications Initiative*, a funding program initiated by the *High Performance Computing and Communication Act of 1991*, one of several computing developments initiated by U.S. Senator Al Gore.[14] Prior to the release of Mosaic, graphics were not commonly mixed with text in web pages, and its popularity was less than older protocols in use over the Internet, such as Gopher and Wide Area Information Servers (WAIS). Mosaic's graphical user interface allowed the Web to become, by far, the most popular Internet protocol.

The World Wide Web Consortium (W3C) was founded by Tim Berners-Lee after he left the European Organization for Nuclear Research (CERN) in October, 1994. It was founded at the Massachusetts Institute of Technology Laboratory for Computer Science (MIT/LCS) with support from the Defense Advanced Research Projects Agency (DARPA)—which had pioneered the → Internet—and the European Commission. By the end of 1994, while the total number of websites was still minute compared to present standards, quite a number of notable websites were already active, many of whom are the precursors or inspiration for today's most popular services.

Connected by the existing Internet, other → websites were created around the world, adding international standards for domain names and the HTML. Since then, Berners-Lee has played an active role in guiding the development of web standards (such as the markup languages in which web pages are composed), and in recent years has advocated his vision of a Semantic Web. The World Wide Web enabled the spread of information over the → Internet through an easy-to-use and flexible format. It thus played an important role in popularizing use of the Internet.[15] Although the two terms are sometimes conflated in popular use, *World Wide Web* is not synonymous with *Internet*.[16] The Web is an application built on top of the Internet.

Function

The terms Internet and World Wide Web are often used in every-day speech without much distinction. However, the Internet and the World Wide Web are not one and the same. The Internet is a global system of interconnected computer networks. In contrast, the Web is one of the services that runs on the Internet. It is a collection of interconnected documents and other resources, linked by hyperlinks and URLs. In short, the Web is an application running on the Internet.[17] Viewing a → web page on the World Wide Web normally begins either by typing the URL of the page into a web browser, or by following a hyperlink to that page or resource. The web browser then initiates a series of communication messages, behind the scenes, in order to fetch and display it.

First, the server-name portion of the URL is resolved into an IP address using the global, distributed → Internet database known as the domain name system, or DNS. This IP address is necessary to contact the Web server. The browser then requests the resource by sending an HTTP request to the Web server at that particular address. In the case of a typical web page, the HTML text of the page is requested first and parsed immediately by the web browser, which then makes additional requests for images and any other files that form parts of the page. Statistics measuring a website's popularity are usually based either on the number of 'page views' or associated server 'hits' (file requests) that take place.

While receiving these files from the web server, browsers may progressively render the page onto the screen as specified by its HTML, CSS, and other web languages. Any images and other resources are incorporated to produce the on-screen web page that the user sees. Most web pages will themselves contain hyperlinks to other related pages and perhaps to downloads, source documents, definitions and other web resources. Such a collection of useful, related resources, interconnected via hypertext links, is what was dubbed a "web" of information. Making it available on the Internet created what Tim Berners-Lee first called the **WorldWideWeb** (in its original CamelCase, which was subsequently discarded) in November 1990.[2]

What does W3 define?

W3, or www, stands for many different things. The main topics being:

- The idea of a boundless information world in which all items have a reference by which they can be retrieved;
- the address system (URL) which the project implemented to make this world possible, despite many different protocols;
- a network protocol (HTTP) used by native W3 servers giving performance and features not otherwise available;
- a markup language (HTML) which every W3 client is required to understand, and is used for the transmission of basic things such as text, menus and simple on-line help information across the net;
- the body of data available on the Internet using all or some of the preceding listed items.

[18]

Linking

Over time, many web resources pointed to by hyperlinks disappear, relocate, or are replaced with different content. This phenomenon is referred to in some circles as "link rot" and the hyperlinks affected by it are often called "dead links". The ephemeral nature of the Web has prompted many efforts to archive web sites. The Internet Archive is one of the best-known efforts; it has been active since 1996.

Graphic representation of a minute fraction of the WWW, demonstrating hyperlinks

Ajax updates

JavaScript is a scripting language that was initially developed in 1995 by Brendan Eich, then of Netscape, for use within web pages.[19] The standardized version is ECMAScript.[19] To overcome some of the limitations of the page-by-page model described above, some web applications also use Ajax (asynchronous JavaScript and XML). JavaScript is delivered with the page that can make additional HTTP requests to the server, either in response to user actions such as mouse-clicks, or based on lapsed time. The server's responses are used to modify the current page rather than creating a new page with each response. Thus the server only needs to provide limited, incremental information. Since multiple Ajax requests can be handled at the same time, users can interact with a page even while data is being retrieved. Some web applications regularly poll the server to ask if new information is available.[20]

WWW prefix

Many web addresses begin with *www*, because of the long-standing practice of naming Internet hosts (servers) according to the services they provide. So, the host name for a web server is often *www* as it is *ftp* for an FTP server, and *news* or *nntp* for a USENET news server etc. These host names then appear as DNS subdomain names, as in "www.example.com". The use of such subdomain names is not required by any technical or policy standard; indeed, the first ever web server was called "nxoc01.cern.ch",[21] and many web sites exist without a *www* subdomain prefix, or with some other prefix such as "www2", "secure" etc. These subdomain prefixes have no consequence; they are simply chosen names. Many web servers are set up such that both the domain by itself (e.g., example.com) and the *www* subdomain (e.g., www.example.com) refer to the same site, others require one form or the other, or they may map two different web sites.

When a single word is typed into the address bar and the return key is pressed, some web browsers automatically try adding "www." to the beginning of it and possibly ".com", ".org" and ".net" at the end. For example, typing 'apple<enter>' may resolve to *http://www.apple.com/* and 'openoffice<enter>' to *http://www.openoffice.org*. This feature was beginning to be included in early versions of Mozilla Firefox (when it still had the working title 'Firebird') in early 2003.[22] It is reported that Microsoft was granted a US patent for the same idea in 2008, but only with regard to mobile devices.[23]

The 'http://' or 'https://' part of web addresses *does* have meaning: These refer to Hypertext Transfer Protocol and to HTTP Secure and so define the communication protocol that will be used to request and receive the page and all its images and other resources. The HTTP network protocol is fundamental to the way the World Wide Web works, and the encryption involved in HTTPS adds an essential layer if confidential information such as passwords or bank details are to be exchanged over the public internet. Web browsers often prepend this 'scheme' part to URLs too, if it is omitted. Despite this, Berners-Lee himself has admitted that the two 'forward slashes' (//) were in fact initially unnecessary[24] . In overview, RFC 2396 defined web URLs to have the following form: <scheme>://<authority><path>?<query>#<fragment>. Here <authority> is for example the web server (like www.example.com), and <path> identifies the web page. The web server processes the <query> (which can be data sent via a form, e.g. terms sent to a search engine), and the returned page depends on it. Finally, <fragment> is not sent to the web server. It identifies the portion of the page which the browser shows first.

In English, *www* is pronounced by individually pronouncing the name of characters (*double-u double-u double-u*). Although some technical users pronounce it *dub-dub-dub* this is not widespread. The English writer Douglas Adams once quipped in The Independent on Sunday (1999): "The World Wide Web is the only thing I know of whose shortened form takes three times longer to say than what it's short for," with Stephen Fry later pronouncing it in his "Podgrammes" series of podcasts as "wuh wuh wuh." In Mandarin Chinese, *World Wide Web* is commonly translated via a phono-semantic matching to *wàn wéi wǎng* (万维网), which satisfies *www* and literally means "myriad dimensional net",[25] a translation that very appropriately reflects the design concept and proliferation of the World Wide Web. Tim Berners-Lee's web-space states that *World Wide Web* is officially spelled as three separate words, each capitalized, with no intervening hyphens.[26]

Privacy

Computer users, who save time and money, and who gain conveniences and entertainment, may or may not have surrendered the right to privacy in exchange for using a number of technologies including the Web.[27] Worldwide, more than a half billion people have used a social network service,[28] and of Americans who grew up with the Web, half created an online profile[29] and are part of a generational shift that could be changing norms.[30] [31] Facebook progressed from U.S. college students to a 70% non-U.S. audience, and in 2009 prior to launching a beta test of the "transition tools" to set privacy preferences,[32] estimated that only 20% of its members use privacy settings.[33]

Privacy representatives from 60 countries have resolved to ask for laws to complement industry self-regulation, for education for children and other minors who use the Web, and for default protections for users of social networks.[34] They also believe data protection for personally identifiable information benefits business more than the sale of that information.[34] Users can opt-in to features in browsers to clear their personal histories locally and block some cookies and advertising networks[35] but they are still tracked in websites' server logs, and particularly web beacons.[36] Berners-Lee and colleagues see hope in accountability and appropriate use achieved by extending the Web's architecture to policy awareness, perhaps with audit logging, reasoners and appliances.[37] Among services paid for by → advertising, Yahoo! could collect the most data about users of commercial websites, about 2,500 bits of information per month about each typical user of its site and its affiliated advertising network sites. Yahoo! was followed by MySpace with about half that potential and then by AOL–TimeWarner, Google, Facebook, Microsoft, and eBay.[38]

Security

The Web has become criminals' preferred pathway for spreading malware. Cybercrime carried out on the Web can include identity theft, fraud, espionage and intelligence gathering.[1] Web-based vulnerabilities now outnumber traditional computer security concerns,[39] [40] and as measured by Google, about one in ten web pages may contain malicious code.[41] Most Web-based attacks take place on legitimate websites, and most, as measured by Sophos, are hosted in the United States, China and Russia.[42] The most common of all malware threats is SQL injection attacks against websites.[43] Through HTML and URIs the Web was vulnerable to attacks like cross-site scripting (XSS) that came with the introduction of JavaScript[44] and were exacerbated to some degree by Web 2.0 and Ajax web design that favors the use of scripts.[45] Today by one estimate, 70% of all websites are open to XSS attacks on their users.[46]

Proposed solutions vary to extremes. Large security vendors like McAfee already design governance and compliance suites to meet post-9/11 regulations,[47] and some, like Finjan have recommended active real-time inspection of code and all content regardless of its source.[48] Some have argued that for enterprise to see security as a business opportunity rather than a cost center,[49] "ubiquitous, always-on digital rights management" enforced in the infrastructure by a handful of organizations must replace the hundreds of companies that today secure data and networks.[50] Jonathan Zittrain has said users sharing responsibility for computing safety is far preferable to locking down the Internet.[51]

Standards

Many formal standards and other technical specifications define the operation of different aspects of the World Wide Web, the Internet, and computer information exchange. Many of the documents are the work of the World Wide Web Consortium (W3C), headed by Berners-Lee, but some are produced by the Internet Engineering Task Force (IETF) and other organizations.

Usually, when web standards are discussed, the following publications are seen as foundational:

*   Recommendations for markup languages, especially HTML and XHTML, from the W3C. These define the structure and interpretation of hypertext documents.
*   Recommendations for stylesheets, especially CSS, from the W3C.
*   Standards for ECMAScript (usually in the form of JavaScript), from Ecma International.
*   Recommendations for the Document Object Model, from W3C.

Additional publications provide definitions of other essential technologies for the World Wide Web, including, but not limited to, the following:

*   *Uniform Resource Identifier* (URI), which is a universal system for referencing resources on the Internet, such as hypertext documents and images. URIs, often called URLs, are defined by the IETF's RFC 3986 / STD 66: *Uniform Resource Identifier (URI): Generic Syntax*, as well as its predecessors and numerous URI scheme-defining RFCs;
*   *HyperText Transfer Protocol (HTTP)*, especially as defined by RFC 2616: *HTTP/1.1* and RFC 2617: *HTTP Authentication*, which specify how the browser and server authenticate each other.

Accessibility

Access to the Web is for everyone regardless of disability including visual, auditory, physical, speech, cognitive, or neurological. Accessibility features also help others with temporary disabilities like a broken arm or the aging population as their abilities change.[52] The Web is used for receiving information as well as providing information and interacting with society, making it essential that the Web be accessible in order to provide equal access and equal opportunity to people with disabilities.[53] Tim Berners-Lee once noted, "The power of the Web is in its universality. Access by everyone regardless of disability is an essential aspect."[52] Many countries regulate web accessibility as a requirement for websites.[54] International cooperation in the W3C Web Accessibility Initiative led to simple guidelines that web content authors as well as software developers can use to make the Web accessible to persons who may or may not be using assistive technology.[52] [55]

Internationalization

The W3C Internationalization Activity assures that web technology will work in all languages, scripts, and cultures.[56] Beginning in 2004 or 2005, Unicode gained ground and eventually in December 2007 surpassed both ASCII and Western European as the Web's most frequently used character encoding.[57] Originally RFC 3986 allowed resources to be identified by URI in a subset of US-ASCII. RFC 3987 allows more characters—any character in the Universal Character Set—and now a resource can be identified by IRI in any language.[58]

Statistics

According to a 2001 study, there were massively more than 550 billion documents on the Web, mostly in the invisible Web, or deep Web.[59] A 2002 survey of 2,024 million Web pages[60] determined that by far the most Web content was in English: 56.4%; next were pages in German (7.7%), French (5.6%), and Japanese (4.9%). A more recent study, which used Web searches in 75 different languages to sample the Web, determined that there were over 11.5 billion Web pages in the publicly indexable Web as of the end of January 2005.[61] As of March 2009[62], the indexable web contains at least 25.21 billion pages.[63] On July 25, 2008, Google software engineers Jesse Alpert and Nissan Hajaj announced that Google Search had discovered one trillion unique URLs.[64] As of May 2009[62], over 109.5 million websites operated.[65] Of these 74% were commercial or other sites operating in the .com generic top-level domain.[65]

Speed issues

Frustration over congestion issues in the → Internet infrastructure and the high latency that results in slow browsing has led to an alternative, pejorative name for the World Wide Web: the *World Wide Wait*.[66] Speeding up the Internet is an ongoing discussion over the use of peering and QoS technologies. Other solutions to reduce the World Wide Wait can be found at W3C.[67] Standard guidelines for ideal Web response times are:[68]

- 0.1 second (one tenth of a second). Ideal response time. The user doesn't sense any interruption.
- 1 second. Highest acceptable response time. Download times above 1 second interrupt the user experience.
- 10 seconds. Unacceptable response time. The user experience is interrupted and the user is likely to leave the site or system.

Caching

If a user revisits a Web page after only a short interval, the page data may not need to be re-obtained from the source Web server. Almost all web browsers cache recently obtained data, usually on the local hard drive. HTTP requests sent by a browser will usually only ask for data that has changed since the last download. If the locally cached data are still current, it will be reused. Caching helps reduce the amount of Web traffic on the Internet. The decision about expiration is made independently for each downloaded file, whether image, stylesheet, JavaScript, HTML, or whatever other content the site may provide. Thus even on sites with highly dynamic content, many of the basic resources only need to be refreshed occasionally. Web site designers find it worthwhile to collate resources such as CSS data and JavaScript into a few site-wide files so that they can be cached efficiently. This helps reduce page download times and lowers demands on the Web server.

There are other components of the Internet that can cache Web content. Corporate and academic firewalls often cache Web resources requested by one user for the benefit of all. (See also Caching proxy server.) Some search engines, such as Google or Yahoo!, also store cached content from websites. Apart from the facilities built into Web servers that can determine when files have been updated and so need to be re-sent, designers of dynamically generated Web pages can control the HTTP headers sent back to requesting users, so that transient or sensitive pages are not cached. Internet banking and news sites frequently use this facility. Data requested with an HTTP 'GET' is likely to be cached if other conditions are met; data obtained in response to a 'POST' is assumed to depend on the data that was POSTed and so is not cached.

See also

- CERN
- Deep web
- Electronic publishing
- List of websites
- Streaming media
- Web 1.0
- Web 2.0
- Web accessibility
- Web archiving
- Web browser
- Web directory
- Web operating system
- Web science
- → Web search engine
- Web services
- Website architecture
- Prestel

References

- Fielding, R.; Gettys, J.; Mogul, J.; Frystyk, H.; Masinter, L.; Leach, P.; Berners-Lee, T. (June 1999). *Hypertext Transfer Protocol — HTTP/1.1* [69]. Request For Comments 2616. Information Sciences Institute.
- Berners-Lee, Tim; Bray, Tim; Connolly, Dan; Cotton, Paul; Fielding, Roy; Jeckle, Mario; Lilley, Chris; Mendelsohn, Noah; Orchard, David; Walsh, Norman; Williams, Stuart (December 15, 2004). *Architecture of the World Wide Web, Volume One* [70]. Version 20041215. W3C.
- Polo, Luciano (2003). "World Wide Web Technology Architecture: A Conceptual Analysis" [71]. *New Devices*. Retrieved July 31, 2005.
- Skau, H.O. (March 1990). "The World Wide Web and Health Information" [71]. *New Devices*. Retrieved 1989.

External links

- Early archive of the first Web site [72]
- Internet Statistics: Growth and Usage of the Web and the Internet [73]
- Living Internet [74] A comprehensive history of the Internet, including the World Wide Web.
- Web Design and Development [75] at the Open Directory Project
- World Wide Web Consortium [76]
- World Wide Web Size [77] Daily estimated size of the World Wide Web.
- Internet Usage statistics and analysis for English websites [78]

References

[1] "Tim Berners Lee - Time 100 People of the Century" (http://www.yachtingnet.com/time/time100/scientist/profile/bernerslee.html). *Time Magazine.* . "He wove the World Wide Web and created a mass medium for the 21st century. The World Wide Web is Berners-Lee's alone. He designed it. He loosed it on the world. And he more than anyone else has fought to keep it open, nonproprietary and free. ."

[2] "Berners-Lee, Tim; Cailliau, Robert (November 12, 1990). "WorldWideWeb: Proposal for a HyperText Project" (http://www.w3.org/Proposal.html). . Retrieved July 27, 2009.

[3] Berners-Lee, Tim. "Pre-W3C Web and Internet Background" (http://www.w3.org/2004/Talks/w3c10-HowItAllStarted/?n=15). World Wide Web Consortium. . Retrieved April 21, 2009.

[4] Wardrip-Fruin, Noah and Nick Montfort, ed (2003). The New Media Reader. Section 54. The MIT Press. ISBN 0-262-23227-8.

[5] "Information Management: A Proposal" (http://www.w3.org/History/1989/proposal.html). March 1989. . Retrieved July 27, 2009.

[6] "Tim Berners-Lee: WorldWideWeb, the first web client" (http://www.w3.org/People/Berners-Lee/WorldWideWeb). W3.org. . Retrieved July 27, 2009.

[7] "First Web pages" (http://www.w3.org/History/19921103-hypertext/hypertext/WWW/TheProject.html). W3.org. . Retrieved July 27, 2009.

[8] "Short summary of the World Wide Web project" (http://groups.google.com/group/alt.hypertext/msg/395f282a67a1916c). Groups.google.com. August 6, 1991. . Retrieved July 27, 2009.

[9] Jean Marie Deken. "The Early World Wide Web at SLAC: Early Chronology and Documents" (http://www.slac.stanford.edu/history/earlyweb/history.shtml). Slac.stanford.edu. . Retrieved July 27, 2009.

[10] "Inventor of the Week Archive: The World Wide Web" (http://web.mit.edu/invent/iow/berners-lee.html). Massachusetts Institute of Technology: MIT School of Engineering. . Retrieved July 23, 2009.

[11] "Ten Years Public Domain for the Original Web Software" (http://tenyears-www.web.cern.ch/tenyears-www/Welcome.html). Tenyears-www.web.cern.ch. April 30, 2003. . Retrieved July 27, 2009.

[12] "Mosaic Web Browser History - NCSA, Marc Andreessen, Eric Bina" (http://www.livinginternet.com/w/wi_mosaic.htm). Livinginternet.com. . Retrieved July 27, 2009.

[13] "NCSA Mosaic - September 10, 1993 Demo" (http://www.totic.org/nscp/demodoc/demo.html). Totic.org. . Retrieved July 27, 2009.

[14] "Vice President Al Gore's ENIAC Anniversary Speech" (http://www.cs.washington.edu/homes/lazowska/faculty.lecture/innovation/gore.html). Cs.washington.edu. February 14, 1996. . Retrieved July 27, 2009.

[15] "Internet legal definition of Internet" (http://legal-dictionary.thefreedictionary.com/Internet). *West's Encyclopedia of American Law, edition 2.* Free Online Law Dictionary. July 15, 2009. . Retrieved November 25, 2008.

[16] "WWW (World Wide Web) Definition" (http://www.techterms.com/definition/www). TechTerms. . Retrieved July 27, 2009.

[17] "The W3C Technology Stack" (http://www.w3.org/Consortium/technology). World Wide Web Consortium. . Retrieved April 21, 2009.

[18] # ^ Wardrip-Fruin, Noah and Nick Montfort, ed (2003). The New Media Reader. The MIT Press. ISBN 0-262-23227-8.

[19] Hamilton, Naomi (July 31, 2008). "The A-Z of Programming Languages: JavaScript" (http://www.computerworld.com.au/article/255293/-z_programming_languages_javascript). *Computerworld.* IDG. . Retrieved May 12, 2009.

[20] Buntin, Seth (23 September 2008). "jQuery Polling plugin" (http://buntin.org/2008/sep/23/jquery-polling-plugin/). . Retrieved 2009-08-22.

[21] "Frequently asked questions by the Press - Tim Berners-Lee" (http://www.w3.org/People/Berners-Lee/FAQ.html). W3.org. . Retrieved July 27, 2009.

[22] "automatically adding www.___.com" (http://forums.mozillazine.org/viewtopic.php?f=9&t=10980). mozillaZine. May 16th, 2003. . Retrieved May 27, 2009.

[23] Masnick, Mike (July 7th 2008). "Microsoft Patents Adding 'www.' And '.com' To Text" (http://www.techdirt.com/articles/20080626/0203581527.shtml). Techdirt. . Retrieved May 27, 2009.

[24] http://news.bbc.co.uk/1/hi/technology/8306631.stm

[25] "MDBG Chinese-English dictionary - Translate" (http://us.mdbg.net/chindict/chindict.php?page=translate&trst=0&trqs=World+Wide+Web&trlang=&wddmtm=0). . Retrieved July 27, 2009.

[26] "Frequently asked questions by the Press - Tim BL" (http://www.w3.org/People/Berners-Lee/FAQ.html). W3.org. . Retrieved July 27, 2009.

[27] Hal Abelson, Ken Ledeen and Harry Lewis (April 14, 2008). "1–2" (http://www.bitsbook.com/). *Blown to Bits: Your Life, Liberty, and Happiness After the Digital Explosion.* Addison Wesley. ISBN 0-13-713559-9. . Retrieved November 6, 2008.

[28] comScore (August 12, 2008). "Social Networking Explodes Worldwide as Sites Increase their Focus on Cultural Relevance" (http://www.comscore.com/press/release.asp?press=2396). Press release. . Retrieved November 9, 2008.

[29] Amanda Lenhart and Mary Madden (April 18, 2007). "Teens, Privacy & Online Social Networks" (http://www.pewinternet.org/pdfs/PIP_Teens_Privacy_SNS_Report_Final.pdf) (PDF). Pew Internet & American Life Project. . Retrieved November 9, 2008.

[30] Schmidt, Eric (Google). (October 20, 2008). *Eric Schmidt at Bloomberg on the Future of Technology* (http://www.youtube.com/watch?v=rD_x9LW5QRg). New York, New York: YouTube. Event occurs at 16:30. . Retrieved November 9, 2008.

[31] Nussbaum, Emily (February 12, 2007). "Say Everything" (http://nymag.com/news/features/27341/). *New York* (New York Media). . Retrieved November 9, 2008.

[32] Wortham, Jenna (July 1, 2009). "Facebook Will Give Users More Control Over Who Sees What" (http://bits.blogs.nytimes.com/2009/07/01/facebook-will-give-users-more-control-over-who-sees-what/). The New York Times Company. . Retrieved July 1, 2009.

[33] Stone, Brad (March 28, 2009). "Is Facebook Growing Up Too Fast?" (http://www.nytimes.com/2009/03/29/technology/internet/29face.html?pagewanted=all). The New York Times. . and Lee Byron (Facebook) (March 28, 2009). "The Road to 200 Million" (http://www.nytimes.com/imagepages/2009/03/29/business/29face.graf01.ready.html). The New York Times. . Retrieved April 2, 2009.

[34] "30th International Conference of Data Protection and Privacy Commissioners" (http://www.privacyconference2008.org/pdf/press_final_en.pdf) (PDF). Press release. October 17, 2008. . Retrieved November 8, 2008.

[35] Cooper, Alissa (October 2008). "Browser Privacy Features: A Work In Progress" (http://www.cdt.org/privacy/20081022_browser_priv.pdf) (PDF). Center for Democracy and Technology. . Retrieved November 8, 2008.

[36] Joshua Gomez, Travis Pinnick, and Ashkan Soltani (June 1, 2009). "KnowPrivacy" (http://www.knowprivacy.org/report/KnowPrivacy_Final_Report.pdf) (PDF). University of California, Berkeley, School of Information. pp. 8–9. . Retrieved June 2, 2009.

[37] Daniel J. Weitzner, Harold Abelson, Tim Berners-Lee, Joan Feigenbaum, James Hendler, Gerald Jay Sussman (June 13, 2007). "Information Accountability" (http://hdl.handle.net/1721.1/37600). MIT Computer Science and Artificial Intelligence Laboratory. . Retrieved November 6, 2008.

[38] Story, Louise and comScore (March 10, 2008). "They Know More Than You Think" (http://www.nytimes.com/imagepages/2008/03/10/technology/20080310_PRIVACY_GRAPHIC.html) (JPEG). . in Story, Louise (March 10, 2008). "To Aim Ads, Web Is Keeping Closer Eye on You" (http://www.nytimes.com/2008/03/10/technology/10privacy.html). The New York Times (The New York Times Company). . Retrieved March 9, 2008.

[39] Christey, Steve and Martin, Robert A. (May 22, 2007). "Vulnerability Type Distributions in CVE (version 1.1)" (http://cwe.mitre.org/documents/vuln-trends/index.html). MITRE Corporation. . Retrieved June 7, 2008.

[40] "Symantec Internet Security Threat Report: Trends for July-December 2007 (Executive Summary)" (http://eval.symantec.com/mktginfo/enterprise/white_papers/b-whitepaper_exec_summary_internet_security_threat_report_xiii_04-2008.en-us.pdf) (PDF). Symantec Corp.. April 2008. pp. 1–2. . Retrieved May 11, 2008.

[41] "Google searches web's dark side" (http://news.bbc.co.uk/2/hi/technology/6645895.stm). BBC News. May 11, 2007. . Retrieved April 26, 2008.

[42] "Security Threat Report" (http://www.sophos.com/sophos/docs/eng/marketing_material/sophos-threat-report-Q108.pdf) (PDF). Sophos. Q1 2008. . Retrieved April 24, 2008.

[43] "Security threat report" (http://www.sophos.com/sophos/docs/eng/papers/sophos-security-report-jul08-srna.pdf) (PDF). Sophos. July 2008. . Retrieved August 24, 2008.

[44] Fogie, Seth, Jeremiah Grossman, Robert Hansen, and Anton Rager (2007) (PDF). Cross Site Scripting Attacks: XSS Exploits and Defense (http://www.syngress.com/book_catalog//SAMPLE_1597491543.pdf). Syngress, Elsevier Science & Technology. pp. 68–69, 127. ISBN 1597491543. . Retrieved June 6, 2008.

[45] O'Reilly, Tim (September 30, 2005). "What Is Web 2.0" (http://www.oreillynet.com/pub/a/oreilly/tim/news/2005/09/30/what-is-web-20.html). O'Reilly Media. pp. 4–5. . Retrieved June 4, 2008. and AJAX web applications can introduce security vulnerabilities like "client-side security controls, increased attack surfaces, and new possibilities for Cross-Site Scripting (XSS)", in Ritchie, Paul (March 2007). "The security risks of AJAX/web 2.0 applications" (http://www.infosecurity-magazine.com/research/Sep07_Ajax.pdf) (PDF). Infosecurity (Elsevier). . Retrieved June 6, 2008. which cites Hayre, Jaswinder S. and Kelath, Jayasankar (June 22, 2006). "Ajax Security Basics" (http://www.securityfocus.com/infocus/1868). SecurityFocus. . Retrieved June 6, 2008.

[46] Berinato, Scott (January 1, 2007). "Software Vulnerability Disclosure: The Chilling Effect" (http://www.csoonline.com/article/221113). CSO (CXO Media): p. 7. . Retrieved June 7, 2008.

[47] Prince, Brian (April 9, 2008). "McAfee Governance, Risk and Compliance Business Unit" (http://www.eweek.com/c/a/Security/McAfee-Governance-Risk-and-Compliance-Business-Unit/). eWEEK (Ziff Davis Enterprise Holdings). . Retrieved April 25, 2008.

[48] Ben-Itzhak, Yuval (April 18, 2008). "Infosecurity 2008 - New defence strategy in battle against e-crime" (http://www.computerweekly.com/Articles/2008/04/18/230345/infosecurity-2008-new-defence-strategy-in-battle-against.htm). ComputerWeekly (Reed Business Information). . Retrieved April 20, 2008.

[49] Preston, Rob (April 12, 2008). "Down To Business: It's Past Time To Elevate The Infosec Conversation" (http://www.informationweek.com/news/security/client/showArticle.jhtml?articleID=207100989). InformationWeek (United Business Media). . Retrieved April 25, 2008.

[50] Claburn, Thomas (February 6, 2007). "RSA's Coviello Predicts Security Consolidation" (http://www.informationweek.com/news/security/showArticle.jhtml?articleID=197003826). InformationWeek (United Business Media). . Retrieved April 25, 2008.

[51] Duffy Marsan, Carolyn (April 9, 2008). "How the iPhone is killing the 'Net" (http://www.networkworld.com/news/2008/040908-zittrain.html). Network World (IDG). . Retrieved April 17, 2008.

[52] "Web Accessibility Initiative (WAI)" (http://www.w3.org/WAI/l). World Wide Web Consortium. . Retrieved April 7, 2009.

[53] "Developing a Web Accessibility Business Case for Your Organization: Overview" (http://www.w3.org/WAI/bcase/Overviewl). World Wide Web Consortium. . Retrieved April 7, 2009.

[54] "Legal and Policy Factors in Developing a Web Accessibility Business Case for Your Organization" (http://www.w3.org/WAI/bcase/pol). World Wide Web Consortium. . Retrieved April 7, 2009.

[55] "Web Content Accessibility Guidelines (WCAG) Overview" (http://www.w3.org/WAI/intro/wcag.php). World Wide Web Consortium. . Retrieved April 7, 2009.

[56] "Internationalization (I18n) Activity" (http://www.w3.org/International/). World Wide Web Consortium. . Retrieved April 10, 2009.

[57] Davis, Mark (April 5, 2008). "Moving to Unicode 5.1" (http://googleblog.blogspot.com/2008/05/moving-to-unicode-51.html). Google. . Retrieved April 10, 2009.

[58] World Wide Web Consortium (January 26, 2005). "World Wide Web Consortium Supports the IETF URI Standard and IRI Proposed Standard" (http://www.w3.org/2004/11/uri-iri-pressrelease.html). Press release. . Retrieved April 10, 2009.

[59] "The 'Deep' Web: Surfacing Hidden Value" (http://www.brightplanet.com/resources/details/deepweb.html). Brightplanet.com. . Retrieved July 27, 2009.

[60] "Distribution of languages on the Internet" (http://www.netz-tipp.de/languages.html). Netz-tipp.de. . Retrieved July 27, 2009.

[61] Alessio Signorini. "Indexable Web Size" (http://www.cs.uiowa.edu/~asignori/web-size/). Cs.uiowa.edu. . Retrieved July 27, 2009.

[62] http://en.wikipedia.org/wiki/World_wide_web

[63] "The size of the World Wide Web" (http://www.worldwidewebsize.com/). Worldwidewebsize.com. . Retrieved July 27, 2009.

[64] Alpert, Jesse; Hajaj, Nissan (July 25, 2008). "We knew the web was big..." (http://googleblog.blogspot.com/2008/07/we-knew-web-was-big.html). *The Official Google Blog.* .

[65] "Domain Counts & Internet Statistics" (http://www.domaintools.com/internet-statistics/). Name Intelligence. . Retrieved May 17, 2009.

[66] "World Wide Wait" (http://www.techweb.com/encyclopedia/defineterm.jhtml?term=world+wide+wait). *TechEncyclopedia.* United Business Media. . Retrieved April 10, 2009.

[67] Khare, Rohit and Jacobs, Ian (1999). "W3C Recommendations Reduce 'World Wide Wait'" (http://www.w3.org/Protocols/NL-PerfNote.html). World Wide Web Consortium. . Retrieved April 10, 2009.

[68] Nielsen, Jakob (from Miller 1968; Card et al. 1991) (1994). "Usability Engineering:" (http://www.useit.com/papers/responsetime.html). Morgan Kaufmann. . Retrieved April 10, 2009.

[69] ftp://ftp.isi.edu/in-notes/rfc2616.txt

[70] http://www.w3.org/TR/webarch/

[71] http://newdevices.com/publicaciones/www/

[72] http://www.w3.org/History/19921103-hypertext/hypertext/WWW/

[73] http://www.mit.edu/people/mkgray/net/

[74] http://www.livinginternet.com/w/w.htm

[75] http://www.dmoz.org/Computers/Internet/Web_Design_and_Development/

[76] http://www.w3.org/

[77] http://www.worldwidewebsize.com/

[78] http://tofocus.info/english-internet-population.php

E-mail

Electronic mail, most commonly abbreviated **email** and **e-mail**, is a method of exchanging digital messages. E-mail systems are based on a store-and-forward model in which e-mail computer server systems accept, forward, deliver and store messages on behalf of users, who only need to connect to the e-mail infrastructure, typically an e-mail server, with a network-enabled device for the duration of message submission or retrieval. Originally, e-mail was always transmitted directly from one user's device to another's; nowadays this is rarely the case.

An electronic mail message consists of two components, the message *header*, and the message *body*, which is the email's content. The message header contains control information, including, minimally, an originator's email address and one or more recipient addresses. Usually additional information is added, such as a subject header field.

Originally a text-only communications medium, email was extended to carry multi-media content attachments, which were standardized in with RFC 2045 through RFC 2049, collectively called, Multipurpose Internet Mail Extensions (MIME).

The foundation for today's global Internet e-mail service was created in the early ARPANET and standards for encoding of messages were proposed as early as 1973 (RFC 561). An e-mail sent in the early 1970s looked very similar to one sent on the Internet today. Conversion from the ARPANET to the Internet in the early 1980s produced the core of the current service.

Network-based email was initially exchanged on the ARPANET in extensions to the File Transfer Protocol (FTP), but is today carried by the Simple Mail Transfer Protocol (SMTP), first published as Internet standard 10 (RFC 821) in 1982. In the process of transporting email messages between systems, SMTP communicates delivery parameters using a message *envelope* separately from the message (headers and body) itself.

Spelling

There are several spelling variations that are occasionally the cause of vehement disagreement.[1] [2]

email is the form officially required by IETF Request for Comments and working groups[3] and is also recognized in most dictionaries.[4] [5] [6] [7] [8] [9]

e-mail is a form still recommended by some prominent journalistic and technical style guides. [10] [11]

Less common forms include *eMail* and simply *mail*.

mail was the form used in the original RFC. The service is referred to as *mail* and a single piece of electronic mail is called a *message*.[12] [13] [14]

eMail, capitalizing only the letter *M*, was common among ARPANET users and early developers from Unix, CMS, AppleLink, eWorld, AOL, GEnie, and Hotmail.

EMail is a traditional form that has been used in RFCs for the "Author's Address"[13] [14] , and is expressly required "*...for historical reasons...*".[15]

Origin

Electronic mail predates the inception of the → Internet, and was in fact a crucial tool in creating the Internet.

MIT first demonstrated the Compatible Time-Sharing System (CTSS) in 1961.[16] It allowed multiple users to log into the IBM 7094[17] from remote dial-up terminals, and to store files online on disk. This new ability encouraged users to share information in new ways. E-mail started in 1965 as a way for multiple users of a time-sharing mainframe computer to communicate. Although the exact history is murky, among the first systems to have such a facility were SDC's Q32 and MIT's CTSS.

Host-based mailsystems

The original email systems allowed communication only between users who logged into the one host or "mainframe", but this could be hundreds or thousands of users within a company or university. By 1966 (or earlier, it is possible that the SAGE system had something similar some time before), such systems allowed email between different companies as long as they ran compatible operating systems, but not to other dissimilar systems.

Examples include BITNET, IBM PROFS, Digital All-in-1 and the original Unix mail.

LAN-based mailsystems

From the early 1980s networked personal computers on LANs became increasingly important - and server-based systems similar to the earlier mainframe systems developed, and again initially allowed communication only between users logged into the one server, but these also could generally be linked between different companies as long as they ran the same email system and (proprietary) protocol.

Examples include cc:Mail, WordPerfect Office, Microsoft Mail, Banyan VINES and Lotus Notes - with various vendors supplying gateway software to link these incompatible systems.

Attempts at Interoperability

- Novell briefly championed the open MHS protocol
- uucp was used as an open "glue" between differing mail systems
- The Coloured Book protocols on UK academic networks until 1992
- X.400 in the early 1990s was mandated for government use under GOSIP but almost immediately abandoned by all but a few — in favour of → Internet SMTP

The rise of ARPANET-based mail

The ARPANET computer network made a large contribution to the development of e-mail. There is one report that indicates experimental inter-system e-mail transfers began shortly after its creation in 1969.[18] Ray Tomlinson is credited by some as having sent the first email, initiating the use of the "@" sign to separate the names of the user and the user's machine in 1971, when he sent a message from one Digital Equipment Corporation DEC-10 computer to another DEC-10. The two machines were placed next to each other.[19] [20] The ARPANET significantly increased the popularity of e-mail, and it became the killer app of the ARPANET.

Most other networks had their own email protocols and address formats; as the influence of the ARPANET and later the Internet grew, central sites often hosted email gateways that passed mail between the Internet and these other networks. Internet email addressing is still complicated by the need to handle mail destined for these older networks. Some well-known examples of these were UUCP (mostly Unix computers), BITNET (mostly IBM and VAX mainframes at universities), FidoNet (personal computers), DECNET (various networks) and CSNet a forerunner of NSFNet.

An example of an Internet email address that routed mail to a user at a UUCP host:

```
hubhost!middlehost!edgehost!user@uucpgateway.somedomain.example.com
```

This was necessary because in early years UUCP computers did not maintain (or consult servers for) information about the location of all hosts they exchanged mail with, but rather only knew how to communicate with a few network neighbors; email messages (and other data such as Usenet News) were passed along in a chain among hosts who had explicitly agreed to share data with each other.

Operation overview

The diagram to the right shows a typical sequence of events[21] that takes place when Alice composes a message using her mail user agent (MUA). She enters the e-mail address of her correspondent, and hits the "send" button.

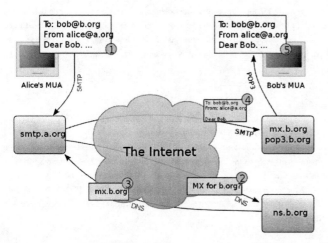

1. Here MUA formats the message in e-mail format and uses the Simple Mail Transfer Protocol (SMTP) to send the message to the local mail transfer agent (MTA), in this case smtp.a.org, run by Alice's Internet Service Provider (ISP).

2. The MTA looks at the destination address provided in the SMTP protocol (not from the message header), in this case bob@b.org. An Internet e-mail address is a string of the form localpart@exampledomain. The part before the @ sign is the **local part** of the address, often the username of the recipient, and the part after the @ sign is a domain name or a fully qualified domain name. The MTA resolves a domain name to determine the fully qualified domain name of the mail exchange server in the Domain Name System.

3. The DNS server for the b.org domain, ns.b.org, responds with any MX records listing the mail exchange servers for that domain, in this case mx.b.org, a server run by Bob's ISP.

4. smtp.a.org sends the message to mx.b.org using SMTP, which delivers it to the mailbox of the user bob.

5. Bob presses the "get mail" button in his MUA, which picks up the message using the Post Office Protocol (POP3).

That sequence of events applies to the majority of e-mail users. However, there are many alternative possibilities and complications to the e-mail system:

- Alice or Bob may use a client connected to a corporate e-mail system, such as IBM Lotus Notes or Microsoft Exchange. These systems often have their own internal e-mail format and their clients typically communicate with the e-mail server using a vendor-specific, proprietary protocol. The server sends or receives e-mail via the Internet through the product's Internet mail gateway which also does any necessary reformatting. If Alice and Bob work for the same company, the entire transaction may happen completely within a single corporate e-mail system.

- Alice may not have a MUA on her computer but instead may connect to a webmail service.

- Alice's computer may run its own MTA, so avoiding the transfer at step 1.

- Bob may pick up his e-mail in many ways, for example using the Internet Message Access Protocol, by logging into mx.b.org and reading it directly, or by using a webmail service.

- Domains usually have several mail exchange servers so that they can continue to accept mail when the main mail exchange server is not available.

- E-mail messages are not secure if e-mail encryption is not used correctly.

Many MTAs used to accept messages for any recipient on the Internet and do their best to deliver them. Such MTAs are called *open mail relays*. This was very important in the early days of the Internet when network connections were unreliable. If an MTA couldn't reach the destination, it could at least deliver it to a relay closer to the destination. The relay stood a better chance of delivering the message at a later time. However, this mechanism proved to be exploitable by people sending unsolicited bulk e-mail and as a consequence very few modern MTAs are open mail relays, and many MTAs don't accept messages from open mail relays because such messages are very likely to be spam.

Message format

The Internet e-mail message format is defined in RFC 5322 and a series of RFCs, RFC 2045 through RFC 2049, collectively called, *Multipurpose Internet Mail Extensions*, or *MIME*. Although as of July 13, 2005, RFC 2822 is technically a proposed IETF standard and the MIME RFCs are draft IETF standards,[22] these documents are the standards for the format of Internet e-mail. Prior to the introduction of RFC 2822 in 2001, the format described by RFC 822 was the standard for Internet e-mail for nearly 20 years; it is still the official IETF standard. The IETF reserved the numbers 5321 and 5322 for the updated versions of RFC 2821 (SMTP) and RFC 2822, as it previously did with RFC 821 and RFC 822, honoring the extreme importance of these two RFCs. RFC 822 was published in 1982 and based on the earlier RFC 733 (see[23]).

Internet e-mail messages consist of two major sections:

- Header — Structured into fields such as summary, sender, receiver, and other information about the e-mail.
- Body — The message itself as unstructured text; sometimes containing a signature block at the end. This is exactly the same as the body of a regular letter.

The header is separated from the body by a blank line.

Message header

Each message has exactly one header, which is structured into fields. Each field has a name and a value. RFC 5322 specifies the precise syntax.

Informally, each line of text in the header that begins with a printable character begins a separate field. The field name starts in the first character of the line and ends before the separator character ":". The separator is then followed by the field value (the "body" of the field). The value is continued onto subsequent lines if those lines have a space or tab as their first character. Field names and values are restricted to 7-bit ASCII characters. Non-ASCII values may be represented using MIME encoded words.

Header fields

The message header should include at least the following fields:

- From: The e-mail address, and optionally the name of the author(s). In many e-mail clients not changeable except through changing account settings.
- To: The e-mail address(es), and optionally name(s) of the message's recipient(s). Indicates primary recipients (multiple allowed), for secondary recipients see Cc: and Bcc: below.
- Subject: A brief summary of the topic of the message. Certain abbreviations are commonly used in the subject, some of which are automatically inserted by the e-mail client, including Re: ("[in] the matter of"), FW: (forward), FYI: (for your information), I: (information), and EOM (end of message, used at the end of the subject when the entire content of the e-mail is contained in the subject and the body remains empty).
- Date: The local time and date when the message was written. Like the *From:* field, many email clients fill this in automatically when sending. The recipient's client may then display the time in the format and time zone local to her.
- Message-ID: Also an automatically generated field; used to prevent multiple delivery and for reference in In-Reply-To: (see below).

Note that the "To:" field is not necessarily related to the addresses to which the message is delivered. The actual delivery list is supplied separately to the transport protocol, SMTP, which may or may not originally have been extracted from the header content. The "To:" field is similar to the addressing at the top of a conventional letter which is delivered according to the address on the outer envelope. Also note that the "From:" field does not have to be the real sender of the e-mail message. One reason is that it is very easy to fake the "From:" field and let a message seem to be from any mail address. It is possible to digitally sign e-mail, which is much harder to fake, but such signatures require extra programming and often external programs to verify. Some Internet service providers do not relay e-mail claiming to come from a domain not hosted by them, but very few (if any) check to make sure that the person or even e-mail address named in the "From:" field is the one associated with the connection. Some Internet service providers apply e-mail authentication systems to e-mail being sent through their MTA to allow other MTAs to detect forged spam that might appear to come from them.

RFC 3864 describes registration procedures for message header fields at the IANA; it provides for permanent [24] and provisional [25] message header field names, including also fields defined for MIME, netnews, and http, and referencing relevant RFCs. Common header fields for email include:

- Bcc: Blind Carbon Copy; addresses added to the SMTP delivery list but not (usually) listed in the message data, remaining invisible to other recipients.
- Cc: Carbon copy; Many e-mail clients will mark e-mail in your inbox differently depending on whether you are in the To: or Cc: list.
- Content-Type: Information about how the message is to be displayed, usually a MIME type.
- In-Reply-To: Message-ID of the message that this is a reply to. Used to link related messages together.
- Precedence: commonly with values "bulk", "junk", or "list"; used to indicate that automated "vacation" or "out of office" responses should not be returned for this mail, eg. to prevent vacation notices from being sent to all other subscribers of a mailinglist.
- Received: Tracking information generated by mail servers that have previously handled a message, in reverse order (last handler first).
- References: Message-ID of the message that this is a reply to, and the message-id of the message the previous was reply a reply to, etc.
- Reply-To: Address that should be used to reply to the message.
- Sender: Address of the actual sender acting on behalf of the author listed in the From: field (secretary, list manager, etc.).
- X-Face: Small icon.

Message body

Content encoding

E-mail was originally designed for 7-bit ASCII.[26] Much e-mail software is 8-bit clean but must assume it will communicate with 8-bit servers and mail readers. The MIME standard introduced character set specifiers and two content transfer encodings to enable transmission of non-ASCII data: quoted printable for mostly 7 bit content with a few characters outside that range and base64 for arbitrary binary data. The 8BITMIME extension was introduced to allow transmission of mail without the need for these encodings but many mail transport agents still do not support it fully. In some countries, several encoding schemes coexist; as the result, by default, the message in a non-Latin alphabet language appears in non-readable form (the only exception is coincidence, when the sender and receiver use the same encoding scheme). Therefore, for international character sets, Unicode is growing in popularity.

Plain text and HTML

Most modern graphic e-mail clients allow the use of either plain text or HTML for the message body at the option of the user. HTML e-mail messages often include an automatically-generated plain text copy as well, for compatibility reasons.

Advantages of HTML include the ability to include inline links and images, set apart previous messages in block quotes, wrap naturally on any display, use emphasis such as underlines and italics, and change font styles. Disadvantages include the increased size of the email, privacy concerns about web bugs, abuse of HTML email as a vector for phishing attacks and the spread of malicious software.[27]

Mailing lists commonly insist that all posts to be made in plain-text[28] [29] [30] for all the above reasons, but also because they have a significant number of readers using text-based e-mail clients such as Mutt.

Some Microsoft e-mail clients have allowed richer formatting by using RTF rather than HTML, but unless the recipient is guaranteed to have a compatible e-mail client this should be avoided.[31]

Servers and client applications

Messages are exchanged between hosts using the Simple Mail Transfer Protocol with software programs called mail transfer agents. Users can retrieve their messages from servers using standard protocols such as POP or IMAP, or, as is more likely in a large corporate environment, with a proprietary protocol specific to Lotus Notes or Microsoft Exchange Servers. Webmail interfaces allow users to access their mail with any standard web browser, from any computer, rather than relying on an e-mail client.

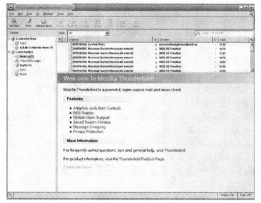

The interface of an e-mail client, Thunderbird.

Mail can be stored on the client, on the server side, or in both places. Standard formats for mailboxes include Maildir and mbox. Several prominent e-mail clients use their own proprietary format and require conversion software to transfer e-mail between them.

Accepting a message obliges an MTA to deliver it, and when a message cannot be delivered, that MTA must send a bounce message back to the sender, indicating the problem.

Filename extensions

Upon reception of e-mail messages, e-mail client applications save message in operating system files in the filesystem. Some clients save individual messages as separate files, while others use various database formats, often proprietary, for collective storage. A historical standard of storage is the *mbox* format. The specific format used is often indicated by special filename extensions:

`.eml`

> Used by many e-mail clients including Microsoft Outlook Express, Windows Mail and Mozilla Thunderbird.[32] The files are plain text in MIME format, containing the e-mail header as well as the message contents and attachments in one or more of several formats.

`.emlx`

> Used by Apple Mail.

`.msg`

> Used by Microsoft Office Outlook.

`.mbx`

> Used by Opera Mail, KMail, and Apple Mail based on the mbox format.

Some applications (like Apple Mail) also encode attachments into messages for searching while also producing a physical copy of the files on a disk. Others separate attachments from messages by depositing them into designated folders on disk.

URI scheme *mailto:*

The URI scheme, as registered with the IANA, defines the `mailto:` scheme for SMTP email addresses. Though its use is not strictly defined, URLs of this form are intended to be used to open the new message window of the user's mail client when the URL is activated, with the address as defined by the URL in the "To:" field. [33]

Use

In society

There are numerous ways in which people have changed the way they communicate in the last 50 years; e-mail is certainly one of them. Traditionally, social interaction in the local community was the basis for communication – face to face. Yet, today face-to-face meetings are no longer the primary way to communicate as one can use a landline telephone, mobile phones, fax services, or any number of the computer mediated communications such as e-mail.

Research has shown that people actively use e-mail to maintain core social networks, particularly when others live at a distance. However, contradictory to previous research, the results suggest that increases in Internet usage are associated with decreases in other modes of communication, with proficiency of Internet and e-mail use serving as a mediating factor in this relationship.[34] With the introduction of chat messengers and video conference there are more ways to communicate.

Flaming

Flaming occurs when a person sends a message with angry or antagonistic content. Flaming is assumed to be more common today because of the ease and impersonality of e-mail communications: confrontations in person or via telephone require direct interaction, where social norms encourage civility, whereas typing a message to another person is an indirect interaction, so civility may be forgotten. Flaming is generally looked down upon by Internet communities as it is considered rude and non-productive.

E-mail bankruptcy

Also known as "e-mail fatigue", e-mail bankruptcy is when a user ignores a large number of e-mail messages after falling behind in reading and answering them. The reason for falling behind is often due to information overload and a general sense there is so much information that it is not possible to read it all. As a solution, people occasionally send a boilerplate message explaining that the e-mail inbox is being cleared out. Stanford University law professor Lawrence Lessig is credited with coining this term, but he may only have popularized it.[35]

In business

E-mail was widely accepted by the business community as the first broad electronic communication medium and was the first 'e-revolution' in business communication. E-mail is very simple to understand and like postal mail, e-mail solves two basic problems of communication: logistics and synchronization (see below). LAN based email is also an emerging form of usage for business. It not only allows the business user to download mail when *offline*, it also provides the small business user to have multiple users e-mail ID's with just *one e-mail connection.*

Pros

- **The problem of logistics**

Much of the business world relies upon communications between people who are not physically in the same building, area or even country; setting up and attending an in-person meeting, telephone call, or conference call can be inconvenient, time-consuming, and costly. E-mail provides a way to exchange information between two or more people with no set-up costs and that is generally far less expensive than physical meetings or phone calls.

- **The problem of synchronization**

With real time communication by meetings or phone calls, participants have to work on the same schedule, and each participant must spend the same amount of time in the meeting or call. E-mail allows asynchrony: each participant may control their schedule independently.

Cons

Most business workers today spend from one to two hours of their working day on e-mail: reading, ordering, sorting, 're-contextualizing' fragmented information, and writing e-mail.[36] The use of e-mail is increasing due to increasing levels of globalization—labour division and outsourcing amongst other things. E-mail can lead to some well-known problems:

- **Loss of Context**: which means that the context is lost forever; there is no way to get the text back.

Information in context (as in a newspaper) is much easier and faster to understand than unedited and sometimes unrelated fragments of information. Communicating in context can only be achieved when both parties have a full understanding of the context and issue in question.

- **Information overload**: E-mail is a push technology—the sender controls who receives the information. Convenient availability of mailing lists and use of "copy all" can lead to people receiving unwanted or irrelevant information of no use to them.
- **Inconsistency**: E-mail can duplicate information. This can be a problem when a large team is working on documents and information while not in constant contact with the other members of their team.

Despite these disadvantages, e-mail has become the most widely used medium of communication within the business world.

Problems

Information overload

A December 2007 New York Times blog post described E-mail as "a $650 Billion Drag on the Economy",[37] and the New York Times reported in April 2008 that "E-MAIL has become the bane of some people's professional lives" due to information overload, yet "none of the current wave of high-profile Internet start-ups focused on e-mail really eliminates the problem of e-mail overload because none helps us prepare replies".[38]

Technology investors reflect similar concerns.[39]

Spamming and computer viruses

The usefulness of e-mail is being threatened by four phenomena: e-mail bombardment, spamming, phishing, and e-mail worms.

Spamming is unsolicited commercial (or bulk) e-mail. Because of the very low cost of sending e-mail, spammers can send hundreds of millions of e-mail messages each day over an inexpensive Internet connection. Hundreds of active spammers sending this volume of mail results in information overload for many computer users who receive voluminous unsolicited e-mail each day.[40] [41]

E-mail worms use e-mail as a way of replicating themselves into vulnerable computers. Although the first e-mail worm affected UNIX computers, the problem is most common today on the more popular Microsoft Windows operating system.

The combination of spam and worm programs results in users receiving a constant drizzle of junk e-mail, which reduces the usefulness of e-mail as a practical tool.

A number of anti-spam techniques mitigate the impact of spam. In the United States, U.S. Congress has also passed a law, the Can Spam Act of 2003, attempting to regulate such e-mail. Australia also has very strict spam laws restricting the sending of spam from an Australian ISP,[42] but its impact has been minimal since most spam comes from regimes that seem reluctant to regulate the sending of spam.

E-mail spoofing

E-mail spoofing occurs when the header information of an email is altered to make the message appear to come from a known or trusted source. It is often used as a ruse to collect personal information.

E-mail bombing

E-mail bombing is the intentional sending of large volumes of messages to a target address. The overloading of the target email address can render it unusable and can even cause the mail server to crash.

Privacy concerns

E-mail privacy, without some security precautions, can be compromised because:

- e-mail messages are generally not encrypted;
- e-mail messages have to go through intermediate computers before reaching their destination, meaning it is relatively easy for others to intercept and read messages;
- many Internet Service Providers (ISP) store copies of e-mail messages on their mail servers before they are delivered. The backups of these can remain for up to several months on their server, despite deletion from the mailbox;
- the Received: fields and other information in the e-mail can often identify the sender, preventing anonymous communication.

There are cryptography applications that can serve as a remedy to one or more of the above. For example, Virtual Private Networks or the Tor anonymity network can be used to encrypt traffic from the user machine to a safer network while GPG, PGP, SMEmail [43] , or S/MIME can be used for end-to-end message encryption, and SMTP STARTTLS or SMTP over Transport Layer Security/Secure Sockets Layer can be used to encrypt communications for a single mail hop between the SMTP client and the SMTP server.

Additionally, many mail user agents do not protect logins and passwords, making them easy to intercept by an attacker. Encrypted authentication schemes such as SASL prevent this.

Finally, attached files share many of the same hazards as those found in peer-to-peer filesharing. Attached files may contain trojans or viruses.

Tracking of sent mail

The original SMTP mail service provides limited mechanisms for tracking a transmitted message, and none for verifying that it has been delivered or read. It requires that each mail server must either deliver it onward or return a failure notice (bounce message), but both software bugs and system failures can cause messages to be lost. To remedy this, the IETF introduced Delivery Status Notifications (delivery receipts) and Message Disposition Notifications (return receipts); however, these are not universally deployed in production.

US Government

The US Government has been involved in e-mail in several different ways.

Starting in 1977, the US Postal Service (USPS) recognized that electronic mail and electronic transactions posed a significant threat to First Class mail volumes and revenue. Therefore, the USPS initiated an experimental e-mail service known as E-COM. Electronic messages were transmitted to a post office, printed out, and delivered as hard copy. To take advantage of the service, an individual had to transmit at least 200 messages. The delivery time of the messages was the same as First Class mail and cost 26 cents. Both the Postal Regulatory Commission and the Federal Communications Commission opposed E-COM. The FCC concluded that E-COM constituted common carriage under its jurisdiction and the USPS would have to file a tariff.[44] Three years after initiating the service, USPS canceled E-COM and attempted to sell it off.[45] [46] [47] [48] [49] [50] [51]

The early ARPANET dealt with multiple e-mail clients that had various, and at times incompatible, formats. For example, in the system Multics, the "@" sign meant "kill line" and anything after the "@" sign was ignored.[52] The Department of Defense DARPA desired to have uniformity and interoperability for e-mail and therefore funded efforts to drive towards unified interoperable standards. This led to David Crocker, John Vittal, Kenneth Pogran, and Austin Henderson publishing RFC 733, "Standard for the Format of ARPA Network Text Message" (November 21, 1977), which was apparently not effective. In 1979, a meeting was held at BBN to resolve incompatibility issues. Jon Postel recounted the meeting in RFC 808, "Summary of Computer Mail Services Meeting Held at BBN on 10 January 1979" (March 1, 1982), which includes an appendix listing the varying e-mail systems at the time. This, in turn, lead to the release of David Crocker's RFC 822, "Standard for the Format of ARPA Internet Text Messages" (August 13, 1982).[53]

The National Science Foundation took over operations of the ARPANET and Internet from the Department of Defense, and initiated NSFNet, a new backbone for the network. A part of the NSFNet AUP forbade commercial traffic.[54] In 1988, Vint Cerf arranged for an interconnection of MCI Mail with NSFNET on an experimental basis. The following year Compuserve e-mail interconnected with NSFNET. Within a few years the commercial traffic restriction was removed from NSFNETs AUP, and NSFNET was privatized.

In the late 1990s, the Federal Trade Commission grew concerned with fraud transpiring in e-mail, and initiated a series of procedures on spam, fraud, and phishing.[55] In 2004, FTC jurisdiction over spam was codified into law in the form of the CAN SPAM Act.[56] Several other US Federal Agencies have also exercised jurisdiction including the Department of Justice and the Secret Service.

See also

Enhancements

- E-mail encryption
- HTML e-mail
- Internet fax
- L- or letter mail, e-mail letter and letter e-mail
- Mule (e-mail)
- Privacy-enhanced Electronic Mail
- Push e-mail
- Google Wave

E-mail social issues

- Anti-spam techniques (e-mail)
- Computer virus
- CompuServe (first consumer service)
- E-card
- E-mail art
- E-mail jamming
- E-mail spam
- E-mail spoofing
- E-mail storm
- Information overload
- Internet humor
- Internet slang
- Netiquette
- Reply All
- Usenet quoting

Clients and servers

- Biff
- E-mail address
- E-mail authentication
- E-mail client, Comparison of e-mail clients
- E-mail hosting service
- Internet mail standards
- Mail transfer agent
- Mail user agent
- Unicode and e-mail
- Webmail

Mailing list

- Anonymous remailer
- Disposable e-mail address
- E-mail encryption
- E-mail tracking
- Electronic mailing list
- Mailer-Daemon
- Mailing list archive

Protocols

- IMAP
- POP3
- SMTP
- UUCP
- X400

External links

- IANA's list of standard header fields [24]
- The History of Electronic Mail [57] is a personal memoir by the implementer of an early e-mail system

References

[1] *"A Matter of (Wired News) Style"*, Tony Long, Wired magazine, 23 October 2000 (http://www.nettime.org/Lists-Archives/ nettime-bold-0010/msg00471.html)

[2] *"Readers on (Wired News) Style"*, Wired magazine, 24 October 2000 (http://www.wired.com/culture/lifestyle/news/2000/10/39651)

[3] "RFC Editor Terms List" (http://www.rfc-editor.org/rfc-style-guide/terms-online-03.txt). IETF. .

[4] AskOxford Language Query team. "What is the correct way to spell 'e' words such as 'email', 'ecommerce', 'egovernment'?" (http://www. askoxford.com/asktheexperts/faq/aboutspelling/email). *FAQ*. Oxford University Press. . Retrieved 4 September 2009. "We recommend email, as this is now by far the most common form"

[5] Reference.com (http://dictionary.reference.com/browse/email)

[6] Random House Unabridged Dictionary, 2006

[7] The American Heritage Dictionary of the English Language, Fourth Edition

[8] Princeton University WordNet 3.0

[9] The American Heritage Science Dictionary, 2002

[10] Microsoft Corporation Editorial Style Board (November 12, 2003). "Microsoft Manual of Style for Technical Publications Third Edition" (http://safari.oreilly.com/0735617465). Microsoft Press. . Retrieved 4 September 2009. "At Microsoft CD-ROM as a general term has become CD and blog has entered our vocabulary. E-mail, however, is still e-mail."

[11] APStylebook.com (http://www.apstylebook.com/ask_editor.php)

[12] RFC 821 (rfc821) - Simple Mail Transfer Protocol (http://www.faqs.org/rfcs/rfc821.html)

[13] RFC 1939 (rfc1939) - Post Office Protocol - Version 3 (http://www.faqs.org/rfcs/rfc1939.html)

[14] RFC 3501 (rfc3501) - Internet Message Access Protocol - version 4rev1 (http://www.faqs.org/rfcs/rfc3501.html)

[15] *"RFC Style Guide"*, Table of decisions on consistent usage in RFC (http://www.rfc-editor.org/rfc-style-guide/terms-online-03.txt)

[16] "CTSS, Compatible Time-Sharing System" (September 4, 2006), University of South Alabama, web: USA-CTSS (http://www.cis. usouthal.edu/faculty/daigle/project1/ctss.htm).

[17] Tom Van Vleck, "The IBM 7094 and CTSS" (September 10, 2004), *Multicians.org* (Multics), web: Multicians-7094 (http://www. multicians.org/thvv/7094.html).

[18] The History of Electronic Mail (http://www.multicians.org/thvv/mail-history.html)

[19] The First Email (http://openmap.bbn.com/~tomlinso/ray/firstemailframe.html)

[20] Wave New World,Time Magazine, October 19, 2009, p.48

[21] *How E-mail Works* (http://www.webcastr.com/videos/informational/how-email-works.html). [internet video]. howstuffworks.com. 2008. .

[22] "RFC Index" (http://www.ietf.org/iesg/1rfc_index.txt). .

[23] Ken Simpson, "An update to the email standards" (October 3, 2008), *blog.mailchannels.com*, web: MailChannels Blog Entry (http://blog. mailchannels.com/2008/10/update-to-email-standards.html).

[24] http://www.iana.org/assignments/message-headers/perm-headers.html

[25] http://www.iana.org/assignments/message-headers/prov-headers.html

[26] Craig Hunt (2002). *TCP/IP Network Administration*. O'Reilly Media. pp. 70. ISBN 978-0596002978.

[27] "Email policies that prevent viruses" (http://advosys.ca/papers/mail-policies.html). .

[28] "When posting to a RootsWeb mailing list..." (http://helpdesk.rootsweb.com/listadmins/plaintext.html)

[29] "...Plain text, 72 characters per line..." (http://www.openbsd.org/mail.html)

[30] "What is wrong with sending HTML or MIME messages?" (http://www.expita.com/nomime.html)

[31] How to Prevent the Winmail.dat File from Being Sent to Internet Users (http://support.microsoft.com/kb/138053)

[32] "File Extension .EML Details" (http://filext.com/file-extension/EML). *FILExt - The File Extension Source*. . Retrieved 2009-09-26.

[33] RFC 2368 section 3 : by Paul Hoffman in 1998 discusses operation of the "mailto" URL.

[34] Stern, Michael J.Information, Communication & Society; Oct2008, Vol. 11 Issue 5, p591-616, 26p. CLB Oklahoma State University, Stillwater, OK, USA.

[35] "All We Are Saying." (http://www.nytimes.com/2007/12/23/weekinreview/23buzzwords.html?ref=weekinreview). New York Times. December 23, 2007. . Retrieved 2007-12-24.

[36] "Email Right to Privacy - Why Small Businesses Care" (http://www.smallbiztrends.com/2007/06/email-has-right-to-privacy-why-small-businesses-care.html). Anita Campbell. 2007-06-19. .

[37] "Is Information Overload a $650 Billion Drag on the Economy?" (http://bits.blogs.nytimes.com/2007/12/20/is-information-overload-a-650-billion-drag-on-the-economy). New York Times. 2007-12-20. .

[38] "Struggling to Evade the E-Mail Tsunami" (http://www.nytimes.com/2008/04/20/technology/20digi.html?_r=2&oref=slogin&oref=slogin). New York Times. 2008-04-20. .

[39] "Did Darwin Skip Over Email?" (http://www.foundrygroup.com/blog/archives/2008/04/did-darwin-skip-over-email.php). Foundry Group. 2008-04-28. .

[40] ITVibe news, 2006, january 02, http://itvibe.com/news/3837/

[41] avalanche of Viagra ads and Rolex pitches http://dir.salon.com/story/tech/feature/2005/01/19/microsoft_spam/index.html

[42] "Spam Bill 2003" (http://www.aph.gov.au/library/pubs/bd/2003-04/04bd045.pdf) (PDF). .

[43] Mohsen Toorani, SMEmail - A New Protocol for the Secure E-mail in Mobile Environments (http://ieeexplore.ieee.org/xpl/freeabs_all.jsp?arnumber=4783292), Proceedings of the Australian Telecommunications Networks and Applications Conference (ATNAC'08), pp.39-44, Adelaide, Australia, December 2008.

[44] In re Request for declaratory ruling and investigation by Graphnet Systems, Inc., concerning the proposed E-COM service, FCC Docket No. 79-6 (September 4, 1979)

[45] History of the United States Postal Service, USPS (http://www.usps.com/history/history/his1.htm)

[46] Hardy, Ian R; The Evolution of ARPANET Email; 1996-05-13; History Thesis; University of California at Berkeley

[47] James Bovard, The Law Dinosaur: The US Postal Service, CATO Policy Analysis (February 1985)

[48] Jay Akkad, The History of Email (http://www.cs.ucsb.edu/~almeroth/classes/F04.176A/homework1_good_papers/jay-akkad.html)

[49] Cybertelecom : Email (http://www.cybertelecom.org/notes/email.htm)

[50] US Postal Service: Postal Activities and Laws Related to Electronic Commerce, GAO-00-188 (http://www.gao.gov/archive/2000/gg00188.pdf)

[51] Implications of Electronic Mail and Message Systems for the U.S. Postal Service , Office of Technology Assessment, Congress of the United States, August 1982 (http://govinfo.library.unt.edu/ota/Ota_4/DATA/1982/8214.PDF)

[52] Jay Akkad, The History of Email (http://www.cs.ucsb.edu/~almeroth/classes/F04.176A/homework1_good_papers/jay-akkad.html)

[53] Email History, How Email was Invented , Living Internet (http://www.livinginternet.com/e/ei.htm)

[54] Cybertelecom : Internet History (http://www.cybertelecom.org/notes/internet_history80s.htm)

[55] Cybertelecom : SPAM Reference (http://www.cybertelecom.org/spam/Spamref.htm)

[56] Cybertelecom : Can Spam Act (http://www.cybertelecom.org/spam/canspam.htm)

[57] http://www.multicians.org/thvv/mail-history.html

Internet

The **Internet** is a global system of interconnected computer networks that use the standard Internet Protocol Suite (TCP/IP) to serve billions of users worldwide. It is a *network of networks* that consists of millions of private and public, academic, business, and government networks of local to global scope that are linked by a broad array of electronic and optical networking technologies. The Internet carries a vast array of information resources and services, most notably the inter-linked hypertext documents of the → World Wide Web (WWW) and the infrastructure to support → electronic mail.

Most traditional communications media, such as telephone and television services, are reshaped or redefined using the technologies of the Internet, giving rise to services such as Voice over Internet

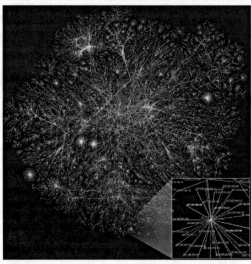

Visualization of the various routes through a portion of the Internet

Protocol (VoIP) and IPTV. Newspaper publishing has been reshaped into Web sites, blogging, and web feeds. The Internet has enabled or accelerated the creation of new forms of human interactions through instant messaging, Internet forums, and social networking sites.

The origins of the Internet reach back to the 1960s when the United States funded research projects of its military agencies to build robust, fault-tolerant and distributed computer networks. This research and a period of civilian funding of a new U.S. backbone by the National Science Foundation spawned worldwide participation in the development of new networking technologies and led to the commercialization of an international network in the mid 1990s, and resulted in the following popularization of countless applications in virtually every aspect of modern human life. As of 2009, an estimated quarter of Earth's population uses the services of the Internet.

The Internet has no centralized governance in either technological implementation or policies for access and usage; each constituent network sets its own standards. Only the overreaching definitions of the two principal name spaces in the Internet, the Internet Protocol address space and the Domain Name System, are directed by a maintainer organization, the Internet Corporation for Assigned Names and Numbers (ICANN). The technical underpinning and standardization of the core protocols (IPv4 and IPv6) is an activity of the Internet Engineering Task Force (IETF), a non-profit organization of loosely-affiliated international participants that anyone may associate with by contributing technical expertise.

Terminology

The terms *Internet* and *World Wide Web* are often used in everyday speech without much distinction. However, the Internet and the → World Wide Web are not one and the same. The Internet is a global data communications system. It is a hardware and software infrastructure that provides connectivity between computers. In contrast, the Web is one of the services communicated via the Internet. It is a collection of interconnected documents and other resources, linked by hyperlinks and URLs.[1] The term *the Internet*, when referring to *the* Internet, has traditionally been treated as a proper noun and written with an initial capital letter. There is a trend to regard it as a generic term or common noun and thus write it as "the internet", without the capital.

History

The USSR's launch of Sputnik spurred the United States to create the Advanced Research Projects Agency (ARPA or DARPA) in February 1958 to regain a technological lead.[2] [3] ARPA created the Information Processing Technology Office (IPTO) to further the research of the Semi Automatic Ground Environment (SAGE) program, which had networked country-wide radar systems together for the first time. J. C. R. Licklider was selected to head the IPTO. Licklider moved from the Psycho-Acoustic Laboratory at Harvard University to MIT in 1950, after becoming interested in information technology. At MIT, he served on a committee that established Lincoln Laboratory and worked on the SAGE project. In 1957 he became a Vice President at BBN, where he bought the first production PDP-1 computer and conducted the first public demonstration of time-sharing.

Professor Leonard Kleinrock with one of the first ARPANET Interface Message Processors at UCLA

At the IPTO, Licklider got Lawrence Roberts to start a project to make a network, and Roberts based the technology on the work of Paul Baran,[4] who had written an exhaustive study for the United States Air Force that recommended packet switching (opposed to circuit switching) to achieve better network robustness and disaster survivability. UCLA professor Leonard Kleinrock had provided the theoretical foundations for packet networks in 1962, and later, in the 1970s, for hierarchical routing, concepts which have been the underpinning of the development towards today's Internet.

After much work, the first two nodes of what would become the ARPANET were interconnected between UCLA's School of Engineering and Applied Science and SRI International (SRI) in Menlo Park, California, on October 29, 1969. The ARPANET was one of the "eve" networks of today's Internet. Following the demonstration that packet switching worked on the ARPANET, the British Post Office, Telenet, DATAPAC and TRANSPAC collaborated to create the first international packet-switched network service. In the UK, this was referred to as the International Packet Switched Service (IPSS), in 1978. The collection of X.25-based networks grew from Europe and the US to cover Canada, Hong Kong and Australia by 1981. The X.25 packet switching standard was developed in the CCITT (now called ITU-T) around 1976.

X.25 was independent of the TCP/IP protocols that arose from the experimental work of DARPA on the ARPANET, Packet Radio Net and Packet Satellite Net during the same time period. Vinton Cerf and Robert Kahn developed the first description of the TCP protocols during 1973 and published a paper on the subject in May 1974. Use of the term "Internet" to describe a single global TCP/IP network originated in December 1974 with the publication of RFC 675, the first full specification of TCP that was written by Vinton Cerf, Yogen Dalal and Carl Sunshine, then at Stanford University. During the next nine years, work proceeded to refine the protocols and to implement them on a wide range of operating systems. The first TCP/IP-based wide-area network was operational by January 1, 1983 when all hosts on the ARPANET were switched over from the older NCP protocols. In 1985, the United States' National Science Foundation (NSF) commissioned the construction of the NSFNET, a university 56 kilobit/second network backbone using computers called "fuzzballs" by their

A plaque commemorating the birth of the Internet at Stanford University

inventor, David L. Mills. The following year, NSF sponsored the conversion to a higher-speed 1.5 megabit/second network. A key decision to use the DARPA TCP/IP protocols was made by Dennis Jennings, then in charge of the Supercomputer program at NSF.

The opening of the network to commercial interests began in 1988. The US Federal Networking Council approved the interconnection of the NSFNET to the commercial MCI Mail system in that year and the link was made in the summer of 1989. Other commercial electronic e-mail services were soon connected, including OnTyme, Telemail and Compuserve. In that same year, three commercial Internet service providers (ISPs) were created: UUNET, PSINet and CERFNET. Important, separate networks that offered gateways into, then later merged with, the Internet include Usenet and BITNET. Various other commercial and educational networks, such as Telenet, Tymnet, Compuserve and JANET were interconnected with the growing Internet. Telenet (later called Sprintnet) was a large privately funded national computer network with free dial-up access in cities throughout the U.S. that had been in operation since the 1970s. This network was eventually interconnected with the others in the 1980s as the TCP/IP protocol became increasingly popular. The ability of TCP/IP to work over virtually any pre-existing communication networks allowed for a great ease of growth, although the rapid growth of the Internet was due primarily to the availability of an array of standardized commercial routers from many companies, the availability of commercial Ethernet equipment for local-area networking, and the widespread implementation and rigorous standardization of TCP/IP on UNIX and virtually every other common operating system.

This NeXT Computer was used by Sir Tim Berners-Lee at CERN and became the world's first Web server.

Although the basic applications and guidelines that make the Internet possible had existed for almost two decades, the network did not gain a public face until the 1990s. On 6 August 1991, CERN, a pan European organization for particle research, publicized the new → World Wide Web project. The Web was invented by English scientist Tim Berners-Lee in 1989. An early popular web browser was ViolaWWW, patterned after HyperCard and built using the X Window System. It was eventually replaced in popularity by the Mosaic web browser. In 1993, the National Center for Supercomputing Applications at the University of Illinois released version 1.0 of Mosaic, and by late 1994 there was growing public interest in the previously academic, technical Internet. By 1996 usage of the word *Internet* had become commonplace, and consequently, so had its use as a synecdoche in reference to the World Wide Web.

Meanwhile, over the course of the decade, the Internet successfully accommodated the majority of previously existing public computer networks (although some networks, such as FidoNet, have remained separate). During the 1990s, it was estimated that the Internet grew by 100 percent per year, with a brief period of explosive growth in 1996 and 1997.[5] This growth is often attributed to the lack of central administration, which allows organic growth of the network, as well as the non-proprietary open nature of the Internet protocols, which encourages vendor interoperability and prevents any one company from exerting too much control over the network.[6] The estimated population of Internet users is 1.67 billion as of June 30, 2009.[7]

Technology

Protocols

The complex communications infrastructure of the Internet consists of its hardware components and a system of software layers that control various aspects of the architecture. While the hardware can often be used to support other software systems, it is the design and the rigorous standardization process of the software architecture that characterizes the Internet and provides the foundation for its scalability and success. The responsibility for the architectural design of the Internet software systems has been delegated to the Internet Engineering Task Force (IETF).[8] The IETF conducts standard-setting work groups, open to any individual, about the various aspects of Internet architecture. Resulting discussions and final standards are published in a series of publications, each called a Request for Comments (RFC), freely available on the IETF web site. The principal methods of networking that enable the Internet are contained in specially designated RFCs that constitute the Internet Standards. Other less rigorous documents are simply informative, experimental, or historical, or document the best current practices (BCP) when implementing Internet technologies.

The Internet Standards describe a framework known as the Internet Protocol Suite. This is a model architecture that divides methods into a layered system of protocols (RFC 1122, RFC 1123). The layers correspond to the environment or scope in which their services operate. At the top is the Application Layer, the space for the application-specific networking methods used in software applications, e.g., a web browser program. Below this top layer, the Transport Layer connects applications on *different hosts* via the network (e.g., client-server model) with appropriate data exchange methods. Underlying these layers are the core networking technologies, consisting of two layers. The Internet Layer enables computers to identify and locate each other via Internet Protocol (IP) addresses, and allows them to connect to one-another via intermediate (transit) networks. Lastly, at the bottom of the architecture, is a software layer, the Link Layer, that provides connectivity between hosts on the same local network link, such as a local area network (LAN) or a dial-up connection. The model, also known as TCP/IP, is designed to be independent of the underlying hardware which the model therefore does not concern itself with in any detail. Other models have been developed, such as the Open Systems Interconnection (OSI) model, but they are not compatible in the details of description, nor implementation, but many similarities exist and the TCP/IP protocols are usually included in the discussion of OSI networking.

The most prominent component of the Internet model is the Internet Protocol (IP) which provides addressing systems (IP addresses) for computers on the Internet. IP enables internetworking and essentially establishes the Internet itself. IP Version 4 (IPv4) is the initial version used on the first generation of the today's Internet and is still in dominant use. It was designed to address up to ~4.3 billion (10^9) Internet hosts. However, the explosive growth of the Internet has led to IPv4 address exhaustion which is estimated to enter its final stage in approximately 2011.[9] A new protocol version, IPv6, was developed in the mid 1990s which provides vastly larger addressing capabilities and more efficient routing of Internet traffic. IPv6 is currently in commercial deployment phase around the world and Internet address registries (RIRs) have begun to urge all resource managers to plan rapid adoption and conversion.[10]

IPv6 is not interoperable with IPv4. It essentially establishes a "parallel" version of the Internet not directly accessible with IPv4 software. This means software upgrades or translator facilities are necessary for every networking device that needs to communicate on the IPv6 Internet. Most modern computer operating systems are already converted to operate with both versions of the Internet Protocol. Network infrastructures, however, are still lagging in this development. Aside from the complex physical connections that make up its infrastructure, the Internet is facilitated by bi- or multi-lateral commercial contracts (e.g., peering agreements), and by technical specifications or protocols that describe how to exchange data over the network. Indeed, the Internet is defined by its interconnections and routing policies.

Structure

The Internet structure and its usage characteristics have been studied extensively. It has been determined that both the Internet IP routing structure and hypertext links of the World Wide Web are examples of scale-free networks. Similar to the way the commercial Internet providers connect via Internet exchange points, research networks tend to interconnect into large subnetworks such as GEANT, GLORIAD, Internet2 (successor of the Abilene Network), and the UK's national research and education network JANET. These in turn are built around smaller networks (see also the list of academic computer network organizations).

Many computer scientists describe the Internet as a "prime example of a large-scale, highly engineered, yet highly complex system".[11] The Internet is extremely heterogeneous; for instance, data transfer rates and physical characteristics of connections vary widely. The Internet exhibits "emergent phenomena" that depend on its large-scale organization. For example, data transfer rates exhibit temporal self-similarity. The principles of the routing and addressing methods for traffic in the Internet reach back to their origins the 1960s when the eventual scale and popularity of the network could not be anticipated. Thus, the possibility of developing alternative structures is investigated.[12]

Governance

The Internet is a globally distributed network comprising many voluntarily interconnected autonomous networks. It operates without a central governing body. However, to maintain interoperability, all technical and policy aspects of the underlying core infrastructure and the principal name spaces are administered by the Internet Corporation for Assigned Names and Numbers (ICANN), headquartered in Marina del Rey, California. ICANN is the authority that coordinates the assignment of unique identifiers for use on the Internet, including domain names, Internet Protocol (IP) addresses, application port numbers in the transport protocols, and many other parameters. Globally unified name spaces, in which names and numbers are uniquely assigned, are essential for the global reach of the Internet. ICANN is

ICANN headquarters in Marina Del Rey, California, United States

governed by an international board of directors drawn from across the Internet technical, business, academic, and other non-commercial communities. The US government continues to have the primary role in approving changes to the DNS root zone that lies at the heart of the domain name system. ICANN's role in coordinating the assignment of unique identifiers distinguishes it as perhaps the only central coordinating body on the global Internet. On November 16, 2005, the World Summit on the Information Society, held in Tunis, established the Internet Governance Forum (IGF) to discuss Internet-related issues.

Modern uses

The Internet is allowing greater flexibility in working hours and location, especially with the spread of unmetered high-speed connections and web applications.

The Internet can now be accessed almost anywhere by numerous means, especially through mobile Internet devices. Mobile phones, datacards, handheld game consoles and cellular routers allow users to connect to the Internet from anywhere there is a wireless network supporting that device's technology. Within the limitations imposed by small screens and other limited facilities of such pocket-sized devices, services of the Internet, including email and the web, may be available. Service providers may restrict the services offered and wireless data transmission charges may be significantly higher than other access methods.

The Internet has also become a large market for companies; some of the biggest companies today have grown by taking advantage of the efficient nature of low-cost → advertising and commerce through the Internet, also known as e-commerce. It is the fastest way to spread information to a vast number of people simultaneously. The Internet has also subsequently revolutionized shopping—for example; a person can order a CD online and receive it in the mail within a couple of days, or download it directly in some cases. The Internet has also greatly facilitated personalized marketing which allows a company to market a product to a specific person or a specific group of people more so than any other advertising medium. Examples of personalized marketing include online communities such as MySpace, Friendster, Facebook, Twitter, Orkut and others which thousands of Internet users join to advertise themselves and make friends online. Many of these users are young teens and adolescents ranging from 13 to 25 years old. In turn, when they advertise themselves they advertise interests and hobbies, which online marketing companies can use as information as to what those users will purchase online, and advertise their own companies' products to those users.

The low cost and nearly instantaneous sharing of ideas, knowledge, and skills has made collaborative work dramatically easier, with the help of collaborative software. Not only can a group cheaply communicate and share ideas, but the wide reach of the Internet allows such groups to easily form in the first place. An example of this is the free software movement, which has produced, among other programs, Linux, Mozilla Firefox, and OpenOffice.org. Internet "chat", whether in the form of IRC chat rooms or channels, or via instant messaging systems, allow colleagues to stay in touch in a very convenient way when working at their computers during the day. Messages can be exchanged even more quickly and conveniently than via e-mail. Extensions to these systems may allow files to be exchanged, "whiteboard" drawings to be shared or voice and video contact between team members.

Version control systems allow collaborating teams to work on shared sets of documents without either accidentally overwriting each other's work or having members wait until they get "sent" documents to be able to make their contributions. Business and project teams can share calendars as well as documents and other information. Such collaboration occurs in a wide variety of areas including scientific research, software development, conference planning, political activism and creative writing. Social and political collaboration is also becoming more widespread as both Internet access and computer literacy grow. From the flash mob 'events' of the early 2000s to the use of social networking in the 2009 Iranian election protests, the Internet allows people to work together more effectively and in many more ways than was possible without it.

The Internet allows computer users to remotely access other computers and information stores easily, wherever they may be across the world. They may do this with or without the use of security, authentication and encryption technologies, depending on the requirements. This is encouraging new ways of working from home, collaboration and information sharing in many industries. An accountant sitting at home can audit the books of a company based in another country, on a server situated in a third country that is remotely maintained by IT specialists in a fourth. These accounts could have been created by home-working bookkeepers, in other remote locations, based on information e-mailed to them from offices all over the world. Some of these things were possible before the widespread use of the Internet, but the cost of private leased lines would have made many of them infeasible in practice. An office worker away from their desk, perhaps on the other side of the world on a business trip or a holiday, can open a remote desktop session into his normal office PC using a secure Virtual Private Network (VPN) connection via the Internet. This gives the worker complete access to all of his or her normal files and data, including e-mail and other applications, while away from the office. This concept is also referred to by some network security people as the Virtual Private Nightmare, because it extends the secure perimeter of a corporate network into its employees' homes.

Services

Information

Many people use the terms *Internet* and *World Wide Web*, or just the *Web*, interchangeably, but the two terms are not synonymous. The → World Wide Web is a global set of documents, images and other resources, logically interrelated by hyperlinks and referenced with Uniform Resource Identifiers (URIs). URIs allow providers to symbolically identify services and clients to locate and address web servers, file servers, and other databases that store documents and provide resources and access them using the Hypertext Transfer Protocol (HTTP), the primary carrier protocol of the Web. HTTP is only one of the hundreds of communication protocols used on the Internet. Web services may also use HTTP to allow software systems to communicate in order to share and exchange business logic and data.

World Wide Web browser software, such as Internet Explorer, Firefox, Opera, Apple Safari, and Google Chrome, let users navigate from one web page to another via hyperlinks embedded in the documents. These documents may also contain any combination of computer data, including graphics, sounds, text, video, multimedia and interactive content including games, office applications and scientific demonstrations. Through keyword-driven Internet research using → search engines like Yahoo! and Google, users worldwide have easy, instant access to a vast and diverse amount of online information. Compared to printed encyclopedias and traditional libraries, the World Wide Web has enabled the decentralization of information.

The Web has also enabled individuals and organizations to publish ideas and information to a potentially large audience online at greatly reduced expense and time delay. Publishing a web page, a blog, or building a website involves little initial cost and many cost-free services are available. Publishing and maintaining large, professional web sites with attractive, diverse and up-to-date information is still a difficult and expensive proposition, however. Many individuals and some companies and groups use *web logs* or blogs, which are largely used as easily updatable online diaries. Some commercial organizations encourage staff to communicate advice in their areas of specialization in the hope that visitors will be impressed by the expert knowledge and free information, and be attracted to the corporation as a result. One example of this practice is Microsoft, whose product developers publish their personal blogs in order to pique the public's interest in their work. Collections of personal web pages published by large service providers remain popular, and have become increasingly sophisticated. Whereas operations such as Angelfire and GeoCities have existed since the early days of the Web, newer offerings from, for example, Facebook and MySpace currently have large followings. These operations often brand themselves as social network services rather than simply as web page hosts.

Advertising on popular web pages can be lucrative, and e-commerce or the sale of products and services directly via the Web continues to grow. In the early days, web pages were usually created as sets of complete and isolated HTML text files stored on a web server. More recently, websites are more often created using content management or wiki software with, initially, very little content. Contributors to these systems, who may be paid staff, members of a club or other organization or members of the public, fill underlying databases with content using editing pages designed for that purpose, while casual visitors view and read this content in its final HTML form. There may or may not be editorial, approval and security systems built into the process of taking newly entered content and making it available to the target visitors.

Communication

→ E-mail is an important communications service available on the Internet. The concept of sending electronic text messages between parties in a way analogous to mailing letters or memos predates the creation of the Internet. Today it can be important to distinguish between internet and internal e-mail systems. Internet e-mail may travel and be stored unencrypted on many other networks and machines out of both the sender's and the recipient's control. During this time it is quite possible for the content to be read and even tampered with by third parties, if anyone considers it important enough. Purely internal or intranet mail systems, where the information never leaves the corporate or organization's network, are much more secure, although in any organization there will be IT and other personnel whose job may involve monitoring, and occasionally accessing, the e-mail of other employees not addressed to them. Pictures, documents and other files can be sent as e-mail attachments. E-mails can be cc-ed to multiple e-mail addresses.

Internet telephony is another common communications service made possible by the creation of the Internet. VoIP stands for Voice-over-Internet Protocol, referring to the protocol that underlies all Internet communication. The idea began in the early 1990s with walkie-talkie-like voice applications for personal computers. In recent years many VoIP systems have become as easy to use and as convenient as a normal telephone. The benefit is that, as the Internet carries the voice traffic, VoIP can be free or cost much less than a traditional telephone call, especially over long distances and especially for those with always-on Internet connections such as cable or ADSL. VoIP is maturing into a competitive alternative to traditional telephone service. Interoperability between different providers has improved and the ability to call or receive a call from a traditional telephone is available. Simple, inexpensive VoIP network adapters are available that eliminate the need for a personal computer.

Voice quality can still vary from call to call but is often equal to and can even exceed that of traditional calls. Remaining problems for VoIP include emergency telephone number dialling and reliability. Currently, a few VoIP providers provide an emergency service, but it is not universally available. Traditional phones are line-powered and operate during a power failure; VoIP does not do so without a backup power source for the phone equipment and the Internet access devices. VoIP has also become increasingly popular for gaming applications, as a form of communication between players. Popular VoIP clients for gaming include Ventrilo and Teamspeak. Wii, PlayStation 3, and Xbox 360 also offer VoIP chat features.

Data transfer

File sharing is an example of transferring large amounts of data across the Internet. A computer file can be e-mailed to customers, colleagues and friends as an attachment. It can be uploaded to a → website or FTP server for easy download by others. It can be put into a "shared location" or onto a file server for instant use by colleagues. The load of bulk downloads to many users can be eased by the use of "mirror" servers or peer-to-peer networks. In any of these cases, access to the file may be controlled by user authentication, the transit of the file over the Internet may be obscured by encryption, and money may change hands for access to the file. The price can be paid by the remote charging of funds from, for example, a credit card whose details are also passed—usually fully encrypted—across the Internet. The origin and authenticity of the file received may be checked by digital signatures or by MD5 or other message digests. These simple features of the Internet, over a worldwide basis, are changing the production, sale, and distribution of anything that can be reduced to a computer file for transmission. This includes all manner of print publications, software products, news, music, film, video, photography, graphics and the other arts. This in turn has caused seismic shifts in each of the existing industries that previously controlled the production and distribution of these products.

Streaming media refers to the act that many existing radio and television broadcasters promote Internet "feeds" of their live audio and video streams (for example, the BBC). They may also allow time-shift viewing or listening such as Preview, Classic Clips and Listen Again features. These providers have been joined by a range of pure Internet "broadcasters" who never had on-air licenses. This means that an Internet-connected device, such as a computer or something more specific, can be used to access on-line media in much the same way as was previously possible only with a → television or → radio receiver. The range of available types of content is much wider, from specialized technical webcasts to on-demand popular multimedia services. Podcasting is a variation on this theme, where—usually audio—material is downloaded and played back on a computer or shifted to a portable media player to be listened to on the move. These techniques using simple equipment allow anybody, with little censorship or licensing control, to broadcast audio-visual material worldwide.

Webcams can be seen as an even lower-budget extension of this phenomenon. While some webcams can give full-frame-rate video, the picture is usually either small or updates slowly. Internet users can watch animals around an African waterhole, ships in the Panama Canal, traffic at a local roundabout or monitor their own premises, live and in real time. Video chat rooms and video conferencing are also popular with many uses being found for personal webcams, with and without two-way sound. YouTube was founded on 15 February 2005 and is now the leading website for free streaming video with a vast number of users. It uses a flash-based web player to stream and show video files. Registered users may upload an unlimited amount of video and build their own personal profile. YouTube claims that its users watch hundreds of millions, and upload hundreds of thousands of videos daily.[13]

Accessibility

The prevalent language for communication on the Internet is English. This may be a result of the origin of the Internet, as well as English's role as a lingua franca. It may also be related to the poor capability of early computers, largely originating in the United States, to handle characters other than those in the English variant of the Latin alphabet. After English (29% of Web visitors) the most requested languages on the → World Wide Web are Chinese (22%), Spanish (8%), Japanese (6%), French (5%), Portuguese and German (4% each), Arabic (3%) and Russian and Korean (2% each).[14] By region, 42% of the world's Internet users are based in Asia, 24% in Europe, 15% in North America, 11% in Latin America and the Caribbean taken together, 4% in Africa, 3% in the Middle East and 1% in Australia/Oceania.[15]

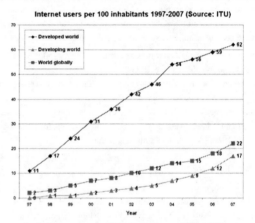

Graph of Internet users per 100 inhabitants between 1997 and 2007 by International Telecommunication Union

The Internet's technologies have developed enough in recent years, especially in the use of Unicode, that good facilities are available for development and communication in most widely used languages. However, some glitches such as *mojibake* (incorrect display of foreign language characters, also known as *kryakozyabry*) still remain.

Common methods of Internet access in homes include dial-up, landline broadband (over coaxial cable, fiber optic or copper wires), Wi-Fi, satellite and 3G technology cell phones. Public places to use the Internet include libraries and Internet cafes, where computers with Internet connections are available. There are also Internet access points in many public places such as airport halls and coffee shops, in some cases just for brief use while standing. Various terms are used, such as "public Internet kiosk", "public access terminal", and "Web payphone". Many hotels now also have public terminals, though these are usually fee-based. These terminals are widely accessed for various usage like ticket booking, bank deposit, online payment etc. Wi-Fi provides wireless access to computer networks, and therefore can do so to the Internet itself. Hotspots providing such access include Wi-Fi cafes, where would-be users need to bring their own wireless-enabled devices such as a laptop or PDA. These services may be free to all, free to customers only, or fee-based. A hotspot need not be limited to a confined location. A whole campus or park, or even an entire city can be enabled. Grassroots efforts have led to wireless community networks. Commercial Wi-Fi services covering large city areas are in place in London, Vienna, Toronto, San Francisco, Philadelphia, Chicago and Pittsburgh. The Internet can then be accessed from such places as a park bench.[16] Apart from Wi-Fi, there have been experiments with proprietary mobile wireless networks like Ricochet, various high-speed data services over cellular phone networks, and fixed wireless services. High-end mobile phones such as smartphones generally come with Internet access through the phone network. Web browsers such as Opera are available on these advanced handsets, which can also run a wide variety of other Internet software. More mobile phones have Internet access than PCs, though this is not as widely used. An Internet access provider and protocol matrix differentiates the methods used to get online.

Social impact

The Internet has enabled entirely new forms of social interaction, activities, and organizing, thanks to its basic features such as widespread usability and access. Social networking websites such as Facebook and MySpace have created a new form of socialization and interaction. Users of these sites are able to add a wide variety of information to their personal pages, to persue common interests, and to connect with others. It is also possible to find a large circle of existing acquaintants, especially if a site allows users to represent themselves by their given names, and to allow communication among existing groups of people. Sites like meetup.com exist to allow wider announcement of groups which may exist mainly for face-to-face meetings, but which may have a variety of minor interactions over their group's site.

In the first decade of the 21st century the first generation is raised with widespread availability of Internet connectivity, bringing consequences and concerns in areas such as personal privacy and identity, and distribution of copyrighted materials. These "digital natives" face a variety of challenges that were not present for prior generations.

The Internet has achieved new relevance as a political tool, leading to Internet censorship by some states. The presidential campaign of Howard Dean in 2004 in the United States was notable for its success in soliciting donation via the Internet. Many political groups use the Internet to achieve a new method of organizing in order to carry out their mission, having given rise to Internet activism. Some governments, such as those of Iran, North Korea, Myanmar, the People's Republic of China, and Saudi Arabia, restrict what people in their countries can access on the Internet, especially political and religious content. This is accomplished through software that filters domains and content so that they may not be easily accessed or obtained without elaborate circumvention.

In Norway, Denmark, Finland[17] and Sweden, major Internet service providers have voluntarily, possibly to avoid such an arrangement being turned into law, agreed to restrict access to sites listed by authorities. While this list of forbidden URLs is only supposed to contain addresses of known child pornography sites, the content of the list is secret. Many countries, including the United States, have enacted laws against the possession or distribution of certain material, such as child pornography, via the Internet, but do not mandate filtering software. There are many free and commercially available software programs, called content-control software, with which a user can choose to block offensive websites on individual computers or networks, in order to limit a child's access to pornographic materials or depiction of violence.

The Internet has been a major outlet for leisure activity since its inception, with entertaining social experiments such as MUDs and MOOs being conducted on university servers, and humor-related Usenet groups receiving much traffic. Today, many Internet forums have sections devoted to games and funny videos; short cartoons in the form of Flash movies are also popular. Over 6 million people use blogs or message boards as a means of communication and for the sharing of ideas. The pornography and gambling industries have taken advantage of the World Wide Web, and often provide a significant source of advertising revenue for other websites. Although many governments have attempted to restrict both industries' use of the Internet, this has generally failed to stop their widespread popularity.

One main area of leisure activity on the Internet is multiplayer gaming. This form of recreation creates communities, where people of all ages and origins enjoy the fast-paced world of multiplayer games. These range from MMORPG to first-person shooters, from role-playing games to online gambling. This has revolutionized the way many people interact while spending their free time on the Internet. While online gaming has been around since the 1970s, modern modes of online gaming began with subscription services such as GameSpy and MPlayer. Non-subscribers were limited to certain types of game play or certain games. Many people use the Internet to access and download music, movies and other works for their enjoyment and relaxation. Free and fee-based services exist for all of these activities, using centralized servers and distributed peer-to-peer technologies. Some of these sources exercise more care with respect to the original artists' copyrights than others.

Many people use the World Wide Web to access news, weather and sports reports, to plan and book vacations and to find out more about their interests. People use chat, messaging and e-mail to make and stay in touch with friends worldwide, sometimes in the same way as some previously had pen pals. Social networking websites like MySpace, Facebook and many others like them also put and keep people in contact for their enjoyment. The Internet has seen a growing number of Web desktops, where users can access their files and settings via the Internet. Cyberslacking can become a serious drain on corporate resources; the average UK employee spent 57 minutes a day surfing the Web while at work, according to a 2003 study by Peninsula Business Services.[18]

See also

- Digital rights
- Electronic publishing
- Freedom of information
- Information continuum
- Internet bias
- Internet democracy
- Internet meme
- Internet organizations
- Internet privacy
- List of cable Internet providers
- List of Internet topics
- Network Neutrality
- Outline of the Internet

References

- Media Freedom Internet Cookbook [19] by the OSCE Representative on Freedom of the Media Vienna, 2004
- Living Internet [20]—Internet history and related information, including information from many creators of the Internet
- First Monday [21] peer-reviewed journal on the Internet
- How Much Does The Internet Weigh? [22] by Stephen Cass, Discover 2007
- Rehmeyer, Julie J. 2007. Mapping a medusa: The Internet spreads its tentacles. Science News 171(June 23):387-388. Available at Sciencenews.org [23]
- Castells, M. 1996. Rise of the Network Society. 3 vols. Vol. 1. Cambridge, MA: Blackwell Publishers.
- Castells, M. (2001), "Lessons from the History of Internet", in "The Internet Galaxy", Ch. 1, pp 9–35. Oxford University Press.
- RFC 1122, Requirements for Internet Hosts—Communication Layers, IETF, R. Braden (Ed.), October 1989
- RFC 1123, Requirements for Internet Hosts—Application and Support, IETF, R. Braden (Ed.), October 1989

External links

- The Internet [24] (National Science Foundation)
- "10 Years that changed the world" — Wired looks back at the evolution of the Internet over last 10 years [25]
- Berkman Center for Internet and Society at Harvard [26]
- CBC Digital Archives—Inventing the Internet Age [27]
- How the Internet Came to Be [28]
- The Internet Society History Page [29]
- RFC 801, planning the TCP/IP switchover [30]
- Preparing Europe's digital future - i2010 Mid-Term Review [31]
- Manjoo, Farhad - The Unrecognizable Internet of 1996 [32] - *Slate*

References

[1] "Links" (http://www.w3.org/TR/html401/struct/links.html#h-12.1). *HTML 4.01 Specification*. World Wide Web Consortium. HTML 4.01 Specification. . Retrieved 2008-08-13. "[T]he link (or hyperlink, or Web link) [is] the basic hypertext construct. A link is a connection from one Web resource to another. Although a simple concept, the link has been one of the primary forces driving the success of the Web."

[2] "ARPA/DARPA" (http://www.darpa.mil/body/arpa_darpa.html). Defense Advanced Research Projects Agency. . Retrieved 2007-05-21.

[3] "DARPA: History" (http://www.darpa.mil/history.html). Defense Advanced Research Projects Agency. . Retrieved 2009-12-07.

[4] Baran, Paul (1964). *On Distributed Communications* (http://www.rand.org/pubs/research_memoranda/RM3767). .

[5] Coffman, K. G; Odlyzko, A. M. (1998-10-02) (PDF). *The size and growth rate of the Internet* (http://www.dtc.umn.edu/~odlyzko/doc/internet.size.pdf). AT&T Labs. . Retrieved 2007-05-21.

[6] Comer, Douglas (2006). *The Internet book*. Prentice Hall. p. 64. ISBN 0132335530.

[7] "World Internet Users and Population Stats" (http://www.internetworldstats.com/stats.htm). *Internet World Stats*. Miniwatts Marketing Group. 2009-06-30. . Retrieved 2009-11-06.

[8] "IETF Home Page" (http://www.ietf.org/). Ietf.org. . Retrieved 2009-06-20.

[9] Huston, Geoff. "IPv4 Address Report, daily generated" (http://www.potaroo.net/tools/ipv4/index.html). . Retrieved 2009-05-20.

[10] "Notice of Internet Protocol version 4 (IPv4) Address Depletion" (https://www.arin.net/knowledge/about_resources/ceo_letter.pdf) (PDF). . Retrieved 2009-08-07.

[11] Walter Willinger, Ramesh Govindan, Sugih Jamin, Vern Paxson, and Scott Shenker (2002). Scaling phenomena in the Internet (http://www.pnas.org/cgi/content/full/99/suppl_1/2573), in *Proceedings of the National Academy of Sciences, 99*, suppl. 1, 2573–2580

[12] "Internet Makeover? Some argue it's time" (http://seattletimes.nwsource.com/html/businesstechnology/2003667811_btrebuildnet16.html). The Seattle Times, April 16, 2007.

[13] "YouTube Fact Sheet" (http://www.youtube.com/t/fact_sheet). YouTube, LLC. . Retrieved 2009-01-20.

[14] Internet World Stats (http://www.internetworldstats.com/stats7.htm), updated June 30, 2009

[15] World Internet Usage Statistics News and Population Stats (http://www.internetworldstats.com/stats.htm) updated June 30, 2009

[16] "Toronto Hydro to Install Wireless Network in Downtown Toronto" (http://www.bloomberg.com/apps/news?pid=10000082&sid=aQ0ZfhMa4XGQ&refer=canada). Bloomberg.com. Retrieved 19-Mar-2006.

[17] "Finland censors anti-censorship site" (http://www.theregister.co.uk/2008/02/18/finnish_policy_censor_activist/). *The Register*. 2008-02-18. . Retrieved 2008-02-19.

[18] "Scotsman.com News - Net abuse hits small city firms" (http://news.scotsman.com/topics.cfm?tid=914&id=1001802003). News.scotsman.com. . Retrieved 2009-08-07.

[19] http://www.osce.org/item/13570.html

[20] http://www.livinginternet.com

[21] http://www.firstmonday.org/

[22] http://discovermagazine.com/2007/jun/how-much-does-the-internet-weigh

[23] http://www.sciencenews.org/articles/20070623/fob2.asp

[24] http://www.nsf.gov/about/history/nsf0050/internet/internet.htm

[25] http://www.wired.com/wired/archive/13.08/intro.html

[26] http://cyber.law.harvard.edu/home/

[27] http://archives.cbc.ca/IDD-1-75-1738/science_technology/internet/

[28] http://www.internetvalley.com/archives/mirrors/cerf-how-inet.txt

[29] http://www.isoc.org/internet/history/brief.shtml

[30] http://www.ietf.org/rfc/rfc801.txt

[31] http://ec.europa.eu/information_society/eeurope/i2010/mid_term_review_2008/index_en.htm

[32] http://www.slate.com/id/2212108/pagenum/all/

Screenplay

A **screenplay** or **script** is a written work that is made especially for a film or television program. Screenplays can be original works or adaptations from existing pieces of writing. A play for television is known as a teleplay.

Format and style

The format is structured in a way that one page usually equates to one minute of screen time. In a "shooting script", each scene is numbered, and technical direction may be given. In a "spec" or a "draft" in various stages of development, the scenes are *not* numbered, and technical direction is at a minimum. The standard font for a screenplay is 12-point Courier.

The major components are action and dialogue. The "action" is written in the present tense. The "dialogue" are the lines the characters speak. Unique to the screenplay (as opposed to a stage play) is the use of slug lines.

The format consists of two aspects:

Sample from a screenplay, showing dialogue and action descriptions.

1. The interplay between typeface/font, line spacing and type area, from which the standard of one page of text per one minute of screen time is derived. Unlike in the United States where US letter size and Courier 12 point are mandatory, Europe uniformly uses A4 as the standard paper size format (but without a uniform font requirement).
2. The tab settings of the scene elements (dialogue, scenes headings, transitions, parentheticals, etc.), which constitute the screenplay's *layout*.

The style consists of a grammar that is specific to screenplays. This grammar also consists of two aspects:

1. A prose that is manifestation-oriented, i.e. focuses largely on what is audible and what is visible on screen. This prose may only supply interpretations and explanation (deviate from the manifestation-oriented prose) if clarity would otherwise be adversely affected.
2. Codified notation of certain technical or dramatic elements, such as scene transitions, changes in narrative perspective, sound effects, emphasis of dramatically relevant objects and characters speaking from outside a scene.

Types of Screenplay

Screenplays can generally be divided into two kinds; a 'spec' screenplay, and a commissioned screenplay.

A speculative screenplay is a script written with no upfront payment, or a promise of payment. The content is usually invented solely by the screenwriter, though spec screenplays can also be based on established works, or real people and events.

A commissioned screenplay is written by a hired writer. The concept is usually developed long before the screenwriter is brought on, and usually has many writers work on it before the script is green lit.

Screenwriting software

Detailed computer programs are designed specifically to format screenplays, teleplays and stage plays. Celtx, DreamaScript, Final Draft, Movie Outline 3.0, FiveSprockets, and Montage are several such programs. Software is also available as web applications, accessible from any computer, and on mobile devices.

See also

- Act structure
- Closet screenplay
- Filmmaking
- Scriptment
- Screenwriter's salary
- Storyboard
- List of film-related topics
- List of screenwriting software
- *Dreams on Spec*
- Guide to Literary Agents
- Writer's Digest

References

- David Trottier (1998). *The Screenwriter's Bible: A Complete Guide to Writing, Formatting, and Selling Your Script*. Silman-James Press. ISBN 1-879505-44-4. - Paperback
- Yves Lavandier (2005). *Writing Drama, A Comprehensive Guide for Playwrights and Scritpwriters*. Le Clown & l'Enfant. ISBN 2-910606-04-X. - Paperback
- Judith H. Haag, Hillis R. Cole (1980). *The Complete Guide to Standard Script Formats: The Screenplay*. CMC Publishing. ISBN 0-929583-00-0. - Paperback
- Jami Bernard (1995). *Quentin Tarantino: The Man and His Movies*. HarperCollins publishers. ISBN 0-002556-44-8. - Paperback
- Riley, C. (2005) *The Hollywood Standard: the complete and authoriative guide to script format and style*. Michael Weise Productions. Sheridan Press. ISBN 0941188949.

External links

- Screenplays [1] at the Open Directory Project

References

[1] http://www.dmoz.org/Arts/Movies/Filmmaking/Screenwriting/Scripts//

Press release

A **press release**, **news release**, **media release**, or **press statement** is a written or recorded communication directed at members of the news media for the purpose of announcing something claimed as having news value. Typically, they are mailed, faxed, or → e-mailed to assignment editors at newspapers, magazines, radio stations, television stations, and/or television networks. Commercial press-release distribution services are also used to distribute them.

The use of a press release is common in the field of public relations, the aim of which is to attract favorable media attention to public relations professional's client and/or provide publicity for → products or events marketed by those clients. A press release provides reporters with the basics they need to develop a news story. Press releases can announce a range of news items such as: scheduled events, personal promotions, awards, news products and services, sales and other financial data, accomplishments, etc. They are often used in generating a feature story or are sent for the purpose of announcing news conferences, upcoming events or change in corporation.

A 1983 IBM (UK) press release

A *press statement* is information supplied to reporters. This is an official statement or account of a news story that is specially prepared and issued to newspapers and other news media for them to make known to the public.

Origins

One anecdote on an origin of modern press releases is about an incident in 1906 involving Ivy Lee, who is often referred to as the first real public relations practitioner. At that time, Lee's agency was working with the Pennsylvania Railroad, which had just fallen victim to a tragic accident. Ivy Lee convinced the company to issue the first press release to journalists, before other versions of the story, or suppositions, could be spread among them and reported. He used a press release, in addition to inviting journalists and photographers to the scene and providing their transportation there, as a means of fostering open communication with the media.

Elements

While there are several types of press releases (such as the general news release, event release, product press release, financial/earnings releases and, more recently, the social media release), press releases very often have several traits of their structure in common. This helps journalists separate press releases from other PR communication methods, such as pitch letters or media advisories. Some of these common structural elements include:

- **Headline** — used to grab the attention of journalists and briefly summarize the news.
- **Dateline** — contains the release date and usually the originating city of the press release.
- **Introduction** — first paragraph in a press release, that generally gives basic answers to the questions of who, what, when, where and why.
- **Body** — further explanation, statistics, background, or other details relevant to the news.
- **Boilerplate** — generally a short "about" section, providing independent background on the issuing company, organization, or individual.
- **Close** — in North America, traditionally the symbol "-30-" appears after the boilerplate or body and before the media contact information, indicating to media that the release is ending. A more modern equivalent has been the "###" symbol. In other countries, other means of indicating the end of the release may be used, such as the text "ends".
- **Media contact information** — name, phone number, email address, mailing address, or other contact information for the PR or other media relations contact person.

Video news releases

Some public relations firms send out video news releases (VNRs) which are pre-taped video programs that can be aired intact by TV stations. Often, the VNRs are aired without the stations' identifying or attributing them as such.

TV news viewers can often detect the use of VNRs within television newscasts; for example, many movie-star "interviews" are actually VNRs, taped on a set which is located at the movie studio and decorated with the movie's logo. Another frequent example of VNRs masquerading as news footage is videotapes of particular medical "breakthroughs," that are really produced and distributed by pharmaceutical companies for the purpose of selling new medicines.

Video news releases can be in the form of full blown productions costing tens of thousands or even hundreds of thousands. They can also be in the TV news format, or even produced for the web.

Recently, many broadcast news outlets have discouraged the use of VNRs. Many stations, citing an already poor public perception, want to increase their credibility. Public relations companies are having a tougher time getting their pre-edited video aired.

VNRs can be turned into podcasts then posted onto newswires. Further to this, a story can be kept running longer by engaging "community websites", which are monitored and commented on by many journalists and features writers.

Embargoed press release

Sometimes a press release is embargoed — that is, news organizations are requested not to report the story until a specified time. For instance, news organizations usually receive a copy of presidential speeches several hours in advance. Product or media reviewers are commonly given a sample or preview of a product ahead of its release date. In such cases, the news organizations generally do not break the embargo. If they do, the agency that sent the release may blacklist them. A blacklisted news organization will not receive any more embargoed releases, or possibly any releases at all. They may also be compelled to honor the embargo via a legally binding non-disclosure agreement.

However, it is very hard to enforce embargoes on journalists, as there is constant pressure by editors to scoop other news outlets. It is unlikely that a PR agency will blacklist a form of media, as other clients may want to be featured in this publication. This problem is sometimes overcome by controlling the timing of a release via email rather than relying on the journalist to do so.

See also

- Electronic press kit (EPK)
- News conference
- Public relations (PR)
- Spokesman

White paper

A **white paper** is an authoritative report or guide that often addresses issues and how to solve them. White papers are used to educate readers and help people make decisions. They are often used in politics and business, and technical subjects. In commercial use, the term "white paper" has also come to refer to documents used by businesses as a marketing or sales tool.

Government white papers

In the Commonwealth of Nations, "white paper" is an informal name for a parliamentary paper enunciating government policy; in the United Kingdom these are mostly issued as "Command papers". White papers are issued by the government and lay out policy, or proposed action, on a topic of current concern. Although a white paper may on occasion be a consultation as to the details of new legislation, it does signify a clear intention on the part of a government to pass new law. By contrast, green papers, which are issued much more frequently, are more open ended. These green papers, also known as *consultation documents*, may merely propose a strategy to be implemented in the details of other legislation or they may set out proposals on which the government wishes to obtain public views and opinion.

White papers published by the European Commission are documents containing proposals for European Union action in a specific area. They sometimes follow a green paper released to launch a public consultation process.

For examples see the following:

- *Russia No 1. A Collection of Reports on Bolshevism in Russia, April 1919*, often referred to as "The White Paper" a collection of telegraphic messages by British officers in Russia, concerning the Bolshevik revolution.
- *Churchill White Paper, 1922*, planning a national home in Palestine for Jews.
- *White Paper of 1939*, calling for the creation of a unified Palestinian state and a limited Jewish immigration and ability to purchase land.
- *White Paper on Full Employment*, 1945, Commonwealth of Australia to recognize state's obligation to given jobs to people.
- *White Paper on Defence*, 1964, led to the unification/creation of the modern Canadian Forces.
- 1966 Defence White Paper, cancelled new British aircraft carriers such as the BAC TSR-2 aircraft.
- *In Place of Strife*, 1969 (later abandoned), to reduce trade union power.
- *1969 White Paper*, 1969 (later abandoned), to abolish the Indian Act in Canada and recognize First Nations as the same as other minorities in Canada, rather than distinct groups.

Commercial white papers

Since the early 1990s, the term "white paper" has also come to refer to documents used by businesses as marketing or sales tools. White papers of this sort argue that the benefits of a particular technology or → product are superior for solving a specific problem.

These types of white papers are almost always → marketing communications documents designed to promote a specific company's solutions or products. As a marketing tool, these papers will highlight information favorable to the company authorizing or sponsoring the paper. Such white papers are often used to generate sales leads, establish thought leadership, make a business case, or to educate customers.

There are three main types of commercial white papers:

- Business-benefits: Makes a business case for a certain technology or methodology
- Technical: Describes how a certain technology works
- Hybrid: Combines high-level business benefits with technical details in a single document

See also

- Green paper
- Persuasive writing

Notes

- Stelzner, Michael (2007). *Writing White Papers: How to capture readers and keep them engaged*. Poway, California: WhitePaperSource Publishing. pp. 214. ISBN 9780977716937.
- Bly, Robert W. (2006). *The White Paper Marketing Handbook*. Florence, Kentucky: South-Western Educational Publishing. pp. 256. ISBN 9780324300826.

References

- White paper [1] EU glossary

References

[1] http://europa.eu/scadplus/glossary/white_paper_en.htm

Mail order

Mail order is a term which describes the buying of goods or services by mail delivery. The buyer places an order for the desired products with the merchant through some remote method such as through a telephone call or web site. Then, the products are delivered to the customer. The products are typically delivered directly to an address supplied by the customer, such as a home address, but occasionally the orders are delivered to a nearby retail location for the customer to pick up. Some merchants also allow the goods to be shipped directly to a third party consumer, which is an effective way to send a gift to an out-of-town recipient.

The cover of the first Eaton's catalog, published in 1884. The Eaton's catalog would continue to be published until 1976.

A **mail-order catalog** is a publication containing a list of general merchandise from a company. Companies who publish and operate mail-order catalogs are referred to as catalogers within the industry. Catalogers buy or manufacture goods then market those goods to prospects (prospective customers). Many catalogers, just as with most retailers, are increasingly buying goods from China. Catalogers "rent" names from list brokers or cooperative databases. The catalog itself is published in a similar fashion as any magazine publication and distributed through a variety of means, usually via a postal service and the → internet.

Sometimes supermarket products do mail-order promotions where people can send in the UPC code plus shipping and handling to get a product made especially for the company.

Few things are not available through mail order.

Mail order in the United States

American magazine advertisement from 1916 offering mail delivery of fish and seafood.

According to The National Mail Order Association (NMOA.org) Benjamin Franklin is believed to have been the first cataloger in the United States. In 1744, he formulated the basic mail-order concept when he produced the first catalog, which sold scientific and academic books. He is also credited with offering the first mail-order guarantee: "Those persons who live remote, by sending their orders and money to B. Franklin may depend on the same justice as if present."

The earliest surviving mail-order business, now known as Hammacher Schlemmer was established by Alfred Hammacher in New York City in 1848. Offering mechanic's tools and builder's hardware, its first catalog was published in 1881. [1] Now known for offering an eclectic, premium assortment of "The Best, The Only, and The Unexpected", it is America's longest running catalog.

In 1872, Aaron Montgomery Ward produced the first mail-order catalog for his Montgomery Ward mail order business. This first catalog was a single sheet of paper with a price list, 8 by 12 inches, showing the merchandise for sale and ordering instructions. Montgomery Ward identified a market of merchant-wary farmers in the Midwest. Within two decades, his single-page list of products grew into a 540-page illustrated book selling over 20,000 items. Almost a decade later, the first Sears catalog was published in the United States. CENCO dominated the field of selling science education equipment through their mail-order catalog.

Other mail order catalogs include JC Penney, The Noble Collection, Spiegel catalog, Welco.

With the invention of the → Internet, a company's → website became the more usual way to order merchandise for delivery by mail, although the term "mail order" is not always used to describe the ordering of goods over the Internet. It is more usual to refer to this as e-commerce or online shopping. Nowadays however most traditional mail order companies also sell over the internet, which makes these two varieties tend to merge.

However, rising paper, printing and postage costs have caused some traditional catalogs such as Bloomingdale's [2] to suspend their printed catalog to focus more on their website. This is a trend that will likely continue in the future as more merchants look to improve their most economical means of developing and retaining customers.

And though the Internet has largely been adopted by most catalog companies, it's important to note that some merchants function as a mail order company without a printed catalog to promote and sell their products. These types of companies are know as "pure plays" or "dot-coms" and their presence is growing everyday.

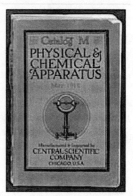

Cover of a mail-order catalog for scientific equipment.

In the United States, an advantage of this type of shopping is that the merchant is typically not required by law to add sales tax to the price of the goods, unless they have a physical presence in the customers' state. Instead, most states require the resident purchaser to pay applicable taxes. There has been periodic discussion about amending the law to make these sales taxable.

In the European Union, the EU VAT union has the principle that the merchant adds the VAT of his own country to the price, and the buyer does not have pay any more tax. If the buyer is a company it deducts that VAT like inside its own country. This makes the EU look more like one country than the US in this respect.

Year Mail Order Catalogs were founded:

- Hammacher Schlemmer: 1848
- Montgomery Ward: 1872
- Sears: 1893
- L.L.Bean: 1912
- Eddie Bauer: 1920
- Miles Kimball: 1935
- Vermont Country Store: 1945
- Walter Drake: 1947
- Cohasset Colonials: 1949
- Lillian Vernon: 1951
- Taylor Gifts: 1952
- Harriet Carter: 1958
- Lands' End: 1963

See also

- Catalog merchant
- E-commerce
- Mail-order bride
- Online shopping
- Pick and pack
- Shipping list
- Specialty catalogs
- Trade literature

External links

- History of Mail Order Catalogue Shopping in the UK [3]
- History of Canadian Mail-order Catalogues [4]
- Mail-order history [5]
- UK places where home shopping is most prevalent [6]
- Hammacher Schlemmer Company History [1]
- C. F. Orvis Company history [7]
- Taylor Gifts history [8]

References

[1] http://www.hammacher.com/about_us/history.asp
[2] http://www.bloomingdales.com/
[3] http://www.thecatalogshop.co.uk
[4] http://www.civilisations.ca/cmc/exhibitions/cpm/catalog/cat0000e.shtml
[5] http://inventors.about.com/library/inventors/blshopping.htm
[6] http://press.experian.com/documents/showdoc.cfm?doc=2318
[7] http://www.orvis.com/detail.asp?subject=9&index=1&dir_id=&cat_id=&group_id=
[8] http://www.taylorgifts.com/custserv/about.asp

Billboard

A **billboard** is a large outdoor advertising structure (a → billing board), typically found in high traffic areas such as alongside busy roads. Billboards present large → advertisements to passing pedestrians and drivers. Typically showing large, ostensibly witty slogans, and distinctive visuals, billboards are highly visible in the top designated market areas. Bulletins are the largest, most impactful standard-size billboards. Located primarily on major highways, expressways or principal arterials, they command high-density consumer exposure (mostly to vehicular traffic). Bulletins afford greatest visibility due not only to their size, but because they allow

Billboards in Times Square, New York

creative "customizing" through extensions and embellishments. Billboards are a great place to advertise business because rather than you having to find your customers, your customers will find your advertising.

Posters are the other common form of billboard advertising, located chiefly in commercial and industrial areas on primary and secondary arterial roads. Posters are a smaller format than bulletins and are viewed principally by residents and commuter traffic, with some pedestrian exposure.

Advertising style

Billboard advertisements are designed to catch a person's attention and create a memorable impression very quickly, leaving the reader thinking about the advertisement after they have driven past it. They have to be readable in a very short time because they are usually read while being passed at high speeds. Thus there are usually only a few words, in large print, and a humorous or arresting image in brilliant color.

Some billboard designs spill outside the actual space given to them by the billboard, with parts of figures hanging off the billboard edges or jutting out of the billboard in three dimensions. An example in the United States around the turn of the 21st century were the Chick-fil-A billboards (a chicken sandwich fast food chain), which had three-dimensional cow figures in the act of painting the billboards with misspelled anti-beef slogans such as "frendz don't let frendz eat beef."

Placement of billboards

Some of the most prominent billboards are alongside highways; since passing drivers typically have little to occupy their attention, the impact of the billboard is greater. Billboards are often drivers' primary method of finding food and fuel on unfamiliar highways. There were approximately 450,000 billboards on United States highways as of 1991. Somewhere between 5,000 and 15,000 are erected each year. In Europe billboards are a major component and source of income in urban street furniture concepts.

An interesting use of billboards unique to highways was the Burma-Shave advertisements between 1925 and 1963, which had 4- or 5-part messages stretched across multiple signs, keeping the reader hooked by the promise of a punchline at the end. This example is in the National Museum of American History at the Smithsonian Institution:

1940s 3AW billboard advertising *For the Term of his Natural Life* in Melbourne

> Shaving brushes
>
> You'll soon see 'em
>
> On a shelf
>
> In some museum
>
> Burma-Shave

These sort of multi-sign advertisements are no longer common, though they are not extinct. One example, advertising for the NCAA, depicts a basketball player aiming a shot on one billboard; on the next one, 90 yards (82 meters) away, is the basket. Another example is the numerous billboards advertising the roadside attraction South of the Border near Dillon, SC, stretching along I-95 for many states.

Many cities have high densities of billboards, especially in places where there is a lot of pedestrian traffic—Times Square in New York City is a good example. Because of the lack of space in cities, these billboards are painted or hung on the sides of buildings and sometimes are free-standing billboards hanging above buildings. Billboards on the sides of buildings create different stylistic opportunities, with artwork that incorporates features of the building into the design, such as using windows as eyes, or for gigantic frescoes that adorn the entire building.

Visual and environmental concerns

The Animal Liberation Front vandalized this Chick-fil-A billboard to support its vegan aims.

Many groups such as Scenic America have complained that billboards on highways cause excessive clearing of trees and intrude on the surrounding landscape, with billboards' bright colors, lights and large fonts making it difficult to focus on anything else, making them a form of visual pollution. Other groups believe that billboards and advertising in general contribute negatively to the mental climate of a culture by promoting products as providing feelings of completeness, wellness and popularity to motivate purchase. One focal point for this sentiment would be the magazine AdBusters, which will often showcase politically motivated billboard and other advertising vandalism, called culture jamming.

In 2000, rooftops in Athens had grown so thick with billboards that it was difficult to see its famous architecture. In preparation for the 2004 Summer Olympics, the city embarked on a successful four-year project demolishing the majority of rooftop billboards to beautify the city for the tourists the games will bring, overcoming resistance from advertisers and building owners. Most of these billboards were illegal, but had been ignored up to then.

In 2007, São Paulo, Brazil instituted a billboard ban because there were no viable regulations of the billboard industry. Today, São Paulo, Brazil, is working with outdoor companies in the region to rebuild the outdoor infrastructure in a way that will reflect the vibrant business climate of the city while adopting good regulations to control growth.

Road safety concerns

In the United States, many cities tried to put laws into effect to ban billboards as early as 1909 (California Supreme Court, Varney & Green vs. Williams) but the First Amendment has made these attempts difficult. A San Diego law championed by Pete Wilson in 1971 cited traffic safety and driver distraction as the reason for the billboard ban, but was narrowly overturned by the Supreme Court in 1981, in part because it banned non-commercial as well as commercial billboards.

Billboards have long been accused of being distracting to drivers and causing accidents. However, this may not necessarily be true, as a study by researchers at the University of North Carolina showed. Released in June 2001, the researchers prepared a thorough report on driver distraction for the AAA Foundation for Traffic Safety. This study said: "The search appears to suggest that some items—such as CB radios, billboards, and temperature controls—are not significant distractions."

Traffic safety experts have studied the relationship between outdoor advertising and traffic accidents since the 1950s, finding no authoritative or scientific evidence that billboards are linked to traffic accidents. However, many of these studies were funded by the Outdoor Advertising Association of America, which has led to accusations of bias. The methodology used in certain studies is also questionable.

The U.S. Department of Transportation, State Department of Transportation and property/casualty insurance companies statistics on fatal accidents indicate no correlation between billboards and traffic accidents. A broad sampling of law enforcement agencies across the country found no evidence to suggest that motor vehicle accidents were caused by billboards. Property and casualty insurance companies have conducted detailed studies of traffic accident records and conclude no correlation between billboards and traffic accidents.

However, studies based on correlations between traffic accidents and billboards face the problem of under-reporting: drivers are unwilling to admit responsibility for a crash, so will not admit to being distracted at a crucial moment. Even given this limitation, some studies have found higher crash rates in the vicinity of advertising using variable message signs[1] or electronic billboards.[2]

It is possible that advertising signs in rural areas reduce driver boredom, which many believe is a contribution to highway safety. On the other hand, drivers may fixate on a billboard which unexpectedly appears in a monotonous landscape, and drive straight into it (a phenomenon known as "highway hypnosis").[3]

Surveys of drivers and road users show that the lighting provided by billboards provide security and visibility to many motorists. The Federal Highway Administration (FHWA) went on record (Federal Register, March 5, 1999) stating that the agency agrees that appropriately regulated billboards do not compromise highway safety. It should be noted that this statement was made before the release of the FHWA report *Research review of potential safety effects of electronic billboards on driver attention and distraction*[2] in 2001. What level of regulation is appropriate for billboards in different areas is still under discussion by road safety experts around the world.

Laws limiting billboards

In 1964, the negative impact of the over-proliferation of signage was abundantly evident in Houston, Texas, and it motivated Lady Bird Johnson to ask her husband to create a law. At the same time the outdoor advertising industry was becoming aware that excessive signs, some literally one in front of the other, was bad for business.

In 1965, the Highway Beautification Act was signed into law. The act applied only to "Federal Aid Primary" and "Defense" highways and limited billboards to commercial and industrial zones created by states and municipalities. It required each state to set standards based on "customary use" for the size, lighting and spacing of billboards, and prohibited city and state governments from removing billboards without paying compensation to the owner. The act requires states to maintain "effective control" of billboards or lose 5% of their federal highway dollars.

The act also required the screening of junk yards adjacent to regulated highways.

Around major holidays, volunteer groups erected highway signs offering free coffee at the next rest stop. These were specifically exempted from the limits in the act.

Currently, four states—Vermont, Alaska, Hawaii, and Maine—have prohibited billboards. Vermont's law went into effect in 1968 [4] , Hawaii's law went into effect in 1927[5] , Maine's law went into effect in 1979[6] , and Alaska's law went into effect upon its achievement of statehood in 1959.

In the UK, billboards are controlled as adverts as part of the planning system. To display such an advert is a criminal offence with a fine of up to £2500 per offence (per poster). All of the large UK outdoor advertisers such as CBS Outdoor [7], JCDecaux, Clear Channel, Titan and Primesight have numerous convictions for such crimes.[8] [9]

In Toronto, Canada, a municipal tax on billboards will be implemented in April 2010. A portion of the tax will help fund arts programs in the city.[10]

Usages

Highway

The now-famous "City of Champions" billboard that once greeted visitors to Pittsburgh in the early 1980's when the Pittsburgh Pirates and Steelers won the World Series and Super Bowl, respectively, in 1979. The billboard was sponsored by Pittsburgh National Bank, which renamed itself PNC Bank in 1982.

Many signs advertise local restaurants and shops in the coming miles, and are crucial to drawing business in small towns. One example is Wall Drug, which in 1931 erected billboards advertising "free ice water" and the town of Wall, South Dakota was essentially built around the 20,000 customers per day those billboards brought in (as of 1981). Some signs were placed at great distances, with slogans such as "only 827 miles to Wall Drug, with FREE ice water." In some areas the signs were so dense that one almost immediately followed the last. This situation changed after the Highway Beautification Act was passed; the proliferation of Wall Drug billboards is sometimes cited as one of the reasons the bill was passed. After the passage of the act, other states (such as Oregon[11]) embarked on highway beautification efforts.

Big name advertisers

Billboards are also used to advertise national or global brands, particularly in more densely populated urban areas. According to the Outdoor Advertising Association of America, the top three companies advertising on billboards as of 2009 were McDonald's, Verizon Long Distance and Pepsi. A large number of wireless phone companies, movie companies, car manufacturers and banks are high on the list as well.

ATB Financial ad, Edmonton

Tobacco advertising

Prior to 1999, billboards were a major venue of cigarette advertising; 10% of Michigan billboards advertise alcohol and tobacco, according to the Detroit Free Press.[12] This is particularly true in countries where tobacco advertisements are not allowed in other media. For example, in the US, tobacco advertising was banned on → radio and → television in 1971, leaving billboards and magazines as some of the last places tobacco could be advertised. Billboards made the news in America when, in the tobacco settlement of 1999, all cigarette billboards were replaced with anti-smoking messages. In a parody of the Marlboro Man, some billboards depicted cowboys riding on ranches with slogans like "Bob, I miss my lung."

Mail Pouch Barn advertisement: A bit of Americana in southern Ohio. Mail Pouch painted the barns for free.

Likely the best-known of the tobacco advertising boards were those for "Mail Pouch" chewing tobacco in the United States during the first half of the 20th century (pictured above). The company agreed to paint two or three sides of a farmer's barn any color he chose in exchange for painting their advertisement on the one or two sides of the structure facing the road. The company has long since abandoned this form of advertising, and none of these advertisements have been painted in many years, but some remain visible on rural highways.

Non-commercial use

Not all billboards are used for advertising products and services—non-profit groups and government agencies use them to communicate with the public. In 1999 an anonymous person created the God Speaks billboard campaign in Florida "to get people thinking about God", with witty statements signed by God. "Don't make me come down there", "We need to talk" and "Keep using my name in vain, I'll make rush hour longer" were parts of the campaign, which was picked up by the Outdoor Advertising Association of America and continues today on billboards across the country.

Non-commercial advertisement is used around the world by governments and non-profit organisations to obtain donations, volunteer support or change consumer behavior.[13]

South of Olympia, Washington is the privately owned Uncle Sam billboard. It features conservative, sometimes inflammatory messages, changed on a regular basis. Chehalis farmer Al Hamilton first started the board during the Johnson era, when the government was trying to make him remove his billboards along interstate 5. He had erected the signs after he lost a legal battle to prevent the building of the freeway across his land. Numerous legal and illegal attempts to remove the Uncle Sam billboard have failed, and it is now in its third location.[14] One message, attacking a nearby liberal arts college, was photographed, made into a postcard and is sold in the College Bookstore.

Governance

The Traffic Audit Bureau for Media Measurement Inc. (TAB) was established in 1933 as a non-profit organization whose historical mission has been to audit the circulation of out-of-home media in the United States. TAB's role has expanded to lead and/or support other major out of home industry research initiatives. Governed by a tripartite board composed of advertisers, agencies and media companies, the TAB acts as an independent auditor for traffic circulation in accordance to guidelines established by its Board of Directors.

Similarly, in Canada, the Canadian Outdoor Measurement Bureau (COMB) was formed in 1965 as a non-profit organization independently operated by representatives composed of advertisers, advertising agencies and members of the Canadian out-of-home advertising industry. COMB is charged with the verification of traffic circulation for the benefit of the industry and its users.

History

Early billboards were basically large posters on the sides of buildings, with limited but still appreciable commercial value. As roads and highways multiplied, the billboard business thrived.

1908 billboard, Salt Lake City, Utah

- 1794 – Lithography was invented, making real posters possible
- 1835 – Jared Bell was making 9x6 posters for the circus in the U.S.
- 1867 – Earliest known billboard rentals (source: OAAA)
- 1872 – International Bill Posters Association of North America was established (now known as the Outdoor Advertising Association of America) as a billboard lobbying group.
- 1889 - The world's first 24 sheet billboard was displayed at the Paris Exposition and later at the 1893 World's Columbian Exposition in Chicago. The format was quickly adopted for various types of advertising, especially for circuses, traveling shows, and movies
- 1908 – The Model T automobile is introduced in the U.S., increasing the number of people using highways and therefore the reach of roadside billboards.
- 1919 - Japanese candy company Glico introduces its building-spanning billboard, the Glico Man
- 1925 – Burma-Shave makes its billboards lining the highways
- 1931 – The Wall Drug billboards start to go up nationwide
- 1960 - The mechanized Kani Doraku billboard is built in Dotonbori, Osaka
- 1965 – the Highway Beautification Act is passed after much campaigning by Lady Bird Johnson
- 1971 – The Public Health Cigarette Smoking Act bans cigarette ads in television and radio, moving that business into billboards
- 1981 – The Supreme Court overturns a San Diego billboard ban, but leaves room open for other cities to ban commercial billboards
- 1997 – Tobacco advertising is no longer allowed on outdoor billboards in America
- 2007 – Industry adopts one sheet plastic poster replacement for paper poster billboards and begins phase-out of PVC flexible vinyl, replacing it with eco-plastics such as polyethylene

Billboard companies

- CBS Outdoor
- Clear Channel
- JCDecaux
- Primesight
- YESCO

See also

- Advertising board
- Human billboard
- Mediascape
- Neon sign
- Publicity
- Sales promotion
- Marquee (sign)
- Truckside advertisement

References

[1] Cairney, P., & Gunatillake, T. (2000). Does roadside advertising really cause crashes? Paper presented at the Road Safety: research, enforcement and policy., Brisbane, Australia.

[2] Farbry, J., Wochinger, K., Shafer, T., Owens, N., & Nedzesky, A. (2001). Research review of potential safety effects of electronic billboards on driver attention and distraction. Washington, DC: Federal Highway Administration

[3] Wallace, B. (2003). Driver distraction by advertising: genuine risk or urban myth? Municipal Engineer, 156, 185-190.

[4] http://www.vpr.net/news_detail/78949/

[5] http://www.wptz.com/automotive/20165541/detail.html

[6] http://pressherald.mainetoday.com/story.php?id=123918&ac=PHnws

[7] http://www.cbsoutdoor.com

[8] http://www.wandsworth.gov.uk/NR/Wandsworth/localpdf/brightside/bside_oct07.pdf

[9] http://es.homesandproperty.co.uk/property_news/articles/writing.html

[10] http://www.cbc.ca/canada/toronto/story/2009/12/07/toronto-billboard-tax693.html

[11] Trevision, Catherine and Wozniacka, Gosia. (http://www.oregonlive.com/news/oregonian/index.ssf?/base/news/118671991861640. xml&coll=7.) "The Oregonian. 12 August 2007. Retrieved December 26, 2007.

[12] http://www.cancer.org/docroot/NWS/content/NWS_2_1x_December_Mixed_Month_for_Tobacco_Opponents.asp

[13] Koekemoer, Ludi; Steve Bird (2004). *Marketing Communications* (http://books.google.es/books?id=T3UUfNBE1DcC). Juta and Company Limited. p. 71. ISBN 0702165093. .

[14] http://seattletimes.nwsource.com/news/nation-world/infocus/mideast/iraq/homefront0402.html

Marketing communications

Marketing Communications (or **MarCom** or **Integrated Marketing Communications**) are messages and related media used to communicate with a market. Those who practice → advertising, branding, direct marketing, graphic design, → marketing, packaging, → promotion, publicity, sponsorship, public relations, sales, sales promotion and online marketing are termed *marketing communicators, marketing communication managers,* or more briefly as *marcom managers.*

Traditionally, marketing communication practitioners focus on the creation and execution of printed marketing collateral; however, academic and professional research developed the practice to use strategic elements of branding and marketing in order to ensure consistency of message delivery throughout an organization - the same "look & feel". Many trends in business can be attributed to marketing communication; for example: the transition from customer service to customer relations, and the transition from human resources to human solutions.

In branding, every opportunity to impress the organization's (or individual's) brand upon the customer is called a *brand touchpoint* (or *brand contact point.*) Examples include everything from TV and other media advertisements, event sponsorships, webinars, and personal selling to even product packaging. Thus, every experiential opportunity that an organization creates for its stakeholders or customers is a brand touchpoint. Hence, it is vitally important for brand strategists and managers to survey all of their organization's brand touchpoints and control for the stakeholder's or customer's experience. Marketing communication, as a vehicle of an organization's brand management, is concerned with the promotion of an organization's brand, product(s) and/or service(s) to stakeholders and prospective customers through these touchpoints.

Marketing communications is focused on product/produce/service as opposed to corporate communications where the focus of communications work is the company/enterprise itself. Marketing communications is primarily concerned with demand generation, product/produce/service positioning while corporate communications deal with issue management, mergers and acquisitions, litigation etc.

External links

- The Journal of Integrated Marketing Communications [1]
- STC Marketing Communication Special Interest Group [2]

References

[1] http://jimc.medill.northwestern.edu/JIMCWebsite/site.htm
[2] http://www.stcsig.org/mc/

Website

A **website** (also spelled **web site**) is a collection of related → web pages, images, videos or other digital assets that are addressed with a common domain name or IP address in an Internet Protocol-based network. A web site is hosted on at least one web server, accessible via a network such as the → Internet or a private local area network.

A web page is a document, typically written in plain text interspersed with formatting instructions of Hypertext Markup Language (HTML, XHTML). A web page may incorporate elements from other websites with suitable markup anchors.

Web pages are accessed and transported with the Hypertext Transfer Protocol (HTTP), which may optionally employ encryption (HTTP Secure, HTTPS) to provide security and privacy for the user of the web page content. The user's application, often a web browser, renders the page content according to its HTML markup instructions onto a display terminal.

All publicly accessible websites collectively constitute the → World Wide Web.

The pages of a website can usually be accessed from a simple Uniform Resource Locator (URL) called the homepage. The URLs of the pages organize them into a hierarchy, although hyperlinking between them conveys the reader's perceived site structure and guides the reader's navigation of the site.

Some websites require a subscription to access some or all of their content. Examples of subscription sites include many business sites, parts of many news sites, academic journal sites, gaming sites, message boards, web-based → e-mail, services, social networking websites, and sites providing real-time stock market data.

History

The → World Wide Web (WWW) was created in 1990 by CERN engineer Tim Berners-Lee.[1] On 30 April 1993, CERN announced that the World Wide Web would be free to use for anyone.[2]

Before the introduction of HTML and HTTP, other protocols such as file transfer protocol and the gopher protocol were used to retrieve individual files from a server. These protocols offer a simple directory structure which the user navigates and chooses files to download. Documents were most often presented as plain text files without formatting or were encoded in word processor formats.

Overview

Organized by function, a website may be

- a personal website
- a commercial website
- a government website
- a non-profit organization website

It could be the work of an individual, a business or other organization, and is typically dedicated to some particular topic or purpose. Any website can contain a hyperlink to any other website, so the distinction between individual sites, as perceived by the user, may sometimes be blurred.

Websites are written in, or dynamically converted to, HTML (Hyper Text Markup Language) and are accessed using a software interface classified as a user agent. Web pages can be viewed or otherwise accessed from a range of computer-based and Internet-enabled devices of various sizes, including desktop computers, laptops, PDAs and cell phones.

A website is hosted on a computer system known as a web server, also called an HTTP server, and these terms can also refer to the software that runs on these systems and that retrieves and delivers the web pages in response to requests from the website users. Apache is the most commonly used web server software (according to Netcraft statistics) and Microsoft's Internet Information Server (IIS) is also commonly used.

Static website

A **static website** is one that has web pages stored on the server in the format that is sent to a client web browser. It is primarily coded in Hypertext Markup Language (HTML).

Simple forms or marketing examples of websites, such as *classic website*, a *five-page website* or a *brochure website* are often static websites, because they present pre-defined, static information to the user. This may include information about a company and its products and services via text, photos, animations, audio/video and interactive menus and navigation.

This type of website usually displays the same information to all visitors. Similar to handing out a printed brochure to customers or clients, a static website will generally provide consistent, standard information for an extended period of time. Although the website owner may make updates periodically, it is a manual process to edit the text, photos and other content and may require basic website design skills and software.

In summary, visitors are not able to control what information they receive via a static website, and must instead settle for whatever content the website owner has decided to offer at that time.

They are edited using four broad categories of software:

- Text editors, such as Notepad or TextEdit, where content and HTML markup are manipulated directly within the editor program
- WYSIWYG offline editors, such as Microsoft FrontPage and Adobe Dreamweaver (previously Macromedia Dreamweaver), with which the site is edited using a GUI interface and the final HTML markup is generated automatically by the editor software
- WYSIWYG online editors which create media rich online presentation like web pages, widgets, intro, blogs, and other documents.
- Template-based editors, such as Rapidweaver and iWeb, which allow users to quickly create and upload web pages to a web server without detailed HTML knowledge, as they pick a suitable template from a palette and add pictures and text to it in a desktop publishing fashion without direct manipulation of HTML code.

Dynamic website

A **dynamic website** is one that changes or customizes itself frequently and automatically, based on certain criteria.

Dynamic websites can have two types of dynamic activity: Code and Content. Dynamic code is invisible or behind the scenes and dynamic content is visible or fully displayed.

Dynamic code

The first type is a website with **dynamic code** hidden inside. The lines of code are constructed dynamically on the fly using active programming language instead of plain, static HTML.

A website with **dynamic code** refers to its construction or how it is built, and more specifically refers to the code used to create a single web page. A dynamic web page is generated on the fly by piecing together certain blocks of code, procedures or routines. A dynamically-generated web page would call various bits of information from a database and put them together in a pre-defined format to present the reader with a coherent page. It interacts with users in a variety of ways including by reading cookies recognizing users' previous history, session variables, server side variables etc., or by using direct interaction (form elements, mouseovers, etc.). A site can display the current state of a dialogue between users, monitor a changing situation, or provide information in some way personalized to the requirements of the individual user.

Dynamic content

The second type is a website with **dynamic content** displayed in plain view. Variable content is displayed dynamically on the fly based on certain criteria, usually by retrieving content stored in a database.

A website with **dynamic content** refers to how its messages, text, images and other information are displayed on the web page, and more specifically how its content changes at any given moment. The web page content varies based on certain criteria, either pre-defined rules or variable user input. For example, a website with a database of news articles can use a pre-defined rule which tells it to display all news articles for today's date. This type of dynamic website will automatically show the most current news articles on any given date. Another example of dynamic content is when a retail website with a database of media products allows a user to input a search request for the keyword Beatles. In response, the content of the web page will spontaneously change the way it looked before, and will then display a list of Beatles products like CD's, DVD's and books.

Purpose of dynamic websites

The main purpose of a dynamic website is automation. A dynamic website can operate more effectively, be built more efficiently and is easier to maintain, update and expand. It is much simpler to build a template and a database than to build hundreds or thousands of individual, static HTML web pages.

Software systems

There are a wide range of software systems, such as Java Server Pages (JSP), the PHP and Perl programming languages, Active Server Pages (ASP), YUMA and Cold Fusion (CFM) that are available to generate dynamic web systems and dynamic sites. Sites may also include content that is retrieved from one or more databases or by using XML-based technologies such as RSS.

Static content may also be dynamically generated either periodically, or if certain conditions for regeneration occur (cached) in order to avoid the performance loss of initiating the dynamic engine on a per-user or per-connection basis.

Plug ins are available to expand the features and abilities of web browsers, which use them to show *active content*, such as Microsoft Silverlight, Adobe Flash, Adobe Shockwave or applets written in Java. Dynamic HTML also provides for user interactivity and realtime element updating within web pages (i.e., pages don't have to be loaded or reloaded to effect any changes), mainly using the Document Object Model (DOM) and JavaScript, support which is built-in to most modern web browsers.

Turning a website into an income source is a common practice for web developers and website owners. There are several methods for creating a website business which fall into two broad categories, as defined below.

Content-based sites

Some websites derive revenue by selling advertising space on the site (see Contextual advertising).

Product- or service-based sites

Some websites derive revenue by offering products or services for sale. In the case of e-commerce websites, the products or services may be purchased at the website itself, by entering credit card or other payment information into a payment form on the site. While most business websites serve as a shop window for existing brick and mortar businesses, it is increasingly the case that some websites are businesses in their own right; that is, the products they offer are only available for purchase on the web.

Websites occasionally derive income from a combination of these two practices. For example, a website such as an online auctions website may charge the users of its auction service to list an auction, but also display third-party advertisements on the site, from which it derives further income.

Spelling

The forms *website* and *web site* are the most commonly used forms, the former especially in British English. The Associated Press Style book, Reuters, Microsoft, academia, book publishing, *The Chicago Manual of Style*, and dictionaries such as Merriam-Webster use the two-word, initially capitalized spelling *Web site*. This is because "Web" is not a general term but a short form of *World Wide Web*. As with many newly created terms, it may take some time before a common spelling is finalized. This controversy also applies to derivative terms such as web page, web master, and web cam.

The Canadian Oxford Dictionary and the Canadian Press Style book list "website" and "web page" as the preferred spellings. The Oxford English Dictionary began using "website" as its standardized form in 2004.[3]

Bill Walsh, the copy chief of *The Washington Post's* national desk, and one of American English's foremost grammarians, argues for the two-word spelling with capital W in his books *Lapsing into a Comma* and *The Elephants of Style*, and on his site, the Slot.[4]

Types of websites

There are many varieties of websites, each specializing in a particular type of content or use, and they may be arbitrarily classified in any number of ways. A few such classifications might include:

- Affiliate: enabled portal that renders not only its custom CMS but also syndicated content from other content providers for an agreed fee. There are usually three relationship tiers. Affiliate Agencies (e.g., Commission Junction), Advertisers (e.g., eBay) and consumer (e.g., Yahoo!).
- Archive site: used to preserve valuable electronic content threatened with extinction. Two examples are: Internet Archive, which since 1996 has preserved billions of old (and new) web pages; and Google Groups, which in early 2005 was archiving over 845,000,000 messages posted to Usenet news/discussion groups.
- Blog (web log): sites generally used to post online diaries which may include discussion forums (e.g., blogger, Xanga).
- Brand building site: a site with the purpose of creating an experience of a brand online. These sites usually do not sell anything, but focus on building the brand. Brand building sites are most common for low-value, high-volume fast moving consumer goods (FMCG).
- City Site: A site that shows information about a certain city or town and events that takes place in that town. Usually created by the city council or other "movers and shakers".
  - the same as those of geographic entities, such as cities and countries. For example, Richmond.com is the geodomain for Richmond, Virginia.
- Community site: a site where persons with similar interests communicate with each other, usually by chat or message boards, such as MySpace or Facebook.
- Content site: sites whose business is the creation and distribution of original content (e.g., Slate, About.com).
- Corporate website: used to provide background information about a business, organization, or service.
- Electronic commerce (e-commerce) site: a site offering goods and services for online sale and enabling online transactions for such sales.
- Forum: a site where people discuss various topics.
- Gripe site: a site devoted to the critique of a person, place, corporation, government, or institution.
- Humor site: satirizes, parodies or otherwise exists solely to amuse.
- Information site: contains content that is intended to inform visitors, but not necessarily for commercial purposes, such as: RateMyProfessors.com, Free Internet Lexicon and Encyclopedia. Most government, educational and non-profit institutions have an informational site.
- Java applet site: contains software to run over the Web as a Web application.
- Mirror site: A complete reproduction of a website.

- News site: similar to an information site, but dedicated to dispensing news and commentary.
- Personal homepage: run by an individual or a small group (such as a family) that contains information or any content that the individual wishes to include. These are usually uploaded using a web hosting service such as Geocities.
- Phish site: a website created to fraudulently acquire sensitive information, such as passwords and credit card details, by masquerading as a trustworthy person or business (such as Social Security Administration, PayPal) in an electronic communication (see Phishing).
- Political site: A site on which people may voice political views.
- Porn site: A site that shows sexually explicit content for enjoyment and relaxation, most likely in the form of an Internet gallery, dating site, blog, social networking, or video sharing.
- Rating site: A site on which people can praise or disparage what is featured.
- Review site: A site on which people can post reviews for products or services.
- School site: a site on which teachers, students, or administrators can post information about current events at or involving their school. U.S. elementary-high school websites generally use k12 in the URL, such as kearney.k12.mo.us.
- → Search engine site: a site that provides general information and is intended as a gateway or lookup for other sites. A pure example is Google, and well-known sites include Yahoo! Search and Bing (search engine).
- Shock site: includes images or other material that is intended to be offensive to most viewers (e.g. rotten.com).
- Social bookmarking site: a site where users share other content from the Internet and rate and comment on the content. StumbleUpon and Digg are examples.
- Social networking site: a site where users could communicate with one another and share media, such as pictures, videos, music, blogs, etc. with other users. These may include games and web applications.
- Video sharing: A site that enables user to upload videos, such as YouTube and Google Video.
- Warez: a site designed to host and let users download copyrighted materials illegally.
- Web portal: a site that provides a starting point or a gateway to other resources on the Internet or an intranet.
- Wiki site: a site which users collaboratively edit (such as Wikipedia and Wikihow).

Some websites may be included in one or more of these categories. For example, a business website may promote the business's products, but may also host informative documents, such as → white papers. There are also numerous sub-categories to the ones listed above. For example, a porn site is a specific type of e-commerce site or business site (that is, it is trying to sell memberships for access to its site). A fan site may be a dedication from the owner to a particular celebrity.

Websites are constrained by architectural limits (e.g., the computing power dedicated to the website). Very large websites, such as Yahoo!, Microsoft, and Google employ many servers and load balancing equipment such as Cisco Content Services Switches to distribute visitor loads over multiple computers at multiple locations.

In February 2009, Netcraft, an Internet monitoring company that has tracked Web growth since 1995, reported that there were 215,675,903 websites with domain names and content on them in 2009, compared to just 18,000 websites in August 1995.

Awards

The Webby Awards are a set of awards presented to the world's best websites, a concept pioneered by Best of the Web in 1994.

See also

- Cognitive metaphor
- Cyberspace
- Downtime
- Extranet website
- Google guidelines
- Intranet website
- List of content management systems
- List of websites
- Rating sites
- Rational (WebSphere) Application Developer
- Real user monitoring
- Search Engine Optimization
- Staging site
- Template engine (web)
- Tim Berners-Lee, the inventor of the → World Wide Web
- Uptime
- Web analytics
- Web application
- Web content management
- Web design
- Web development
- Web hosting
- Web service
- Web Services Security
- Webmaster
- Website architecture
- Website awards
- Website Design Process Steps
- Website monetizing
- Website monitoring
- Website templates
- World Wide Web Consortium (Web standards)
- Yahoo! Site Explorer

External links

- Internet Corporation For Assigned Names and Numbers (ICANN) [5]
- World Wide Web Consortium (W3C) [76]
- The Internet Society (ISOC) [6]

References

[1] "The website of the world's first-ever web server" (http://info.cern.ch/). . Retrieved 2008-08-30.

[2] Cailliau, Robert. "A Little History of the World Wide Web" (http://www.w3.org/History.html). . Retrieved 2007-02-16.

[3] "Ask Oxford: How should the term *website* be written in official documents and on the web?" (http://www.askoxford.com/asktheexperts/faq/usage/website?view=uk). *Oxford Dictionaries Online*. . Retrieved 2007-02-23.

[4] "The Slot—Sharp Points: Here We Go Again—Eeee!" (http://www.theslot.com/email.html). . Retrieved 2007-02-25.

[5] http://www.icann.org/

[6] http://www.isoc.org/

PageRank

PageRank is a link analysis algorithm, named after Larry Page,[1] used by the Google Internet search engine that assigns a numerical weighting to each element of a hyperlinked set of documents, such as the → World Wide Web, with the purpose of "measuring" its relative importance within the set. The algorithm may be applied to any collection of entities with reciprocal quotations and references. The numerical weight that it assigns to any given element E is also called the *PageRank of* E and denoted by $PR(E)$.

The name "PageRank" is a trademark of Google, and the PageRank process has been patented (U.S. Patent 6285999 [2]). However, the patent is assigned to Stanford University and not to Google. Google has exclusive license rights on the patent from Stanford University. The university received 1.8 million shares of Google in exchange for use of the patent; the shares were sold in 2005 for $336 million.[3] [4]

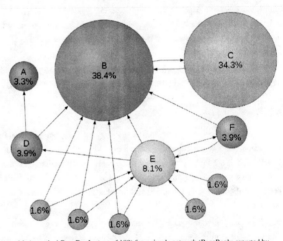

Mathematical **PageRanks** (out of 100) for a simple network (PageRanks reported by Google are rescaled logarithmically). Page C has a higher PageRank than Page E, even though it has fewer links to it; the link it has is of a much higher value. A web surfer who chooses a random link on every page (but with 15% likelihood jumps to a random page on the whole web) is going to be on Page E for 8.1% of the time. (The 15% likelihood of jumping to an arbitrary page corresponds to a damping factor of 85%.) Without damping, all web surfers would eventually end up on Pages A, B, or C, and all other pages would have PageRank zero. Page A is assumed to link to all pages in the web, because it has no outgoing links.

Description

Google describes PageRank:[5]

PageRank relies on the uniquely democratic nature of the web by using its vast link structure as an indicator of an individual page's value. In essence, Google interprets a link from page A to page B as a vote, by page A, for page B. But, Google looks at more than the sheer volume of votes, or links a page receives; it also analyzes the page that casts the vote. Votes cast by pages that are themselves "important" weigh more heavily and help to make other pages "important".

In other words, a PageRank results from a "ballot" among all the other pages on the World Wide Web about how important a page is. A hyperlink to a page counts as a vote of support. The PageRank of a page is defined recursively and depends on the number and PageRank metric of all pages that link to it ("incoming links"). A page that is linked to by many pages with high PageRank receives a high rank itself. If there are no links to a web page there is no support for that page.

Google assigns a numeric weighting from 0-10 for each webpage on the Internet; this PageRank denotes a site's importance in the eyes of Google. The PageRank is derived from a theoretical probability value on a logarithmic scale like the Richter Scale. The PageRank of a particular page is roughly based upon the quantity of inbound links as well as the PageRank of the pages providing the links. It is known that other factors, e.g. relevance of search words on the page and actual visits to the page reported by the Google toolbar also influence the PageRank. In order to prevent manipulation, spoofing and Spamdexing, Google provides no specific details about how other factors influence PageRank.

Numerous academic papers concerning PageRank have been published since Page and Brin's original paper.[6] In practice, the PageRank concept has proven to be vulnerable to manipulation, and extensive research has been devoted to identifying falsely inflated PageRank and ways to ignore links from documents with falsely inflated PageRank.

Other link-based ranking algorithms for Web pages include the HITS algorithm invented by Jon Kleinberg (used by Teoma and now Ask.com), the IBM CLEVER project, and the TrustRank algorithm.

History

PageRank was developed at Stanford University by Larry Page (hence the name *Page*-Rank[7]) and later Sergey Brin as part of a research project about a new kind of search engine. The first paper about the project, describing PageRank and the initial prototype of the Google search engine, was published in 1998[6] : shortly after, Page and Brin founded Google Inc., the company behind the Google search engine. While just one of many factors which determine the ranking of Google search results, PageRank continues to provide the basis for all of Google's web search tools.[5]

PageRank has been influenced by citation analysis, early developed by Eugene Garfield in the 1950s at the University of Pennsylvania, and by Hyper Search, developed by Massimo Marchiori at the University of Padua (Google's founders cite Garfield's and Marchiori's works in their original paper[6]). In the same year PageRank was introduced (1998), Jon Kleinberg published his important work on HITS.

Algorithm

PageRank is a probability distribution used to represent the likelihood that a person randomly clicking on links will arrive at any particular page. PageRank can be calculated for collections of documents of any size. It is assumed in several research papers that the distribution is evenly divided between all documents in the collection at the beginning of the computational process. The PageRank computations require several passes, called "iterations", through the collection to adjust approximate PageRank values to more closely reflect the theoretical true value.

A probability is expressed as a numeric value between 0 and 1. A 0.5 probability is commonly expressed as a "50% chance" of something happening. Hence, a PageRank of 0.5 means there is a 50% chance that a person clicking on a random link will be directed to the document with the 0.5 PageRank.

Simplified algorithm

Assume a small universe of four web pages: **A**, **B**, **C** and **D**. The initial approximation of PageRank would be evenly divided between these four documents. Hence, each document would begin with an estimated PageRank of 0.25.

In the original form of PageRank initial values were simply 1. This meant that the sum of all pages was the total number of pages on the web. Later versions of PageRank (see the below formulas) would assume a probability distribution between 0 and 1. Here a simple probability distribution will be used- hence the initial value of 0.25.

If pages **B**, **C**, and **D** each only link to **A**, they would each confer 0.25 PageRank to **A**. All PageRank **PR( )** in this simplistic system would thus gather to **A** because all links would be pointing to **A**.

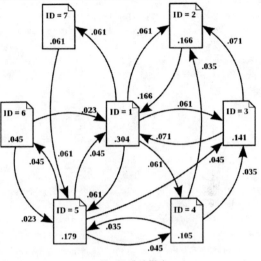

How PageRank Works

$$PR(A) = PR(B) + PR(C) + PR(D).$$

This is 0.75.

Again, suppose page **B** also has a link to page **C**, and page **D** has links to all three pages. The *value of the link-votes is divided among all the outbound links on a page*. Thus, page **B** gives a vote worth 0.125 to page **A** and a vote worth 0.125 to page **C**. Only one third of **D**'s PageRank is counted for **A**'s PageRank (approximately 0.083).

$$PR(A) = \frac{PR(B)}{2} + \frac{PR(C)}{1} + \frac{PR(D)}{3}.$$

In other words, the PageRank conferred by an outbound link is equal to the document's own PageRank score divided by the normalized number of outbound links **L( )** (it is assumed that links to specific URLs only count once per document).

$$PR(A) = \frac{PR(B)}{L(B)} + \frac{PR(C)}{L(C)} + \frac{PR(D)}{L(D)}.$$

In the general case, the PageRank value for any page **u** can be expressed as:

$$PR(u) = \sum_{v \in B_u} \frac{PR(v)}{L(v)},$$

i.e. the PageRank value for a page **u** is dependent on the PageRank values for each page **v** out of the set **B**$_u$ (this set contains all pages linking to page **u**), divided by the number $L(v)$ of links from page **v**.

Damping factor

The PageRank theory holds that even an imaginary surfer who is randomly clicking on links will eventually stop clicking. The probability, at any step, that the person will continue is a damping factor d. Various studies have tested different damping factors, but it is generally assumed that the damping factor will be set around 0.85.[8]

The damping factor is subtracted from 1 (and in some variations of the algorithm, the result is divided by the number of documents in the collection) and this term is then added to the product of the damping factor and the sum of the incoming PageRank scores.

That is,

$$PR(A) = 1 - d + d\left(\frac{PR(B)}{L(B)} + \frac{PR(C)}{L(C)} + \frac{PR(D)}{L(D)} + \cdots\right)$$

or (N = the number of documents in collection)

$$PR(A) = \frac{1-d}{N} + d\left(\frac{PR(B)}{L(B)} + \frac{PR(C)}{L(C)} + \frac{PR(D)}{L(D)} + \cdots\right).$$

So any page's PageRank is derived in large part from the PageRanks of other pages. The damping factor adjusts the derived value downward. The second formula above supports the original statement in Page and Brin's paper that "the sum of all PageRanks is one".[6] Unfortunately, however, Page and Brin gave the first formula, which has led to some confusion.

Google recalculates PageRank scores each time it crawls the Web and rebuilds its index. As Google increases the number of documents in its collection, the initial approximation of PageRank decreases for all documents.

The formula uses a model of a *random surfer* who gets bored after several clicks and switches to a random page. The PageRank value of a page reflects the chance that the random surfer will land on that page by clicking on a link. It can be understood as a Markov chain in which the states are pages, and the transitions are all equally probable and are the links between pages.

If a page has no links to other pages, it becomes a sink and therefore terminates the random surfing process. However, the solution is quite simple. If the random surfer arrives at a sink page, it picks another URL at random and continues surfing again.

When calculating PageRank, pages with no outbound links are assumed to link out to all other pages in the collection. Their PageRank scores are therefore divided evenly among all other pages. In other words, to be fair with pages that are not sinks, these random transitions are added to all nodes in the Web, with a residual probability of usually $d = 0.85$, estimated from the frequency that an average surfer uses his or her browser's bookmark feature.

So, the equation is as follows:

$$PR(p_i) = \frac{1-d}{N} + d\sum_{p_j \in M(p_i)} \frac{PR(p_j)}{L(p_j)}$$

where $p_1, p_2, \ldots, p_N$ are the pages under consideration, $M(p_i)$ is the set of pages that link to p_i, $L(p_j)$ is the number of outbound links on page p_j, and N is the total number of pages.

The PageRank values are the entries of the dominant eigenvector of the modified adjacency matrix. This makes PageRank a particularly elegant metric: the eigenvector is

$$\mathbf{R} = \begin{bmatrix} PR(p_1) \\ PR(p_2) \\ \vdots \\ PR(p_N) \end{bmatrix}$$

where $\mathbf{R}$ is the solution of the equation

$$
\mathbf{R} = \begin{bmatrix} (1-d)/N \\ (1-d)/N \\ \vdots \\ (1-d)/N \end{bmatrix} + d \begin{bmatrix} \ell(p_1,p_1) & \ell(p_2,p_1) & \cdots & \ell(p_N,p_1) \\ \ell(p_1,p_2) & \ddots & & \vdots \\ \vdots & & \ell(p_i,p_j) & \\ \ell(p_1,p_N) & \cdots & & \ell(p_N,p_N) \end{bmatrix} \mathbf{R}
$$

where the adjacency function $\ell(p_i,p_j)$ is 0 if page p_i does not link to p_j, and normalised such that, for each i

$$
\sum_{i=1}^{N} \ell(p_i,p_j) = 1,
$$

i.e. the elements of each column sum up to 1. This is a variant of the eigenvector centrality measure used commonly in network analysis.

Because of the large eigengap of the modified adjacency matrix above, [9] the values of the PageRank eigenvector are fast to approximate (only a few iterations are needed).

As a result of Markov theory, it can be shown that the PageRank of a page is the probability of being at that page after lots of clicks. This happens to equal t^{-1} where t is the expectation of the number of clicks (or random jumps) required to get from the page back to itself.

The main disadvantage is that it favors older pages, because a new page, even a very good one, will not have many links unless it is part of an existing site (a site being a densely connected set of pages, such as Wikipedia). The Google Directory (itself a derivative of the Open Directory Project) allows users to see results sorted by PageRank within categories. The Google Directory is the only service offered by Google where PageRank directly determines display order. In Google's other search services (such as its primary Web search) PageRank is used to weigh the relevance scores of pages shown in search results.

Several strategies have been proposed to accelerate the computation of PageRank.[10]

Various strategies to manipulate PageRank have been employed in concerted efforts to improve search results rankings and monetize advertising links. These strategies have severely impacted the reliability of the PageRank concept, which seeks to determine which documents are actually highly valued by the Web community.

Google is known to penalize link farms and other schemes designed to artificially inflate PageRank. In December 2007 Google started *actively* penalizing sites selling paid text links. How Google identifies link farms and other PageRank manipulation tools are among Google's trade secrets.

Variations

Google Toolbar

The Google Toolbar's PageRank feature displays a visited page's PageRank as a whole number between 0 and 10. The most popular websites have a PageRank of 10. The least have a PageRank of 0. Google has not disclosed the precise method for determining a Toolbar PageRank value, previously it could still be found by visiting: http:// www. google. com/ search?client=navclient-auto& ch=6-1484155081& features=Rank& q=info:http:/ / www. wikipedia. org/ (NOTE: this link generates a Google error in the form of a Terms of Service violation as of 2009.08.10) where www.wikipedia.org is the website name.

The following one-line Javascript performs the URL substitution and used to be usable as a bookmarklet in any browser bookmark bar (including Google Chrome which presently lacks a Google Toolbar add-in):

```
javascript:location.href='http:\/\/www.google.com\/search?client=navclient-auto&ch=6-1484
```

(NOTE: The above two techniques generate a 403 Forbidden error as of 10 Sept 2009)

The Google Toolbar is updated approximately 5 times a year, so often shows out of date values. It was last updated on 31 December, 2009 [11].

SERP Rank

The SERP (Search Engine Results Page) is the actual result returned by a search engine in response to a keyword query. The SERP consists of a list of links to web pages with associated text snippets. The SERP rank of a web page refers to the placement of the corresponding link on the SERP, where higher placement means higher SERP rank. The SERP rank of a web page is not only a function of its PageRank, but depends on a relatively large and continuously adjusted set of factors,[12] [13] commonly referred to by internet marketers as "Google Love"[14] . → SEO (Search Engine Optimization) is aimed at achieving the highest possible SERP rank for a website or a set of web pages.

Google directory PageRank

The Google Directory PageRank is an 8-unit measurement. These values can be viewed in the Google Directory. Unlike the Google Toolbar which shows the PageRank value by a mouseover of the green bar, the Google Directory does not show the PageRank as a numeric value but only as a green bar.

False or spoofed PageRank

While the PageRank shown in the Toolbar is considered to be derived from an accurate PageRank value (at some time prior to the time of publication by Google) for most sites, it must be noted that this value used to be easily manipulated. A previous flaw was that any low PageRank page that was redirected, via a HTTP 302 response or a "Refresh" meta tag, to a high PageRank page caused the lower PageRank page to acquire the PageRank of the destination page. In theory a new, PR 0 page with no incoming links could have been redirected to the Google home page - which is a PR 10 - and then the PR of the new page would be upgraded to a PR10. This spoofing technique, also known as 302 Google Jacking, was a known failing or bug in the system. Any page's PageRank could have been spoofed to a higher or lower number of the webmaster's choice and only Google has access to the real PageRank of the page. Spoofing is generally detected by running a Google search for a URL with questionable PageRank, as the results will display the URL of an entirely different site (the one redirected to) in its results.

Manipulating PageRank

For → search-engine optimization purposes, some companies offer to sell high PageRank links to webmasters.[15] As links from higher-PR pages are believed to be more valuable, they tend to be more expensive. It can be an effective and viable marketing strategy to buy link advertisements on content pages of quality and relevant sites to drive traffic and increase a webmaster's link popularity. However, Google has publicly warned webmasters that if they are or were discovered to be selling links for the purpose of conferring PageRank and reputation, their links will be devalued (ignored in the calculation of other pages' PageRanks). The practice of buying and selling links is intensely debated across the Webmaster community. Google advises webmasters to use the nofollow HTML attribute value on sponsored links. According to Matt Cutts, Google is concerned about webmasters who try to game the system, and thereby reduce the quality and relevancy of Google search results.[15]

The intentional surfer model

The original PageRank algorithm reflects the so-called random surfer model, meaning that the PageRank of a particular page is derived from the theoretical probability of visiting that page when clicking on links at random. However, real users do not randomly surf the web, but follow links according to their interest and intention. A page ranking model that reflects the importance of a particular page as a function of how many actual visits it receives by real users is called the *intentional surfer model*[16] . The Google toolbar sends information to Google for every page visited, and thereby provides a basis for computing PageRank based on the intentional surfer model. The introduction of the nofollow attribute by Google to combat Spamdexing has the side effect that webmasters commonly use it on outgoing link to increase their own PageRank. This causes a loss of actual links for the Web crawlers to follow, thereby making the original PageRank algorithm based on the random surfer model potentially unreliable. Using information about users' browsing habits provided by the Google toolbar partly compensates for the loss of information caused by the nofollow attribute. The SERP rank of a page, which determines a page's actual placement in the search results, is based on a combination of the random surfer model (PageRank) and the intentional surfer model (browsing habits) in addition to other factors [17].

Other uses

A version of PageRank has recently been proposed as a replacement for the traditional Institute for Scientific Information (ISI) impact factor,[18] and implemented at eigenfactor.org [19]. Instead of merely counting total citation to a journal, the "importance" of each citation is determined in a PageRank fashion.

A similar new use of PageRank is to rank academic doctoral programs based on their records of placing their graduates in faculty positions. In PageRank terms, academic departments link to each other by hiring their faculty from each other (and from themselves). [20]

PageRank has been used to rank spaces or streets to predict how many people (pedestrians or vehicles) come to the individual spaces or streets.[21] [22] It has also been used to automatically rank WordNet synsets according to how strongly they possess a given semantic property, such as positivity or negativity. [23]

A dynamic weighting method similar to PageRank has been used to generate customized reading lists based on the link structure of Wikipedia. [24]

A Web crawler may use PageRank as one of a number of importance metrics it uses to determine which URL to visit next during a crawl of the web. One of the early working papers [25] which were used in the creation of Google is *Efficient crawling through URL ordering* [26] , which discusses the use of a number of different importance metrics to determine how deeply, and how much of a site Google will crawl. PageRank is presented as one of a number of these importance metrics, though there are others listed such as the number of inbound and outbound links for a URL, and the distance from the root directory on a site to the URL.

The PageRank may also be used as a methodology [27] to measure the apparent impact of a community like the Blogosphere on the overall Web itself. This approach uses therefore the PageRank to measure the distribution of attention in reflection of the Scale-free network paradigm.

In any ecosystem, a modified version of PageRank may be used to determine species that are essential to the continuing health of the environment.[28]

Google's `rel="nofollow"` option

In early 2005, Google implemented a new value, "nofollow"[29] , for the rel attribute of HTML link and anchor elements, so that website developers and bloggers can make links that Google will not consider for the purposes of PageRank — they are links that no longer constitute a "vote" in the PageRank system. The nofollow relationship was added in an attempt to help combat spamdexing.

As an example, people could previously create many message-board posts with links to their website to artificially inflate their PageRank. With the nofollow value, message-board administrators can modify their code to automatically insert "rel='nofollow'" to all hyperlinks in posts, thus preventing PageRank from being affected by those particular posts. This method of avoidance, however, also has various drawbacks, such as reducing the link value of actual comments. (See: Spam in blogs#nofollow)

In an effort to manually control the flow of PageRank among pages within a website, many webmasters practice what is known as PageRank Sculpting[30] - which is the act of strategically placing the nofollow attribute on certain internal links of a website in order to funnel PageRank towards those pages the webmaster deemed most important. This tactic has been used since the inception of the nofollow attribute, but the technique has been thought by many to have lost its effectiveness.[31]

Removal from Google Webmaster Tools

On October 14, 2009, Google employee Susan Moskwa confirmed that the company had removed PageRank from its Webmaster Tools section. Her post said in part, "We've been telling people for a long time that they shouldn't focus on PageRank so much; many site owners seem to think it's the most important metric for them to track, which is simply not true." [32] PageRank was still displayed on the Google Toolbar web appliance two days after Moskwa's confirmation.

See also

- EigenTrust — a decentralized PageRank algorithm
- Google bomb
- Google guidelines
- Google search
- Google matrix
- Hilltop algorithm
- Link love
- PigeonRank
- Power method — the iterative eigenvector algorithm used to calculate PageRank
- → Search engine optimization
- SimRank - a measure of object-to-object similarity based on random-surfer model
- Topic-Sensitive PageRank
- TrustRank

References

- Langville, Amy N.; Meyer, Carl D. (2006). *Google's PageRank and Beyond: The Science of Search Engine Rankings*. Princeton University Press. ISBN 0-691-12202-4.
- Page, Lawrence; Brin, Sergey; Motwani, Rajeev and Winograd, Terry (1999). *The PageRank citation ranking: Bringing order to the Web* [33].
- Richardson, Matthew; Domingos, Pedro (2002). "The intelligent surfer: Probabilistic combination of link and content information in PageRank" [34] (PDF). Proceedings of Advances in Neural Information Processing Systems. **14**.
- Cheng, Alice; Eric J. Friedman (2006-06-11). "Manipulability of PageRank under Sybil Strategies" [35] (PDF). Proceedings of the First Workshop on the Economics of Networked Systems (NetEcon06). Ann Arbor, Michigan. Retrieved 2008-01-22.
- Altman, Alon; Moshe Tennenholtz (2005). "Ranking Systems: The PageRank Axioms" [36] (PDF). Proceedings of the 6th ACM conference on Electronic commerce (EC-05). Vancouver, BC. Retrieved 2008-02-05.
- Haveliwala, Taher; Jeh, Glen and Kamvar, Sepandar (2003). "An Analytical Comparison of Approaches to Personalizing PageRank" [37] (PDF). Stanford University Technical Report.

External links

- Our Search: Google Technology [38] by Google
- How Google Finds Your Needle in the Web's Haystack [39] by the American Mathematical Society
- Original PageRank U.S. Patent- Method for node ranking in a linked database [40] - September 4, 2001
- PageRank U.S. Patent - Method for scoring documents in a linked database [41] - September 28, 2004
- PageRank U.S. Patent - Method for node ranking in a linked database [42] - June 6, 2006
- PageRank U.S. Patent - Scoring documents in a linked database [43] - September 11, 2007

References

[1] "Google Press Center: Fun Facts" (http://www.google.com/press/funfacts.html). www.google.com. . Retrieved 2009-10-05.

[2] http://www.google.com/patents?vid=6285999

[3] Lisa M. Krieger (1 December 2005). "Stanford Earns $336 Million Off Google Stock" (http://www.redorbit.com/news/education/318480/ stanford_earns_336_million_off_google_stock/). San Jose Mercury News, cited by redOrbit. . Retrieved 2009-02-25.

[4] Richard Brandt. "Starting Up. How Google got its groove" (http://www.stanfordalumni.org/news/magazine/2004/novdec/features/ startingup.html). Stanford magazine. . Retrieved 2009-02-25.

[5] Google Technology (http://www.google.com/technology/)

[6] "The Anatomy of a Large-Scale Hypertextual Web Search Engine" (http://dbpubs.stanford.edu:8090/pub/1998-8). Brin, S.; Page, L. 1998.

[7] David Vise and Mark Malseed (2005). The Google Story (http://www.thegooglestory.com/). pp. 37. ISBN ISBN 0-553-80457-X. .

[8] Sergey Brin and Lawrence Page (1998). "The anatomy of a large-scale hypertextual Web search engine" (http://www-db.stanford.edu/ ~backrub/google.html). Proceedings of the seventh international conference on World Wide Web 7. Brisbane, Australia. pp. 107–117 (Section 2.1.1 Description of PageRank Calculation). .

[9] Taher Haveliwala and Sepandar Kamvar. (March 2003). "The Second Eigenvalue of the Google Matrix" (http://www-cs-students.stanford. edu/~taherh/papers/secondeigenvalue.pdf) (PDF). Stanford University Technical Report. .

[10] "Fast PageRank Computation via a Sparse Linear System (Extended Abstract)" (http://citeseerx.ist.psu.edu/viewdoc/summary?doi=10. 1.1.118.5422). Gianna M. Del Corso, Antonio Gullí, Francesco Romani. .

[11] Google PageRank dates http://www.1websitedesigner.com/google-pagerank#dates

[12] Aubuchon, Vaughn, "Google Ranking Factors - SEO Checklist" (http://www.vaughns-1-pagers.com/internet/google-ranking-factors. htm),

[13] Fishkin, Rand; Jeff Pollard (April 2, 2007). "Search Engine Ranking Factors - Version 2" (http://www.seomoz.org/article/ search-ranking-factors). seomoz.org. . Retrieved May 11, 2009.

[14] http://article-blog.thephantomwriters.com/google-love/2008/08/09/

[15] "How to report paid links" (http://www.mattcutts.com/blog/how-to-report-paid-links/). mattcutts.com/blog. April 14, 2007. . Retrieved 2007-05-28.

[16] Jøsang, A. (2007), "Trust and Reputation Systems" (http://www.unik.no/people/josang/papers/Jos2007-FOSAD.pdf), in Aldini, A. (PDF), Foundations of Security Analysis and Design IV, FOSAD 2006/2007 Tutorial Lectures., Springer LNCS 4677, pp. 209–245, doi: 10.1007/978-3-540-74810-6 (http://dx.doi.org/10.1007/978-3-540-74810-6),

[17] SEOnotepad, "Myth of the Google Toolbar Ranking" (http://www.seonotepad.com/search-engines/google-seo/ myth-of-the-google-toolbar-ranking/),

[18] Johan Bollen, Marko A. Rodriguez, and Herbert Van de Sompel. (December 2006). "Journal Status" (http://www.arxiv.org/abs/cs.GL/ 0601030). Scientometrics 69 (3). .

[19] http://www.eigenfactor.org

[20] Benjamin M. Schmidt and Matthew M. Chingos (2007). "Ranking Doctoral Programs by Placement: A New Method" (http://www.people. fas.harvard.edu/~chingos/rankings_paper.pdf) (PDF). PS: Political Science and Politics 40 (July): 523–529. .

[21] Jiang B. (2006). "Ranking spaces for predicting human movement in an urban environment" (http://arxiv.org/abs/physics/0612011) (PDF). International Journal of Geographical Information Science 23: 823–837. .

[22] Jiang B., Zhao S., and Yin J. (2008). "Self-organized natural roads for predicting traffic flow: a sensitivity study" (http://arxiv.org/abs/ 0804.1630). Journal of Statistical Mechanics: Theory and Experiment P07008. .

[23] Andrea Esuli and Fabrizio Sebastiani. "PageRanking WordNet synsets: An Application to Opinion-Related Properties" (http://nmis.isti. cnr.it/sebastiani/Publications/ACL07.pdf) (PDF). In Proceedings of the 35th Meeting of the Association for Computational Linguistics, Prague, CZ, 2007, pp. 424-431. . Retrieved June 30, 2007.

[24] Wissner-Gross, A. D. (2006). " Preparation of topical readings lists from the link structure of Wikipedia (http://www.alexwg.org/ ICALT2006.pdf)". Proceedings of the IEEE International Conference on Advanced Learning Technology (Rolduc, Netherlands): 825. doi: 10.1109/ICALT.2006.1652568 (http://dx.doi.org/10.1109/ICALT.2006.1652568).

[25] "Working Papers Concerning the Creation of Google" (http://dbpubs.stanford.edu:8091/diglib/pub/projectdir/google.html). Google. . Retrieved November 29, 2006.

[26] Cho, J., Garcia-Molina, H., and Page, L. (1998). " Efficient crawling through URL ordering (http://dbpubs.stanford.edu:8090/pub/ 1998-51)". *Proceedings of the seventh conference on World Wide Web* (Brisbane, Australia).

[27] http://de.scientificcommons.org/23846375

[28] http://news.bbc.co.uk/2/hi/science/nature/8238462.stm

[29] "Preventing Comment Spam" (http://googleblog.blogspot.com/2005/01/preventing-comment-spam.html). *Google*. . Retrieved January 1, 2005.

[30] http://www.seomoz.org/blog/pagerank-sculpting-parsing-the-value-and-potential-benefits-of-sculpting-pr-with-nofollow

[31] http://www.mattcutts.com/blog/pagerank-sculpting/

[32] Susan Moskwa, "PageRank Distribution Removed From WMT" (http://www.google.com/support/forum/p/Webmasters/ thread?tid=6a1d6250e26e9e48&hl=en), , retrieved October 16, 2009

[33] http://dbpubs.stanford.edu:8090/pub/showDoc.Fulltext?lang=en&doc=1999-66&format=pdf&compression=

[34] http://www.cs.washington.edu/homes/pedrod/papers/nips01b.pdf

[35] http://www.cs.duke.edu/nicl/netecon06/papers/ne06-sybil.pdf

[36] http://stanford.edu/~epsalon/pagerank.pdf

[37] http://www-cs-students.stanford.edu/~taherh/papers/comparison.pdf

[38] http://www.google.com/technology/

[39] http://www.ams.org/featurecolumn/archive/pagerank.html

[40] http://patft.uspto.gov/netacgi/nph-Parser?patentnumber=6,285,999

[41] http://patft1.uspto.gov/netacgi/nph-Parser?Sect1=PTO1&Sect2=HITOFF&d=PALL&p=1&u=%2Fnetahtml%2FPTO%2Fsrchnum. htm&r=1&f=G&l=50&s1=6,799,176.PN.&OS=PN/6,799,176&RS=PN/6,799,176

[42] http://patft.uspto.gov/netacgi/nph-Parser?Sect1=PTO2&Sect2=HITOFF&u=%2Fnetahtml%2FPTO%2Fsearch-adv.htm&r=1&p=1& f=G&l=50&d=PTXT&S1=7,058,628.PN.&OS=pn/7,058,628&RS=PN/7,058,628

[43] http://patft.uspto.gov/netacgi/nph-Parser?Sect1=PTO2&Sect2=HITOFF&u=%2Fnetahtml%2FPTO%2Fsearch-adv.htm&r=1&p=1& f=G&l=50&d=PTXT&S1=7,269,587.PN.&OS=pn/7,269,587&RS=PN/7,269,587

Web search engine

A **web search engine** is a tool designed to search for information on the → World Wide Web. The search results are usually presented in a list of results and are commonly called *hits*. The information may consist of → web pages, images, information and other types of files. Some search engines also mine data available in databases or open directories. Unlike Web directories, which are maintained by human editors, search engines operate algorithmepically or are a mixture of algorithmic and human input.

History

Time line (full list)		
Year	**Engine**	**Event**
1993	W3Catalog	Launch
	Ali web	Launch
	JumpStation	Launch
1994	WebCrawler	Launch
	Infoseek	Launch
	Lycos	Launch
1995	AltaVista	Launch
	Open Text Web Index	Launch[1]
	Magellan	Launch
	Excite	Launch
	SAPO	Launch

1996	Dogpile	Launch
	Inktomi	Founded
	HotBot	Founded
	Ask Jeeves	Founded
1997	Northern Light	Launch
	Yandex	Launch
1998	Google	Launch
1999	AlltheWeb	Launch
	GenieKnows	Founded
	Naver	Launch
	Teoma	Founded
	Vivisimo	Founded
2000	Baidu	Founded
	Exalead	Founded
2003	Info.com	Launch
2004	Yahoo! Search	Final launch
	A9.com	Launch
	Sogou	Launch
2005	MSN Search	Final launch
	Ask.com	Launch
	GoodSearch	Launch
	SearchMe	Founded
2006	wikiseek	Founded
	Quaero	Founded
	Ask.com	Launch
	Live Search	Launch
	ChaCha	Beta Launch
	Guruji.com	Beta Launch
2007	wikiseek	Launched
	Sproose	Launched
	Wikia Search	Launched
	Blackle.com	Launched

2008	Powerset	Launched
	Picollator	Launched
	Viewzi	Launched
	Cuil	Launched
	Boogami	Launched
	LeapFish	Beta Launch
	Forestle	Launched
	VADLO	Launched
	Sperse! Search	Launched
	Duck Duck Go	Launched
2009	Bing	Launched
	search2.net	Launched
	Miiner :: Data/Text Mining	Launched
	Yebol	Beta Launch
	Mugurdy	Launched
Goby	Launched	

Before there were web search engines there was a complete list of all webservers. The list was edited by Tim Berners-Lee and hosted on the CERN webserver. One historical snapshot from 1992 remains.[2] As more and more webservers went online the central list could not keep up. On the NCSA site new servers were announced under the title "What's New!" but no complete listing existed any more.[3]

The very first tool used for searching on the Internet was Archie.[4] The name stands for "archive" without the "v." It was created in 1990 by Alan Emtage, a student at McGill University in Montreal. The program downloaded the directory listings of all the files located on public anonymous FTP (File Transfer Protocol) sites, creating a searchable database of file names; however, Archie did not index the contents of these sites.

The rise of Gopher (created in 1991 by Mark McCahill at the University of Minnesota) led to two new search programs, Veronica and Jughead. Like Archie, they searched the file names and titles stored in Gopher index systems. Veronica (Very Easy Rodent-Oriented Net-wide Index to Computerized Archives) provided a keyword search of most Gopher menu titles in the entire Gopher listings. Jughead (Jonzy's Universal Gopher Hierarchy Excavation And Display) was a tool for obtaining menu information from specific Gopher servers. While the name of the search engine "Archie" was not a reference to the Archie comic book series, "Veronica" and "Jughead" are characters in the series, thus referencing their predecessor.

In the summer of 1993, no search engine existed yet for the web, though numerous specialized catalogues were maintained by hand. Oscar Nierstrasz at the University of Geneva wrote a series of Perl scripts that would periodically mirror these pages and rewrite them into a standard format which formed the basis for W3Catalog, the web's first primitive search engine, released on September 2, 1993[5].

In June 1993, Matthew Gray, then at MIT, produced what was probably the first web robot, the Perl-based World Wide Web Wanderer, and used it to generate an index called 'Wandex'. The purpose of the Wanderer was to measure the size of the World Wide Web, which it did until late 1995. The web's second search engine Aliweb appeared in November 1993. Aliweb did not use a web robot, but instead depended on being notified by website administrators of the existence at each site of an index file in a particular format.

JumpStation (released in December 1993[6]) used a web robot to find web pages and to build its index, and used a web form as the interface to its query program. It was thus the first WWW resource-discovery tool to combine the three essential features of a web search engine (crawling, indexing, and searching) as described below. Because of the limited resources available on the platform on which it ran, its indexing and hence searching were limited to the titles and headings found in the web pages the crawler encountered.

One of the first "full text" crawler-based search engines was WebCrawler, which came out in 1994. Unlike its predecessors, it let users search for any word in any webpage, which has become the standard for all major search engines since. It was also the first one to be widely known by the public. Also in 1994 Lycos (which started at Carnegie Mellon University) was launched, and became a major commercial endeavor.

Soon after, many search engines appeared and vied for popularity. These included Magellan, Excite, Infoseek, Inktomi, Northern Light, and AltaVista. Yahoo! was among the most popular ways for people to find web pages of interest, but its search function operated on its web directory, rather than full-text copies of web pages. Information seekers could also browse the directory instead of doing a keyword-based search.

In 1996, Netscape was looking to give a single search engine an exclusive deal to be their featured search engine. There was so much interest that instead a deal was struck with Netscape by 5 of the major search engines, where for $5Million per year each search engine would be in a rotation on the Netscape search engine page. These five engines were: Yahoo!, Magellan, Lycos, Infoseek and Excite.[7] [8]

Search engines were also known as some of the brightest stars in the Internet investing frenzy that occurred in the late 1990s.[9] Several companies entered the market spectacularly, receiving record gains during their initial public offerings. Some have taken down their public search engine, and are marketing enterprise-only editions, such as Northern Light. Many search engine companies were caught up in the dot-com bubble, a speculation-driven market boom that peaked in 1999 and ended in 2001.

Around 2000, the Google search engine rose to prominence. The company achieved better results for many searches with an innovation called → PageRank. This iterative algorithm ranks web pages based on the number and PageRank of other web sites and pages that link there, on the premise that good or desirable pages are linked to more than others. Google also maintained a minimalist interface to its search engine. In contrast, many of its competitors embedded a search engine in a web portal.

By 2000, Yahoo was providing search services based on Inktomi's search engine. Yahoo! acquired Inktomi in 2002, and Overture (which owned AlltheWeb and AltaVista) in 2003. Yahoo! switched to Google's search engine until 2004, when it launched its own search engine based on the combined technologies of its acquisitions.

Microsoft first launched MSN Search in the fall of 1998 using search results from Inktomi. In early 1999 the site began to display listings from Looksmart blended with results from Inktomi except for a short time in 1999 when results from AltaVista were used instead. In 2004, Microsoft began a transition to its own search technology, powered by its own web crawler (called msnbot).

Microsoft's rebranded search engine, Bing, was launched on June 1, 2009. On July 29, 2009, Yahoo! and Microsoft finalized a deal in which Yahoo! Search would be powered by Microsoft Bing technology.

According to Hitbox,[10] Google's worldwide popularity peaked at 82.7% in December, 2008. July 2009 rankings showed Google (78.4%) losing traffic to Baidu (8.87%), and Bing (3.17%). The market share of Yahoo! Search (7.16%) and AOL (0.6%) were also declining.

In the United States, Google held a 63.2% market share in May 2009, according to Nielsen NetRatings.[11] In the People's Republic of China, Baidu held a 61.6% market share for web search in July 2009.[12]

How web search engines work

A search engine operates, in the following order

1. Web crawling
2. Indexing
3. Searching

Web search engines work by storing information about many web pages, which they retrieve from the html itself. These pages are retrieved by a Web crawler (sometimes also known as a spider) — an automated Web browser which follows every link on the site. Exclusions can be made by the use of robots.txt. The contents of each page are then analyzed to determine how it should be indexed (for example, words are extracted from the titles, headings, or special fields called meta tags). Data about web pages are stored in an index database for use in later queries. A query can be a single word. The purpose of an index is to allow information to be found as quickly as possible. Some search engines, such as Google, store all or part of the source page (referred to as a cache) as well as information about the web pages, whereas others, such as AltaVista, store every word of every page they find. This cached page always holds the actual search text since it is the one that was actually indexed, so it can be very useful when the content of the current page has been updated and the search terms are no longer in it. This problem might be considered to be a mild form of linkrot, and Google's handling of it increases usability by satisfying user expectations that the search terms will be on the returned webpage. This satisfies the principle of least astonishment since the user normally expects the search terms to be on the returned pages. Increased search relevance makes these cached pages very useful, even beyond the fact that they may contain data that may no longer be available elsewhere.

When a user enters a query into a search engine (typically by using key words), the engine examines its index and provides a listing of best-matching web pages according to its criteria, usually with a short summary containing the document's title and sometimes parts of the text. The index is built from the information stored with the data and the method by which the information is indexed. Unfortunately, there is not one search engine that allows to search documents by date. Most search engines support the use of the boolean operators AND, OR and NOT to further specify the search query. Boolean operators are for literal searches that allow the user to refine and extend the terms of the search. The engine looks for the words or phrases exactly as entered. Some search engines provide an advanced feature called proximity search which allows users to define the distance between keywords. There is also concept-based searching where the research involves using statistical analysis on pages containing the words or phrases you search for. As well, natural language queries allow the user to type a question in the same form one would ask it to a human. A site like this would be ask.com.

The usefulness of a search engine depends on the relevance of the **result set** it gives back. While there may be millions of web pages that include a particular word or phrase, some pages may be more relevant, popular, or authoritative than others. Most search engines employ methods to rank the results to provide the "best" results first. How a search engine decides which pages are the best matches, and what order the results should be shown in, varies widely from one engine to another. The methods also change over time as Internet usage changes and new techniques evolve. There are two main types of search engine that have evolved: one is a system of predefined and hierarchically ordered keywords that humans have programmed extensively. The other is a system that generates an "inverted index" by analyzing texts it locates. This second form relies much more heavily on the computer itself to do the bulk of the work.

Most Web search engines are commercial ventures supported by → advertising revenue and, as a result, some employ the practice of allowing advertisers to pay money to have their listings ranked higher in search results. Those search engines which do not accept money for their search engine results make money by running search related ads alongside the regular search engine results. The search engines make money every time someone clicks on one of these ads.

Game search engines

A game search engine is similar to a web search engine, but it only includes results related to the video game industry. The growing market of video game industry demands a more specific search platform to find game information, game resources, game videos, game blogs and bloggers, game download websites and importantly game industry news.

Some specialist websites have incorporated a search facility that only brings in game related results. Examples include GamePublic, Gamespot, KakaGames, and GameSpider.

Also in existence are video game specific search engines based on Google custom searches. Examples include AllGameSearch and GameCurry.

See also

- Collaborative search engine
- List of search engines
- → Internet
- Metasearch engine
- Natural language search engine
- OpenSearch
- Search engine marketing
- → Search engine optimization
- Search oriented architecture
- Selection-based search
- Semantic Web
- Social search
- Spell checker
- Web indexing
- Web search query
- Website Parse Template

References

- GBMW: Reports of 30-day punishment, re: Car maker BMW had its German website bmw.de delisted from Google, such as: Slashdot-BMW [13] (05-Feb-2006).
- INSIZ: Maximum size of webpages indexed by MSN/Google/Yahoo! ("100-kb limit"): Max Page-size [14] (28-Apr-2006).

[1] http://www.highbeam.com/doc/1G1-16636341.html
[2] http://www.w3.org/History/19921103-hypertext/hypertext/DataSources/WWW/Servers.html
[3] http://home.mcom.com/home/whatsnew/whats_new_0294.html
[4] "Internet History - Search Engines" (from Search Engine Watch), Universiteit Leiden, Netherlands, September 2001, web: LeidenU-Archie (http://www.internethistory.leidenuniv.nl/index.php3?c=7).
[5] Oscar Nierstrasz (2 September 1993). "Searchable Catalog of WWW Resources (experimental)" (http://groups.google.com/group/comp. infosystems.www/browse_thread/thread/2176526a36dc8bd3/2718fd17812937ac?hl=en&lnk=gst&q=Oscar+ Nierstrasz#2718fd17812937ac) (html). .
[6] Archive of NCSA what's new in December 1993 page (http://web.archive.org/web/20010620073530/http://archive.ncsa.uiuc.edu/ SDG/Software/Mosaic/Docs/old-whats-new/whats-new-1293.html)
[7] Yahoo! And Netscape Ink International Distribution Deal (http://files.shareholder.com/downloads/YHOO/701084386x0x27155/ 9a3b5ed8-9e84-4cba-a1e5-77a3dc606566/YHOO_News_1997_7_8_General.pdf),
[8] Browser Deals Push Netscape Stock Up 7.8% (http://articles.latimes.com/1996-04-01/business/fi-53780_1_netscape-home), Los Angeles Times, 1 April 1996,

[9] Gandal, Neil (2001). "The dynamics of competition in the internet search engine market". *International Journal of Industrial Organization* **19** (7): 1103–1117. doi: 10.1016/S0167-7187(01)00065-0 (http://dx.doi.org/10.1016/S0167-7187(01)00065-0).

[10] http://marketshare.hitslink.com/search-engine-market-share.aspx?qprid=5&qpdt=1&qpct=4&qptimeframe=M&qpsp=103&qpnp=25

[11] http://en-us.nielsen.com/rankings/insights/rankings/internet

[12] http://risetothetop.techwyse.com/internet-marketing/search-engine-market-share-july-2009/

[13] http://slashdot.org/article.pl?sid=06/02/05/235218

[14] http://www.sitepoint.com/article/indexing-limits-where-bots-stop

Further reading

- For a more detailed history of early search engines, see Search Engine Birthdays (http://searchenginewatch. com/showPage.html?page=3071951) (from Search Engine Watch), Chris Sherman, September 2003.
- Steve Lawrence; C. Lee Giles (1999). "Accessibility of information on the web". *Nature* **400**: 107. doi: 10.1038/21987 (http://dx.doi.org/10.1038/21987).
- Bing Liu (2007), *Web Data Mining: Exploring Hyperlinks, Contents and Usage Data* (http://www.cs.uic.edu/ ~liub/WebMiningBook.html). Springer, ISBN 3540378812
- Levene, Mark (2005). *An Introduction to Search Engines and Web Navigation*. Pearson.
- Hock, Randolph (2007). *The Extreme Searcher's Handbook*. ISBN 978-0-910965-76-7
- Javed Mostafa (February 2005). "Seeking Better Web Searches" (http://www.sciam.com/article. cfm?articleID=0006304A-37F4-11E8-B7F483414B7F0000). *Scientific American Magazine*.
- Ross, Nancy; Wolfram, Dietmar (2000). "End user searching on the Internet: An analysis of term pair topics submitted to the Excite search engine". *Journal of the American Society for Information Science* **51** (10): 949–958. doi: 10.1002/1097-4571(2000)51:10<949::AID-ASI70>3.0.CO;2-5 (http://dx.doi.org/10.1002/ 1097-4571(2000)51:10<949::AID-ASI70>3.0.CO;2-5).
- Xie, M.; *et al.* (1998). "Quality dimensions of Internet search engines". *Journal of Information Science* **24** (5): 365–372. doi: 10.1177/016555159802400509 (http://dx.doi.org/10.1177/016555159802400509).

External links

- Search Engines (http://www.dmoz.org/Computers/Internet/Searching/Search_Engines//) at the Open Directory Project
- History of Search Engines (http://www.searchenginehistory.com/)
- Search Engines in every country in the world (http://www.searchenginesindex.com/)
- How Stuff Works explanation of Search Engines (http://www.howstuffworks.com/search-engine.htm)

Game search engines

- KakaGames (http://www.kakagames.com/)
- AllGameSearch (http://www.allgamesearch.com)
- GameCurry (http://www.gamecurry.com)
- GameSpider (http://www.gamespider.com/)
- GamePublic (http://www.gamepublic.com)

Search engine optimization

A typical search engine results page

Internet marketing
Display advertising
E-mail marketing
E-mail marketing software
Interactive advertising
Social media optimization
Web analytics
Cost per impression
Affiliate marketing
Cost per action
Contextual advertising
Revenue sharing
Search engine marketing
→ Search engine optimization
Pay per click advertising
Paid inclusion
Search analytics
Mobile advertising

Search engine optimization (SEO) is the process of improving the volume or quality of traffic to a web site from search engines via "natural" or un-paid ("organic" or "algorithmic") search results as opposed to search engine marketing (SEM) which deals with paid inclusion. Typically, the earlier (or higher) a site appears in the search results list, the more visitors it will receive from the search engine. SEO may target different kinds of search, including image search, local search, video search and industry-specific vertical search engines. This gives a web site web presence.

As an Internet marketing strategy, SEO considers how search engines work and what people search for. Optimizing a website primarily involves editing its content and HTML and associated coding to both increase its relevance to specific keywords and to remove barriers to the indexing activities of search engines.

The acronym "SEO" can refer to "search engine optimizers," a term adopted by an industry of consultants who carry out optimization projects on behalf of clients, and by employees who perform SEO services in-house. Search engine optimizers may offer SEO as a stand-alone service or as a part of a broader marketing campaign. Because effective SEO may require changes to the HTML source code of a site, SEO tactics may be incorporated into web site development and design. The term "search engine friendly" may be used to describe web site designs, menus, content management systems, images, videos, shopping carts, and other elements that have been optimized for the purpose of search engine exposure.

Another class of techniques, known as black hat SEO or spamdexing, use methods such as link farms, keyword stuffing and article spinning that degrade both the relevance of search results and the user-experience of search engines. Search engines look for sites that employ these techniques in order to remove them from their indices.

History

Webmasters and content providers began optimizing sites for search engines in the mid-1990s, as the first search engines were cataloging the early → Web. Initially, all a webmaster needed to do was submit the address of a page, or URL, to the various engines which would send a spider to "crawl" that page, extract links to other pages from it, and return information found on the page to be indexed.[1] The process involves a search engine spider downloading a page and storing it on the search engine's own server, where a second program, known as an indexer, extracts various information about the page, such as the words it contains and where these are located, as well as any weight for specific words, and all links the page contains, which are then placed into a scheduler for crawling at a later date.

Site owners started to recognize the value of having their sites highly ranked and visible in search engine results, creating an opportunity for both white hat and black hat SEO practitioners. According to industry analyst Danny Sullivan, the phrase *search engine optimization* probably came into use in 1997.[2]

Early versions of search algorithms relied on webmaster-provided information such as the keyword meta tag, or index files in engines like ALIWEB. Meta tags provide a guide to each page's content. But using meta data to index pages was found to be less than reliable because the webmaster's choice of keywords in the meta tag could potentially be an inaccurate representation of the site's actual content. Inaccurate, incomplete, and inconsistent data in meta tags could and did cause pages to rank for irrelevant searches.[3] Web content providers also manipulated a number of attributes within the HTML source of a page in an attempt to rank well in search engines.[4]

By relying so much on factors such as keyword density which were exclusively within a webmaster's control, early search engines suffered from abuse and ranking manipulation. To provide better results to their users, search engines had to adapt to ensure their results pages showed the most relevant search results, rather than unrelated pages stuffed with numerous keywords by unscrupulous webmasters. Since the success and popularity of a search engine is determined by its ability to produce the most relevant results to any given search, allowing those results to be false would turn users to find other search sources. Search engines responded by developing more complex ranking algorithms, taking into account additional factors that were more difficult for webmasters to manipulate.

Graduate students at Stanford University, Larry Page and Sergey Brin, developed "backrub," a search engine that relied on a mathematical algorithm to rate the prominence of web pages. The number calculated by the algorithm, → PageRank, is a function of the quantity and strength of inbound links.[5] PageRank estimates the likelihood that a given page will be reached by a web user who randomly surfs the web, and follows links from one page to another. In effect, this means that some links are stronger than others, as a higher PageRank page is more likely to be reached by the random surfer.

Page and Brin founded Google in 1998. Google attracted a loyal following among the growing number of Internet users, who liked its simple design.[6] Off-page factors (such as PageRank and hyperlink analysis) were considered as well as on-page factors (such as keyword frequency, meta tags, headings, links and site structure) to enable Google to avoid the kind of manipulation seen in search engines that only considered on-page factors for their rankings. Although PageRank was more difficult to game, webmasters had already developed link building tools and schemes to influence the Inktomi search engine, and these methods proved similarly applicable to gaming PageRank. Many sites focused on exchanging, buying, and selling links, often on a massive scale. Some of these schemes, or link farms, involved the creation of thousands of sites for the sole purpose of link spamming.[7]

By 2004, search engines had incorporated a wide range of undisclosed factors in their ranking algorithms to reduce the impact of link manipulation. Google says it ranks sites using more than 200 different signals.[8] The leading search engines, Google and Yahoo, do not disclose the algorithms they use to rank pages. Notable SEOs, such as Rand Fishkin, Barry Schwartz, Aaron Wall and Jill Whalen, have studied different approaches to search engine optimization, and have published their opinions in online forums and blogs.[9] [10] SEO practitioners may also study patents held by various search engines to gain insight into the algorithms.[11]

In 2005 Google began personalizing search results for each user. Depending on their history of previous searches, Google crafted results for logged in users.[12] In 2008, Bruce Clay said that "ranking is dead" because of personalized search. It would become meaningless to discuss how a website ranked, because its rank would potentially be different for each user and each search.[13]

In 2007 Google announced a campaign against paid links that transfer PageRank.[14] On June 15 2009, Google disclosed that they had taken measures to mitigate the effects of PageRank sculpting by use of the nofollow attribute on links. Matt Cutts, a well known software engineer at Google, announced that Google Bot would no longer treat nofollowed links in the same way, in order to prevent SEOs from using nofollow for PageRank sculpting[15]. As a result of this change the usage of nofollow leads to evaporation of pagerank. In order to avoid the above, SEOs developed alternative techniques that replace nofollowed tags with obfuscated Javascript and thus permit PageRank sculpting. Additionally several solutions have been suggested that include the usage of iframes, flash and javascript.[16]

In December 2009 Google announced it would be using the web search history of all its users in order to populate search results [17].

Real-time-search was introduced in late 2009 in an attempt to make search results more timely and relevant. Historically site administrators have spent months or even years optimizing a website to increase search rankings. With the growth in popularity of social media sites and blogs the leading engines made changes to their algorithms to allow fresh content to rank quickly within the search results. [18] This new approach to search places importance on current, fresh and unique content.

Relationship with search engines

By 1997 search engines recognized that webmasters were making efforts to rank well in their search engines, and that some webmasters were even manipulating their rankings in search results by stuffing pages with excessive or irrelevant keywords. Early search engines, such as Infoseek, adjusted their algorithms in an effort to prevent webmasters from manipulating rankings.[19]

Due to the high marketing value of targeted search results, there is potential for an adversarial relationship between search engines and SEOs. In 2005, an annual conference, AIRWeb, Adversarial Information Retrieval on the Web,[20] was created to discuss and minimize the damaging effects of aggressive web content providers.

SEO companies that employ overly aggressive techniques can get their client websites banned from the search results. In 2005, the Wall Street Journal reported on a company, Traffic Power, which allegedly used high-risk techniques and failed to disclose those risks to its clients.[21] Wired magazine reported that the same company sued blogger and SEO Aaron Wall for writing about the ban.[22] Google's Matt Cutts later confirmed that Google did in fact ban Traffic Power and some of its clients.[23]

Some search engines have also reached out to the SEO industry, and are frequent sponsors and guests at SEO conferences, chats, and seminars. In fact, with the advent of paid inclusion, some search engines now have a vested interest in the health of the optimization community. Major search engines provide information and guidelines to help with site optimization.[24] [25] [26] Google has a Sitemaps program[27] to help webmasters learn if Google is having any problems indexing their website and also provides data on Google traffic to the website. Google guidelines are a list of suggested practices Google has provided as guidance to webmasters. Yahoo! Site Explorer provides a way for webmasters to submit URLs, determine how many pages are in the Yahoo! index and view link information.[28]

Methods

Getting indexed

The leading search engines, such as Google and Yahoo!, use crawlers to find pages for their algorithmic search results. Pages that are linked from other search engine indexed pages do not need to be submitted because they are found automatically. Some search engines, notably Yahoo!, operate a paid submission service that guarantee crawling for either a set fee or cost per click.[29] Such programs usually guarantee inclusion in the database, but do not guarantee specific ranking within the search results.[30] Two major directories, the Yahoo Directory and the Open Directory Project both require manual submission and human editorial review.[31] Google offers Google Webmaster Tools, for which an XML Sitemap feed can be created and submitted for free to ensure that all pages are found, especially pages that aren't discoverable by automatically following links.[32]

→ Search engine crawlers may look at a number of different factors when crawling a site. Not every page is indexed by the search engines. Distance of pages from the root directory of a site may also be a factor in whether or not pages get crawled.[33]

Preventing crawling

To avoid undesirable content in the search indexes, webmasters can instruct spiders not to crawl certain files or directories through the standard robots.txt file in the root directory of the domain. Additionally, a page can be explicitly excluded from a search engine's database by using a meta tag specific to robots. When a search engine visits a site, the robots.txt located in the root directory is the first file crawled. The robots.txt file is then parsed, and will instruct the robot as to which pages are not to be crawled. As a search engine crawler may keep a cached copy of this file, it may on occasion crawl pages a webmaster does not wish crawled. Pages typically prevented from being crawled include login specific pages such as shopping carts and user-specific content such as search results from internal searches. In March 2007, Google warned webmasters that they should prevent indexing of internal search results because those pages are considered search spam.[34]

Increasing prominence

A variety of other methods are employed to get a webpage shown up at the search results. These include:

- Cross linking between pages of the same website. Giving more links to main pages of the website, to increase → PageRank used by search engines.[35] Linking from other websites, including link farming and comment spam. However, link spamming can also have a bad impact on your search result position.
- Writing content that includes frequently searched keyword phrase, so as to be relevant to a wide variety of search queries.[36] Adding relevant keywords to a web page meta tags, including keyword stuffing.
- URL normalization of web pages accessible via multiple urls, using the "canonical" meta tag.[37]

White hat versus black hat

SEO techniques can be classified into two broad categories: techniques that search engines recommend as part of good design, and those techniques of which search engines do not approve. The search engines attempt to minimize the effect of the latter, among them spamdexing. Some industry commentators have classified these methods, and the practitioners who employ them, as either white hat SEO, or black hat SEO.[38] White hats tend to produce results that last a long time, whereas black hats anticipate that their sites may eventually be banned either temporarily or permanently once the search engines discover what they are doing.[39] **White hat seo** An SEO technique is considered white hat if it conforms to the search engines' guidelines and involves no deception. We can say the legal seo is a white hat seo. As the search engine guidelines[24] [25] [26] [40] are not written as a series of rules or commandments, this is an important distinction to note. White hat SEO is not just about following guidelines, but is about ensuring that the content a search engine indexes and subsequently ranks is the same content a user will see. White hat advice is generally summed up as creating content for users, not for search engines, and then making that content easily accessible to the spiders, rather than attempting to trick the algorithm from its intended purpose. White hat SEO is in many ways similar to web development that promotes accessibility,[41] although the two are not identical.

Black hat SEO attempts to improve rankings in ways that are disapproved of by the search engines, or involve deception. One black hat technique uses text that is hidden, either as text colored similar to the background, in an invisible div, or positioned off screen. Another method gives a different page depending on whether the page is being requested by a human visitor or a search engine, a technique known as cloaking.

Search engines may penalize sites they discover using black hat methods, either by reducing their rankings or eliminating their listings from their databases altogether. Such penalties can be applied either automatically by the search engines' algorithms, or by a manual site review. Infamous examples are the February 2006 Google removal of both BMW Germany and Ricoh Germany for use of deceptive practices.[42] and the April 2006 removal of the PPC Agency BigMouthMedia.[43] All three companies, however, quickly apologized, fixed the offending pages, and were restored to Google's list.[44]

Many Web applications employ back-end systems that dynamically modify page content (both visible and meta-data, for example the page title or meta-keywords) and are designed to increase page relevance to search engines based upon how past visitors reached the original page. This dynamic search engine optimization and tuning process can be (and has been) abused by criminals in the past. Exploitation of Web applications that dynamically alter themselves can be *poisoned*.[45]

Gray hat techniques

Gray hat techniques are those that are neither really white nor black hat. Some of these gray hat techniques may be argued either way. These techniques might have some risk associated with them. A very good example of such a technique is purchasing links. The average price for a text link depends on the page rank of the linking page.

While Google is against sale and purchase of links there are people who subscribe to online magazines, memberships and other resources for the purpose of getting a link back to their website.

Another widely used gray hat technique is a webmaster creating multiple 'micro-sites' which he controls for the sole purpose of cross linking to the target site. Since it is the same owner of all the micro-sites, this is a violation of the principles of the search engine's algorithms (by self-linking) but since ownership of sites is not traceable by search engines it is impossible to detect and therefore they can appear as different sites, especially when using separate Class-C IPs.

As a marketing strategy

Eye tracking studies have shown that searchers scan a search results page from top to bottom and left to right (for left to right languages), looking for a relevant result. Placement at or near the top of the rankings therefore increases the number of searchers who will visit a site.[46] However, more search engine referrals does not guarantee more sales. SEO is not necessarily an appropriate strategy for every website, and other Internet marketing strategies can be much more effective, depending on the site operator's goals.[47] A successful Internet marketing campaign may drive organic traffic to web pages, but it also may involve the use of paid advertising on search engines and other pages, building high quality web pages to engage and persuade, addressing technical issues that may keep search engines from crawling and indexing those sites, setting up analytics programs to enable site owners to measure their successes, and improving a site's conversion rate.[48]

SEO may generate a return on investment. However, search engines are not paid for organic search traffic, their algorithms change, and there are no guarantees of continued referrals. (Some trading sites such as eBay can be a special case for this, it will announce how and when the ranking algorithm will change a few months before changing the algorithm)Due to this lack of guarantees and certainty, a business that relies heavily on search engine traffic can suffer major losses if the search engines stop sending visitors.[49] It is considered wise business practice for website operators to liberate themselves from dependence on search engine traffic.[50] A top-ranked SEO blog Seomoz.org[51] has suggested, "Search marketers, in a twist of irony, receive a very small share of their traffic from search engines." Instead, their main sources of traffic are links from other websites.[52]

International markets

Optimization techniques are highly tuned to the dominant search engines in the target market. The search engines' market shares vary from market to market, as does competition. In 2003, Danny Sullivan stated that Google represented about 75% of all searches.[53] In markets outside the United States, Google's share is often larger, and Google remains the dominant search engine worldwide as of 2007.[54] As of 2006, Google had an 85-90% market share in Germany.[55] While there were hundreds of SEO firms in the US at that time, there were only about five in Germany.[55] As of June 2008, the marketshare of Google in the UK was close to 90% according to Hitwise.[56] That market share is achieved in a number of countries.[57]

As of 2009, there are only a few large markets where Google is not the leading search engine. In most cases, when Google is not leading in a given market, it is lagging behind a local player. The most notable markets where this is the case are China, Japan, South Korea, Russia and Czech Republic where respectively Baidu, Yahoo! Japan, Naver, Yandex and Seznam are market leaders.

Successful search optimization for international markets may require professional translation of web pages, registration of a domain name with a top level domain in the target market, and web hosting that provides a local IP address. Otherwise, the fundamental elements of search optimization are essentially the same, regardless of language.[55]

Legal precedents

On October 17, 2002, SearchKing filed suit in the United States District Court, Western District of Oklahoma, against the search engine Google. SearchKing's claim was that Google's tactics to prevent spamdexing constituted a tortious interference with contractual relations. On May 27, 2003, the court granted Google's motion to dismiss the complaint because SearchKing "failed to state a claim upon which relief may be granted."[58] [59]

In March 2006, KinderStart filed a lawsuit against Google over search engine rankings. Kinderstart's web site was removed from Google's index prior to the lawsuit and the amount of traffic to the site dropped by 70%. On March 16, 2007 the United States District Court for the Northern District of California (San Jose Division) dismissed KinderStart's complaint without leave to amend, and partially granted Google's motion for Rule 11 sanctions against KinderStart's attorney, requiring him to pay part of Google's legal expenses.[60] [61]

See also

- List of search engines
- Image search optimization
- Search engine optimization copywriting

External links

- Google Webmaster Guidelines [62]
- Yahoo! Webmaster Guidelines [63]
- Bing Webmaster Guidelines [64]
- Ask.com Webmaster Guidelines [65]

References

[1] Brian Pinkerton. "Finding What People Want: Experiences with the WebCrawler" (http://www.webir.org/resources/phd/pinkerton_2000. pdf) (PDF). The Second International WWW Conference Chicago, USA, October 17–20, 1994. . Retrieved 2007-05-07.

[2] Danny Sullivan (June 14, 2004). "Who Invented the Term "Search Engine Optimization"?" (http://forums.searchenginewatch.com/ showpost.php?p=2119&postcount=10). Search Engine Watch. . Retrieved 2007-05-14. See Google groups thread (http://groups.google. com/group/alt.current-events.net-abuse.spam/browse_thread/thread/6fee2777dc17b8ab/3858bff94e56aff3?lnk=st&q="search+engine+ optimization"&rnum=1#3858bff94e56aff3).

[3] Cory Doctorow (August 26, 2001). "Metacrap: Putting the torch to seven straw-men of the meta-utopia" (http://www.e-learningguru.com/ articles/metacrap.htm). e-LearningGuru. . Retrieved 2007-05-08.

[4] Pringle, G., Allison, L., and Dowe, D. (April 1998). "What is a tall poppy among web pages?" (http://www.csse.monash.edu.au/~lloyd/ tilde/InterNet/Search/1998_WWW7.html). Proc. 7th Int. World Wide Web Conference. . Retrieved 2007-05-08.

[5] Brin, Sergey and Page, Larry (1998). "The Anatomy of a Large-Scale Hypertextual Web Search Engine" (http://www-db.stanford.edu/ ~backrub/google.html). Proceedings of the seventh international conference on World Wide Web. p. 107–117. . Retrieved 2007-05-08.

[6] Thompson, Bill (December 19, 2003). "Is Google good for you?" (http://news.bbc.co.uk/1/hi/technology/3334531.stm). BBC News. . Retrieved 2007-05-16.

[7] Zoltan Gyongyi and Hector Garcia-Molina (2005). "Link Spam Alliances" (http://infolab.stanford.edu/~zoltan/publications/ gyongyi2005link.pdf) (PDF). Proceedings of the 31st VLDB Conference, Trondheim, Norway. . Retrieved 2007-05-09.

[8] "Google Keeps Tweaking Its Search Engine" (http://www.nytimes.com/2007/06/03/business/yourmoney/03google.html). New York Times. June 3, 2007. . Retrieved 2007-06-06.

[9] Danny Sullivan (September 29, 2005). "Rundown On Search Ranking Factors" (http://blog.searchenginewatch.com/blog/ 050929-072711). Search Engine Watch. . Retrieved 2007-05-08.

[10] "Search Engine Ranking Factors V2" (http://www.seomoz.org/article/search-ranking-factors). SEOmoz.org. April 2, 2007. . Retrieved 2007-05-14.

[11] Christine Churchill (November 23, 2005). "Understanding Search Engine Patents" (http://searchenginewatch.com/showPage. html?page=3564261). Search Engine Watch. . Retrieved 2007-05-08.

[12] "Google Personalized Search Leaves Google Labs - Search Engine Watch (SEW)" (http://searchenginewatch.com/3563036). searchenginewatch.com. . Retrieved 2009-09-05.

[13] "Will Personal Search Turn SEO On Its Ear?" (http://www.webpronews.com/topnews/2008/11/17/seo-about-to-get-turned-on-its-ear). www.webpronews.com. . Retrieved 2009-09-05.

[14] "8 Things We Learned About Google PageRank" (http://www.searchenginejournal.com/8-things-we-learned-about-google-pagerank/5897/). www.searchenginejournal.com. . Retrieved 2009-08-17.

[15] "PageRank sculpting" (http://www.mattcutts.com/blog/pagerank-sculpting/). Matt Cutts. . Retrieved 2010-01-12.

[16] "Google Loses "Backwards Compatibility" On Paid Link Blocking & PageRank Sculpting" (http://searchengineland.com/google-loses-backwards-compatibility-on-paid-link-blocking-pagerank-sculpting-20408). searchengineland.com. . Retrieved 2009-08-17.

[17] "Personalized Search for everyone" (http://googleblog.blogspot.com/2009/12/personalized-search-for-everyone.html). Google. . Retrieved 2009-12-14.

[18] "Relevance Meets Real Time Web" (http://googleblog.blogspot.com/2009/12/relevance-meets-real-time-web.html). Google Blog. .

[19] Laurie J. Flynn (November 11, 1996). "Desperately Seeking Surfers" (http://query.nytimes.com/gst/fullpage.html?res=940DE0DF123BF932A25752C1A960958260). New York Times. . Retrieved 2007-05-09.

[20] "AIRWeb" (http://airweb.cse.lehigh.edu/). Adversarial Information Retrieval on the Web, annual conference. . Retrieved 2007-05-09.

[21] David Kesmodel (September 22, 2005). "Sites Get Dropped by Search Engines After Trying to 'Optimize' Rankings" (http://online.wsj.com/article/SB112714166978744925.html?apl=y&r=947596). Wall Street Journal. . Retrieved 2008-07-30.

[22] Adam L. Penenberg (September 8, 2005). "Legal Showdown in Search Fracas" (http://www.wired.com/news/culture/0,1284,68799,00.html). Wired Magazine. . Retrieved 2007-05-09.

[23] Matt Cutts (February 2, 2006). "Confirming a penalty" (http://www.mattcutts.com/blog/confirming-a-penalty/). mattcutts.com/blog. . Retrieved 2007-05-09.

[24] "Google's Guidelines on Site Design" (http://www.google.com/webmasters/guidelines.html). google.com. . Retrieved 2007-04-18.

[25] "Site Owner Help: MSN Search Web Crawler and Site Indexing" (http://search.msn.com/docs/siteowner.aspx?t=SEARCH_WEBMASTER_REF_GuidelinesforOptimizingSite.htm). msn.com. . Retrieved 2007-04-18.

[26] "Yahoo! Search Content Quality Guidelines" (http://help.yahoo.com/l/us/yahoo/search/basics/basics-18.html). help.yahoo.com. . Retrieved 2007-04-18.

[27] "Google Webmaster Tools" (http://www.google.com/webmasters/sitemaps/login). google.com. . Retrieved 2007-05-09.

[28] "Yahoo! Site Explorer" (http://siteexplorer.search.yahoo.com). yahoo.com. . Retrieved 2007-05-09.

[29] "Submitting To Search Crawlers: Google, Yahoo, Ask & Microsoft's Live Search" (http://searchenginewatch.com/showPage.html?page=2167871). Search Engine Watch. 2007-03-12. . Retrieved 2007-05-15.

[30] "Search Submit" (http://searchmarketing.yahoo.com/srchsb/index.php). searchmarketing.yahoo.com. . Retrieved 2007-05-09.

[31] "Submitting To Directories: Yahoo & The Open Directory" (http://searchenginewatch.com/showPage.html?page=2167881). Search Engine Watch. 2007-03-12. . Retrieved 2007-05-15.

[32] "What is a Sitemap file and why should I have one?" (http://www.google.com/support/webmasters/bin/answer.py?answer=40318&topic=8514). google.com. . Retrieved 2007-03-19.

[33] Cho, J., Garcia-Molina, H. (1998). "Efficient crawling through URL ordering" (http://dbpubs.stanford.edu:8090/pub/1998-51). Proceedings of the seventh conference on World Wide Web, Brisbane, Australia. . Retrieved 2007-05-09.

[34] "Newspapers Amok! New York Times Spamming Google? LA Times Hijacking Cars.com?" (http://searchengineland.com/070508-165231.php). Search Engine Land. May 8, 2007. . Retrieved 2007-05-09.

[35] (http://www.clickz.com/3623372) Link Development"

[36] (http://www.clickz.com/3623372) "keyword rich text"

[37] "Bing - Partnering to help solve duplicate content issues - Webmaster Blog - Bing Community" (http://www.bing.com/community/blogs/webmaster/archive/2009/02/12/partnering-to-help-solve-duplicate-content-issues.aspx). www.bing.com. . Retrieved 2009-10-30.

[38] Andrew Goodman. "Search Engine Showdown: Black hats vs. White hats at SES" (http://searchenginewatch.com/showPage.html?page=3483941). SearchEngineWatch. . Retrieved 2007-05-09.

[39] Jill Whalen (November 16, 2004). "Black Hat/White Hat Search Engine Optimization" (http://www.searchengineguide.com/whalen/2004/1116_jw1.html). searchengineguide.com. . Retrieved 2007-05-09.

[40] "What's an SEO? Does Google recommend working with companies that offer to make my site Google-friendly?" (http://www.google.com/webmasters/seo.html). google.com. . Retrieved 2007-04-18.

[41] Andy Hagans (November 8, 2005). "High Accessibility Is Effective Search Engine Optimization" (http://alistapart.com/articles/accessibilityseo). A List Apart. . Retrieved 2007-05-09.

[42] Matt Cutts (February 4, 2006). "Ramping up on international webspam" (http://www.mattcutts.com/blog/ramping-up-on-international-webspam/). mattcutts.com/blog. . Retrieved 2007-05-09.

[43] seobook (April 4, 2006). "Big Mouth Media Banned for Excessive Hidden Text Spamming - Google's Matt Cutts Confirms Hand Job" (http://www.threadwatch.org/node/6276). threadwatch.org. . Retrieved 2007-05-09.

[44] Matt Cutts (February 7, 2006). "Recent reinclusions" (http://www.mattcutts.com/blog/recent-reinclusions/). mattcutts.com/blog. . Retrieved 2007-05-09.

[45] Gunter Ollmann (August, 2008). "SEO Code Injection" (http://www.technicalinfo.net/papers/SEOCodeInjection.html). Technicalinfo.net. .

[46] "A New F-Word for Google Search Results" (http://searchenginewatch.com/showPage.html?page=3488076). Search Engine Watch. March 8, 2005. . Retrieved 2007-05-16.

[47] "What SEO Isn't" (http://blog.v7n.com/2006/06/24/what-seo-isnt/). blog.v7n.com. June 24, 2006. . Retrieved 2007-05-16.

[48] Melissa Burdon (March 13, 2007). "The Battle Between Search Engine Optimization and Conversion: Who Wins?" (http://www. grokdotcom.com/2007/03/13/the-battle-between-search-engine-optimization-and-conversion-who-wins/). Grok.com. . Retrieved 2007-05-09.

[49] Andy Greenberg (April 30, 2007). "Condemned To Google Hell" (http://www.forbes.com/technology/2007/04/29/ sanar-google-skyfacet-tech-cx_ag_0430googhell.html?partner=rss). Forbes. . Retrieved 2007-05-09.

[50] Jakob Nielsen (January 9, 2006). "Search Engines as Leeches on the Web" (http://www.useit.com/alertbox/search_engines.html). useit.com. . Retrieved 2007-05-14.

[51] "SEOmoz: Best SEO Blog of 2006" (http://www.searchenginejournal.com/seomoz-best-seo-blog-of-2006/4195/). searchenginejournal.com. January 3, 2007. . Retrieved 2007-05-31.

[52] "A survey of 25 blogs in the search space comparing external metrics to visitor tracking data" (http://www.seomoz.org/article/ search-blog-stats#4). seomoz.org. . Retrieved 2007-05-31.

[53] "The search engine that could" (http://www.usatoday.com/tech/news/2003-08-25-google_x.htm). USA Today. 2003-08-26. . Retrieved 2007-05-15.

[54] Greg Jarboe (2007-02-22). "Stats Show Google Dominates the International Search Landscape" (http://searchenginewatch.com/ showPage.html?page=3625072). Search Engine Watch. . Retrieved 2007-05-15.

[55] Mike Grehan (April 3, 2006). "Search Engine Optimizing for Europe" (http://www.clickz.com/showPage.html?page=3595926). Click. . Retrieved 2007-05-14.

[56] Jack Schofield (2008-06-10). "Google UK closes in on 90% market share" (http://www.guardian.co.uk/technology/blog/2008/jun/10/ googleukclosesinon90mark). Guardian. . Retrieved 2008-06-10.

[57] Alex Chitu (2009-03-13). "Google's Market Share in Your Country" (http://googlesystem.blogspot.com/2009/03/ googles-market-share-in-your-country.html). Google Operating System. . Retrieved 2009-05-16.

[58] "Search King, Inc. v. Google Technology, Inc., CIV-02-1457-M" (http://www.docstoc.com/docs/618281/ Order-(Granting-Googles-Motion-to-Dismiss-Search-Kings-Complaint)) (PDF). docstoc.com. May 27, 2003. . Retrieved 2008-05-23.

[59] Stefanie Olsen (May 30, 2003). "Judge dismisses suit against Google" (http://news.com.com/2100-1032_3-1011740.html). CNET. . Retrieved 2007-05-10.

[60] "Technology & Marketing Law Blog: KinderStart v. Google Dismissed—With Sanctions Against KinderStart's Counsel" (http://blog. ericgoldman.org/archives/2007/03/kinderstart_v_g_2.htm). blog.ericgoldman.org. . Retrieved 2008-06-23.

[61] "Technology & Marketing Law Blog: Google Sued Over Rankings—KinderStart.com v. Google" (http://blog.ericgoldman.org/archives/ 2006/03/google_sued_ove.htm). blog.ericgoldman.org. . Retrieved 2008-06-23.

[62] http://www.google.com/support/webmasters/bin/answer.py?hl=en&answer=35769

[63] http://help.yahoo.com/l/us/yahoo/search/basics/basics-18.html

[64] http://help.live.com/help.aspx?mkt=en-us&project=wl_webmasters&querytype=&query=&tmt=&domain=help.live.com& format=b1

[65] http://about.ask.com/en/docs/about/webmasters.shtml

Strategy

A **strategy** is a plan of action designed to achieve a particular goal. The word strategy has military connotations, because it derives from the Greek word for *general*.[1]

Strategy is distinct from tactics. In military terms, tactics is concerned with the conduct of an engagement while strategy is concerned with how different engagements are linked. In other words, how a battle is fought is a matter of tactics: the terms that it is fought on and whether it should be fought at all is a matter of strategy. Military strategy is the overarching, long-term plan of operations that will achieve the political objectives of the nation. It is part of the four levels of warfare: political goals, strategy, operations, and tactics.

Strategies in game theory

In game theory, a *strategy* refers to one of the options that a player can choose. That is, every player in a non-cooperative game has a set of possible strategies, and must choose one of the choices.

A strategy must specify what action will happen in each contingent state of the game - e.g. if the opponent does A, then take action B, whereas if the opponent does C, take action D.

Strategies in game theory may be random (mixed) or deterministic (pure). That is, in some games, players choose mixed strategies. Pure strategies can be thought of as a special case of mixed strategies, in which only probabilities 0 or 1 are assigned to actions.

Noted texts on strategy

Classic texts such as Chanakya's *Arthashastra* written in the 3rd century BC, Sun Tzu's *The Art of War*, written in China 2,500 years ago, the political strategy of Niccolò Machiavelli's *The Prince*, written in 1513, or Carl von Clausewitz's *On War*, published in 1832, as with the Japanese classic The book of five rings by Miyamoto Mushashi written in 1645, are still well known, and highly influential. In the twentieth century, the subject of strategic management has been particularly applied to organisations, most typically to business firms and corporations.

The nature of historic texts differs greatly from area to area, and given the nature of strategy itself, there are some potential parallels between various forms of strategy (noting, for example, the popularity of the *The Art of War* as a business book). Each domain generally has its own foundational texts, as well as more recent contributions to new applications of strategy. Some of these are:

- Political strategy

  - *The Prince*, published in 1532 by Niccolò Machiavelli
  - *Arthashastra*, written in the 4th century BC by Chanakya
  - *The Book of the Courtier* by Baldassare Castiglione
- Military strategy:

  - *The Art of War*, written in the 6th century BC by Sun Tzu
  - *The Art of War*, written in the 19th century AD by Baron Antoine Henri de Jomini
  - *Strategikon*, written in the 6th century AD by the Byzantine emperor Maurice
  - *Taktikon*, by the Byzantine emperor Leo VI the Wise
  - *On War*, by Carl von Clausewitz (19th century)
  - → *Strategy*, by Basil Liddell Hart
  - *On Guerrilla Warfare*, by Mao Zedong
  - *The Influence of Sea Power upon History*, by Alfred Thayer Mahan
  - *The Air Campaign*, by Colonel John A. Warden, III
  - *Makers of Modern Strategy*, edited by Peter Paret

- *Strategy*, by Edward N. Luttwak
- Economic strategy
  - *General Theory of Employment, Interest and Money*, published in 1936 by John Maynard Keynes
- Business strategy
  - *Demystifying Competitive Intelligence*, Estelle Metayer, Ivey Business Journal, Nov 1999
  - *Competitive Strategy*, by Michael Porter
  - *Strategy Concept I: Five Ps for Strategy* and *Strategy Concept II: Another Look at Why Organizations Need Strategies*, by Henry Mintzberg
  - *Winning In FastTime* by John A. Warden, III and Leland A. Russell, 2002.
- General strategy
  - *Strategy Safari*, by Henry Mintzberg, Bruce Ahlstrand and Joseph Lampel.
  - *Strategic Studies-Intelligence and strategy*,by Gagliano Giuseppe, Uniservice, Nov 2009
- Others
  - Marcel Détienne and Jean-Pierre Vernant, *Les Ruses de l'intelligence*, Paris: Flammarion, 1993 (on the role of the Greek *Metis*)

See also

- American football strategy
- Business biomimetics
- Nuclear strategy
- Odds algorithm (Odds strategy)
- Plan
- Poker strategy
- Strategic planning
- Strategy game
- Synergy
- Tactics

External links

- Strategy Definition and Fundamentals [2]
- Math Strategies [3]

References

[1] *Oxford English Dictionary* (2 ed.). Oxford, England: Oxford University Press. 1989.
[2] http://www.easy-strategy.com/strategy-definition.html
[3] http://educationalblog.exploringchild.com/learning/math/math-strategies

Web page

A **webpage** or **web page** is a document or resource of information that is suitable for the → World Wide Web and can be accessed through a web browser and displayed on a computer screen.

This information is usually in HTML or XHTML format, and may provide navigation to other webpages via hypertext links.

Webpages may be retrieved from a local computer or from a remote web server. The web server may restrict access only to a private network, e.g. a corporate intranet, or it may publish pages on the World Wide Web. Webpages are requested and served from web servers using Hypertext Transfer Protocol (HTTP).

A screenshot of a webpage.

Webpages may consist of files of static text stored within the web server's file system (static webpages), or the web server may construct the (X)HTML for each webpage when it is requested by a browser (dynamic webpages). Client-side scripting can make webpages more responsive to user input once in the client browser.

Color, typography, illustration and interaction

Webpages usually include information as to the colors of text and backgrounds and very often also contain links to images and sometimes other media to be included in the final view. Layout, typographic and color-scheme information is provided by Cascading Style Sheet (CSS) instructions, which can either be embedded in the HTML or can be provided by a separate file, which is referenced from within the HTML. The latter case is especially relevant where one lengthy stylesheet is relevant to a whole → website: due to the way HTTP works, the browser will only download it once from the web server and use the cached copy for the whole site. Images are stored on the web server as separate files, but again HTTP allows for the fact that once a webpage is downloaded to a browser, it is quite likely that related files such as images and stylesheets will be requested as it is processed. An HTTP 1.1 web server will maintain a connection with the browser until all related resources have been requested and provided. Web browsers usually render images along with the text and other material on the displayed webpage.

Dynamic behavior

Client-side computer code such as JavaScript or code implementing Ajax techniques can be provided either embedded in the HTML of a webpage or, like CSS stylesheets, as separate, linked downloads specified in the HTML. These scripts may run on the client computer, if the user allows.

Browsers

A web browser can have a Graphical User Interface, like Internet Explorer, Mozilla Firefox and Opera, or can be text-based, like Lynx.

Web users with disabilities often use assistive technologies and adaptive strategies to access webpages.[1] Users may be color blind, may or may not want to use a mouse perhaps due to repetitive stress injury or motor-neurone problems, may be deaf and require audio to be captioned, may be blind and using a screen reader or braille display, may need screen magnification, etc.

Disabled and able-bodied users may disable the download and viewing of images and other media, to save time, network bandwidth or merely to simplify their browsing experience. Users of mobile devices often have restricted displays and bandwidth. Anyone may prefer not to use the fonts, font sizes, styles and color schemes selected by the webpage designer and may apply their own CSS styling to the page.

The World Wide Web Consortium (W3C) and Web Accessibility Initiative (WAI) recommend that all webpages should be designed with all of these options in mind.

Elements of a webpage

A *webpage*, as an information set, can contain numerous types of information, which is able to be seen, heard or interact by the end user:

Perceived (rendered) information:

- *Textual information*: with diverse render variations.
- *Non-textual information*:
  - *Static images* on raster graphics, typically GIF, JPEG or PNG; or vector formats as SVG or Flash.
  - *Animated images* typically Animated GIF and SVG, but also may be Flash, Shockwave, or Java applet.
  - Audio, typically MIDI or WAV formats or Java applets.
  - Video, WMV (Windows), RM (Real Media), FLV (Flash Video), MPG, MOV (QuickTime)
- *Interactive information*: more complex, glued to interface; see dynamic webpage.
  - For "on page" interaction:
    - *Interactive text*: see DHTML.
    - *Interactive illustrations*: ranging from "click to play" image to games, typically using *script orchestration*, Flash, Java applets, SVG, or Shockwave.
    - *Buttons*: forms providing alternative interface, typically for use with *script orchestration* and DHTML.
  - For "between pages" interaction:
    - *Hyperlinks*: standard "change page" reactivity.
    - *Forms*: providing more interaction with the server and server-side databases.

Internal (hidden) information:

- *Comments*
- *Linked Files through Hyperlink (Like DOC,XLS,PDF,etc).*
- *Metadata* with semantic meta-information, Charset information, Document Type Definition (DTD), etc.
- *Diagramation and style information*: information about rendered items (like image size attributes) and visual specifications, as Cascading Style Sheets (CSS).
- *Scripts*, usually JavaScript, complement interactivity and functionality.

  Note: on server-side the webpage may also have "Processing Instruction Information Items".

The webpage can also contain dynamically adapted information elements, dependent upon the rendering browser or end-user location (through the use of IP address tracking and/or "cookie" information).

From a more general/wide point of view, some information (grouped) elements, like a navigation bar, are uniform for all website pages, like a standard. These kind of "website standard information" are supplied by technologies like web template systems.

Rendering

Webpages will often require more screen space than is available for a particular display resolution. Most modern browsers will place scrollbars (the bar at the side of the screen that allows you to move down) in the window to allow the user to see all content. Scrolling horizontally is less prevalent than vertical scrolling, not only because those pages do not print properly, but because it inconveniences the user more so than vertical scrolling would (because lines are horizontal; scrolling back and forth for every line is much more inconvenient than scrolling after reading a whole screen; also most computer keyboards have page up and down keys, and many computer mice have vertical scroll wheels, but the horizontal scrolling equivalents are rare).

When webpages are stored in a common directory of a web server, they become a → website. A website will typically contain a group of webpages that are linked together, or have some other coherent method of navigation. The most important webpage to have on a website is the index page. Depending on the web server settings, this index page can have many different names, but the most common is index.html. When a browser visits the homepage for a website, or any URL pointing to a directory rather than a specific file, the web server will serve the index page to the requesting browser. If no index page is defined in the configuration, or no such file exists on the server, either an error or directory listing will be served to the browser.

A webpage can either be a single HTML file, or made up of several HTML files using frames or Server Side Includes (SSIs). Frames have been known to cause problems with web accessibility, copyright,[2] navigation, printing and search engine rankings [3] , and are now less often used than they were in the 1990s.[4] [5] Both frames and SSIs allow certain content which appears on many pages, such as page navigation or page headers, to be repeated without duplicating the HTML in many files. Frames and the W3C recommended alternative of 2000, the <object> tag,[4] also allow some content to remain in one place while other content can be scrolled using conventional scrollbars. Modern CSS and JavaScript client-side techniques can also achieve all of these goals and more.

When creating a webpage, it is important to ensure it conforms to the World Wide Web Consortium (W3C) standards for HTML, CSS, XML and other standards. The W3C standards are in place to ensure all browsers which conform to their standards can display identical content without any special consideration for proprietary rendering techniques. A properly coded webpage is going to be accessible to many different browsers old and new alike, display resolutions, as well as those users with audio or visual impairments.

URL

Typically, webpages today are becoming more dynamic. A dynamic webpage is one that is created server-side when it is requested, and then served to the end-user. These types of webpages typically do not have a permalink, or a static URL, associated with them. Today, this can be seen in many popular forums, online shopping, and even on Wikipedia. This practice is intended to reduce the amount of static pages in lieu of storing the relevant webpage information in a database. Some search engines may have a hard time indexing a webpage that is dynamic, so static webpages can be provided in those instances.

Viewing a webpage

In order to graphically display a webpage, a web browser is needed. This is a type of software that can retrieve webpages from the → Internet. Most current web browsers include the ability to view the source code. Viewing a webpage in a text editor will also display the source code, not the visual product.

Creating a webpage

To create a webpage, a text editor or a specialized HTML editor is needed. In order to upload the created webpage to a web server, traditionally an FTP client is needed.

The design of a webpage is highly personal. A design can be made according to one's own preference, or a premade web template can be used. Web templates let webpage designers edit the content of a webpage without having to worry about the overall aesthetics. Many people publish their own webpages using products like Geocities from Yahoo, Tripod, or Angelfire. These web publishing tools offer free page creation and hosting up to a certain size limit.

Other ways of making a webpage is to download specialized software, like a Wiki, CMS, or forum. These options allow for quick and easy creation of a webpage which is typically dynamic.

Saving a webpage

While one is viewing a webpage, a copy of it is saved locally; this is what is being viewed. Depending on the browser settings, this copy may be deleted at any time, or stored indefinitely, sometimes without the user realizing it. Most GUI browsers will contain all the options for saving a webpage more permanently. These include, but are not limited to:

- Saving the rendered text without formatting or images - Hyperlinks are not identified, but displayed as plain text
- Saving the HTML file as it was served - Overall structure will be preserved, although some links may be broken
- Saving the HTML file and changing relative links to absolute ones - Hyperlinks will be preserved
- Saving the entire webpage - All images will be saved, as well as links being changed to absolute
- Saving the HTML file including all images, stylesheets and scripts into a single MHTML file. This is supported by Internet Explorer, Firefox and Opera. Firefox only support this if the MAF plugin has been installed. An MHTML file is based upon the MHTML standard.

Common web browsers, like Mozilla Firefox, Internet Explorer and Opera, give the option to not only print the currently viewed webpage to a printer, but optionally to "print" to a file which can be viewed or printed later. Some webpages are designed, for example by use of CSS, so that hyperlinks, menus and other navigation items, which will be useless on paper, are rendered into print with this in mind. Space-wasting menus and navigational blocks may be absent from the printed version; other hyperlinks may be sh the end.

See also

- Dead link
- Domain name
- Guestbook
- Homepage
- Linked data page
- SEO Copywriting
- Web document

References

[1] "How People with Disabilities Use the Web" (http://www.w3.org/WAI/EO/Drafts/PWD-Use-Web/). W3C. 5 May 2005. . Retrieved 2009-05-01.

[2] Tysver, Dan (1996-2008). "Linking and Liability - Problems with Frames" (http://www.bitlaw.com/internet/linking.html#Frames). Minneapolis, USA: Beck & Tysver. . Retrieved 2009-05-01.

[3] Frames Problems - ITC Web Development (http://www.itc.virginia.edu/desktop/web/frames_problems.html)

[4] "HTML Techniques for Web Content Accessibility Guidelines 1.0 - Frames" (http://www.w3.org/TR/WCAG10-HTML-TECHS/#frames). W3C. 6 November 2000. . Retrieved 2009-05-01. "In the following sections, we discuss how to make frames more accessible. We also provide an alternative to frames that uses HTML 4.01 and CSS and addresses many of the limitations of today's frame implementations."

[5] Steinmetz, Israel (2 November 1999). "Frames Free!" (http://www.noframes.org/). . Retrieved 2009-05-01.

Article Sources and Contributors

Copywriting *Source*: http://en.wikipedia.org/w/index.php?title=Copywriting *Contributors*: 16@r, A monkey named 'Naught', Aapo Laitinen, AbsolutDan, Admonkey, Adrian, Alandaviddoane, Allonline, Annemoss, Annie Chung, Aosune, Artemgy, Bedesboy, Beland, Caap, Cairo123, Can't sleep, clown will eat me, ChannelNewsAsiaFanatic, Ckatz, Cl52059, ContBur, Damian Yerrick, Dekisugi, Deli nk, Discospinster, Dittmandavid, Drew.sonne, Duckax, Dudi Scraba, Elphion, Eplater, Femto, Flowanda, FlyHigh, Forrestlaw71, Freelancer1234, FreplySpang, Furrykef, Gazpacho, Globaledits, Gnusmas, GraemeL, Gwernol, HJ Mitchell, Haakon, Hechung, HerbFirestone, Hu12, IanD, ImmortalDragon02, Invertzoo, Inwind, James Roome, Jamesb01, Jokestress, Kal.Sawa, Kencalhoun, Kingofcopy.com, KristymcNillan, Leafyplant, LegitimateAndEvenCompelling, Liface, Linkspamremover, LittleOldMe, Locatelli, Lumpio-, Majorly, Marsiat, Maurreen, Mgcsinc, Mikecatherall, Ml1369, Mmehdi.g, Mrtea, Mwanner, NaamaOren, NawlinWiki, Ohnoitsjamie, Oicumayberight, PapaWhitman, Philosophizer, Phoe, Piano non troppo, Rasmus Faber, Renochka, RexNL, Rjwilmsi, Robocoder, Roisterer, Ronz, Samirdude21, Sarahaddyman, ShakingSpirit, Shimeru, Sirena evklad, Smalljim, Snalwibma, Someguy1221, Soph, Splintax, Stevefleming, Sub grega, Superwritergirl, Ungluedtoo, Unitanode, V333, Victoriagirl, Viridae, Woohookitty, 189 anonymous edits

Person *Source*: http://en.wikipedia.org/w/index.php?title=Person *Contributors*: "alyosha", 77persons, Aarktica, Acswoops, AdultSwim, Ahoerstemeier, Aka042, Alan Rockefeller, Alansohn, Ale jrb, AlexHillan, Alienus, AliveFreeHappy, Alksub, Altenmann, Anarchia, Ancheta Wis, AndonicO, Andrew Maiman, Android Mouse, Andycjp, AngelOfSadness, Anthony Krupp, Arakunem, Aranae, Aranel, Aranherunar, Arbor, Archanamiya, Armenianweirdo, Arthur Rubin, Assyria 90, AzaToth, Aznmatthias12345, Backslash Forwardslash, Baiji, Baileyfav, Benno Briton, Bennychains, Bhuston, Bibliophylax, Big billy bob, Bladestorm, Blanchardb, Bleh999, Bleistift, BoNoMoJo (old), Bobo192, Boccobrock, Bogdangiusca, Bongwarrior, Brad.leach, BrianH123, Brianjd, Bucephalus, COMPFUNK2, CSWarren, Caltas, Camw, Can't sleep, clown will eat me, Caprenicus11, Capricorn42, Catboy32528, Catgut, Ch358223ob, CharlesGillingham, Chocoforfriends, Chris fluppy, Cjmnyc, Claynayton, Cometstyles, Cooper.g, Copperwing0, Corkmastercheeseface, CrazyLegsKC, Cremepuff222, Cuddlyable3, Cybercobra, DMacks, DVD R W, Dafyddperry, DanielCD, Danny lost, Darthgate, DeadEyeArrow, Debresser, Deeptrivia, Delldot, DeluxNate, DerHexer, Derek Andrews, DesmondRavenstone, Deusveritasest, Devin122, Dfrg.msc, Discospinster, Docboat, Dolphindreamer67, Doulos Christos, Dpark, Dreftymac, Dysepsion, El estremeñu, Elmer92413, Emeraude, Enzo Aquarius, Epbr123, EpiVictor, Epskionline, Euchiasmus, Evan Robidoux, Evercat, Everyking, Eviloldman, ExistentialEudaimonia, FT2, Face5678, FayssalF, FetchcommsAWB, Fgtr, Foliowned, Fourohfour, Fred Bauder, Frehley, Frencheigh, Freyr, Gabbe, Gazimoff, Generalvador, GeorgeMoney, Gilliam, Gingerluvr, Go for it!, Godardesque, Goferhoney, Gogo Dodo, Goluszkamax, Gordonrox24, GraemeL, Gregbard, Growlie2, Guitarking6045, Gurch, Gwernol, Gökhan, Hadal, HalfShadow, HamatoKameko, HamburgerRadio, Hdt83, Hebrides, Hezzy, Hmrox, HobosTakeMyCash, Holyzoibe, Hoof Hearted, HorsePunchKid, Howcheng, Hrundi Bakshi, Hsteach, Huntthetroll, Hypergeometric2F1(a,b,c,x), II MusLiM HyBRiD II, Iamaperson123, Iancarter, Ideletealot2, Ihcoyc, Insorak, Itschris, Ixfd64, Izehar, J.delanoy, JASpencer, JForget, JaGa, Jagger88, Jamesofur, Janus Shadowsong, Jay, Jennavecia, Jerzy, Jfdwolff, Jfraatz, Jjamesj, Jni, John254, JohnCD, Jojit fb, Joriki, Joseph Solis in Australia, Juliancolton, Jusdafax, Karol Langner, Kazzyfromky 08, Keilana, KillerChihuahua, Killiondude, Kinu, Kirby04, Konadawg, Ksy92003, Kukini, Kurieeto, Kuru, L.Kenzel, LOL, Lambda, Lapaz, Lexor, Lightbourne7, Lights, LittleOldMe, LjL, Lol0075, Loremaster, LucaviX, Lucy-marie, Lurlock, Lycurgus, Lynn Wilbur, M00npirate, MER-C, MONGO, MVP0079, Malo, MarkS, Mary katsika, Mateo LeFou, Mayooranathan, Melchoir, Mendaliv, Metamagician3000, Michael Devore, Michael Hardy, Mickyc30, Midway, Mild Bill Hiccup, Milos2000, Miss Mondegreen, Mochachocca, Montrealais, Moreschi, Mr. Billion, MrJones, Nakomis, Nakon, Navy Blue, NawlinWiki, Neelix, Neverquick, NewEnglandYankee, Newbyguesses, Nihiltres, No Guru, Nsaa, Nutiketaiel, OOO15, Obey, Oda Mari, Olderthanwiser, Onevalefan, Ontoraul, Orangemike, Otashiro, Paradisevalleycampground, Pbrane, Persian Poet Gal, Phaedriel, Philip Trueman, Philwelch, Phlyght, Piano non troppo, Pit, Postpartisannotbipartisan, Ppntori, Prophêcy, Pyfan, Quizkajer, RG2, Radagast83, Radiant!, RadioKirk, Radiosband, RainbowOfLight, Random166352, Rdsmith4, Rebroad, Red Thunder, RehmanK786, Rich Farmbrough, Rmhermen, Roleplayer, Ruby.red.roses, S19991002, SableSynthesis, Saintofbladez, Samw, Sardanaphalus, Senator Palpatine, Sentience, Seraphimblade, Shanoman, Shirulashem, Shrommer, Sirex98, Siroxo, Skapur, Skyezx, SlimVirgin, Slugger, Snigbrook, Snowolf, Spellcast, Spliffy, Spotfixer, Steevven1, SteinbDJ, Stephen G. Brown, Susan118, SweetNightmares, Swpb, Tasham12, The Famous Movie Director, The Thing That Should Not Be, The Transhumanist, The undertow, TheFarix, Thingg, Tiddly Tom, Tiptoety, Tkn20, Tktktk, Tobycat, Trevyn, Ukexpat, Umqothu, Una Smith, Uncle Dick, UninvitedCompany, Universitytruth, Unyoyega, Useight, Veledan, Vishnava, Voxpuppet, Vsmith, Walljordan, Warrington, Whalebond, WhisperToMe, Will Beback, William Avery, Willking1979, Wknight94, Wndl42, Woohookitty, Xelgen, Yamamoto Ichiro, Yekrats, Yidisheryid, Zach fisher, Zahd, Zanaq, Zodon, Zondor, Zsinj, Zzuuzz, 806 anonymous edits

Business *Source*: http://en.wikipedia.org/w/index.php?title=Business *Contributors*: -Kerplunk-, 10metreh, 334a, 417.417, 97parnellj, A8UDI, AaronEJ, Abdullais4u, AbsolutDan, Academic Challenger, Acegenesis, AdjustShift, Adochka, Adrest4, Aeden2, Againme, Agers, Aitambong, Ajeet, Akram1978, Al.locke, Alan Liefting, Alansohn, Alex earlier account, Alexius08, Aliyevramin, Alkiviadis, All Male Action, Allank6, Allstargold, Altenmann, AnaLondon, Andoceo, Andre Engels, Andrewharold, Andrewpmk, Andycjp, Anetode, Angela, Angr, Anna Lincoln, Antandrus, Anthony, Anthony Appleyard, Arbitrarily0, Ardonik, Ariaconditzione, Arsene, Arthur Markham, Aryawat, Asimnazar, Audriusa, Auroranorth, Avono, Azmax007, Azzix, BD2412, BSTemple, Bact, Balaam42, Barcelova, Bartledan, Battlecry, Beano, Bebestbe, Beetstra, Belinrahs, Belovedfreak, Bemoeial, BennyQuixote, Blake-, Blanchardb, Blue520, Bobby Ironsights, Bobo192, Bogdan08, Bongwarrior, Boreas231, Bradjamesbrown, Brian0918, Brocky9, Bruguiea, Bsadowski1, BusinessAsUnusual, Businesstopics, CUSENZA Mario, CactusWriter, Caknuck, Calidore Chase, Camw, Can't sleep, clown will eat me, Capricorn42, Capturetheworld, Careless hx, Carnildo, Caseylebaker, Casperdc, Catgut, Ccacsmss, Cenarium, Ceo, Cesco, Chcknwnm, Chennaiseo, Chinneeb, Chuckiesdad, Ckatz, Closedmouth, Closermac, Computerjoe, Conquer 59, Cool Hand Luke, Cornellrockey, CorporationBuilder, Covington, Crimz2k8, Ctbolt, Cuecla, Curps, Cyktsui, DMacks, DVD R W, Da monster under your bed, DancingPenguin, Danielspencer91, David Underdown, Davidkazuhiro, Davisftaylor, Dbc06, Dcarafel, Dcoetzee, Ddr, Ddstretch, Degress, Delldot, DerHexer, Derob ecnirp, Deus Ex, DigsPeanuts, Discospinster, DocWatson42, Docu, Dreadstar, Drew R. Smith, Durkalurks, ESkog, Edgar181, Editerdude, Ehheh, El C, Enterprise Guru, Enviroboy, Enzo Aquarius, Epbr123, Eplekake, Eric Chang, Eric Larcher, Eric ausente, Esiegel3, Espen, Essjay, Etlsen, Eugene van der Pijll, Evalowyn, Everyking, Examtester, Excirial, FT2, Faithlessthewonderboy, Faradayplank, Felix116, FelixKaiser, FisherQueen, Fitzkie, Fitzkie1, Flewis, Flutterfly, FocusAndFinish, Foggy Morning, Fplay, Frank, Frankenpuppy, Frecklefoot, Fred Bauder, Fredouil, Frisco21, Fusionmix, Fvasconcellos, Gail, Gaius Cornelius, Galoubet, Garfield226, Gavin Kettis!, Geneb1955, Geof, Georgiakatopodis, Georgieboi123, GetPhunk, Gilliam, Gimme danger, Girolamo Savonarola, Glenn, Gobonobo, Gogo Dodo, Goodoldpolonius2, GraemeL, Guy Peters, Gwernol, Gwyndon, Haakon, Hadal, Halojoe94, Haza-w, Hclim65, Hdt83, Heightwatcher, Hellraiser160791, Henning Wiekhorst, Henrik, Hephaestos, HereToHelp, Heron, Hezarfenn, Hhalladay, Hmrox, Hohoho1, Hojimachong, Hopiakuta, Houseofcosby, Hu12, IRP, Icairns, Imran, Imrek, Insanephantom, Insomanic, Interestingstuffadder, Iridescent, Ironholds, IslandHopper973, Istartfires, Iterator12n, J.delanoy, JD554, JForget, Jackofwiki, Jackp, Jackp11213, James086, JamesWalker-ntu, Jamiemilbourne, Jareha, Jay, Jeffrey Mall, Jerryseinfeld, Jiang, Jim Douglas, JimVC3, Jj137, Jni, John, JohnCD, JohnDoe0007, JohnOwens, Joka, Jonny-mt, Jonovision, Jose77, Joshn3, JoshuaZ, Jossi, Jukcoder, Jummai, Jurusie, KFP, Kabad2008, Kaihsu, Kanehdian, Kangphil, Karl-Henner, Karnesky, Kashi0341, Kasschei, Keilana, Kelly Martin, Kelvinwkw, Khatru2, Khoikhoi, Khukri, Kiand, Killiondude, Kingpin13, KissL, Kotniski, Kozuch, Kpharvey1, Krakfly, Krawi, Krupo, Kubigula, Kungfuadam, Kuru, L0b0t, LZFVBNM, La Pianista, LaggedOnUser, Lamaar, Larry Lawrence, Lbunited, LeeG, Levineps, Lewis-teck, Lights, Limimim, Limit0, Linkspamremover, Llamadog903, Logical8, Lolb^u, Longhair, Lordddraconius, Loren.wilton, LouGeorge, LouI, Lradrama, Luapnampahc, Luinwe, Luk, Luna Santin, MER-C, MONGO, Mac Davis, Madchester, Magnuschubb, Malo, MarceloB, MarkSutton, Martarius, Martin Jensen, Martin451, Matt Crypto, Matthew238, Maurreen, Maxim, Maximus Rex, Maxis ftw, Mayumashu, Mcbumnugit, Mejor Los Indios, MeltBanana, Mendaliv, Mendel, Meursault2004, Mic, Michael Snow, Midnightcomm, Mike 7, Mike Omaley, Miketear27, MisfitToys, Mkoval, Moonriddengirl, Moris43, Mr Stephen, MrOllie, Mthampi, Muchness, Muppet317, Muriel Gottrop, Mwalimu59, Mydogategodshat, Nagy, Nancylyy, NawlinWiki, Ndkartik, Nerijus valskis, Nerval, Netoholic, Neverquick, NewEnglandYankee, Nicholas Tam, Nigholith, Nightsturm, Nikai, Ninja43, Nmacpherson, Notinasnaid, Nsaa, NuclearWarfare, Nurg, Nuttycoconut, ObjectivityAlways, Oblomoff, Oda Mari, Ohnoitsjamie, Olathe, Old Moonraker, Oleg Alexandrov, Olegwiki, Olexandr Kravchuk, Omicronpersei8, Omm nom nom nom, Omoide, Oneiros, Onorem, Optimale, Oraclelocal, Orgwiki, Oslolso, Otisjimmy1, Otolemur crassicaudatus, Owen, PGPirate, Paintman, Palladmial, PamD, Pamri, Parmarossa, Passportguy, Passw0rd, Patrick, PatrickFlaherty, Patstuart, Patxunan, Paul August, Pavel Vozenilek, Pax:Vobiscum, Paxse, Pb30, Pdogsi, Pedant17, Pedro, Pegship, Peshko, Ph.D.Nikki, Phantomsteve, Phoebe, PiMaster3, Piano non troppo, Pinkadelica, Plinkit, Pobably, Poeloq, Poohpooh817, Poor Yorick, Poweroid, Ppntori, Prolog, Prototime, Psy guy, Questionaire99, REDyellowGreenBLUE, RJII, RJN, RadioKirk, RanchoRosco, Ratherhaveaheart, RazorICE, RedHillian, Redsome, Remi0o, RexNL, Rfc1394, Rgvandewalker, Rhobite, Rich257, Richard D. LeCour, RichardF, Rick Block, Rm w a vu, RobLa, Rocket976, Roni you, Ronniefaron, Ronreed, Rossami, Royli57, RxS, SCEhardt, SUL, Sachindole, Salasks, Samwisedagr8, Sango123, Sanjaymca, Sannse, SarahJBull, Sarahviolin, SchfiftyThree, Scriberius, Secretlondon, Selmo, Sgtslash93, Shadowjams, Sharpsage, Shatrughan, Shishir.krs, Shlomke, Sid007, Silsor, SimonP, SineWave, Skidude9950, Smallman12q, Smilesfozwood, Smitty, Snowolf, Socs, Sokker30, Spiritualism, Sprachpfleger, Spudmuffin, Srushe, StaticGull, Stepbigboss, Stephenb, Stevertigo, SueHay, Sumimu, SuperHamster, SvenAERTS, Svick, THEN WHO WAS PHONE?, TachyonP, Taggard, Tallcitikid, Tannin, TastyPoutine, Tbb9216, Ted Longstaffe, Tehsilvercock, Teleszczupak, Templarion, Tempodivalse, Tgv8925, Tharshman, The Original Economist, The Rambling Man, The Thing That Should Not Be, The Transhumanist, The Transhumanist (AWB), TheBusinessCoach, Thebigpalooka, Thehappyjew, Tide rolls, Tim Song, Timmothias, Tiptopmovie, Tnxman307, Todd Vierling, Tombomp, Tony Fox, Transity, Trusilver, Twooars, Tyir, Tzartzam, USCFE, Uncemaster3000, Universalpayroll, Useight, Utcursch, Valerie Funderburg, Veinor, Versus22, Vipul pratap, Vman475, Walden, Walor, WarthogDemon, Weregerbil, Wgoetsch, Whatifound, Whiner01, Why Not A Duck, WikiGee, WikiLaurent, Wikidestroyer114, Wikihater114, Wikikiller65, Williambeaufoy, Willking1979, Windrunr, Wise Willie, Wizardman, Xhaoz, Yangyang2036, Yansa, Ybbor, Yhkhoo, Yidisheryid, Yintan, Zafiroblue05, ZimZalaBim, Zitie, Zragon, Zundark, Zvn, Zzuuzz, 百家姓之四, 1096 anonymous edits

Opinion *Source*: http://en.wikipedia.org/w/index.php?title=Opinion *Contributors*: 4twenty42o, Afil, Alansohn, AngryBadger28, Antandrus, Blanchardb, Blubbermuffin, Bogdangiusca, Bongwarrior, Borgx, Brian0918, Brisvegas, COMPFUNK2, Captain-tucker, Charles Matthews, Chaser, Christopher Parham, Claytorious, Cpl Syx, DHooke1973, Damortseam, Dcoetzee, Discospinster, DivineAlpha, Dorftrottel, Draziw66, Drini, Eastlaw, Emersoni, Epbr123, Everdictorg, Evil Genius, FCSundae, Fbd, FlabZ, Fredrik, GaryColemanFan, Gawaxay, Granpuff, Gregbard, Grumpyyoungman01, Grutness, Guanaco, Gurch, Halmstad, Happysmileyface, Horselove004, IShadowed, Ilyanep, Inko Inko, Insanity Incarnate, Iridescent, J.delanoy, JCO312, JJRR10, Jaymax, Jeeves, Jetru, Jmlk17, JoelHuang, Josephprymak, Juliancolton, KF, Kahkonen, Katefan0, Killjoy12, Kwamikagami, La goutte de pluie, Luna Santin, Maurice Carbonaro, Maurits, Micfri, Mike4ty4, Mmmbeer, Mtilda, Nakon, Neelix, NewEnglandYankee, Otto ter Haar, Pearle, Persian Poet Gal, Pianoplonkers, Pollinosisss, PubliusFL, PullUpYourSocks, RG2, RLipstock, Rabbethan, Ragusan, RedSpruce, Rfc1394, RumoriousBIG, Sam Spade, Scaian, ScorpO, Sjakkalle, Sm1969, Smee, Smithfarm, Speedevil, SpuriousQ, Stefanomione, The 13th 4postle, Thegn, TigerShark, TimmyandTammy, Transfinite, Txomin, Ukexpat, Versageek, Vestigial Thumb, Vikramsahil98, Wasthere, Wikidemon, Wuffyz, Yaris678, Yidisheryid, Zorro CX, ZuluPapa5, 152 anonymous edits

Idea *Source*: http://en.wikipedia.org/w/index.php?title=Idea *Contributors*: 16@r, Akhilleus, Alex756, Alpt, AndriuZ, Anurag online, Aranel, Barticus88, Bastique, Bcjordan, Bill.albing, Bird, Blue wave, Bomac, Bongwarrior, Brettz9, COMPFUNK2, CaSe, Carlos-alberto-teixeira, Cgingold, Chameleon, Charles Matthews, CharlieNisser, Ched Davis, Cobain, Commander Shepard, Corporate.legal, DCDuring, Dan Polansky, Danny lost, Darbouka International, Davepape, Dchmelik, Denis C., Diberri, Discospinster, Dorftrottel, Doug Coldwell, Download, Dpv, Eaefremov, Edcolins, EivindJ, Epbr123, Esperant, Everyking, Fan-1967, Feezo, Fnarf999, Fuzzbox, GPJohnson, Gabinho, Gianfranco, Glogger, Goethean, Gogo Dodo, Gregbard, Gunmetal Angel, Hallenrm, Hede2000, Hermeneus, Hersfold, Hihi234, Hveziris, Ideamapping, J04n, Jaberwocky6669, Jamacfarlane, Jeff Silvers, JimStyle61093475, Johnrpenner, Jon Awbrey, Joonasl, Julian Mendez, Jvdpahlen, Kbthompson, Kenny sh, Kernow, Kku, Kstinch, Lapaz, Lar, Lestrade, Lolobee, Lugnuts, MER-C, MISHCLIF, Mark Nez, Maurreen, Meelar, Mel Etitis, Meldor, Mikaelbook, NathanoNL, Nikai, Noamdanon, Oscar, Oxymoron83, Pakimark, Pammylove, Pavel Vozenilek, Philogo, Phronima, Piano non troppo, Poa, Prolog, Psychicdiva, Ranveig, Rd232, Reflex Reaction, Rodrigo Cornejo, Romanc19s, Roundhouse0, Rudd-O, Sabbut, Samw, Sander123, Savant13, SimonP, SofieElisBexter, Stefanomione, SteveMcCluskey, Stsang, Sunray, Swerty, T g7, TakuyaMurata, The Tetrast, The Thing That Should Not Be, Therealbrendan31, TinyMark, Twipley, WRK, Wareh, Washdivad, Westendgirl, Woohookitty, Yair rand, Yidisheryid, Yoninah, ZachCrichfield, Zfr, Zoicon5, Zzuuzz, 158 anonymous edits

Copy (written) *Source*: http://en.wikipedia.org/w/index.php?title=Copy_%28written%29 *Contributors*: Adrian, Beland, BesigedB, Bodnotbod, Ehn, Fvw, Gnusmas, Jeff3000, Locatelli, Maurreen, Nurg, Piastu, Ravanacker, Rbanzai, Schissel, Shizhao, Soph, TimNelson, Vermiculus, Walden, 11 anonymous edits

Advertising *Source*: http://en.wikipedia.org/w/index.php?title=Advertising *Contributors*: SyD!, -- April, -Midorihana-, 10kweeks, 119, 2D, 63.195.83.xxx, A little insignificant, A.abdo, A. B., A8UDI, ACBest, AEF, ALargeElk, Aapo Laitinen, Aaron Brenneman, Abaddon314159, Abbeyvet, Abrech, AbsolutDan, Accurizer, Ace ETP, AdPrin, Adam7davies, Aducation, Advanced, Advertiser88, Aff123a, Ag1979, Aggieuk, Ahoerstemeier, Ais.bul, Aitias, Ajaxkroon, Akki1994, Akubra, Alanjpage, Alansohn, Ale jrb, Alex43223, Alexkin, AlistairMcMillan, All Is One, Allagainsteverything311, Alphachimp, Alsandro, Altenmann, Alwaysepic, Amizani, Ancheta Wis, Anders.Warga, AndrewHowse, Andrewpmk, AndriuZ, Andypandy.UK, Angel Cupid, Annabell2310, Anonywiki, Antandrus, Anthony Appleyard, AnupMukherjee, ArglebargleIV, ArielGold, Arjayay, Armour Hotdog, Arnon Chaffin, Artfikan, Ascidian, Asriel86, Atenea26, Atif.t2, Atlantima, Avian, AxelBoldt, AySz88, Aymatth2, BD2412, Back door90, Baratunde, Barce, Bavandongen, Baxter42, Baylink, Beach drifter, Beam er, Bearian, Beetstra, Belovedfreak, Benapgar, Betacommand, Bhadani, Bhound89, Bhuston, BigCow, Bigbluefish, Bigtop, Biscuit.trippz, Bissinger, Bkatong, Blanchardb, BlastOButter42, Bletch, Bob A, Bobblewik, Bobiosfred, Bobo192, Bombastus, Bonadea, Bongwarrior, Boothy443, Born2cycle, Boronzbiz, Brandalone, Brianga, Brnelson, Bryan Derksen, Bsadowski1, Build your own community, Burzmali, Byronsharp, CDN99, CIreland, CWii, Calan, CallamRodya, Caltas, CalumH93, Calvin 1998, Calvin ngan, CambridgeBayWeather, Camw, Can't sleep, clown will eat me, CanisRufus, Canley, Capricorn42, Careless hx, Cartoon3321, Catgut, CatherineMunro, Ccpark, Chase me ladies, I'm the Cavalry, Chcknwnm, Chendy, Chenzw, Chewypup, Chill Pill Bill, Chiminoul, Chovain, Chris 73, Chris j wood, Chrislk02, Chzz, Circeus, Citimobile1, Civil Engineer III, Clark89, Claudek7, CliffC, Closedmouth, CloudNine, Cmontero, Coffee, Cohesion, ColtM4, Cometstyles, CommonsDelinker, Confused monk, Conversion script, Coolcaesar, Coolmedia, Coredesat, Correogsk, CraigDDunn, Cream147, Creativecopywriter, Crystallina, Ctjf83, Ctw3333, Cyanoa Crylate, Cyberstrike3000X, Cyp01, D, D tonack, D. Recorder, DA3N, DDerby, DEEJAY JPM, DMacks, DVD R W, Da monster under your bed, Dajohndeerefarmer, Dalmation, Damcy, Dan198792, Dangomba, Daniel, DanielCD, DanielPenfield, DanielRigal, Darktemplar222, Dasani, Dave6, DaveG12345, David Esrati, David T Tokyo, DavidLevinson, DavidMarciano, Davidcharle, Davodd, Dcastlebeck, Deizk, Dcooper, Ddj, Ddxc, DeadEyeArrow, DeadlyAssassin, Defekt7x, Deli nk, Delicious carbuncle, Delight74, Deor, DerHexer, Derek.cashman, Dersh, Descendall, Devatipan, Dharmabum420, Diegopen, Dieter Simon, Diligent, Dino, Dinosaurdarrell, DirectEdge, Discospinster, Djcam, Djinn112, Djlayton4, Dlohcierekim, Dm2ablur, Docu, DougsTech, Download, Draicone, Dranzer19, DraxusD, Drbreznjev, Dreaded Walrus, DreamGuy, Dreblowski, Drini, Drmies, Dtodd, Dubhdara, Duck7, Duncanson, Dureo, Durova, Dylan Lake, EJF, Eaglecbr, Earlkohn, Echoray, EdBever, Edgar181, Edward, Edward301, Ehheh, El C, El jefe, Eli77e, Eliz81, Elliskev, Emmalf, Emsépé, Emurphy42, Enkrates, Enric Naval, Epbr123, Equazcion, Eric outdoors, Ericaherb, Erik Chevrier, Erik9, Erikas123, Erkcan, EsonLinji, Estoy Aquí, Ethanpilot787, Euniana, Everyking, Everyone Dies In the End, Ewawer, Ewok9, Exander, Excirial, Exert, Experto Crede, FJPB, Fadingad, Fairsing, Faithx5, Fareeha007, Fastily, FayssalF, Fcoulter, FiP, Finlay McWalter, Fireworking, FisherQueen, Flaming, FlowerSniffer, Fluffythemonkey, Folajimi, Former user 2, Fourmiz59, Fourohfour, Francis Schonken, FrancisTyers, Franes2000, Frankandvinnyrule!, Fraser J Allison, Freckles.10.6.2005, FrenchIsAwesome, Friginator, Fruckert, Fudoreaper, Furrykef, Futurebird, Futureobservatory, GT5162, GUllman, Gabbe, Gabr, Gadfium, Gaius Cornelius, Gakrivas, Galoubet, Galwhaa, Gareth Cash, Garyruskin, Genius101, Gilliam, Gingerzilla, Gixxy123, Godlessharry, Gogo Dodo, Gracenotes, GraemeL, Graemecodrington, Grapeman, Gregalton, Gregbrown, Gregory Welteroth Advertising, Gromlakh, Grooveadv, Ground, Guitarist Nick, Gurch, Guvna, Guy Peters, GuyRo, Gwernol, Gökhan, H, HJ Mitchell, Haakon, Haham hanuka, Haiduc, HamburgerRadio, Harleydavidsons, Hatarchive, Hateless, Hdt83, Heebiejeebieclub, Heimstern, Herbythyme, Hinto, Hitmanad, Hiwk, Hk linus, Hornblack, Horoshi1820, Hostile Amish, Hotfuzz1234567890, Hu12, Hurricanehink, Husond, Hussein fazal, I.DIESELMAN, ILorbb, Iambbscom, Ian Pitchford, Iandoh2, Icephoenix26, Idtabije, Ignatzmice, Infrogmation, Internus, Intgr, Intothewoods29, Iridescent, Iris lorain, Irunongames, Isn1015, IstvanWolf, Itub, Ixfd64, J. Nguyen, J.delanoy, JForget, JLaTondre, JYolkowski, JaGa, Jack Phoenix, Jahsonic, James086, Jamesggilmore, JammydodgerUK, Jamyskis, Janejellyroll, Jannadada, Japanese Searobin, Jastrow, Jatkins, Jauerback, JavierMC, JayKeaton, Jayden54, Jb lance plumber, Jclemens, Jeff G., Jeffrey Mall, Jeffrey.Kleykamp, Jehochman, Jennyfromny1, Jerbaby9, JeremyA, Jet sat 07, JiFish, Jiggalo09, Jimmy Flores, Jimphilos, Jj137, Jjron, Jleboeuf, Jobgoom, JodyB, JoeLatics, JoeSmack, John Broughton, John254, John5170, Johnny Au, JohnnyB256, Jokestress, Jonathan Hall, JosephGleeson, Josesaturn, Jossi, JuJube, Juckum, Juicystyle, Juliancolton, Jusdafax, Jusjih, JustJeddeh, Jyarmey, KChiu7, KSchutte, Kafziel, Kanenas, Karol Langner, Katharine908, Kcnonfiction, Ken Gallager, Kerotan, Kharkless, Kilo-Lima, Kingturtle, Kipkipuk, KirchnerE07, Knowledge Seeker, KnowledgeOfSelf, Knpepper, Koavf, Kompas, Korath, Kronos299, Ktownt., Kukini, Kungfuadam, Kurieeto, Kurt Shaped Box, Kuru, Kuyan, Kxjtaz, La Parka Your Car, La vita è dolce, Lar, Lawbrn67, Leadtoasia, LeaveSleaves, Lee M, Lee gregz, LegCircus, Lennytim, Lenoxus, Leranedo, LiamUK, Liface, Light of Shadow, Lightmouse, Lihaas, LilHelpa, Likdre7760, Lindsayluckadoo, Linkspamremover, Littledanno, Localcustomerconnect, Longwood58, LordofPens, Lowellian, Lpxz, Lucky 6.9, LuigiManiac, Luja Manandhar, Luk, Luna Santin, Lvken7, Lvsubram, M fic, MER-C, MSGJ, Maddie!, Malik Shabazz, Malinaccier, Malo, Mamawrites, Man It's So Loud In Here, Mandy80326, Marinaforina, Mark, Mark9739, Markonen, Markus Büchele, Martarius, Martin Jensen, MartinDK, Mashmallow273, Master Deusoma, Mateo SA, Mattbrundage, Matthk, Mattisse, Maurreen, Mav, Maximus Rex, Maxpower0113, Mbaird1119, Mboverload, McSly, Mecflo99, Meaghan, Mediaexpert, MementoVivere, Meor, Merc25, Merphant, Metronews, Michael Hardy, MickWest, Miel Patterson, Miernik, Mike Rosoft, Mike.lifeguard, Millisits, Mintleaf, Mion, MiracleMat, Miranda, Mitch Ames, Mm40, Modemac, Modernist, Modulatum, Moh.elguindy, Moltare, Monkeyman, Moondial, Mostlymostly, Moweryg, Mozzerati, MrOllie, Mrand, Mrzaius, Mschel, Msdollars, Muchobueno, Muhgcee, Muhile, Muro de Aguas, Music soul 29, Mustufashah, Mxn, My Cat inn, Mycroft.Holmes, Mydogategodshat, Mykl1812, N1h1l, N5iln, NMChico24, Nakon, Naraht, Natalie Erin, NawlinWiki, Ndgorg1, Needles27, Neelix, Neep, Nehrams2020, NeilN, Neverquick, Ni ck ii xx!xx, Nialsh, Nick, NickBurns, NickelShoe, Nightscream, Nikzbitz, Nivix, Nixeagle, Njthomes, NoIdeaNick, Noahgh, Nogard363, Nol888, Noncompliant one, Nukeless, Nv8200p, Odie5533, Ohnoitsjamie, Oicumayberight, Ojuice5001, Omicronpersei8, OneVeryBadMan, Osucrew983, Otolemur crassicaudatus, Otus, OwenX, Oxymoron83, PTSE, Pablo2garcia, Padense, PapaWhitman, Paramountpublishing, Parhamr, Patrick, Paul Barlow, PaulGS, Pax:Vobiscum, Pb30, Pcjabber, Pedapod, Penbat, Penubag, Perfecto, Perspectoff, Peter Clarke, Peter Fleet, Peter Lawless, Peterbisset, Peterhuang9604, Peteryh, Pgk, Ph89, Phil Boswell, Philip Trueman, Philwiki, Phoe, Phonefinder2007, Piano non troppo, Pimlottc, Pir, Pjbrockmann, Plinkit, Postdlf, Poweroid, Premeditated Chaos, Presario3000, Promodirect, Promotingspace, PromotionalCurrency, Psyche825, Puchiko, Puri.pallavi, Qtroger, Quadell, Quarl, Qx41120, Qxz, R0ssr0ss, Racklever, Racula, Raelx, RainbowOfLight, Rainer Wasserfuhr, RandomP, Rasmus Faber, Rastaman 99, RazielZero, Rcawsey, Rcephuk, Redlentil, Reetawowfactor, Regibox, Renski, Rettetast, RevRagnarok, RexNL, ReyBrujo, Rhobite, Riana, Rich Farmbrough, Rich Janis, Richard W.M. Jones, Richardwarren, Richchum, Richyli, RickK, Rigadoun, Riverhelp, Rizoglou, Rjcain, Rjd0060, Rjgibb, Rjwilmsi, Rlevse, Rlitwin, Rlsheehan, Robert Skyhawk, RockMFR, Rockdrum12, Rockfang, Romanm, Ron prince51, Ronhjones, Ronnyedwards, Ronz, Rosedb, Rotem Dan, Roux, RoyBoy, Roychonggfc, Rror, Rubikubism, Ruled, Ryanyahoo, S0me l0ser, ST47, SWAdair, Saccerzd, Sade, Saihtam, Salamurai, Salgueiro, Salmanazar, Sam Francis, Samaritan, Sampi, Samuraispy, Samw, Sannse, Saorlab, Savidan, Scarian, SchfiftyThree, Schmackity, Schoolassignment, Schroeder74, Schwallex, Scientizzle, Sdbmaranello, Sdornan, Seddon, Selket, Semolina Pilchard, Sert, Seth Ilys, Sewing, Shackel21, Shaddack, Shadow1, ShadowyCaballero, Shandris, Shanimoshe, Sheldon Rampton, Shihosakamoto, Shoessss, Shoujun, Shoy, Shreshth91, Silverbackwireless, Silversurfer3000, SimonP, Sin-man, Singhalawap, Sir Lewk, Sjakkalle, Skizzik, Slakr, Smokizzy, Smpickens, Snalwibma, Snowolf, SoCalSuperEagle, Soilguy5, Someguy1221, Spalding, Spartan, Spellcast, Spirelli, Spiritia, Spyfilms2007, Squash, Squid661, Srinivas.pasham, Sroc, Stars4change, StaticGull, Stefan Kögl, Stefanbocck, Stefanomione, Stephenb, Sterry2607, Stevelemming, Stormie, Suffusion of Yellow, Sujithc, Sukritsmasher, Sunainakhurana, Sundar1, Sunsfan1797, SuperDude115, Supergeo, Swordman182, Swpb, TFCforever, TMNolan, TUF-KAT, Taak, Tail, Tanthalas39, Targeman, Tbonejoo, Teddey, Tgumport, That Guy, From That Show!, Thaurisil, The Anome, The Land of Smeg, The Thing That Should Not Be, The undertow, TheAsocialApe, TheInvisibleHomepage, TheKMan, TheSuave, Thebigted, Themfromspace, Themicemen, Theone00, Thexray, Thingg, Think outside the box, Thomas H. Larsen, Thrash242, TiLK, Tide rolls, Tiernuchin, Tinucherian, Titoxd, Tnxman307, Tom9d, Tomchiukc, Tomeliot, Tomi T Ahonen, Tomt, Tony Corsini, Tony Fox, Tony1, TonyTheTiger, Tonywalton, Tophernator, Topory, Topspeedracer, Tpbradbury, Tresiden, Trevor MacInnis, Trgl317, Tri400, Trialsanderrors, Trounce, Turgan, Twooars, Tzartzam, Uberveritas, Ugochuku, Ujake5, Undead Kangaroo, Unschool, Unwiserohit, Useight, Utcursch, Van helsing, Vasanth.telebuy, Veinor, Ventur, Versageek, Versus22, Vikingstad, Vildricianus, Violetriga, Voceditenore, Väsk, WAS 4.250, WATP, WAvegetarian, Wai Wai, Walden, Waterjuice, Wavelength, Wayward, Webmarketer55, Weregerbil, Weyes, WhisperToMe, Why Not A Duck, WibblyLeMoende, Wiki alf, Wikidudeman, Wikiklrsc, Wikilibrarian, Wilderr67, William Avery, Willwaugh, Wimt, Wisdombank, Witty lama, Wmahan, Woohookitty, Wordmonkey2, Work permit, Wrp103, Wtmitchell, XXx radio xXx, Xanderall, Xhaoz, Xxplayboi965xx, Xy7, YUL89YYZ, Yansa, Yashtulsyan, Yeti Hunter, Yidisheryid, Yorrick, Yousaf465, YuriSanCa, Z3ugmatic, Zaheen, Zaki Usman, Zanimum, Zantastik, Zepheus, Zzuuzz, Zzyzx11, 2242 anonymous edits

Television *Source*: http://en.wikipedia.org/w/index.php?title=Television *Contributors*: *drew, -Midorihana-, 02hansona, 0kdal, 119, 12.252.66.xxx, 12.64.180.xxx, 16@r, 1bobby93, 2004-12-29T22:45Z, 203.170.3.xxx, 234abc, 24.93.53.xxx, 3MP, 63.192.137.xxx, A-giau, A2Kafir, ACupOfCoffee, AEMoreira042281, AOEU, Abductive, Abtract, Abu badali, Acalamari, Accurizer, Acroterion, AdRock, Adamm, Adamrush, AderakConsteen, Adrian, Adveragejoe, After Midnight, Ahoerstemeier, Ai4ijoel, Aitias, Ajplmr, Alai, Alan Liefting, Alasdair, AlbertSM, Aldie, AlexiusHoratius, Alfio, Algocu, Ali, Ali K, AliceJMarkham, AlistairMcMillan, Alksub, All in, Alphachimp, Altenmann, AltiusBimm, Am088, Amaccormack, Amazon10x, Amazonien, Amberrock, AmiDaniel, Anakin908, Andre Engels, Andreas -horn- Hornig, Andrewjharvey1, Andrewpmk, Andrey Isakov, Andy G, Andy M. Wang, Andy Marchbanks, Andycjp, Andylandandrew, Andypandy.UK, Anetode, Angela, Angilbas, Angmering, Animemeg, Ann Stouter, Anonywiki, Antaeus Feldspar, Antandrus, Anthony Appleyard, AntonioMartin, Antony the genius, AppleJordan, AppleMacReporter, Applejuicefool, Arado, Arjun01, Arronax50, Art LaPella, Arteitle, Artorius, Asav, Ascidian, Atlan, AuburnPilot, Audin, AussieLegend, Avant Guard, Avilezj, Avt tor, AxG, AxiomShell, AySz88, Aznoble, B, B1atv, BRG, Badgernet, Bakkima, Barkingdoc, Barrettmagic, Barticus88, Basawala, Bass fishing physicist, Bawjaws123, Bbrownp, Beetstra, Beier5, Benc, Berkay0652, Bhadani, Bhuston, Bidgee, Bigbluefish, Bigfoot's Curse of the Wild, Bigturtle, Bill Marsh, Bill Wrigley, Billinghurst, Binksternet, Bkd, Blackjack48, BlankVerse, BlinkingBlimey, Blub Klub, BlueNovember, Bluemask, Bluetooth954, Bmdavll, Bob A, Bobblewik, Bobo192, Boffob, Boffy b, Bonadea, Bongwarrior, BorgQueen, Boston-fashionista, Bovineone, BozMo, Bradeos Graphon, Brand93, Breakfast100, Bremen, Brian the Fat, Brian0918, BrianGV, Bryan Derksen, Bryce Zabel, Bsroiaadn, Btubbb, Bucs, Buddha24, Budisov, Bumhoolery, BurnDownBabylon, Burt Harris, Bwalters, C. Trifle, C0nanPayne, C1k3, CALR, CIreland, CNicol, CS46, Cab88, Cabiria, Caesartheking, Caldorwards4,

Calicocat, Calieber, Calmypal, Caltas, Calvin 1998, CambridgeBayWeather, Camembert, Cameronmas214, Can't sleep, clown will eat me, Canadiana, CanisRufus, Canjth, Cantus, CapitalR, CaptainVindaloo, Carey Evans, Carl.bunderson, Carlroller, Carterandreid, Cartoon-Fan, Casper2k3, Casperdog2227, Catbar, CatherineMunro, Ccacsmss, Cdc, Cdog1, Celebration1981, Ceyockey, Cflm001, Chanting Fox, Chaojoker, CharlotteWebb, Chaser, Chetvorno, Chight, Chitrapa, Chocolateboy, Chocowulf, Chris 42, Chris 73, Chris Roy, Chrislk02, Chriswiki, Chuq, Cjboffoli, Clarenceville Trojan, Clawson, Closedmouth, Cmdrjameson, CoJaBo, Codex Sinaiticus, Coemgenus, Coffee Atoms, Coinchon, Colin99, Colleenthegreat, Cometstyles, Commander Keane, CommonsDelinker, Computer97, Conversion script, Cool joshua1991, Coolpeople, Cordell, Corpx, Covernoiseloveshakespeare, Cowlord7, Craigy144, Cremepuff222, Crimmer, Csoyars, CunningLinguist, Cursit, Cutler, Cyan, D. D. Recorder, DASonnenfeld, DHN, DVD R W, Da monster under your bed, DabMachine, Dainamo, Dale Arnett, Dalek Cab, Damalexandra, Damian Yerrick, Dan Atkinson, DanDud88, DanMS, DancingForRain, DancingMan, Dancingqueenrl, Dane Sorensen, Daniel.Cardenas, Daniel5127, DanielCohen, Dannybu2001, Dannyc77, Dark Mage, Darkieboy236, Darkiller414, Dave dean, Davemcarlson, DavidA, DavidFarmbrough, DavidWJohnson, Davidcottis0100, Davidrubenstern, Dawnseeker2000, Daymas214, Dbemont, Dbo789, Deflyer, Depc0807, Ddxc, DeadEyeArrow, Deb, December21st2012Freak, Deepred6502, Deewiant, Dekisugi, Deli nk, Delldot, Demmy, Denelson83, Deor, DerHexer, Derek Ross, Derek.cashman, Deskruns, Devestator74, Dgreg, Dhartung, Dhp1080, Diagonalfish, Dicka, Dicklyon, Diego001, Digitalme, Dirkbb, Dirt licker, Discospinster, Djdannyp, Djg2006, Djgregory, Dlohcierekim, Dmhoch720, Dmn, Doc glasgow, DocWatson42, Doctormach, Dominykas Blyze, Dooky, Downwards, Dpeters11, DrAjitParkash, DrFrench, DrThompson, Draicone, Dravecky, Dreadstar, Drini, Dskluz, Dualshock2, Duk, Dunks58, DurotarLord, Dwight666, Dwilso, Dycedarg, Dysepsion, Dysprosia, DéRahier, E mozza, Eagle4000, Eaglesdude1525, Echuck215, Ecurb12, Ed g2s, Edison, Editor at Large, Editornumber2, Edward, Edwinabner, Efghij, Eiler7, Eivind F Øyangen, Ekem, El Cid, Elaragirl, Eleuther, Elfguy, Eliyak, Eliz81, Ellsworth, Ember of Light, Emcee2k, Emitron1, Emmwashere71, Emx, Enochlau, EoGuy, Epbr123, Eran of Arcadia, Erebus555, Erik33, EronMain, Esanchez7587, Esprit15d, Essjay, Euchiasmus, Eurosong, Evercat, Everettvlai, Everyking, Evice, Ewlyahoocom, Eyreland, FFLH100, FJPB, Fabometric, Fabzzap, Fang Aili, Fantastic fred, Farosdaughter, FastLizard4, Father Goose, Fayenatic london, Fbhi, Fedallah, Feedmecereal, Feitclub, Felizdenovo, Ferday, Filelakeshoe, Filmutea, Fingal, Fire Kamer, Firestorm190, Firsfron, FisherQueen, Flafybob, FlavrSavr, Fleiger, Flubbit, Fmjennif, Fnfd, Focus mankind, Frap, Frazz, Freakofnurture, FreeKresge, Freedomlinux, FreemanMAS214, Frelsun, Fremsley, FreplySpang, Fritzpoll, Froggydarb, Ftazero, Func, Funkatram, Funke73, Future Perfect at Sunrise, Fuzheado, Fvw, G1MFG, GSSAGE7, GUllman, Gaff, Gaidheal, Gaius Cornelius, Galoubet, Gamer1682, GarnetRChaney, Garyruskin, Gatewaycat, Gbleem, Geologyguy, Gergerballball, Gert7, Ghiraddje, Gidds, Giftlite, Gikwik, Gilliam, Gimboid13, Gimmetrow, Girolamo Savonarola, Glenn, Glloq, Glover, Go link!, Goatasaur, GodofPH, Gointv, Golbez, Goldglover07, Gottadmit, GraYoshi2x, Gracenotes, GraemeL, GrahamN, Greatgavini, GreenLocust, Greenag, Greenrd, GregAsche, GregU, Gregly, Grey Shadow, GreyCat, Greyhood, Greyscale, Grm wnr, GrooveDog, Grumpyyoungman01, Gtorell, Guanaco, Guitarmas5, Gurch, Gurchzilla, Gutza, Gwandoya, Gwernol, Gwest1, Gypsum Fantastic, HTGuru, HTurtle, Haakon, Hadal, HaeB, Haham hanuka, Haiduc, Hardtouch, Harley peters, Harryboyles, Hauskalainen, Hayabusa future, Haydenirren, Hbackman, Hdt83, Heimstern, Hellisp, Hellotarget, Hemanshu, HenryLi, Henrymo2, Hephaestos, Heron, Hhartel, Himomm, Hippietrail, Hitladen, Hitman000, Hokeman, Hongandthegang, Horseman951, Houshuang, Howabout1, Howardjones57, Hsan22, Hu12, Hveziris, Hyacinth, Hydrargyrum, Hyper Summer, IGod, ILOVEJOHNNYDEPP, ILovePlankton, INkubusse, IRelayer, IamLucas1, IanHarvey, Ianblair23, Icairns, Iced Kola, Icewedge, Icey, Icurite, Ideletestuffforfun, Ihatepotsmokinghippies, Iicatsii, Ilovevanessa23, Iluv2write, Im a little person, Imabeast187, Imcool4, Indon, Insanity Incarnate, Interested2, Invincible Ninja, Ipooponu334, Iridescent, Itisalive, Ixfd64, Izuna498, J.delanoy, JDspeeder1, JForget, JHeinonen, JNW, JSpung, Ja 62, Jacarv, Jacek Kendysz, Jackery joe, Jacobko, Jagged 85, James086, JamesR, JammydodgerUK, Jaranda, Jareha, Jasow, Jauerback, Jaxl, Jaxsonjo, Jay Litman, Jayjg, Jazz77, Jdhogg, JeLuF, Jebba, Jecowa, Jedi Shadow, Jedi6, Jeff8765, Jengod, JeremyA, JesseW, Jestermas214, Jh51681, Jhkft, Jigesh, Jim.henderson, Jll, JlmMUFC, Jmccormac, JoanneB, Joao, John Chamberlain, John Fader, John254, Johnnybuchanan, Johnsomething, Johnson 1234 rth, Jonemerson, Jonny-mt, Jorunn, Jose77, Joseph Solis in Australia, Josiah Rowe, Josquius, Jossi, Jpbowen, Jpers36, Jpower3, Jrkarp, Jrobinson5, Jrockley, Jrsnbarn, Jscofield55, JuJube, Judson Farnsworth, Julianortega, Jumbo Snails, Justme89, Juventus5, Jörn, K1Bond007, KGV, KJS77, Kafuffle, Kaisershatner, Kanabekobaton, Kashjbk, Katalaveno, Kate, Kathleen.wright5, Kbthompson, Kchishol1970, Kcordina, Kedi the tramp, Keepus, Keilana, KelleyCook, KellyCoinGuy, Kenny sh, Kesmekes, Keycard, Kilo-Lima, Kindian, King Lopez, Kingturtle, Kirjtc2, Kittybrewster, Kizor, Kkv123, Klemen Kocjancic, Kluko, Kmg90, Kneale, Knowledge Seeker, KnowledgeOfSelf, Knowledgeum, Kolblood, Korny O'Near, Kotukunui, Kozuch, Kraalg, KrakatoaKatie, Krawi, Krupo, Kueh, Kui97, Kukini, Kurmis, KuroFalcon, KurtRaschke, Kurtbw, Kuru, Kwirky88, Kwsn, Kyarichy, Kylu, KyraVixen, LACameraman, Lakers, Lambiam, Lancers, Lanieandcourtney, Latka, Laudaka, Laughcosts, Laukster, Lc2288, Lcarscad, Lemortensen, Lee M, Leejghappy, Leekwanyew, Legoboy1129, Legotech, LeighvsOptimvsMaximvs, Lemonander, LenoerdG, LeoNomis, Leon7, LetsGiggle, Levi93, Levineps, Lewisdg2000, Lexi Marie, Lexor, Liftarn, Lightmouse, Lights, Lil.j-boy, LimoWreck, LinkSpamCop, Linkspamremover, Ljmar, Lkopeter, Llamadog903, Llort, Locateliam, Lohengrin1991, Lovenoble, Lpgeffen, Lradrama, Lsy098, Lucyin, Luk, Luna Santin, Luokehao, Luvyduvy0110, Lyght, Lynx46, M-le-mot-dit, M3tal H3ad, MARTIN VILLAFUERTE, MCB, MER-C, MIT Trekkie, MK8, MKoltnow, MMuzammils, MPLX, MPerel, MaGioZal, Mac, Mac Davis, MacGyverMagic, MacRusgail, Macgreco, Mackensen, Madnesstosadness, MagicFan, Mais oui!, Majorclanger, Majorly, MakeRocketGoNow, Makelifeeasy, Makemi, Makveli, Malcontent, Malinaccier, Mani1, Manning Bartlett, Manuel Trujillo Berges, Marina T., Mark, Marknyc, Markt3, Maroux, Martarius, MartinVillafuerte85, Marysunshine, Maser Fletcher, Master of Puppets, MasterTournesol, Matagascar, Mathx314, Matt B., Matt Gies, Matt5091, Mattbr, Mattbrundage, Matthewmayer, Matticus78, Matty9879, Maurice Carbonaro, Maurreen, Mav, Max Naylor, Maxamegalon2000, Maxim, Maximus Rex, Mboverload, McDutchie, McGeddon, McTavidge, Mcmachete, Mdrejhon, Mdwh, Mediumemu, MeekMark, Meepmoo, MegA, Meggem, Melaniesharrison, Melhod, Melo1055, Melsaran, Mentifisto, Mercenary90, Merceris, Mercury, Mhking, Mibblepedia, Michael Greiner, Michael Hardy, MichaelMaggs, Michaelas10, MickeyTheDog, Microfoot, Mieciu K, Miguel.mateo, Mike Rosoft, Mike Winters, Mindmatrix, Minesweeper, Minghong, Mintguy, Miranda, Mirror of nothingness, Miss Madeline, Misza13, Mkill, Mnemeson, Mnts, Modemac, Modernist, Modulatum, MonoMark, Montgomery '39, Moocow12345, Mooo, Morapasten, Mpbx3003, Mr. Lefty, Mr. Yooper, Mr.bonus, MrBlockHaus, MrBoo, MrSomeone, Mrand, Mrceleb2007, Mrdingdong505, Mrhazelj, Mrlee321, Mrschimpf, Mrwetmore, Mschel, Muelo1000, Mufka, Mulad, Muriel Gottrop, Mushroom, Musical Linguist, Myanw, Mycroft7, Mydotnet, MykReeve, Mysdaao, NB, NMChico24, NYScholar, Nakon, Namazu-tron, Natalie22372, Natl1, Navid7, NawlinWiki, Ndenison, Neal ricketts, NeilN, Neilrieck, Nemissimo, NeonMerlin, Netkinetic, Netoholic, Netsnipe, Nev2, New World Man, NewEnglandYankee, Newfers, Newnoise, Nick Cooper, NickBush24, Nielspeterqm, Nigholith, Nikai, Niteowlneils, Nivix, Nlnnet, Nlu, Noisy, Noitall125, Notheruser, Notjake13, Notmicro, Nua eire, NuclearFunk, Nuggetboy, Nunocordeiro, Nv8200p, O, Ocatecir, Odonian, Oh, Oh! TV!, Oli Filth, Ollie, OnBeyondZebrax, Onathinwhiteline, Oneqtpie93, Opelio, Orderinchaos, OregonD00d, Oregongirl0407, OriginalGamer, Ouishoebean, Outoftunebassguitar, OverlordQ, OwenX, Oxymoron83, Ozdaren, Ozzmosis, PACO, PFHLai, Paco1991, Palwill, Paranoid, Pascal.Tesson, Patrick, Patrick Bernier, Paul26uk, Paulcurrion, Paxsimius, Pebene, Pepepe, PeaceNT, PedroPVZ, Peg557, Peruvianllama, Peter Horn, PeterSymonds, Pethan, Pethr, PhantomS, Phgao, Phil Holmes, Philip Cross, Philip1992, Physics8, Picapica, PierreAbbat, Pigsonthewing, Pill, Pilotguy, Piolinfax, Piotrus, Pit-yacker, Pixeltoo, PizzaBox, Pku1, Plasma east, PlayStation 69, Plerdsus, PlzCreateAnotherName, Pm215, Pne, Poccil, Polluxian, Pomegranate, Poohman0, Poor Yorick, Poorleno, Portermas214, Possum, Postdlf, Postoak, PrestonH, Prewitt81, Proabivouac, ProhibitOnions, Prolog, Pupster21, Pyrospirit, Qazx, Quadell, Quendus, Quiddity, Quiensabe, Quinsareth, Qxz, R3m0t, RAMChYLD, RC T., RCRC, RHaworth, RJASE1, RadiantRay, Radiojon, Radiopathy, Radon210, Ram4eva, Rami R, RandomXYZb, Rasmus Faber, Ratiocinate, Raul654, Rawling, Ray Radlein, Raymondwinn, Razorflame, Rcingham, RcktScientistX, Rdsmith4, ReZips, Rebornsoldier, Rebroad, Red Thunder, Red dwarf, Reddi, Refsworldlee, Reinthal, Remurmur, Renauldo64, Retiono Virginian, Reuillerocks, Revotfel, RexNL, Rfc1394, Rhobite, Richdude24, Richie123098, Richjkl, Rico402, Rigadoun, Riphamilton, Rizdaddy, Rjd0060, Rjdainty1, Rje, Rjwilmsi, Rklawton, Rlquall, Rmhermen, Roaming, RobLa, Robert Bond, RobertDahlstrom, Robth, Roger and me, RogerMGrace, Romanm, Ron Burgundy, Rotten tomatoes, Rounddot5827, RoyBoy, Royboycrashfan, Rronline, Rror, Rsalazar12, Rueberm, RxS, Ryan, RyanParis, Ryanmcdaniel, Ryulong, SDC, SJP, SNIyer12, SOLVE INFERNIS, Saforrest, Saikiri, Sajman12, Sam Hocevar, Sam Korn, Sam sung, SamuraiClinton, Sandahl, Sandeep marwah, Sango123, Sarah.liz, SarahEMBH, SarekOfVulcan, Sarenne, Satori Son, Saurabhmangal, Scarian, Sceptre, Schaugle, Scientizzle, Scottmsg, SeanMack, Searchme, Sephiroth BCR, September 7th 2006, Seqsea, Seraphim, Sexperts, Sfoskett, ShakataGaNai, ShakingSpirit, Shanes, Shappy, ShaunES, Shawnc, ShayDC, Shenme, Sherool, Shibboleth, Shino137, Shinton, Shoeofdeath, Shorty 274, Shortyboy192, Shoshonna, Shotput king, Shreshth91, Sigmig, Silencer556, Siliconov, Silsor, SimonLyall, SineWave, Sintaku, Sir Nicholas de Mimsy-Porpington, SirVulture, Sitto, Sjakkalle, Sjwk, Sk8erking85, Skizzik, Skvns, Skyezx, Slady, Slakr, Slark, Slowking Man, Sluzzelin, Smallmas214, Smile a While, Smilestone, Smylei, Snacky, Sniper1646, Snowolf, Sobolewski, Soccergeek43, Solarguy17, SonicBlue, Sorin93, South Bay, Sowff, Spartan-James, Spartan212, SpeedyGonsales, Spellcast, Splash, Splateagle, Spliffy, SpookyMulder, SpuriousQ, SqueakBox, Squirrelist, Srleffler, StAn, Stan J Klimas, Stears159, Stears81, Stefanomione, Stemonitis, Stephan Leeds, Stephenb, SteveSims, Steven Zhang, StevenBradford, StevenMcwillimas, Stickguy, Stiggy04, Stirling Newberry, Stozball, Straw Cat, Stubblyhead, Stupidtest, Super-Magician, SuperDude115, SusanLesch, Suttipongkanasaimas214, Swedish fusilier, Swidge, Swirlygig, Sympleko, SyntaxError55, Sześćsetsześćdziesiątsześć, Szlam, T-borg, Talmadge666, Talmage, Tangmas214, Tanthalas39, Tarasworld, Tashnmic, Tassadaru, Tavilis, Tencv, Tdangkhoa, TeaDrinker, Ted Wilkes, Tedius Zanarukando, TednAZ, Telecineguy, Terence, TerriersFan, Terry on Telly, TexasAndroid, Thalakan, The Dean of Cincinnati, The Font, The Man in Question, The Moneycruncher, The Mystery Man, The eBay reminder, The silent assasin, The undertow, The-G-Unit-Boss, TheBlazikenMaster, TheCatalyst31, TheCoffee, TheCustomOfLife, TheDJ, TheGWO, TheGreenEditor, TheHugmonsters, TheOracl3, TheRealFennShysa, TheStick, Thelb4, Themfromspace, Themissinglint, Thennessey8910, Theriac, Thesoftbulletin82, Thewikipedian, Thingg, Think outside the box, Thismightbezach, Thumperward, Tiddly Tom, Time, Timwi, Tintin1000, Tiptoety, Titansolaris, Titoxd, Tjl666, Tjmayerinsf, Tmopkisn, Tnxman307, Tohd8BohaithuGh1, Tom.k, TomGreen, Tonsofpcs, Tony Sidaway, Tony1, Tothebarricades.tk, Toytoy, Tpbradbury, Trainra, Trakon, Traroth, Travis jorde, Tregoweth, Trekphiler, Tripledot, Trusilver, Ts1388, Tsunaminoai, TulsaTV, Turner93, TuukkaH, Twang, Twistor, Tyler Magician, Tysto, Ungvichian, Unsplosion, Uriber, Usboy12, Useight, Userisme, Username271, Usertaffy3, VMS Mosaic, VT hawkeye, Vegaswikian, Vendettax, Versageek, Vidshow, Vina, Violetriga, Vizcarra, VolatileChemical, Vrlobo888, Vrrayman2005, Vsmith, Väsk, WDaltAYN, WRK, Waggers, Walksonground, Walloon, Walter Arthur, Walter Humala, Wangi, Warpedshadow, WarthogDemon, WatcherWatcher, Wavelength, Wayland, Wayward, Wbrameld, Webfan29, Weightlessness, WellsSt, Wenli, Wenteng, Werneke kid, Wernher, West wikipedia, Wfeidt, Whomp, Wiki alf, WikiCats, Wikibofh, Wikidudeman, Wikihelp1a, Wilson58801, Wimt, Winchelsea, Winhunter, Winnow, Wisdom89, Wk muriithi, Wknight94, Wmahan, Woddfellow2, Woohookitty, Wowow123, Wtshymanski, Ww2censor, Wwitv, Xaosflux, Xcohen, Xenon54, Xiahou, Xjbrad, Xoloverox95, Xwu, XxTimberlakexx, Xy7, Y control, Yah Hoo :) I'm Happy, Yahadreas, Yakky, Yamamoto Ichiro, Yiddophile, Yidisheryid, Yik Lin Khoo, Yofool100, Yomama444, Zac31, Zachbe, Zanimum, ZayZayEM, Zcherry15, Ziggurat, Zimbabwe23, Zoe, Zoney, ZooFari, Zpb52, Zsero, Zsinj, Zzcorge, Zzuuzz, Zzyzx11, Ødipus sic, Александьр, Саша Стефановић, 2845 anonymous edits

Radio *Source*: http://en.wikipedia.org/w/index.php?title=Radio *Contributors*: 206.30.58.xxx, 208.187.134.xxx, 21655, 21stCenturyGreenstuff, 2help, 500million, 7&6=thirteen, A. Parrot, ABF, Aarchiba, Aashleynj, Abdullais4u, Abrech, AbsolutDan, Abu badali, Academic Challenger, Acroterion, Adrian, Ahoerstemeier, Akanemoto, Alai, Alansohn, Aldaron, Almazi, Alsandro, Alvinrune, Amerika, AndonicO, Andrejj, Andrewjuren, Andromeda321, Andy, Andyl620, AngelOfSadness, Angr, Anilbg, Anonymi, Anquiliquest, Antandrus, Anthony Appleyard, Anthonypunk1, Archer3, Aristokrata, Armeria, ArmitageShanks, ArnoldReinhold, Arnon Chaffin, Arteitle, Arthuralee, Arthurs1212, Ascidian, Asher196, Astatine-210, Atomicfro, AuburnPilot, Aude, Audemat, Axel22, Az1568, B0Rn2bL8, Badbilltucker, Badgernet, Bannanas, Baronnet, Barış uçurum, Batesmas214, Bdean1963, Beachyboy, Beenturns23, BenBreen2003, Bendzh, BesselDekker, Best 24, Bgs022, BillC, Biokinetica, Birdhurst, Blacky111, Blainster, Blue borg, Blueboy96, Bluemask, Bob sagget jr., Bobblewik, Bobo192, Bonadea, Bongwarrior, Bonus Onus, Book M, Bookofjude, Borislav, Boud, Brandon5485, Brian the Editor, Brian0918, Brianhe, Brion VIBBER, Bucketsofg, Burntsauce, Butler david, CMYK, CUTKD, Cabe6403, Calor, Caltas, CambridgeBayWeather, Can't sleep, clown will eat me, Canderson7, Capricorn42, Captain-tucker, CardinalDan, Carl.bunderson, Carlosguitar, Cassamine, Centrx, Chalyres, Chaser, Chelseax3rose, Chill doubt, Chris Roy, Chrisjustinparr, Christian List, Chun-hian, Ck lostsword, Clawson, Click23, Cmacd123, Cmapm, Cometstyles, Command5, Conical Johnson,

Futureobservatory, Fvw, Gary D, Garyruskin, Gen6k, Gene Lieb, Geni, Ggurumohan, Ghormax, Gilliam, Gimmetrow, Glenn, Glenn Koenig, Glisenti, Gp93, GraemeL, Gravecat, Gregh, GregorAnton, GregorB, Greudin, Grochim, Grunt, Gscshoyru, Gunsmith, Gurch, GuyRo, Gwernol, Gyokomura, Gökhan, H Bruthzoo, H ackerman005, HR DORA, Haakon, Hadal, Hamiltro, Hayne, HelenGold, Hezink8, High Elf, Hiyaoooo, Hmwith, Hollih, Horoshi1820, Hotlorp, Huntthetroll, Husond, Hut 8.5, Iamdalto, Icewedge, Ihcoyc, Ike9898, Ikonoblast, Infoapex, Inwind, Iris lorain, Irjesusbiatch, Isabelking, Isogolem, Ixfd64, J Di, J. Nguyen, J.delanoy, JForget, JHMM13, JNW, JaGa, Jag100, Jake Wartenberg, Jamesontai, Jardinessardine, JarlaxleArtemis, Jason Leach, Jasviru, Jazzeur, Jbuddle, Jcbrd, Jdrewitt, Jeff G., Jeffnaz, Jehochman, JerLlo, JeremyA, Jim Sterne, JimSym, Jinxed, Jlao04, Joebloggs1234567, John Pretty 1, John Quiggin, John Reaves, JohnGriffinLatimer, JohnOwens, Jojit fb, Jon Shl, Jonas August, Joshua, Joveblue, Jowe84, Juggernaut316, Jusdafax, Just James, Justinfr, Jvdwalt, Jychao, Kaabi, Kablammo, Kameir, Kangphil, Kanonkas, Karto, Katalaveno, Kazrak, Kbh3rd, Kenonfiction, Keilana, Kenneth M Burke, Khalid hassani, Kimbayne, Kingpin13, Klemen Kocjancic, Krawi, Krith23, Kruchka, Kuru, Kuyabribri, Kuzaar, Kuzmo, Kylie perry, Kyriakos, L'Aquatique, LaMenta3, Lafiedler, Lambertb, Learningtousewiki, Leedeth, Lehi53, Leliro19, Leopoldogomez, LeroyWilkins, Leuko, Levineps, Lights, LittleDan, LittleOldMe, Livitup, LizardJr8, Lollerskates, Longhair, Lordmac, Loren.wilton, Louern, Lourdes0717, Lu Wunsch-Rolshoven, Luckyz, LuigiManiac, Lumos3, M3taphysical, MER-C, MZMcBride, MacMed, Macadon, MadAboutMarketing, Madhero88, Maksdo, Mallika nawal, MalwareSmarts, Mandelman, Maneuveringthought, Maniktushar, Mantality, Marcje, Mardus, Mariokempes, Markerting consultant, Marketing professor, Marketing64, MarketingWizard, Marketingman1, Masterpiece2000, MattieTK, Maurreen, Mav, Maven111, Max Naylor, Maybethisnamewontgetblockedall thetime, Mboverload, McSly, Mdebets, Meaghan, Mediathink, Meeples, Mg0314b, Michael Hardy, Michael Snow, Michaelfavia, Michaelmoran, MidgleyDJ, Mig21fishbed, Mike Rosoft, Million Moments, Mindmajick, Minghong, Mini-Geek, Mjwalshe, Mlease, Moenada, Monkeyman, Monotonehell, MoogleEXE, Mooreseo, Mosca, Mouse Nightshirt, MrOllie, Msharaiha, Munazanjum, Myanw, Mycatharsis, Mydogategodshat, Mykej, Mythdon, N2e, N5iln, Nabler, Nakon, NarSakSasLee, Natewrite, NawlinWiki, Nburden, Needles27, Nemesis of Reason, Netsnipe, Nicholas Drayer, NickBarrowman, Nifky?, NightFalcon90909, Niloobushweller, Nivelh, No Parking, Notapennymore, Nrcjersey, Nubin wiki, Nuttycoconut, Odie5533, Ohnoitsjamie, Oicumayberight, Ojigiri, Oleg Alexandrov, Olly150, Omicronpersei8, Onorem, Operativem, Optakeover, Optimization, Oscara, Ossmann, Otolemur crassicaudatus, OverlordQ, OwenX, Oxinabox, Oxymoron83, Paddles, Pandaplodder, Pankaj.multimedia, PapaWhitman, PaterMcFly, Patrick, PatrickFlaherty, Paul Magnussen, Paul1000, Pavel Vozenilek, Pedapod, Pedro, Peschomd, Peter Lawless, PeterSymonds, Pezzzer, Phaedriel, Phantomsteve, PhilKnight, Philip Trueman, Philippe31, Piano non troppo, Pill, Pixelface, Plinkit, Pmauchard, Pnautilus, Poccil, Pogogunner, Poor Yorick, Populus, Portgame, Preetam purbia, Presario3000, ProcureNET, Prodman121, PromotionalCurrency, Ptdecker, Pulkit bajaj, Quadell, Qwerty Binary, Qxz, RUL3R, RadRafe, RadioFan2 (usurped), RainbowOfLight, Ramu50, Random contributor, Rasmus Faber, Realkyhick, Redvers, Reedy, Rege, Retinarow, Rettetast, ReviewDude, RexNL, Rfzaman, Riana, Rich Farmbrough, Richard D. LeCour, Richard0612, RichardF, Rick Block, Rintrah, Rjcain, Rjette, Rjwilmsi, Rkaminsky, Rlsheehan, Robertson-Glasgow, RoboAction, Robowurmz, Rogerthat, Rohan Jayasekera, Ron prince51, Ronz, Rotem Dan, Rrburke, Rrc2soft, Runewiki777, Ryan Postlethwaite, S3000, SJP, SMC, SNowwis, SWAdair, Sachintellusys, Saga City, Sakaa, Sam mishra, Sanjeev.rbs.edu, Sanwar, Sarper, Sceptre, SchfiftyThree, Schlinkdizzle, SchubertCommunications, Sciurinæ, Scorpion agency, Sdbmaranello, Sdornan, Sdudah, Se91an, Semitransgenic, Sengkang, Sephiroth BCR, Serein (renamed because of SUL), Sesu Prime, SevDrape, Shadowjams, Shally87, Shanes, Shengii, Shirarae, Silverxxx, SimonP, SineSoftware, SiobhanHansa, SirTwitch, Skeezix1000, Skew-t, Skunkboy74, SkydiveMike, Slakr, Slaphappy, Smalljim, Smashville, Snezzy, Snghmiranda, So-eZ, SoLando, SoLxStephen, Softbiz, Solipsist, Somedoodfromtheqoob, Soosed, Soyweiser, Sp, Sp3, SpaceFlight89, Spellcast, Spencerk, Spinacia, Spitfire, Springnuts, Srleffler, SteinbDJ, Stellis, Stephanspencer, Stephchristie, Stephen C. Carlson, Stephenb, Stephenbez, Stephenginns, Steve simple, Steven Zhang, Stevertigo, Stk006, Strongsauce, Studio1st, Studiobanks, Stui, Sturm55, Sunsfan1797, Super-Magician, SuperLuigi31, Suruena, Susan118, Svenceone, Svetovid, T2 studios, T5741, TAMilo, TFoxton, THEN WHO WAS PHONE?, TKD, Tabrez, Tainted Sausage, Tamás Kádár, Tao of tyler, Tarret, TastyPoutine, Tawker, Tbonejoo, Tedder, Teejay17, Telenet, Tempodivalse, TenPoundHammer, TerryForsey, Thatguyflint, The Anome, The Gaffer, The Thing That Should Not Be, The Transhumanist (AWB), The undertow, TheGrimReaper NS, Thekohser, Themoose20, Thingg, Think outside the box, Thiseye, Thom0711, Tide rolls, Tiffany.Remo, Tilla, Tiptoety, Titansolaris, Toby Desforges, Tom, Tomayres, Topspeedracer, TravisAF, Tregoweth, Trevor MacInnis, Tricky Victoria, Triona, Tslocum, Tucaz, Twaz, Tzartzam, USMarketingGuy, Ukexpat, Uncle G, VI, VISHAL DESAI, VMS Mosaic, Van helsing, Veinor, Velen117, Versageek, Versus22, VerticalDrop, Vikingstad, Violetriga, Vipinhari, Viridae, Vishnava, Vision Thing, Vodu, Vogue99, Vyceron, Wackymacs, WadeSimMiser, Wafulz, Wahoona, Walkerpercy, Wardizzy2, WarthogDemon, Washburnmav, Wavelength, WebRank, Weeliljimmy, Westendgirl, Wewe100, Wgardner, White Agent, Wik, Wiki Raja, Wiki World, Wiki alf, WikiLaurent, Wikiklrsc, Wikiman01, William Avery, Williamsrus, Wine Guy, WinterSpw, Wireweb, Wkoleszar, Wmahan, Woohookitty, Workman, Woz2, Wuhwuzdat, X!, Xenacn, Xyzzyplugh, Yamamoto Ichiro, Ydriuf, Yeajilike, Yhkhoo, Yidisheryid, Yintan, Ywimc, Zaid Ibrahim, Zdravko mk, Zigo1232, Zip3, Zundark, Zvika, Zzuuzz, 2408 anonymous edits

Promotion (marketing) *Source*: http://en.wikipedia.org/w/index.php?title=Promotion_%28marketing%29 *Contributors*: Alexius08, Alfredxz, Amontron, Ampersandexplainer, Ancheta Wis, AndrewHowse, Apokryltaros, Battamer, Bobo192, Bonadea, Briaboru, Cacycle, Camw, Can't sleep, clown will eat me, Cape cod naturalist, ChiragPatnaik, Ckatz, Csus814, DMacks, DasBub, Decltype, Deor, Discospinster, DéRahier, Fenice, Flowerparty, Fourohfour, Furrykef, Futureobservatory, Gec118, Glen, Glenn.isaac, GraemeL, Grochim, Hclim65, Husond, J.delanoy, JHunterJ, JLaTondre, Jjjchang, Johnleemk, Jusdafax, Kelly, Kingpin13, Kwlovell, Levineps, Linkspamremover, Lommer, MagnusA, Mattisse, Maurreen, Michael Devore, Myataya, NawlinWiki, ONUnicorn, Occlasty, Oxymoron83, Pangweb, Patrick, Pelangiholiday, Petr Kopač, Phynicen, RHaworth, Rosehu, Rosenjon, Rossami, Sesu Prime, Spiritia, Stevertigo, Surridge89, Tide rolls, Tom, Tree Biting Conspiracy, Utcursch, Versageek, Wafulz, Wizzzzman, Woohookitty, Zzuuzz, 106 anonymous edits

Persuasion *Source*: http://en.wikipedia.org/w/index.php?title=Persuasion *Contributors*: -Ozone-, 16@r, 212.67.105.xxx, Alro, Altenmann, Andrew Ross-Parker, Andycjp, Anonymi, Ashenai, Beatagreen, Bobo192, Bongwarrior, Bookandcoffee, Bradjamesbrown, Bytwerk, C14ism, CWSault, Camembert, Charlesatencio, Cleared as filed, Comm&emotion, Conversion script, Dagoblin, Darkfred, Darth Panda, Decltype, Delicious carbuncle, Derekrogerson, Dresdnhope, Elmschrat, Emperorbma, Epbr123, Everyking, Firsfron, GraemeL, Henninb, Hughcharlesparker, Icut4you, J.delanoy, Jackfork, Jan E. Schreiber, Jcbutler, Jennavecia, Jim Douglas, Johnkarp, Johnteslade, Joie de Vivre, Jrockley, Kaypoh, Kenny sh, Kevinalewis, Khalid hassani, Kingpin13, Kraybilr, Kristen Eriksen, Madhero88, Marcika, Mathmo, MaxHund, MrOllie, Naddy, Neelix, Nemhun, Oli Filth, Ot, Patrick, Paul A, Penbat, Peter S., Pikiwyn, Pseudomonas, Publictransport, Quaeler, Radiojon, Reneeholle, RichardF, Ronz, Rossami, SEWilco, Salishsea, Sam Francis, Sara161616, Spotcream, Staffwaterboy, TastyPoutine, Terrek, The Anome, Thebrainsalad, ThirteenthGreg, Tophernator, Tothebarricades.tk, Trondarild, Van helsing, Vantage01, Wars, Wavelength, WilliamDavidRogers, Zappaz, Zombiebaron, 178 anonymous edits

Product (business) *Source*: http://en.wikipedia.org/w/index.php?title=Product_%28business%29 *Contributors*: 7, A3RO, AdnanSa, Agathoclea, Ahouseholder, Alania14, Alias777, Allstarecho, Alveolate, Amnesiac86, Appleseed, Beland, BiteComms, Bloodshedder, Blue Pixel, Bobo192, Busy Stubber, Bwithh, Carajou, Cfsenel, Cherylb, Chris the speller, Cnbrb, Comp8956, Dom Padden, Dzied Bulbash, Egon Eagle, Epbr123, Ferengi, Fieldday-sunday, Fredsmith2, Fromedessa, Futureobservatory, GHe, Gidonb, Giraffedata, Glenn, Greudin, Greyskinnedboy, Gurch, Gurlukovich, Hakan Uğur, HammerHeadHuman, Henrymrx, Hohum, Hotcrocodile, Hyacinth, Ian Pitchford, IceKarma, Ikonoblast, Iterator12n, Ixfd64, J04n, JRHorse, Jim.henderson, KaiSeun, Kingpin13, Knuckles sonic8, Kozuch, Kwamikagami, Layonard, LeoNomis, Levineps, Lfratilla, MER-C, Magdach, Masterpiece2000, MauriceMB, Maurreen, Mikeo, Mkoval, Mr seo writer, MrOllie, Muchness, Mydogategodshat, Nemvocalist, Nick UA, Nixeagle, Onevalefan, Periscope123, Piano non troppo, Pion, Pizza Puzzle, Quoth, Qxz, Radiojon, Randommouse, Ricketgt, Rob Hooft, Ronz, Roscoe x, SJP, SRE.K.A.L.24, Sam mishra, Sarah777, Sectryan, Sesshomaru, Shoessss, Signalhead, Silsor, Sinuhe, Smsarmad, Softbiz, Spinacia, Stanislav87, Svenboatbuilder, TOR, Taka, The Thing That Should Not Be, Theleftorium, TigerShark, VeryVerily, Vikas jain59, Washdivad, Wavelength, Welsh, Wiki alf, WikipedianMarlith, Windharp, Wine Guy, Wlodzimierz, Wossi, Xezbeth, ZimZalaBim, Zoe, Zundark, 220 anonymous edits

Perspective (cognitive) *Source*: http://en.wikipedia.org/w/index.php?title=Perspective_%28cognitive%29 *Contributors*: AbsolutDan, Altenmann, Americanadian, Beland, Bluemoose, Borgx, BritishWatcher, Capricorn42, CrazyChemGuy, Eaefremov, Epolk, Hede2000, Little Mountain 5, Luna Santin, MC10, Mdd, Meaningful Username, Micfri, Michael Hardy, Misuchi, N2e, Nadyes, Pip2andahalf, Quiddity, Rd2destiny, RichardF, Senator Palpatine, Srleffler, The Evil IP address, Wireless Keyboard, Wyatt915, 54 anonymous edits

Advertising mail *Source*: http://en.wikipedia.org/w/index.php?title=Advertising_mail *Contributors*: ABurness, Ajcheema, All Is One, BananaFiend, Bedford2000, Beland, Blanchardb, Bobo192, Capricorn42, Chris the speller, Ckatz, Csteiner27, Deli nk, Dethme0w, Duncanson, Edeskonline, Gail, Gary6flavor, Gcsmithjr, Greenguy109, Greentopia, Ilaiho, JaGa, Jlazerus, Justdaiwil, Kuyabribri, Leoniana, List-logic, Madalberta, Maeshowe, Mark marten, Martacaricato, Michael Romanov, Michaelprintingstudent, Mikkele, Mild Bill Hiccup, MrOllie, Muckelroy06, N5iln, Nakon, NawlinWiki, NellieBly, Onlinecitizen, P1ayer, Paalappoo, Pacificus, Psulioninks, Quercus basaseachicensis, Rickproquo, Rjwilmsi, SEWilco, Saintswithin, Sanjiv swarup, Sevela.p, SiobhanHansa, Skothr, Stephan Leeds, Struthious Bandersnatch, Szyslak, Thingg, Timneu22, Tresiden, Trystan, Veinor, Wasted Time R, 52 anonymous edits

Jingle *Source*: http://en.wikipedia.org/w/index.php?title=Jingle *Contributors*: Adam850, After Midnight, Airodyssey, Amorrow, Andy, Angr, ApJilly, Ashnoise, Badagnani, Barticus88, Bennybp, Bilgin adem, Bluemoose, Bobo192, Bongwarrior, Brian Geppert, Bunchofgrapes, Bunthorne, Cabe6403, Capricorn42, ChKa, Chill Pill Bill, Cocoroco, Daja2k, Dallben, Daniiliscool1, Dantadd, DaveOinSF, Deltabeignet, Deville, Donmccullen, Ellywa, Eridisc, Ev, FTIII, Gilliam, Graham87, Grassynoel42, Guitarist6987876, Haikupoet, HamburgerRadio, Hasanisawi, Infrogmation, JYi, Jinglecompany, Jono1034, Jsandwich01, KPH2293, Karol Langner, Kesla, Khukri, Killiondude, Kingpin13, Kiwidominic, KnowledgeOfSelf, Kosunen, Kymacpherson, Larrymcp, Lee Cremeans, Macaddct1984, Malimar, Mani1, Martin451, McGeddon, Megamanfan3, Mephistophales, Mike Russell, Mike Selinker, Mikeydred, MonteChristof, Mr ethanboy, Nakon, Neo-Jay, NrDg, Oatmeal batman, Optiplex740, Orayzio, Oveyamo, Pearle, Philip Cross, Piksou, Pilotguy, Pronkman, Qxz, Racky, Rankiogo, Roadrunner3000, RogerMGrace, Rpcaudio, Rpremuz, Schappacher, Secfan, ShakingSpirit, SidP, Solipsist, SteinbDJ, Stuhacking, TMC1221, TUF-KAT, TWCarlson, Tedernst, Tedgrant, The sunder king, TheCustomOfLife, Theyonnie, Timeleeeee, Titoxd, Treehole, Treeholes, Tregoweth, Unmake, Video killed the radiostar, Vividenblem, W guice, W.graphique, Wahkeenah, Warko, Wikitown, WpZurp, Wphid01, Wuhwuzdat, YUiCiUS, Yakudza, 239 anonymous edits

Lyrics *Source*: http://en.wikipedia.org/w/index.php?title=Lyrics *Contributors*: -x-dannii-x-, 13alexander, 16@r, 5theye, ABF, ARC Gritt, Academic Challenger, Adam Bishop, Adavidw, Ageekgal, ALlocke, Alexfrance250291, AlistairMcMillan, Altermike, Andycjp, Anthony5429, Antonio Lopez, Apoc2400, Apparition11, ArielGold, Art LaPella, Asterion, Asxvideos, Baim78, Bernis, Bhamv, Blade76, Blm07, Bobet, Bobo192, Brianga, Bunnyhop11, CFCF, Can't sleep, clown will eat me, Canterbury Tail, Captain-tucker, Carinemily, CaseyIsCool, Cdc, Cedders, Cethegus, Charles Matthews, Chase me ladies, I'm the Cavalry, ChrisCork, Contact@music-free-download.net, CoramVobis, CryptoDerk, Csmaster2005, Damian Yerrick, Dantadd, DavidRF, Deeplogic, Defunkt, Deltabeignet, Diaby, Diddi, Dragoburaggo, Dylan Lake, ERcheck, EamonnPKeane, Eclecticology, Elipongo, Elonka, Eloquence, Emmedenney, Enviroboy, Enzo Aquarius, Epbr123, Eric the Rexman, Fennec, Flatfoot4444, Friedenbach, Frogfusious, Garo, Gimme danger, GregAsche, Hadal, HappyCamper, Henry Flower, Hu12, Hyacinth, II MusLiM HyBRiD II, IP 84.5, Iglam, J.delanoy, Jacklee, Jbinder, Jeggish105, Jennavecia, Jerry, Jklin, Jls33fsls, Jmundo, John254, JohnCub, Johnnyw, Jorunn, Jwy, Kairosis, Kazvorpal, Kent Wang, Kerii57, Ks0stm, Kukini, La Pianista, Lafraia, Lathspell, Mac, Macrazy, Madder, Mandarax, Mark.deane, MarkBollett, Martin451, Max Naylor, Merenta, Minesweeper, MinuteHand, Mister Floyd, Mrmanhattanproject, Mxipp, My name, N Shar, NCurse, Nakon, Nanenj, NawlinWiki, Nbrett1, Nemanjakron, Nightkey, No Guru, Notinasnaid, Nuggetman, OMGitsCTC, Osmosis, Paddles,

Patstuart, Pavel Vozenilek, Pewwer42, Pibwl, Pietaster, Pinko1977, Pip2andahalf, Pkoden, Possum, Ptanham, Pyrope, Quill, RMFan1, RadiantRay, RedWolf, Reflex Reaction, Rholton, Rls, Robert Foley, RockMFR, RoyBoy, Ryulong, SColombo, Saberwyn, Sannse, Sean Patrick Griffiths, Seriema, SilkTork, Soliloquial, Sridharinfinity, Ss112, Stephen4800, Stereotek, Struway2, Supastabi, TUF-KAT, Tedder, Thatdog, The Thing That Should Not Be, TheMadBaron, Tigers boy, Tiptoety, Toktosunov, Topbanana, Trysha, Unmesh.bhosle, Vinithehat, Vxlover, Wayland, WebJunkie, Weyes, Willirennen, Willking1979, WinterSpw, Wpbmma, Wtmitchell, Yachtsman1, Yumegusa, Yvil, Zazaban, Zgvozden, 405 anonymous edits

World Wide Web *Source*: http://en.wikipedia.org/w/index.php?title=World_Wide_Web *Contributors*: *feridiák, -Kerplunk-, 16@r, 194.109.232.xxx, 20coconuts, 2206, 3rdTriangle, 5theye, 75th Trombone, A Stop at Willoughby, ABF, AJR, AL3X TH3 GR8, AMHR285, AVand, AaronTownsend, Abarry, Abatres, Abce2, Abd, Abdel.a.saleh, Abovemost, Abrech, AdamXgamer, Adashiel, Adrian.benko, Aeolien, Aesopos, Af648, Ageekgal, Agendum, Agent Smith (The Matrix), Ahoerstemeier, Akendall, Al guy, Alansohn, AlefZet, Alerante, AlexWangombe, Alexf, Alexius08, Alexjohnc3, AlistairMcMillan, Alokchakrabarti, Alphachimp, Alvestrand, Amillar, Amplitude101, AmyzzXX, Andre Engels, Andrea Parri, Andrew D. Jones, Android Mouse, Andromeda321, Andyjsmith, Angela, Anomalocaris, Anonymous Dissident, Anonymous101, Antandrus, Anthony, AntiVan, Aodonnel, Applechair, ArchonMagnus, Argonistic professor, Arnon Chaffin, Art LaPella, Arthena, Artw, Astrobloby, Autopilots, Avono, Avram, Awanta, Balloomc, Bambuway, Bananaclaw, Barek, Barras, Bbatsell, Bdesham, Beavis6325, Beddingplane, Beetstra, Beland, Bender235, Bendy1, Benqish, Bevo, Bgs264, Bibi Saint-Pol, Big Bird, BigHaz, BilCat, BillFlis, Billoraani123, Bk0, BlackAndy, Blahcake666, Bloodshedder, Bo, Bo Lindbergh, Bobblewik, Bobet, Bobo192, Boccobrock, Boerman, Bongwarrior, Bookandcoffee, Bookofjude, Boraxx, Boris Allen, Borislav, Boriszex, Bornhj, Bossk-Office, Bostonian Mike, Bounce1337, Branddobbe, Brian0918, Brianga, Brion VIBBER, Bronger, Brougham96, Bryan Derksen, Buchanan-Hermit, BudSipkiss, BuffStuffer, Bumm13, Burto88, BziB, CSEditor, CUTKD, Cabbatime, Cailliau, Calvin 1998, Camster342, Can't sleep, clown will eat me, Canadian-Bacon, CanadianLinuxUser, Capricorn42, CaptainVindaloo, CardinalDan, Carlsotr, Cenarium, Centrx, Charraksus, Chbarts, Chininazu12, Chip1990, Chris 73, Chris G, ChrisLoosley, ChrisO, Christian List, Christopher Parham, Chuckiesdad, CiaPan, Cielomobile, Claidheamohmor, Classicfilms, Claud1996, Closedmouth, Clpo13, Coflo1994, Coldfire82, Colijunior, CommonsDelinker, Computerjoe, Conversion script, Coolcaesar, Coolninja98, Coplston, CoramN, Corpx, Correctingothers, Corvus cornix, Cov87, CrazyChemGuy, Crazycomputers, Cuahl, Cwolfsheep, Cyclopia, Cyde, D, D6, DJ Clayworth, DRBar, Daaah5, Daedelus, Damian Yerrick, Dan100, Dancter, Danny5000, Darkenn, Darkwind, Darth Panda, Dave6, Daveblack, Daverocks, Daverose 33, Daveydweeb, David Gerard, David Latapie, David.Mestel, DavidLevinson, Davnor, Davodd, Dbsanfte, DeadEyeArrow, DearPrudence, Deathtopudding, Decltype, Deepugn, Den fjättrade ankan, Denis C., DennyColt, DerHexer, Diamond2, Diberri, DigbyDalton, Dina, DirkvdM, Discospinster, Dispenser, Djavidan, Djg2006, Dlrohrer2003, DocWatson42, Docbug, Doggieman159, Dogmavskarma, Dominic, DoubleBlue, Dputig07, DragonHawk, Drbb01, DreamGuy, DriveMySol, Drunken Pirate, Dube-k Nkiribari, DugDownDeep, Dustinasby, Dwilz, Dylan Damien, Dynaflow, Dzhatse, E Wing, EagleFan, Eagleamn, Eamonn sullivan, Earlebird, EarthPerson, EatMyShortz, Editmaniac, Edward Zimmermann, EdwinHJ, Efitu, Ehsan™, El C, Eloquence, Eluchil404, EmeryD, Emperorbma, Eneville, Enil, Epbr123, Erick.Antezana, Esanchez7587, Everyking, Eyu100, Ezeu, Falexi, FatalError, FeldBum, Fenrisulfr, Fireice, Flewis, Florentino floro, Flowerparty, Flowerpotman, Flyer 13, Fmccown, Foxwolfblood, Freakingme, Freakofnurture, Frederik S, Ftu78, Func, Furrykef, G2g2day, GDonato, GW Simulations, Gail, Gaius Cornelius, Garion96, Gary King, Gary the gnome, Gdo01, Geniac, Gholson, Giftlite, Giggy, Gilliam, GlassCobra, Glenn, Gman124, Gooday.1, Goplat, Gracenotes, GraemeL, Grantglendinning, Grawity, Graylorde, Greatbigtwit, Grison, Gsandi, Gscshoyru, Gsklee, Gurch, Gustav von Humpelschmumpel, Gwernol, H2g2bob, Hadal, Hailey C. Shannon, Hairy Dude, HamburgerRadio, Happy darrenchong, Hardyplants, Harfi66, Harmil, Harryboyles, Haseo9999, Hashar, Hellisp, Hendry, Henry Flower, Herehere, HexaChord, Highonhendrix, Hillgentleman, Hoof Hearted, Hotcrocodile, Howdoesthiswo, Hrvoje Simic, Hung3rd, Husond, Hydrogen Iodide, I amm Beowulf!, I dream of horses, IByte, II MusLiM HyBRiD II, IMSoP, IRP, IShadowed, IW.HG, Icairns, Icrutt, Ignatzmice, Imnotminkus, Informatic17, Inter, Invistec, Ipso2, Iridescent, Ironrd, Irrbloss, Isam, Isilanes, Ixfd64, J.delanoy, JFG, JForget, JHMM13, JNW, Ja2k8el, Jackol, JacobCurtis, Jacobolus, Jake Wartenberg, Jake-515-, Jatkins, Javidan, Jayhawk of Justice, Jblatt, Jedsayaman, Jeff G., Jeffq, Jeffreylkk, Jehfes, Jeltz, Jengod, JeremyA, Jeveteca, Jfdwolff, Jhessela, JialiangGao, Jimmi Hugh, Jj137, Jjshapiro, Jleedev, Jnc, Joanjoc, Joel1miles, JoeOnSunset, Joeblakesley, JohanL, John, John Broughton, John Carter, John Fader, JohnI, JohnOwens, JohnPritchard, JohnTechnologist, Johnwrw, JokelineUK, JonHarder, Jonathan Drain, Jonvvv2, JordeeBec, Jorel314, Jorunn, Joseph Solis in Australia, Josephf, Joshthegreat, Joshua, Josquius, Jovianeye, Joy, Jpbowen, Jpo, Jrockley, Jsmestad, Jtiza, Jufert, Jugander, Juliancolton, Junnel, Junon, Justinfr, JzG, Jzylstra, KYPark, Kaiyir Minoia, Karen Johnson, Karl Stas, Karmona, Kate, Katieh5584, Kbolino, Kbrose, Keilana, Kenny sh, Kezze, Khalid, Kim Bruning, Kirbytime, Knutux, Koavf, Korath, Korg, Kornfan71, Kpwa gok, KrakatoaKatie, Krishvanth, Krothor, Kvasilev, Kwamikagami, Kwlothrop, Kyle1278, LUUSAP, Lachatdelarue, Lakefall, Lars Trebing, Lars Washington, Ldg2135a-14, Leafyplant, Lee Carre, Lee Daniel Crocker, Lee S. Svoboda, Legedevin, Leonig Mig, Letdorf, Levineps, Lifefeed, Lightmouse, Ligulem, Little Mountain 5, LittleOldMe, LizardJr8, Loalhe, Loki500, Longhair, LorenzoB, Lowellian, Luk, Luna Santin, Lykoyrgos, MBisanz, MER-C, MITBeaverRocks, MONGO, Mac, Macy, Maestrosync, Magicxcian, Mail4james, Mailer diablo, Malatesta, Malcolm Farmer, Manop, Marek69, Mark Foskey, Markaci, Mars fenix, Martinp, Master Jay, Master of Puppets, Masterhomer, Matt Gies, Matt McIrvin, Matt Yeager, Matteh, Matthieupinard, Mattisse, Matusz, Maurreen, Mav, Maxamegalon2000, Maxis ftw, Maxschmelling, Mayooranathan, Mayor Westfall, Mbell, McSly, Mcalliph, Mcm, Mdbest, Mditto, Meigwil, Mentifisto, Meowkittymeow, Mervyn, Meshach, Metao, Mets501, Michael Hardy, MichaelJanich, MikeWren, Mindmatrix, Minghong, Mini-Geek, Mirt Tenk, MisterCharlie, Mjb, Mjgw, Mlouns, Modemac, Mohitngm, Mooquackwooftweetmeow, Mr random, Mr. Lefty, Mrqueen, Mrzaius, Mschel, Msikma, Mttcmbs, Mumia-w-18, Musicandnintendo, Mvuijlst, Mxn, My favourite teddy bear, Mywyb2, NCurse, NEO369, NHRHS2010, Naerii, Nakon, Nanshu, NantonosAedui, Nantoseiken, Nathanlandis, NawlinWiki, Nbarth, NeilN, Nepenthes, Nertzy, Netoholic, Netvor, Neutrino007, NewEnglandYankee, Newmac, Newmanbe, Nicholasstorriearce, Nick C, NickBush24, Nigelj, Nihiltres, Nikai, Nishkid64, Nivix, Nixeagle, Noah Salzman, Noisy, Noldoaran, Not home, Nubiatech, Nurg, Oberst, Oblivious, Of, Ohnoitsjamie, Ohsayanything, Okiefromokla, Olgerd, Oliver Pereira, Olivier Debre, Onorem, Open4D, Orderinchaos, OregonD00d, Oroso, Ours, Outriggr, Oxymoron83, Oysterguitarist, P3d0, Paliku, Patelmihirb, Patrick, Paul Ebermann, PaulGarner, Pedxing585, Pemboid, Persian Poet Gal, Peter Campbell, Petskratt, Pgan002, Phact, PhantomS, Pharaoh of the Wizards, Phil Boswell, Phoenix Hacker, Piano non troppo, Pigsonthewing, Pinkadelica, Pintopc, Porqin, Possum, Postlewaight, Poulpy, Poweroid, Ppk01, Ppp, Prender101, PrestonH, Prestonmcconkie, Pretty Green, Proofreader, PseudoSudo, Psy guy, Publicly Visible, Putanginanyo, Pádraic MacUidhir, Qmt, Quebec99, Qwanqwa, Qxz, RJaguar3, RUL3R, Radar scanner, RadioActive, Raeky, Ragesoss, Rainbow sprinkle, RainbowOfLight, Raining girl, Rama, RandomP, Randomreturn, Rasmus Faber, Rathfalguni, Raul654, Rav77, Raven in Orbit, Rawr, Razorflame, Rbellin, Rbrwr, Recognizance, Red1 D Oon, RedWolf, Redtroll, Remember the dot, RememberSammyJankis, Reneeholle, Res2216firestar, Rettetast, RexNL, Rhopkins8, Rich Farmbrough, RichardF, RickK, Rmccue, Roadrunner, Robert4668, RobertG, Robertvan1, Robomanx, RockMFR, Rompe, Ronhjones, Ronkronk, Ronz, RossPatterson, Rrburke, Rrfayette, Ruch37, Rws591, Ryan Postlethwaite, Ryan Roos, RyanGerbil10, Ryguillian, Ryulong, S.K., SDC, SGBailey, SNIyer12, SQL, ST47, Sabariganesh, Saebjorn, Sam Korn, Samwb123, Sander Säde, Sango123, SasiSasi, Satori Son, Savidan, Sbrentegani, Scalkin, Scandum, SchuminWeb, Schweiwikist, Scohoust, Sean William, Securityadvisor, Seedat, Septagram, Seraphim, Sesshomaru, Seth Ilys, Sh4rk4tt4ck, Shanimoshe, Shantavira, Sharon08tam, Shii, Shirik, Shot, Shotwell, Siebrand, Simetrical, SimonD, Sionus, Sjh, Sjjupadhyay, Sjmtlewy, Skeejay, Skizzik, Sky Attacker, Sligocki, Sliker Hawk, Slovakia, Snarl, Someguy1221, Someone else, Sonjaaa, SpNeo, Spam kj, Speer320, Spitfire19, Splarka, SpuriousQ, Ssolbergj, Staeiou, Staticfree, Stbalbach, Stephan Leeds, Stephenb, Steven Weston, Steven Zhang, Stirling Newberry, Sue Anne, Suffusion of Yellow, Sugarbeartrio, Sundar, Sunkorg, Superm401, Supten, Surfingslovak, SusanLesch, Susokukan47, Susurrus, Swatje, SweetNeo85, Synthe, Syrthiss, T3chl0v3r, TMC, Ta bu shi da yu, Tangotango, TarkanAttila, TarmoK, Tarquin, Tbutzon, Tcncv, Technopat, Tellyaddict, Tempshill, TenOfAllTrades, Tfmb, That Guy, From That Show!, ThatWikiGuy, The Anome, The JPS, The Man in Question, The Rambling Man, The Random Editor, The Thing That Should Not Be, The sock that should not be, The sunder king, The wub, TheDevilOnLine, TheNoise, TheRhani, Theblackplague, Theraven, Thespian, Thingg, Thinktdub, Thomas For., Thrustinj, Thue, Thundercross16, Tide rolls, TimTomTom, Timbl, Timlane, Timmywimmy, Timrollpickering, Timwi, Tiptoety, Tiramisoo, Tomos, Torgo, Towel401, Tpbradbury, Trakesht, Travis99, Tregoweth, Trenchcoatjedi, Trialsanderrors, Troy 07, True Scaffold, Tsmith189, Ttwol101, TuukkaH, Twang, Twinsday, Tyciol, UBeR, UU, UberScienceNerd, Ukulele, Ulmanor, Ultimus, Uman, Unyoyega, Uriah923, Useight, Usergreatpower, Utcursch, VMS Mosaic, Verne Equinox, Versageek, Viajero, Vicoar, Virii, Vishnava, Vladkornea, VolatileChemical, Vycanis, Wacco, Waggers, Wanderingstan, Wang ty87916, Wangi, Wasssupman2000, Webmaven, Weevil, Weyes, Whazzit, Wikibofh, Wikid77, Wikidudeman, Wikieditor06, Wikimancer, Wildman7856, Willking1979, Wimt, Windharp, Wizofaus, Wknight94, Woohookitty, Wrinehart, Wsxx, Wtmitchell, Wwwwolf, XXBassmanXx, Xdenizen, Xezbeth, Xithen, Yacht, Yama, Yamla, YellowMonkey, Yemal, Yizhenwilliam, Yori, Yvesnimmo, Z3ugmatic, Zaf, Zealotgi, Zenohockey, Zhente, ZimZalaBim, Zondor, Zoney, Zundark, Zzuuzz, 1862 anonymous edits

E-mail *Source*: http://en.wikipedia.org/w/index.php?title=E-mail *Contributors*: 100110100, 16@r, 194.236.5.xxx, 228086, 2D, A More Perfect Onion, A purple wikiuser, Abkovalenko, AdSR, Adw2000, Aesopos, Aff123a, Agather, Agent2693, Ahoerstemeier, AlainV, Alan Liefting, Alanpratt05, Alansohn, Ale2006, AlexWaelde, Alexius08, Alexjohnc3, Aliza250, Allynnc, Amire80, Anastrophe, Andareed, Andrejj, Andrzej P. Wozniak, Andyiou52, Andylkl, Angela, Ann Stouter, Anna Lincoln, Anomalocaris, Antoine854, AntonioMartin, Anwar saadat, Arakunem, ArchonMagnus, Arjuno3, Armando49, Art LaPella, Asdasd12324, Aspandphp, Bachrach44, Badcop666, Baiji, Barefootguru, Barry26, Bayle Shanks, Bearly541, Beesman, Beland, Belugaperson, Benwildeboer, Bettia, Bhadani, Bhobbit, Big Bird, Bigbluefish, Bigderom, Biggity, Birdman1, Bkil, Blitzinteractive, Blue520, Bluemask, Bnorrie, Bob98133, Bobzayton489, Bomac, Bonadea, Bongwarrior, Boothy443, Boyhampus, Bubba hotep, Buckinghampalace101, Butros, C'est moi, C+C, C777, Caesura, Cafeduke, Calliopejen1, Callmejosh, Caltas, Calvin 1998, CambridgeBayWeather, Cameforu, Can't sleep, clown will eat me, Canaima, Canihaveacookie, Canterbury Tail, CapitalR, CapitalSasha, Capricorn42, CaptainCat, CardinalDan, CattleGirl, Causa sui, Cboy676, Ccacsmss, CellMan0677, CesarB, Cfp, Charles Gaudette, Chato, Chivasboi345, Chmod007, Chowbok, Chris G, Chrislk02, Chrismaster1, Christopher Parham, Chuq, Ckatz, Classfun, Classicfilms, ClaudineChionh, Closedmouth, Cometstyles, Comm 212 8, Commander, Comodo, Compo, Computerjoe, Conan, Conversion script, CoolChris99, Corti, Crackerwashere, CrazyInSane, Crazyperson324, Credema, Crismas, Ctjf83, Cutechar, Cyanoa Crylate, Cybercobra, D. Recorder, DRosenbach, DXRAW, Da monster under your bed, Da.skitz, Dalesgay, Dan D. Ric, Dangerousdanman, Daniel C. Boyer, Daniel Quinlan, Danorton, Darac, Darkride, Darth Panda, Dave souza, Davecrocker, DavidCary, DavidWBrooks, Davidcannon, Davidx2, Dawn Bard, Dawnseeker2000, Dean, December21st2012Freak, Demitsu, DerHexer, Derek Ross, Dhaun, Dhoom4, Digitalme, Discospinster, Dmccreary, Doc marseille, Domitori, Dr.s.t.ruggling, DragonHawk, Dreadstar, Dreammixtr, Drilnoth, Drini, Drj, DropDeadGorgias, Drumsac, Duncan Keith, Durcar86, Dwo, DylanW, Dysprosia, Dzordzm, Długosz, ESkog, Eaefremov, EatMyShortz, Eclecticology, Ed Poor, Edgerck, El pobre Pedro, ElKevbo, Eliezer Aharon, Ellywa, Emailexperiencecouncil, Emily GABLE, Emmy.rose, Emperorbma, EncMstr, Enviroboy, Epbr123, Erdal Ronahi, Eric-Wester, ErikWarmelink, EscapingLife, Etacar11, Etz Haim, Everyking, Ewlyahoocom, Faisal.akeel, Farawayfrom, FastLizard4, Fatbroker, FayssalF, Fearless Son, Feedmecereal, Fieldday-sunday, Fisc, Fl, Fleminra, Flockmeal, Fnlayson, Foodlol123, FrancoGG, Frecklefoot, Fredrik, Frehley, FreplySpang, Frodet, Fubar Obfusco, Furrykef, Fuzzie, Galaxy250, Galoubet, Garkbit, Gary King, Gdr, Gejigeji, Ghemachandar, Gianfranco, Giftlite, Gilliam, Giseburt, Gogo Dodo, Gollobt, Graham87, Green caterpillar, Gribeco, Grosscha, Grumpyyoungman01, Gsklee, Guppy, Gurch, Guy Harris, Guybrush, Gzkn, Hadal, Hanoman, Hans Carlos Hofmann, Hardyplants, Harej, Harris7, Harryboyles, HeikoEvermann, Heinzi.at, Hello32020, Heron, Hew, HexaChord, Hilgers08, Hobomason, Hoplon, Hu12, Hullbr3ach, Hymek, IRP, Ibizr, Icairns, Icewedge, Iflynet, Ignacioerrico, Ilmari Karonen, Ilya-108, Imran, Inkington, Insanephantom, Inspector 34, Intgr, Ioapetraka, Iridescent, Irishguy, Itai, Ivan Pozdeev, J-Star, J.delanoy, JForget, JLaTondre, JRM, JTN, Jackzhp, Jaizanuar, Jan eissfeldt, JayJasper, Jddphd, Jdforrester, Jebba, Jeff G., Jer10 95, JeremyA, Jesse Viviano, Jfdwolff, Jfire, Jiddisch, Jj137, Jjl33, Jlandis, Jmundo, Jnc, Jnk, Jnothman, Jodi.a.schneider, JodyB, John Covert, John a s, JohnOwens, Jomunro, Jon Harald Søby, JonHarder, Joseph Solis in Australia, Josh the Nerd, Joshhirstwood, Joy, Jredmond, Ju66l3r, JuJube, Juliancolton, Jumbuck, Jusdafax, Jusjih, KC., KF, KPH2293, KPWM Spotter, Ka-Ping Yee, Kafuffle, Kaliumfredrik, Karcamp, Kaszeta, Katalaveno, Kazikameuk, Kbrose, Keilana, Kiamde, Kingpin13, Kingturtle, Kjkolb, Klykken, KnowledgeBased, KnowledgeOfSelf, Koenige, Kooljay253, Kowey, Krushdiva, Kuru, Kwshaw1, LC, LX, La Parka Your Car, LaFoiblesse, Lacrimosus, LarryQ, Last Avenue, Lathama, Leandrod, Lee Daniel Crocker, LeighvsOptimvsMaximvs, Lerdsuwa, Levineps, Liamob1993, Liftarn, Lightdarkness, Lilac Soul, Lineface, Lisabelleg, Llykstw, Llywrch, Lomonline, Longhair,

Lordmac, Louie Franco, Lucasik, Lucky 6.9, Luckylive, Lunboks, Lupo, MER-C, MFH, MIT Trekkie, MWelchUK, Mabdul, Mac, Magnus Manske, Maheshkale, Majorly, Makro, Mani1, Manticore, Maralia, Marcus Brute, Mark, MarkGallagher, MarkSweep, Martaw22, Masaruemoto, Mattbr, Matteh, Mboverload, MccowattMAS229, Mcr314, Mdwyer, Meand, Meekywiki, Meelar, MelcomRSA, Mendors, Mentifisto, Merry Devil, Mets501, Mhackmer, Michaelbusch, Midnightcomm, Mifter, Mike Payne, Mike Rosoft, Mikker, Minghong, Mm40, Mogglewump, Monkey Bounce, Moondyne, Motor, Mozillar, MrPrada, Mrlee321, Mschel, Msikma, Msrafiq, Mtlk, Mu, Mwalimu59, Mxn, Mystical504, NHRHS2010, Nabeth, Nanshu, Naohiro19, NatusRoma, NawlinWiki, Nealmcb, Nebula17, Nehtefa, Nelson50, Nemo, Neon white, Neurolysis, Neustradamus, NewEnglandYankee, Newportm, Nick, Nick C, Nick Garvey, NickdelaG, Nickptar, NigelR, Nightscream, Nikai, Nikola Smolenski, Nilfanion, Niqueco, Nivix, Njál, No barometer of intelligence, Nol888, Not telling, Notsocoolkid, Novasource, Nsaum75, Nubiatech, Numbo3, Nuttycoconut, Nxu009, Nzseries1, Ohadgliksman, Ohnoitsjamie, Ojw, OlEnglish, Olgerd, Oliphaunt, Oliver Pereira, Oliver202, Olivier, OlivierM, Ombudsman, Omegatron, Omegium, Omicronpersei8, Omniplex, OneWeirdDude, Orayzio, Oxymoron83, P.L.A.R., PCHS-NJROTC, Param0r33, Parmesan, Pat80, Patrick, PatrickFlaherty, Paul August, Paul Stansifer, Paul-L, Pax85, Pd THOR, PengiFergie, Pernoctus, Peschomd, Pfahlstrom, PhJ, Phantomsteve, Pharaoh of the Wizards, Phatom87, Phgao, PiMaster3, Piano non troppo, PierreAbbat, PinchasC, Pinotgris, Pipedreamergrey, Plasticup, Plugwash, Pomte, Poor Yorick, Porkchop28, Prof Wrong, Programarium, Prowikipedians, Prozac1980, Pseudomonas, Qaqaq, Qxz, RCVenkat, RJaguar3, Rajeevtco, RandalSchwartz, Randallrobinstine, Raphel M. Markez, Raryel, Rasmus Faber, Rbpickup, Rcannon100, Rdsmith4, Red Sunset, Refsworldlee, Remi Arntzen, Retodon8, Rettetast, RexNL, Reyk, Rhsatrhs, Rich Farmbrough, Richard Arthur Norton (1958-), Richi, Rick Block, Rjwilmsi, Roedelius, Rohasnagpal, Roland45, Rory096, RoyBoy, Rrburke, Rubicon, Rulesdoc, Runningeek, Ryan Roos, Ryulong, SCGC, SMC89, Safedoctor, Sam Blacketer, Sam Hocevar, Sam Staton, Samtheboy, Sander Säde, Sander123, Sandstein, Sarasvathi, SasiSasi, Sbluen, ScottyWZ, Sd324, Sean 1996, Sentausa, Serpent-A, Sexdemon89, Shadow1, Shadowjams, Shaior, Shanes, Sheehan, Sheliak, Shotwell, Sidhekin, Sietse Snel, Silas S. Brown, Silvery, SimonD, Sina, Sionus, Sir Nicholas de Mimsy-Porpington, Sirping, Skarebo, SkerHawx, Skomorokh, Skpatel20, SkyWalker, Skyezx, Skylerfatfacewrwe, Skyscrap27, Slady, Slakr, Sleske, Slowking Man, Smalljim, Smit, Smokyjohnpipe, Smpwiki, Smtc123, Snori, Snowflake7, Snowmanradio, Snoyes, Solipsist, Someoneinmyheadbutit'snotme, Sorsoup, Spaceman85, Spoirier, Spookfish, Spork the Great, Sroeben, Srpnor, Startvtk, SteinbDJ, Stephen Gilbert, Stephenb, SteveSims, Steven Zhang, Stevietheman, Stirling Newberry, Stolen Account 1, Strait, Stratocracy, Stwalkerster, Styrofoam1994, Superm401, Supermennn, SusanLesch, SystemBuilder, Syvanen, TGNobby, THEN WHO WAS PHONE?, TNLNYC, Taargus taargus 1, Tabletop, Tad Lincoln, TakuyaMurata, Tasc, Taw, TeaDrinker, Terence, TerriersFan, The Anome, The Epopt, The Thing That Should Not Be, The Wild Falcon, The wub, Thebigmc2, Thehornet, Thingg, Thomas H. Larsen, Thue, Thuja, Thumperward, Thunderboltz, Thunderwing, Tide rolls, TigerShark, Tikiwont, Tim Ivorson, Timir Saxa, Todd Gallagher, Trevor mendham, Trnj2000, UkPaolo, Ukexpat, Uncle G, Unforgettableid, Unfree, UnicornTapestry, Unschool, Uriah923, Useight, Vaikulepak, VasilievVV, Veinor, Versageek, Vinnivince, Viskonsas, WadeSimMiser, Wafulz, Warren, Wavelength, Weregerbil, Wes!, Wfeidt, Who, WikHead, Wiki alf, Wikid77, Wikieditor1988, Wikilibrarian, WikipedianMarlith, WillV, WilliamRoper, Wimt, Wj32, Wmahan, Wolfkeeper, Wolfmankurd, Woods229, Wrs1864, Xdenizen, Xp54321, Xwildfire316x, Yahel Guhan, Yama, Yekrats, Yonatan, Ysangkok, Yuva raju raj, Yzmo, Zanimum, Zer0faults, Zip123, Zivha, Zoe, Zointer, Zondor, Zouavman Le Zouave, Zundark, Zzuuzz, Саша Стефановић, محبوب عالم, सुभाष राउत, ლევანი, 1405 anonymous edits

Internet *Source*: http://en.wikipedia.org/w/index.php?title=Internet *Contributors*: -Majestic-, 000o, 0waldo, 12.235.7.xxx, 16@r, 199.196.144.xxx, 2dogs, 3idiot, 424242, 75th Trombone, 802geek, A. B., ABCD, AJR, AaronKaplan, Abbos, Abrooke, Accurizer, Acdx, Acprisip, Acroterion, Adashiel, Administration, Adw2000, Aervanath, Agather, Agathoclea, Ageekgal, Ageing Geek, AgentPeppermint, Ahmad halawani, Ahoerstemeier, Ahruman, Aitias, Akamad, AlMac, Aladdin Sane, AlanBarrett, Alansohn, Aldie, AlefZet, Alem800, Alexf, AlexiusHoratius, Alexwcovington, Alias Flood, AlistairMcMillan, All Is One, Allr0und, Allyoursanity, Alphachimp, Altzinn, Alvestrand, Alyeska, Am088, Ambrose Brightside, AmiDaniel, Amillar, Amire80, Amitesh3011, AndonicO, Andre Engels, Andre3k1, Andres, Andrevan, Andrew Kelly, AndrewHowse, Andreworkney, Andrewpmk, Andris, AndyBQ, Andyiou52345, Andypandy.UK, Anetode, AngelOfSadness, Angela, Angr, Animum, Ankiththegreat, Ann Stouter, Annexia, Anonymasity, Anonymous Dissident, Anonymous anonymous, Anonymous editor, AnotherDeadPerson, Antandrus, Anthony, Anthony Appleyard, Antimatter15, Antonrojo, Antony, joseph, Aphilo, Aranel, Arekku`xx, Arfan, ArielGold, Arienh4, Arsenal0328, Art LaPella, Aruton, Arx Fortis, Asdfghty, Ashenai, Asmo86, AstroHurricane001, Astroview120mm, Atgthatsme, Atomic23112, Atropos, Aujlakam, Auroranorth, Autocracy, Avalean, Aviaris, Avochelm, Avraham, Avuton, Awolf002, AxelBoldt, Az1568, Azkar, AznShortBoi8021, B9 hummingbird hovering, BK08, BWD, Babyface123, Bad Bud, Bambuway, Bandan, Bandj, Barberio, Barefootguru, Barneca, Bart133, Bayerischermann, Baylink, Bband11th, Bbao, Bbatsell, Beland, Ben D., Bennettchipper, Bentonmas214, Berk, Berro9, Bethenco, Bevo, Bhuvanneshsat, Biederman, Big Brother 1984, Bigbrotha3, Bigtimepeace, Bigwig77, Billlion, Bimach, Biruitorul, Bisqwit, Bitbit, Bjb, Blahma, Blake-, Blcarson, Blightsoot, Bloodshedder, Blossom the Awesome, Blowdart, BlueAg09, Bluemask, Bluemoose, Bob A, Bob f it, Bobblewik, Bobet, Bobo192, Bodnotbod, Bogdangiusca, Bonadea, Bongwarrior, Bookh, Bookuser, Bordello, Borislav, BossOfTheGame, Brandmeister, Brandork, Bratsche, Breakmoved, Brendan Moody, Breno, Brezzo, Briaboru, Brian0918, BrianRecchia, Brianga, BrokenSegue, Bryan Derksen, Burner0718, Bushytails, Bwaav, C'est moi, CF90, CIreland, CJLL Wright, CLW, CMW275, CWY2190, Cahk, Calliopejen1, Callipides, Caltas, Cam809, CambridgeBayWeather, CameronHarris, Cameronmas214, Camw, Can't sleep, clown will eat me, Canadian-Bacon, Canaima, Captain Disdain, Carbonite, CaribDigita, Carlsotr, Carmen.banea, Casper2k3, Cbaxter1, Cdc, Cdxnolan, Ceas webmaster, Cenarium, Centered1, Central2, Centrx, CesarB, Ceyockey, Cferrero, Cgeorge316, Chabby, Chalybs, Chanting Fox, Charles7, Charlesblack, Charlesincharge, Chcknwnm, Chensiyuan, Cheung1303, ChewT, Chime Shinsen, Chmod007, Choalbaton, Chocolateboy, Chodorkovskiy, Chotisornmas214, Chris 73, Chris21192, Christian List, Christopherlin, Chroniclev, Chun-hian, Chunky Rice, Cimon Avaro, Cirt, Citicat, Classicfilms, ClockworkSoul, Clothed so hardsm, CloudNine, Clpo13, CobraWiki, Cocklip, Codus, Coelacan, Collin, CommodoreAngryy, CommonsDelinker, Complex, Computageek95, Computerjoe, Conversion script, Coolcaesar, CopperMurdoch, Corrupt one, Cortalux, Cotoco, Couchpotato99, Cpom, Crazycomputers, Cremepuff222, Curps, Cyan, Cybaxter, Cybercobra, Cyberevil, Cyberitis, Cyclopia, Cynical, Cyp01, D. Recorder, DJ Clayworth, DVD R W, Daemon8666, Damian Yerrick, Dan larsen, Dana60Cummins, Daniel, Daniel5127, Danny, Danscool, Danski14, Darius Bacon, Darrendeng, DarthVader, Daveb, Daveg, David.Monniaux, DavidJGW, Davodd, Dbeilhartz, Dchall1, DeadEyeArrow, Deedub1983, Deflagro, Dekisugi, Delirium, Delldot, Den fjättrade ankan, DerHexer, Dess, Dethme0w, Devonreilly, Dforest, Dicklyon, Diderot, Didimos, DigitalSorcerer, Digresser, Dijxtra, Diletante, Dillard421, Dinardi, Dinestysfaith, Dinosaur puppy, DirkvdM, Discharger12, Discospinster, Diverock, Djegan, Djjkxbox, Djr xi, Dlohcierekim, Dnas, Doc glasgow, Dodecki, Domstabsdogs, Dooky, Dorftrottel, Dorgan65, Dotancohen, DoubleBlue, Dpiccuirro, Dr Debug, Dr Zen, Dr. Blofeld, Dr.K., Drappel, Drat, Dreadstar, Dream Focus, DreamGuy, Drew thomas amirault, Drew46, Driftwoodzebulin, Drini, Drivera90, Drn8, DropDeadGorgias, Drosera, Drunkenmonkey, Dryice2ooo, Drzoidberg, Dtcdthingy, Dusso Janladde, Dust Filter, Dvc214, Dwheeler, Dylan Lake, DylanW, E. Sn0 =31337=, EKN, ESkog, EVula, Eaaiscool, EagleOne, EamonnPKeane, Ebaur5, Echuck215, Ederjar, Editmachine, Edonovan, Edwina Storie, Edwy, Eirik (usurped), Ekjon Lok, ElBenevolente, Elcobbola, Eleassar777, Elmidmibbs, Elonka, Eloquence, Eltonhoyantam, Emijrp, Enchantian, Enerccio, Entirety, Entrpy, EoGuy, Epidown, Eran of Arcadia, Eric outdoors, Erik9, Erikringmar, Eriktoto, EronMain, Erzengel, EthanNeuen, Eurosong, Euryalus, EventHorizon, Evercat, Everyking, Evil Monkey, Evil saltine, EvilZak, Evilphoenix, Excelsior f, Excirial, Exeunt, Expert at this, Expertu, Eybaybay, Eyu100, Fab, Fabricationary, Fadookie, FaerieInGrey, Fan-1967, Fantasy, Faseidman, FelixtheMagnificent, Fennec, Filelakeshoe, Firetrap9254, Fishal, Flowerpotman, Flubberdubbe, Fluppy, Flyingember, Foboy, Folajimi, Foodmarket, Fortethefourthversion, Fountain09, FrancoGG, Frap, Frazzydee, Freakofnurture, Fredbauder, Fredrik, Freewayeric, FreplySpang, Freshacconci, Freshbakedpie, Freyr, Frigglinn, Fujifisher, Fulldecent, FundieBuster, Funky Monkey, Fuzheado, Fvw, G0dsweed, GDonato, GHe, GMR5, GUllman, Gadfium, Galwhaa, Gamahucheur, Gamefreek76, Gamer007, Gannzor, Gantster, Gardar Rurak, Garfield 80, Garfield226, Gary King, Gblxyz, Geape, Geekmax, GeorgeTheCar, Gianfranco, Giftlite, Gimmeurm0ney, Gingaspice, Gioto, Glenn, Gluttenus, Gnoluyr, Gobonobo, Goeagles4321, Goel madhur, Gogo Dodo, Golbez, Golfballock, Goobergunch, Good Olfactory, GoodStuff, Goodnewsfortheinsane, Goodnightmush, Goplat, Gppande, Gracenotes, GraemeL, Grafen, Graham87, Grandpafootsoldier, Grassmaker, Graue, GreatLiver, Greatflyingsock, Green caterpillar, GregAsche, GregNorc, Grenavitar, Grich, Grison, Gronky, Grunt, Gscshoyru, Gsklee, Gsociology, Gtrmp, Guade00, Guaka, Guanaco, Gurch, Gurchzilla, Guthrie, Guy M, Guy Peters, Gwernol, Gwylim a, H3llbringer, HJV, HackerOnSteroids69, Hadal, Hadrians, Haemo, Haham hanuka, Hairy Dude, Handface, HappyCamper, HappyInGeneral, Hardcoregayslaveman, HardwareBob, HarryMcDeath, Harrystown, Haukurth, Hawaiian717, Hazr0x, Hdt83, Hegiiman, Heimstern, Hekxcieksdl, Helios Entity 2, Helix84, Henry Flower, Hephaestos, Herdrick, Heron, Hetar, Hhhhgoteam, Hhhhhh, HiB2Bornot2B, Hiddenfromview, Hiii98, Hirschtick3, HisSpaceResearch, HistoryStudent113, Hm2k, Hobbit fingers, Hrvatska, HulleGranz, Hunter-Ing, Hydrajr, Hyperthermia, I Am Not Willy On Wheels, I amm Beowulf!, ICTlogist, INVERTED, IRelayer, IamYossarian, Iceflamephoenix, Icewindfiresnow, Iconoclast, Ida Shaw, Igoldste, Ihope127, Ilmari Karonen, Imacg3, Imthesmartdude, InShaneee, Incnis Mrsi, Indon, Inkypaws, Insiriusdenial, Interflop, Intgr, Intiendes, Into The Fray, Invincible Ninja, Iridescent, Irish Souffle, Irrelivant, Irtrav, Irvingbird, Isomega, Isotope23, Istiamar, Italianboy931, Ixfd64, Izwalito, J.J., J.delanoy, J.puckett, JHunterJ, JIMBO WALES, JLaTondre, JMJimmy, JRod451, Jacek Kendysz, Jack slack, Jacobko, Jacoplane, Jacotto, Jade wezel, Jaffo Gonzales, Jag123, Jahiegel, Jake Nelson, Jamesontai, Jamott, Jaqen, Jaranda, JaredInsanity, Jaxl, Jay-d123, JayEsJay, Jayan13, Jazzilla, Jdforrester, Jecowa, Jeffthejiff, Jeltz, Jeph paul, JeremyMcCracken, Jersey Devil, Jerzy, JesseGarrett, JesseW, Jfire, Jflash, Jgeer, Jigesh, Jimbo D. Wales, Jivadent, Jiy, Jj137, Jkasd, Jkh.gr, Jklin, Jleedev, Jmchuff, Jmundo, Jnavas, Jnc, JoanneB, JodyB, Joeblakesley, Joeikin, Joel delahunty, Joelscorp, John, John Fader, Johnleemk, Johnny-5, Johnnysfish, Jojit fb, Joke321, Jolt76, JonHarder, Jonathan P. Chen, Jonathunder, Jonnabuz, Jonny, Jons63, Jooler, Jops, Jorvik, Jose77, Joseph Solis in Australia, JoshG, JoshuaZ, Jossi, Joy, Joycloete, Joyous!, Jp5508, Jpbowen, Jpgordon, Jreferee, Jschwa1, Jsheehy, Jskleckner, Jsnruf, Jsoffer, Jtkiefer, JuJube, Juansidious, Julie Deanna, Jumborulz, Junie dilitori, Junipercwc, Juro, Jusjih, JustJoe, JustPhil, Justin Eiler, Justin.purvis, Justin050190, Justin5117, Justinwiki324, Jwinius, Jworld2, Jwrosenzweig, K00LKid, KMcD, KYPark, Kabads, Kablammo, Kaihsu, Kaobear, Karen Johnson, Karimarie, Kariteh, Karl Meier, Karstimmer, Katalaveno, KatherineTurnbull, KathrynLybarger, Kbdank71, Kbh3rd, Kbrose, Keilana, KeithTyler, Kelly Martin, Kemkem, KenFehling, Kencf0618, Kenmcfa, Kenny sh, Kenyon, Kernow, Keryst, Kesaloma, Kevin Breitenstein, Kevin66, Kevkoch5, Khanlarian, Khefri, Kiba, KidAirbag, Kidutsu, Kieff, KieranL, KillaDilla, KillerCRS, Kilo-Lima, Kim Bruning, Kinema, King Lopez, King of Hearts, Kingbob2, Kinghy, Kinneyboy90, Kirils, Klenje, Klingoncowboy4, Kmg90, KnightLago, KnowBuddy, Knowledge Seeker, KnowledgeOfSelf, Knows lots, Knutux, Koavf, Kostas.karachalios, Koyaanis Qatsi, Kozuch, KrakatoaKatie, Kramden4700, Krapface, Krawi, Krich, KrisW6, Kubigula, Kuka369, Kukini, Kungfuadam, Kupojsin, Kuru, Kwekubo, Kwirky88, Kznf, LOL, LOLPEAR, LPedroMachado, Laboobala, Lahiru k, Lakefall, Lcarscad, Lee Daniel Crocker, Lee J Haywood, LeilaniLad, Leithp, Lemmio, Lemonflash, Lennartgoosens, Lenoxus, Leonidasthespartan, Levineps, Liddlerebel, Lightdarkness, Lightmouse, Lights, Ligulem, Lilac Soul, Link 991, Linkspamremover, Linnell, Linux Rocks, Little Mountain 5, Little guru, Littleduty2, Livajo, Locatelli, Logan.aggregate, Logan590, Lol at Lilo, Longcatislooooooooooooong, Loodog, Loonymonkey, Lousyd, Lowellian, Lradrama, Luckycatfu, Luis Dantas, Lumaga, Luna Santin, Lupo, Luxurius, M.nelson, M8al, MCBastos, MER-C, MIT Trekkie, MKoltnow, MMuzammils, MODS=FAIL, MONGO, MacMed, Macs, Madmax vii, Mafioosnik, Majorly, Makemebad, Makemi, Maksdo, Malcolm, Mallocks, Malnourish, Malo, Malunis T, Man vyi, Manchurian candidate, MangaFreak0, Mangy Cheshire Cat, Manop, MansonP, Manywindows, Mapper76, Marc Mongenet, MarcRS, Marcin Suwalczan, Marcschulz, Marcusvtos, Marianocecowski, Mark Elliott, Marklar689, Marnanel, Marshallharsh, Marskell, Martinkunev, Martysanders, Marymary, Matt Britt, Matteh, Matthewccna, Mattworld, Maurice Carbonaro, Maurreen, Mav, Max Naylor, Max Schwarz, MaxD, Maxamegalon2000, Maxim, Maximillion Pegasus, Maximus Rex, Maxtremus, Mcmillin24, Mdd, Mditto, MeBee, Meekywiki, Meelar, Meneth, Mentifisto, Merbabu, Mercurywoodrose, Merope, Mgoerner, Michael Hardy, Michael Podgorski, MichaelBillington, Michaelhaslip, Midway, Miffy900, Mike Cherim, Mike Christie, Mike Rosoft, Mike hayes, Mike.lifeguard, MikeWren, Mikeblas, Mikefzhu, Mikker, Millifoo, Millisits, MindlessXD, Mindmatrix, Minesweeper, Minghong, Mini-Geek, Mintguy, Miranda, Mirror Vax, MisfitToys, Missionary, Missy Prissy, Misza13, Mitchumch, Mithent, Mjb, Mlewis000, Mmeri, Mmx1, Moarmudkipzlulz, Modelun88, Modster, Modulatum, Moe Epsilon, Moe kuwait, Moink, Monkeyman, Monkeyman393, Monsier Pie, Montrealais, MoogleEXE, Moonriddengirl, Moreschi, Morganp7, Mr Adequate, Mr pand, Mr. Billion, Mr. Lefty, Mr.Z-man, Mr.happy, MrSnow, Mrcharliexcore, Mrguythefourth, Mristroph, Mschel, Muad, Muchness, Mulad, Mulder416, Muraad kahn, Murali nmv, Mushroom, Musicmaniac15, Mvelicko, Mwilso24, Mxn, MysteryDog, N-true, NCDS, NHRHS2010, NPhoenix, Nakon, Nanshu, Natalie Erin, Natalina smpf,

Article Sources and Contributors

Nathan8225, Nathanrdotcom, Navigatr85, NawlinWiki, NeilN, Neilc, Neonstarlight, Nessdude14, Netizen, Network master, Neutrality, NewEnglandYankee, Newmanbe, Nick125, NickD310, NigelR, Nigelj, Nikk32, Nintendude, Nitishg, NitroOx, Niubrad, Nivix, Nixeagle, Nohat, Noisy, NorthernThunder, Northgrove, Not Zilla3, NrDg, Numbo3, Nurg, Nuttycoconut, Nuutti, Nyceco, OFX, Oakesy, Obarskyr, Obradovic Goran, Octopus-Hands, Oda Mari, Oden, Ohnoitsjamie, Olavandreas, Old Guard, Oldrock666, Olgerd, Oli Filth, Oliver Lineham, Oliverdl, Oliverisyourdaddy, Omghgomg, Omicronpersei8, Ominousguardian, Omniplex, Onevalefan, Oni Ookami Alfador, Oogadabaga, Opelio, Operator tore, OracleGD, Orangemike, Orangutan, Orbitalwow, Orbst, OregonD00d, Oreo Priest, Orphic, Ostaph7, OwenX, Oxymoron83, P0lyglut, PARA19, PCHS-NJROTC, Pagw, Pakaran, Paladinwannabe2, Palica, Paranoid, Parhamr, Parkinn, Patrick, Patrick-br, PatrickFisher, Pchov, Pearle, Pedro, Pegasus1138, Percy Snoodle, PerpetualSX, Persian Poet Gal, Perspectoff, Peruvianllama, Petchboo, Peteark, Peter, Peter Campbell, Peter S., PeterSymonds, Pgk, Pguerra, Ph.D.Nikki, Ph1r35p4wn, PhJ, Phaedriel, PhilHibbs, Philip Trueman, PhilipO, Phillejay, Phil, Pianokid54, Picaroon, Piercetheorganist, Pigsonthewing, PileOnades, Pilotguy, Pinaki ghosh, Piotrus, Piuneer, PizzaMan (usurped), Pjvpjv, Pkoppenb, Plek, Plrk, Plumbago, Pmsyyz, Poeloq, Pointer1, Politik426, Pomte, Poor Yorick, PopeMas214, Popedawg, Populus, Porqin, Poser-xox, Poweroid, Ppk01, Pratyeka, President Rhapsody, PrestonH, Prestonmcconkie, Primate, PrimroseGuy, Prodego, Promodulus, Proofreader, Psy guy, Psychcf, Public Menace, Publicly Visible, Puchiko, PureLogic, Puremind, Purgatory Fubar, Pxma, Quadell, Quendus, Quintessent, Quintote, Qwqrty, Qxz, R Pollack, RJII, RWolf, RadiantRay, RadiantSeabass, RadicalBender, Ragib, Rajah, Ral315, RanchoRosco, Rasmasyean, Rasmus Faber, Ratiocinate, RattleMan, Rattlesnake, Raudys, Raul654, Ravensfan5252, Rawmessalphy, Raydomingo, Rharreira, Rcannon100, Rdmoore6, Rdsmith4, Readro, Reaper X, Reaverdrop, Rebent, Rebroad, RedWolf, Redvers, Redwolf24, Reedy, Regibox, Reisio, Relly Komaruzaman, Remember the dot, Renaissance Man, Resslerdylan, Rettetast, RexNL, ReyBrujo, Reymysterio01, Rfl, Rflorenc, Rhobite, Riana, Rich Farmbrough, Richard Weil, RichardF, Richemond, Rick Block, RickK, Riguy, Rinothan2, Rjwilmsi, Rklawton, Robchurch, Robomaeyhem, RockMFR, Rockhall, Rockinduck, Ronz, Ronz91, Roozbeh, Rory096, RossPatterson, RoyBoy, Roybadami, Rp, Rpgprog, Rrburke, Rsabbatini, Rscash22, RucasHost, Rud Hud Hudibras, Rumping, RunOrDie, RunningBon, Ruud Koot, RxS, Ryan, Ryan Postlethwaite, Ryt, Ryulong, S M Woodall, SEOXpert, SJP, SNIyer12, SSZ, ST47, STA654, Saga City, Saghar2, Sam Ii, Samir, Samj72, Samsara, Samuel Curtis, Sandahl, Saposcat, Sarenne, SasiSasi, Satori Son, Savantpol, Savidan, Sawdon2, Saxmaniac777, Scepia, Sceptre, Schneelocke, Schoolproject2, SchulteMAS214, Schzmo, Sciurine, Scott981992, Scottbell, Scrolls, Scurra, Sdornan, Seav, Sega381, Seinfreak37, Serpent-A, Seth Hs, Seth662, Severa, Sfmammamia, Shadanan, Shade11sayshello, Shadowlynk, Shady Hippo, Shane3x, ShaneCavanaugh, Shanes, Shangrilaista, Shantavira, Shantu123, Sharprs, ShaunES, Shawry00, Shebaboy102, Shengii, Shenme, Shervink, Shii, Shimgray, Shoeofdeath, Sidepocket, SignorSimon, Siliconov, Simetrical, SimonP, SimonShlosberg, Sinn, Sinnerwiki, Sir Nicholas de Mimsy-Porpington, Sirexo, Sjakkalle, Sjjupadhyay, Skb8721, SkyWalker, Skyhupervat, SI, SI021, Slakr, Slark, Slayerteez, Skepyasthesouth, Sloud74, Slowking Man, Sm8900, Smalljim, Sman24, Smeira, Smilesfozwood, Smokizzy, Smoothy, Snoom hapluh, SnowFire, Snoyes, Solipsist, Solitude, Solphusion, Spedwehavedisabilaty, Speedysam, Spellcast, Spellmaster, Spencer, Spick And Span, SpigotMap, Splarka, Spliffy, SpookyMulder, SpuriousQ, SpyMagician, Spyke411, SqueakBox, Squiquifox, Srice13, Srnelson, Sstrader, St tth, Stagefrog2, Staile, Stardust8212, Starnestommy, Stateguy, Steel, Steinberger, Stephan Leeds, Stephen, Stephen B Streater, Stephen Shaw, Stephenb, Stephenchou0722, Stereotek, Steverapaport, Stevey7788, Stevietheman, Sthow, Stickguy, Stirling Newberry, Stormy Waters, Stratocracy, Striver, Student17, Stwalkerster, Subsumilamguy, Syvanen, THEODORMAS214, THEemu, TI85, Taimaster, TakuyaMurata, Tale, TangoFett, Tangotango, Tannin, Tapir Terrific, Tarret, Taskmaster99, Teamcoltra, Tech2blog, Technician2, Technobadger, Tehmechapope, TekeeTakShak, Tenpin477, Terence, Terrx, Texture, Tfcollective, Thatdog, The Anome, The Flying Purple Hippo, The JPS, The Thing That Should Not Be, The Transhumanist (AWB), The teller of all 666, The undertow, The-secret-asian-man, TheIpato, TheDoctor10, TheFloppyOne, TheJosh, TheKMan, TheLeopard, TheObtuseAngleOfDoom, TheRhani, TheStick, Thedjatclubrock, Theguns, Thehelpfulone, Themightyone, Thewallowmaker, Thingg, Thiseye, Thparkth, Thryduulf, Thue, Tiddly Tom, Tiggerjay, Tim Chambers, TimMartin, Timir Saxa, Timkneft, Tiptoety, Tiramiseo, Titoxd, Tkeller, Tktktk, Tkynerd, Tmh, Tobias Bergemann, Tobias Wolter, Tocino, Tokyogirl119, Tomatoe, Tommstein, Tomsega, Tony1, TonyClarke, TonySt, TonyTheTiger, Toolingu, Tothwolf, Tovias, Traroth, Trashday03, TreasuryTag, Tregoweth, Trekkie711, Trevor MacInnis, Trollminator, Tronno, Trusilver, Tsavage, Tuuuuuuudes, Tverbeek, Tylermillersucks, Tzhourdeka, Tznkai, UBeR, URBOSAUR, Uberdude85, UniQue tree, Untame Zerg, Unyoyega, UpTheBracket, Urhixidur, UrsaLinguaBWD, Vidgmchtr, VigilancePrime, Vignaux, Vilerage, Violetriga, Viriditas, Vjlenin, Vocation44, Voice of All, Voyagerfan5761, Voyajer, Vulcanstar6, W1k13rh3nry, WIkiHorseMan, WJBscribe, West Brom 4ever, West wikipedia, Weyes, Whale plane, Where, Whiney, WhisperToMe, Whosh, Wiggleintatter, Wiki Edit 12, Wiki alf, WikiWikiMan, Wikibob, Wikidogia, Wikigreatest, Wompa99, Wonderstruck, Woodshed, Wordsmith, Wossi, Wrs1864, Wutasumi, Www06, X!, XJamRastafire, Xagent86, Xaosflux, Xavier86, Xaxafrad, Xeddy, Xeo-Wizzard, Xeysz, Xezbeth, Yet-another-user, YixilTesiphon, Yonatan, Yosri, You must have cookies enabled to log in to Wikipedia., YourEyesOnly, Ytmnd6, Zachary, ZakTek, Zavon25, Zeno McDohl, ZerD, Zerak-Tul, Zeroinbarnotation, Zhente, Zib redlektab, Zidane tribal, ZimZalaBim, Zizzybaluba, Zombi333, Zondor, Zsinj, Zundark, Zungaphile, Zzuuzz, Zzyzx11, ^demon, Ô, على الله, 3030 anonymous edits

Hilary1123, Hokeman, Howardjacobson, Howcheng, Hughdbrown, Indon, Ingolfson, Inwind, Iridescent, Irishkid, Istartfires, JOSamsung, JamieS93, Jbinder, Jgera5, Jj137, Jkeiser, Jmabel, Joelr31, John Gohde, Joseph Solis in Australia, Jrleighton, JuJube, Juan2x, Jusdafax, Jyarmey, Ke4roh, Kencf0618, Kidynomite, King Butter Turtle, Kingturtle, Korath, Kurieeto, LAX, LFaraone, Lambiam, Larno Man, Laudaka, Lawrence Cohen, Lemon-s, Leonard Outdoor, Lexor, LittleOldMe, Lode (Germany), Lomn, Longhair, Lop239, Lord Emsworth, LorenzoB, Lupin, MC MasterChef, Mani1, Marskell, Matt Crypto, Maurreen, Mav, Maximus Rex, Mbb1184, Mediaexpert, Meelar, Melos Antropon, Melsaran, MeltBanana, Midnightcomm, MightyAtom, Mlmcvinney, Mobilemaster, Mosca, Moto239, Mpeduto, Mshonle, Mulad, Mwanner, Mydogategodshat, Myke2020, Mütze, New World Man, Newpemberly, Nikai, Norm, Not home, NotFromUtrecht, Oblivious, Ohnoitsjamie, Oicumayberight, Oom Agent, Ortegajenkins, Otolemur crassicaudatus, Outdoor guy, OutdooradTime, Outofhomebillboard, Pasd, Patstuart, Paul Erik, Pekinduck, Peter Ellis, Picapica, Plutor, Poshua, Quiddity, Rachel's T-Shirt, RadioKirk, Radon210, Random832, RandomP, Raul654, RedWolf, Remag Kee, Rhobite, Rigadoun, Rjwilmsi, Rmhermen, Roadshaer, RobertG, SPUI, Sable232, SandyGeorgia, Sanguinity, Savethemooses, Scott Burley, Scottk, Sekicho, Serenata, Seth Ilys, Sfreitas, Simoes, SimonP, Sinuhe, Smjc, Snoyes, SoccerD, Sohal 25, Somebody in the WWW, Squids and Chips, Stepa, StudyWiz, Stupid Corn, Susurrus, Swift, Taestell, Taikos, Tarabella, Taxee, Template namespace initialisation script, TheProject, Thinking of England, Tillman, Timulthyus, Tony Sidaway, TonyTheTiger, Tooto, Trounce, Turkishbob, Tyrenius, Vegaswikian, Vegetator, Verne Equinox, Versageek, Violetriga, Vossanova, Vraya, Wavelength, Wmahan, Woohookitty, Yahel Guhan, Yintan, Yinyang042, Ymendel, Yoshih9, Zepheus, Zfowler12, Zumbo, Zzuuzz, 297 anonymous edits

Marketing communications *Source*: http://en.wikipedia.org/w/index.php?title=Marketing_communications *Contributors*: A. B., Adraeus, Andyjsmith, Atauder, Babrinton, Bdubois, Boson, Can't sleep, clown will eat me, Caravaca, Chris j wood, ContBur, Dbielawa, Dpr, Ehheh, Eskim5, Feraya, GTBacchus, Gabriel.zhou, Gilliam, Goldenrowley, GraemeL, Graham87, Gscshoyru, Itcousin, Jbuddle, John, Juristiltins, KnightRider, Liface, Maurreen, Mindmatrix, MrOllie, Mydogategodshat, OMathelot, Ojaars, PRNWilkinson, Plinkit, Plomion, Ppsassociates, Rardell, Sarper, Spinacia, Spitfire, Swtechwr, Texasbbq, Tizio, Unclefeet, Woohookitty, Woz2, Zeebah360, 47 anonymous edits

Website *Source*: http://en.wikipedia.org/w/index.php?title=Website *Contributors*: (jarbarf), *drew, 07murphyj, 0kdal, 119, 12dstring, 16@r, 1locs, 208.60.198.xxx, 21655, 23skidoo, 24cx, 64.34.161.xxx, 7sharks, ABF, Abce2, Academic Challenger, Adam Zivner, Adcaito, AdeMiami, AdjustShift, Adolphus79, Aeons, Afsar Khan, Ageekgal, Ahoerstemeier, Aidarhaynes5, Aishisheep, Aiyda, Ajchen, Akaala, Akmalakapoola, Alansohn, Aldie, Aleenf1, Alexius08, Alexjohnc3, Alexreid2, AlistairMcMillan, Allaboutgq, Allhalofiles, Altenmann, Amitch, Amitsahab, Andmig, Andoceo, Andreeamanea, Andrejj, Andrew, Andycjp, Andyiou52345, Angela, Angr, Animalsanimals, Ansiansiansi, Appleseed, Apyule, Argon233, ArielGold, Arthurian Legend, Asbestos, Assasin23, Atif.t2, Atlantima, Avij, Avochelm, AyJay, Az1568, Azzer007, BYTEmeCITY, Bacchus87, Bagatelle, Barek, Baronnet, BarretBonden, Bcorr, Bdbbdb, Belovedfreak, BenFrantzDale, Bfigura, Bidabadi, Bigtop, Bjc461, Blanchardb, Blitzboy, Blowdart, Blue bear sd, Bobby-hobby, Bobet, Bobo192, Bogdangiusca, Bomac, Bonadea, Bongwarrior, Booyabazooka, Bosox95, Bpeh, Bradjamesbrown, Brandon, Brian0918, Brianga, Brianhe, Brumski, Brunocip, Bugfreeintruder, BuickCenturyDriver, CANUTELOOL3, CIreland, Caesura, Caknuck, Calabraxthis, CalendarWatcher, Calibr8, Caltas, CambridgeBayWeather, Camw, Can't sleep, clown will eat me, CanadianLinuxUser, Capricorn42, Cardamon, Causa sui, Cdbridgeman, Cenarium, Cendyn, Ceoil, CesarB, Ceyockey, Cflm001, Chaojoker, Charles Matthews, Chasindream, Chasingsol, CheeToS, ChidoV.E.K, Chocolateboy, ChrisLoosley, Chrishw, Cjewell, Ckatz, Cleanupman, Click23, Cody Cooper, Coffee, Cohesion, Colonies Chris, Cometstyles, Commander, Concrete angel, Condem, Contactaadi, Conversion script, Corti, Corvus cornix, Cpl Syx, CrazyRob926, Crazycomputers, Crazyfurf, Cristivivo, Cst17, Ctbolt, Cupflppr, Curtisannev, DKqwerty, DS1953, DXL, Da monster under your bed, Daitenchi, Daniel C. Boyer, DanielSwannie, Dave.Dunford, Davehi1, Davewho2, Davewild, David Eppstein, DavidWBrooks, Dawnseeker2000, Db099221, Dbabbitt, Dbzanime, Dealasite, Dekisugi, Delldot, DemiAndSese, Deon, Derik davidson, DevDev212, Devildog67, Dfrg.msc, Dgies, Dieselpham, DildDork, Dinmo, Discospinster, Djg2006, Dlae, DocWatson42, Dochar, Dodo48, DogFaceBoy, Dokareht, Donbert, DoubleBlue, Doulos Christos, Dr. Blofeld, Drbreznjev, Dread4600, Dreadstar, Dreamafter, Drewhamilton, Drini, Drwolffenstein, Dspradau, Dust Filter, Dylan620, DylanW, EALacey, Eagleal, Ed Poor, Edenrage, Edison, Edward321, Eeekster, Eequor, EhJJ, ElTyrant, Elassint, Eldadzakay, Elhector, Elipongo, Elisar39, EllenkampGuus, Emathew1, Emmanuel.keller, Emre D., Endroit, Enrico Dirac, Epbr123, Eric119, Erichvee, Erik Raven, ErinKM, Evercat, Everyguy, Evil saltine, Examtester, Eyashwant, Ezeu, Fabiform, Faithlessthewonderboy, Figgles49, Filemon, Finbarr Saunders, Finngall, Firetrap9254, Fnlayson, Foobaz, Forsfortis, Foxboy18, FreakFish, Frecklefoot, Fredrik, Freedomlinux, Frehley, FreplySpang, Fri ke, Friginator, Fussahvex, Fvw, Fyyer, GRRE, GTBacchus, Gail, Gaius Cornelius, Galaxiaad, Gen. von Klinkerhoffen, General Synopsis, Geoffr, Giftlite, Gogo Dodo, Goldieloxmn, Goobergunch, Gooddudemanbro, Gracenotes, GraemeL, Graham87, Gridlinked, Grm wnr, Grunt, Guinanie, Gunmetal Angel, Guppy, Gurch, Gwernol, Gzornenplatz, Halstonl, Hanvanthu, Happybird, Hardyplants, Harej, Hargurnaz, Hayabusa future, HelloImStorm, Heron, HexaChord, Hooverbag, Hotheelz, Hotsoccerchic12, Hp4023, Hsaqib, Hung3rd, Hydrargyrum, Hydrogen Iodide, Hyper flyin', II MusLiM HyBRiD II, IRP, Ida Shaw, Imad1987, Inclusivedisjunction, Infiniteshadow, Inkington, Intersection360, Ioanaki, Irene1949, Iridescent, Irishguy, Itisdesign, J.delanoy, J89sd kegh32\, JCCamp, JDoorjam, JHMM13, JW1805, JaGa, Jacek Kendysz, Jackrajiv, Jaericho, Jake Wartenberg, Jamesooders, Jamie Bunting, Janadore, Jareme, JarlaxleArtemis, Jasynnash2, Jay3216, Jaydawg3000, Jaymondo911, Jboeckman, Jeffrey Mall, Jeroen, Jerry, Jessicaaaaa, Jesss96, Jester1799, JetLover, Jh12, Jnc, Jnutting512, Joeblakesley, Joer80, Joerite, John254, JohnChrichton, JohnClarknew, JohnLai, Johnadonovan, Johnuniq, Jojhutton, Jojit fb, Jon186, Jose77, Joseph Solis in Australia, Josephfrancis, Jpsk69, Jredmond, Jtjacques, Jtnoonan90, JuJube, Julia Rossi, Jusdafax, Jusjih, Jweiss11, Jzcool, KJS77, KOMBA, Kabab, Kafziel, Kaidra3, Kakofonous, Kandar, Kateshortforbob, Katieh5584, Kazrak, Kbh3rd, Kbrose, Kcc039, Kehrbykid, Keilana, Kennii, Kerii57, Kevin Breitenstein, Kgfleischmann, KillerCRS, Killerdude555, Killiondude, Kimse, Kingpin13, Kjb14086, KnowBuddy, KnowledgeOfSelf, Kostisl, KramarDanIkabu, Krauss, Krawi, Kribbeh, Ktdreyer, Kukini, Kwekubo, Lajolla014dix, Lakinekaki, Laura, Lawrence King, LeaveSleaves, Lecath, Leenewton, LegitBud12, Leifs1, Lenehey, Leszek Jańczuk, LethalReflex, Levineps, Lindmere, Linkspamremover, Lir, Lisanola, Liveindia, LizardJr8, Loalhe, Loser6, Loul, Lowellian, Lozzalicious, Lradrama, Luboogers25, Lucyin, Luk, M.Imran, MBlue2020, MER-C, MK8, MacApple33, Madman, Maggie9416, Mahinda, Majorly, Maln1995, Manop, MansonP, Marek69, Marks27, Martin Jensen, Martin451, Martinurquhart, Martinwilke1980, Martpol, Martynas Patasius, Masiano, Matty2288, Matěj Grabovský, Maxim, Maximus Rex, Mayalld, McSly, Mdwh, Meaghan, Meisjake, Meldor, Melsaran, Meno25, Mermaid from the Baltic Sea, Merovingian, Metagraph, Metatheorem, Mets501, Mgunter93, Michael Shields, MightyWarrior, Mike R, Minderbinder, Mindmatrix, MindstormsKid, Minesweeper, Minghong, MisterCharlie, Misza13, Mmxx, Modulatum, Monkeyman, Moonwhisper, Morganeason, Motoxguy47, Mouats, Mr.Bauer WN, MrOllie, Mt devv, MuZemike, Mudaber, Mudaber123, Muffinmankk, Mushroom, Muthudesigner, Muthukumar32, MuzikJunky, Mwanner, Mxn, My Blogger, My7dream2002, NAHID, Nanshu, Nasimit, Naudefj, NawlinWiki, Nazrila, Nbpandya, NeilN, Neutrality, Nevaski, Neverquick, Nevst, Newkai, Newsaholic, Nickandgino, Nicksmi7h, Nightmarerich, Nis81, Nkayesmith, Noalslob, Nobull67, Non-dropframe, Nsaa, NuclearWarfare, NurAzije, Nuttycoconut, Off!, Ohnoitsjamie, Olorin28, Omello, Omicronpersei8, Orange gold, Osmanseo, Otolemur crassicaudatus, OverlordQ, Parakalo, Patelchetan9, Patoloco2142, Patrick, Patstuart, Pavel Vozenilek, Pb30, Peak, Pedro, Perfecto, Persian Poet Gal, Peruvianllama, PeterSymonds, Pgk, Phantomsteve, Phgao, PhilKnight, Pi, Pinkadelica, Piyush ujawane, Piyushkujawane, Pjdeshann1, Pjoef, Polly, Poweroid, Prari, Princess Clown, Proper Spelling, Protonk, Pxma, Qst, Quadra23, Que?, Quintote, RC-0722, RHaworth, Raelus, Rainman31, Rajeevtco, Rajesh Bagri, Ral315, RandomHumanoid, Rangs2009, Rantforeve, Ranveig, Rathee, Ravnatelj, Rbgij, Rdsmith4, Recognizance, RedSpruce, Redreth, Redrocket, Ṛedthoreau, Redvers, Reinhard Kraasch, Remember the dot, Rettetast, RexNL, Reywas92, RianC, Rich rowan, Richone, Ricobornia, Rjwilmsi, Rnb, Robert Skyhawk, Robocoder, Robosoldier, RockMFR, Rodii, Rohitgavai, Ronz, Ross Feldman, Rpongcojr, Rror, RunOrDie, Ryno502, Rzelnik, S.Örvarr.S, SCJohnson77, SDSandecki, SF007, SWAdair, Sabritextiles, Sajeevdas, Sam8, SamMichaels, Sammyho, Samohyl Jan, Sandblaster, Sandi 007, Sango123, Sangthebirds, Sanyasanya123, Sasha Slutsker, Saturn star, SaveThePoint, Saviiz, Sawran, Scarian, Sean Whitton, Serezniy, Sergeykozich, Shantavira, Sharkface217, ShelfSkewed, Shell Kinney, Shirik, Shirulashem, Shorty 274, Sigma 7, Signalhead, Silivrenion, SimonD, SimonP, Sinneed, Skidude9950, Skinnydude19, Sky Attacker, Slakr, Slowking Man, Smalljim, Snowolfd4, Snoyes, SoCalSuperEagle, Soler97, Somnium, Sonjaaa, South Bay, SpaceFlight89, SparrowsWing, SpikeToronto, SpuriousQ, Star1021Scott, Stephen B Streater, Stephen Gilbert, Stephenb, SteveLoughran, Stevefarwell, Stevietheman, Stewartadcock, Stillnotelf, Suisui, Sunlois, Sunnykapoor111, Sunsfan1797, Susaneh47, Svetovid, Synchronism, Synthesisworld, TEA14, Tabletoptuna, Tails123125, Tangotango, Tarekabosaif, Tarotcards, Tarquin, Tasc, TastyPoutine, Technolojik, Tedickey, Tenebrae, Terrillja, That Guy, From That Show!, Thatguyflint, The Epopt, The Rambling Man, The Thing That Should Not Be, The undertow, TheKMan, TheToiletFlusher, Thepulse2007, Thomas Blomberg, Thrustinj, Tide rolls, TigerShark, Tim1357, Tissot, Tobogganoggin, Tombomp, Toodiesel, Topboy, Topleveldomainuser53, Tosunny, Total Reptiles, Towel401, TreasuryTag, Trengarasu, Tresiden, TrickyM, Tsemii, TubularWorld, Tuggler, Tyler, UBeR, Uahygcfr Fordingham, Ultimus, Ump2152, Uncle Dick, Unisouth, UnitedStatesian, Untchbl, Unused0013, Useight, Usrnme h8er, Uyuyuy99, VI, Vcelloho, Vdavid23, VegitaU, Veinor, Ventusa, Versageek, Vic6318, Vietsmall, Violetriga, Wangi, Wavelength, Wavetravel, Wayfarer, Webcitypages, WereSpielChequers, WhisperToMe, Wiccan Quagga, WikHead, Wiki alf, Wiki006, Wikidemon, William Pietri, Willking1979, Wimt, WinterSpw, Wirbelwind, Wj32, Wm, WojPob, Wolf grey, Wolfsteritory, Woohookitty, Wsanders, Wwtex, Xeysz, Xyzzy288, Xyzzyplugh, Y0u, Yekrats, Yidisheryid, Yogesh111, Youjustgotdeleted, Yurik, Z3n0s, ZX81, Zaqaz, Zondor, Ztyler90, Zvar, Zzuuzz, రవిచందర్, 1508 anonymous edits

PageRank *Source*: http://en.wikipedia.org/w/index.php?title=PageRank *Contributors*: -Midorihana-, 133u, 2008UEFA, 345Kai, A. B., AKA MBG, ALargeElk, Aapo Laitinen, Aaronhill, Academic Challenger, Adambro, Afluent Rider, Ageekgal, Alabalababayaga, Alerante, Alexwg, Alma Pater, Alnokta, Alon, Aminto, Amitkn, Ams80, Anandnadaar, Andreas Kaufmann, Andrei Stroe, Appraiser, Areldyb, ArmadilloFromHell, Arvindn, Asafe, Asgsoft, Audaciter, Aude, Ausref, Avsa, AxelBoldt, Banus, Barek, Bbatsell, Beetstra, Beland, Biars, Bill Slawski, Binjiangwiki, BlaiseFEgan, Blase40, BlueYellowRed, Bobmutch, Bonadea, Booles, Brat32, Brockert, Bruce404, Bryan Derksen, Bugkai, CWii, Camster342, Can't sleep, clown will eat me, Canadian Monkey, Capricorn42, Carmitsp, Casey Abell, Chato, Clausen, Cody.feilding.nz, Collonell, Cometstyles, Commander, CommonsDelinker, Computerjoe, Conversion script, Cumbrowski, D.scain.farenzena, Damian Yerrick, Dan D. Ric, DanKeshet, Daniel.Cardenas, Dave Runger, David Eppstein, DavidWBrooks, Davidpairey, DeadEyeArrow, Deathphoenix, Deror avi, Dimator, Dimitar petrov, Dirkbb, Discospinster, Dispenser, Doc z, Dorward, Doulos Christos, DrQuincy, Ds825, Dspradau, Durova, Dwo, Dysprosia, ESkog, Earth, Ecopetition, Edward, Efe, Efitu, Efren, Elangokp, ElizabethFong, Emile Barker, Engunneer, Ento, Er.punit, Erin Lox, Esteban Zissou, Esthr, Eugman, Euryalus, Evenmadderjon, Evil saltine, FML, Fattyjwoods, Fmccown, Foot, Fran Rogers, FrummerThanThou, Furrykef, Fvw, Gaius Cornelius, Galwhaa, Gamkiller, Gangaz, Gargaj, Gary King, Garyzx, Gennaro Prota, George124, Giftlite, Gingerginger, Gnix, Gomm, Gpanterov, GraemeL, Greatlijo, Greyabernethy, Gurchzilla, Gurubrahma, Guruweb, Gwernol, Haakon, Hadal, HaeB, Hankwang, Haosusays, Harald Hansen, Harej, Hayabusa future, Helix84, Hgranqvist, Hopelessless, HorsePunchKid, Hu12, Hubsauthorities, Husond, Iapetus, Ibjhb, Ibnuasad, Ikescs, IngSoc BigBrother, Inky, J, J.delanoy, J04n, JGXenite, JLaTondre, JaGa, Jamesday, Jamie Mercer, Jarix, Jay Vravos, JeffMHoward, Jehochman, Jeremy Visser, Jimregan, Jmchuff, JoanneB, Johnbibby, JonathanBennaim, Jonyyb, Josang, JoshuaZ, Jpbowen, Jpgordon, Jsnow, Junkinbomb, Just Another Dan, Karnpatel18, Kbdank71, Kemrin, Kenniejyoung, Kesla, Khalid hassani, Kharri1073, KingsOfHearts, Knownot, Knudvaneeden, Korg, LaMenta3, Laura SIMMONS, Legoktm, Leif902, Lethe, Lightdarkness, LilHelpa, LinguistAtLarge, Linkexperts, Linkspamremover, Lisaedesign, LittleDan, Lizorkin, Lomonline, Lumingz, Luna Santin, MECU, MER-C, Macrakis, Macshiva, Madhero88, MansonP, MarkSweep, Martin Jensen, Matt Crypto, MaxVeers, Maximus Rex, Mentisock, Michael Hardy, Michael Martinez, Michaelas10, Mickeynguyen2107, Midgrid, Mido321, Mikeshaws, Mindmatrix, Mion, MissDanni, Misza13, Mqchen, Mr. Random, Ms2ger, MuZemike, MustafaeneS, Nabla, NathanHurst, Necenzurat, Nekroshorume, Neurolysis, NeuronExMachina, Nichtich, Nikaggar, Nochargebacks, Not a dog, Notheruser, Noveltysystems, NuclearWarfare, OSUKid7, Ohnoitsjamie, Oli Filth, Orderud, Ortolan88, Pagerank10, Panther.ru, Paps34c, Paragon12321, Parkerh, Pataya1, Patelmiteshb, Paul Matthews, Paulomi333, Pd THOR, Pde, Pedrito, Pellucidity, Penmachine, Pgluck, Phatalbert, Plrk, Pmc, Postcrypto, Poweroid, Prodego, Pruneau, Pseen, Pseudomonas, Psychonaut, Pxma, Quintote, Ram18y, Rasmus Faber, Rhraunwa, Redvers, Reinyday, Retodon8, RexNL, Rheun, Rhobite, Rhomboid, Rich Farmbrough, Rickington, Rjwilmsi, Robykiwi, Rotational, Royg73, Rsm99833, RubySS, Ruud Koot, SDSandecki, Sbluen, Schalling, Schneelocke, Schnolle, Scott McNay, ShAd0w N1nJa, Sharcho, Showdown, Shreevatsa, Shubhransu, Shuffdog, SideScape, Simon Lacoste-Julien, Singingwolfboy, SiobhanHansa, Sivasankar1984, Skittleys, SnappingTurtle,

Snoyes, Spiff666, SpuriousQ, SqueakBox, Stannered, Steeev, Steel, Steeven1, Stephen, Stevenj, Stochata, Stratocracy, Stringerace, StuffOfInterest, Subaru, SyntaxError55, TNeloms, Taa, Tangotango, Taw, Teoden44, TerriersFan, Tgr, The Anome, The Thing That Should Not Be, Theoklanarchist, Thingg, Thorpe, Thumperward, Thv, Tintinobelisk, Tobias Bergemann, Tom-, TomDubai, Toytoy, Tracy Hall, Travelbird, Tree Biting Conspiracy, Tregoweth, Trigger hurt, Trivialist, Triwbe, Turkingside, Uttaddmb, VINNIEs, Vary, Veinor, Versageek, Vogtadj, WODUP, WaldoJ, Wavelength, Webrescue, Whosasking, William M. Connolley, Willsmith, Wmahan, WouterBolsterlee, Wox2, Wrathchild, Wysprgr2005, X7q, Xevfgv123456, Xs08, Yboord028, Youandme, Zealotgi, ZeroOne, Zhoog, ZimZalaBim, Zizzybaluba, ZombieDance, Zzuuzz, 912 anonymous edits

Web search engine Source: http://en.wikipedia.org/w/index.php?title=Web_search_engine Contributors: 123b, 123c, 123f, 16@r, 7, A. B., Accl.news, Accurizer, Aep itah, Ajkovacs, Ajmint, Alan Liefting, Alansohn, Aliweb, Ambassador29, Andreas Kaufmann, Andrew Duffell, Andropod, Anspar, Anvilmedia, Aragor, Arctic Fox, Aseld, Athaenara, BIGGOOGIES, Badgernet, Banaticus, Bebo77, Beland, Benaya, Bender235, Bjelli, Blehfu, Blogger11, Bloxxy, Bobo192, Bonadea, Bsadowski1, Bugnot, Cacуninet, Caffeinejolt, Capone7722, Capricorn42, Captain-tucker, with a red beard, Credibly Witless, Crows1985, Cst17, Cut Bravo, DGG, DRogers, DSRH, DancingPhilosopher, Dawn Bard, Ddloe, Demarie, Dgiul, DiIlonpg1, Doxin45, Drmadskills, Drmies, ESkog, EdJohnston, Edward Elric 1308, Elipongo, Elkman, Enigmaman, Epipkin, Espoo, Fences and windows, Fmccown, Foogus, Foreigner82, Francis Irving, Frap, Fzamith, G-Yenn123, Gail, Gemirates, Ggallucci, Ggrefen, Gihangamos, Ginadavis, GoHuskies9904, Gogo Dodo, GrantGD, Gregman2, Gurch, HFadeel, HPJoker, Haakon, Heavyweight Gamer, Hillwilliam6, Hkreiger, Hoverfish, Hu12, Hydrogen Iodide, INkubusse, Indian2493, Inetmonster, Insanity Incarnate, J.delanoy, JForget, JNW, Jamesontai, JavierMC, JeanCaffou, Jfroelich, Jiddisch, Jingle bigballs, John Vandenberg, Johnuniq, Jose Gervasio, Jozef.kutej, Jreconomy, K-ray913, K4m1y4, Katr67, Kazastankas, Kc03, Kendalfong, Ketsuekigata, Kiranoush, Kiransarv99, Klutzy, Kmmhasan, Kuru, Kvasilev, Leevanjackson, Legaleagle86, Leuko, Levineps, Likmo123, Llamafirst, Loderuner, Lsolan, Ltkmerlini, Luv len, MBisanz, Mac, Macrakis, Makemi, Mandarax, Mangaman27, Martin451, Mathiaslylo, Mattgirling, Mattnneloson, Maximus2000, Mbelaunde, McSly, Meemore, MercZ, Mhha, Midgrid, Mitu10520, Mlo0352, MoeenKhurshid, Moeenkhurshids, Mooglesearch, MrOllie, Mstrehlke, Nadeem12345, Nainawalli, NawlinWiki, Ndenison, Nenya17, Nono-1966, Nubicsearch, NuclearWarfare, Nurasko, Nurg, Ohnoitsjamie, Ooyyo, Oscar.nierstrasz, PLA y Grande Covián, PakRise, Phantomsteve, Philip Trueman, PhoenixLightInc, Piano non troppo, Plenderj, Poeloq, Possum, Prari, PseudoOne, Puchiko, RW Marloe, Rathee, Ray3055, RazorXX8, Regisbates, Res2216firestar, Richard31415, Ronhjones, Ronz, Rosariomorgan, Rz1115, SDSandecki, SF007, Samdutton, Sampi, Sceptre, Schwarzenneger, Scurless, SnowFire, Srinivas, Steele, Stephenb, Steve.bassey, StuffOfInterest, StuffyProf, SuperHamster, Suzukiboy04, TastyPoutine, Tencv, Tedickey, Think outside the box, Thinktdub, Thomas humphrey12, Thunderbird2, Toussaint, Versageek, Vicenarian, Voyagerfan5761, Waldir, Wikiolap, Wikipedia314, Wizardist, Wmartin08, XDaniX, Xcohen, Xiaoshuang, Xin0427, Xlxfjh, Xmarkmanx, Yamaha07, Yegg13, Yerpo, Yoursvivek, ZeeknayTzfat, ZimZalaBim, Zzuuzz, फ्रेम फ्रेम, 493 anonymous edits

Search engine optimization Source: http://en.wikipedia.org/w/index.php?title=Search_engine_optimization Contributors: 1-555-confide, 1searchking, 8harleydog, A. B., ACDJ, ALargeElk, Aajvcad, Aapo Laitinen, Academic Challenger, Acidburn24m, Aff123a, Ageekgal, Agentbleu, Ahmansoor, Ahoerstemeier, Aiseo, Aitias, Akamad, Alanpog, Alansohn, AlexandiaGrahamBell, Alexius08, Alfio, Alias Flood, Allister MacLeod, Allstarecho, AlphaShroom, Alphaseo, Aman.bahl, Ambulnick, Ameliorate!, Amir Hussein Latifi, Ams80, Anchoress, Andres, Andrew Hampe, Andrewlp1991, AndyKeith, Angela, Angelusc, Angr, AnimeGod, AnonEMouse, Antandrus, Aomarks, Apm expert, Arltomem, Arteworks, Aryavartjewelry1, As847618, Asbestos, Asiftahir, Askild, Athaenara, Avinash.avala, Avtar2006, Aymerkez, Aynom, Bagdad-bob, Balddog, Bass fishing physicist, Bastardk, Batmanand, Beanstalk, Beego2008, Beetstra, Benblackwell, Benhood, Bepcyc, Bevo, Bill Slawski, Bill.albing, Billu999, Billy the Impaler, Billystut, Biot, BizWebCoach, Bjhanifin, Blogger11, Bloodshedder, Boated idea s, Bobby9101, Bonadea, Bongwarrior, Borgx, Bovfb, Braders17, Bradhenry, Brandt Luke Zorn, Brian Kendig, Brianhalacy, Bruce404, Businessjohn, Bvlax2005, Bücherwürmlein, C777, Caesura, Calebschmidt, Calmer Waters, Caltas, CharlotteWebb, Chicago god, Chintu1992, Chochopk, Chocolateboy, Chovy, Chris 73, Chrisk02, Circeus, Citicat, Cka zug, Ckatz, Clasione, Clbass1, Clearwriter, Cleverclick, CliffC, Closedmouth, CloudNine, Coccyx Bloccyx, Coetzeen, Collonell, Cometstyles, Cosmic Latte, Cpl Hicks, CrazyAboutTech, Cretog8, Crithit5000, CrizCraig, Cruddy, Crystalfina, Cumbrowski, Da Dcoetzee, Deathphoenix, Debjitbiswas, Dekisugi, DerHexer, Deramisan, Derek Andrews, DevastatorIIC, Developer2005, Devilzadvokat, Dexteritymedia, Dhaliwal, Diberri, Digitalme, Dimitar a, Dspradau, Dudi Scraba, Duilen, Dunemaire, Dynamicseo, Earthlyreason, Edokter, Edvf1000r, Edward, Eeekster, Eequor, El C, Elcobbola, Eleland, Emre D., Enhanz, Enkrates, Enuffrain26, Epbr123, Eran of Arcadia, Estesce, Ethan01, Euphoricweb, EurekaLott, Euvinlam, Eve1213, FCYTravis, Fahadumer, FatalError, Fc liam, Felyza, Ferdiaob, Fireman biff, Flandidlydanders, FIcelloguy, Fmccown, Foober, Frost110, FrostBoost, Fubar Obfusco, Furrykef, Futurix, Fuzheado, Fuzzie, Fvw, G18industries, Gaius Cornelius, Gallerysites, Gautammarwaha, GeoFan49, Getafreeseo, Gfhlite, Giggy, Gladstein, Glen, Globalinflatables, Globalmarketexposure, GlobeGores, Globefrog, Gmazeroff, Gogo Dodo, Gpridor, GraemeL, Graham87, Graphitesmoothie, Great Mans Job, Greyblogs, Grim-Gym, Gtl13, Guruweb, Gwernol, HVH, Haakon, Hackaback, Hadal, Hagene, HalfShadow, Hardyplants, Harrigan, Harrybias, Harryboyles, Iglew, Igorberger, Imaseo, Imasleepviking, Indiazseo, IndigoLeftRight, Infoserve, Inrv, Internasol, Inspector 34, Intacart, Inter, InternalStatic, Internetseo, Iowasmiles, Iridescent, IslandsTropicalMan, Israelbeach, ItBangladesh, Iwebwriter, Izno, J S Pannu, J.delanoy, JYi, Jaheal200, James.nichole, Jamesday, Jameshacksu, Janbellows, Janet.hightower, Jasfan971, Jason Jnbwebpromotion, Joer80, Joeychgo, John Fader, Jonathan Hall, Jonhenshaw, JordeeBec, Josh Parris, Jpgordon, Jukcoder, Julyo, JurgenG, Jushi, KD5TVI, Kaediem, Kamalchandran, Kardana, KnightRider, Knighty123, Korg, Kozuch, KrakatoaKatie, Krator, Krith23, Krnntp, Kuru, KyraVixen, LDVO30, Labnics, Lamatrice, Latinpafa, Laxminarayan108, LazyFox, Lazyjai, LeaveSleaves, Lev, Lightbulbs, Lightmouse, LinguistAtLarge, LinkKingCJ, Linkspamremover, Lior1075, LisaAndrew, LittleDan, Lkutaj, Lordmac, Lordthees, Luk, Lumingz, Luna Santin, Luwilt, M150565, MER-C, MK8, MKoltnow, Mackan, Mahahahaneapneap, Majorly, Malcolm Farmer, Managedspaces, MansonP, Maple626, Margareta, Markus Kuhn, Markworthen, Masoodsabir, Masteruser23, Mathsci, Mattisse, Mattonline, Max1900, MaxPowers, Mayankgates, Mbp, Md8834, Mdomengeaux, Meinhaj, Mentisock, Meow, Mets501, Micburnet, Michael Devore, Michael J Swassing, Michael Martinez, MichaelCrawford, Michaelbluejay, Mike22222, MikeCapone, Minghong, Misterseo, Mjlissner, Monkeyman, Mononomic, MonsieurLi, Moondyne, Moreschi, Morven, Motanel, MrOllie, Mrseo1, Mspraveen, Mushroom, Mwanner, Mythoughts2, NYCBrokerFREE, Nadine Peschl, NeilN, Nel03004, NellieBly, Northernhenge, Not a dog, Notheruser, Npowell, Nuclear696, Nvidura, Nyeguy, Obe1989, ObseloV, Octahedron80, Oda Mari, Oddity-, Oden, Ohnoitsjamie, Oicumayberight, Oiskas, Oli Filth, Pentagonsoft, Penworthy, Pepperpiggle, Perfecto, PeteWailes, Peter Chastain, PeterMottola, Petrosianii, Pharaoh of the Wizards, Phgao, Philip Trueman, PhilipO, Philwiki, Piano non troppo, Pigsonthewing, Pimlottc, Pjvpjv, Pmg2007, Pne, Pobrien, Poindexter Propellerhead, Polonium, PopularOutcast, Poweroid, Prakash Malayalam, Pravars, Priyankarules, Project mosaic, Projectphp, Pryzbilla, Purse9644, Pyrospirit, Pyrrhus16, Quadszilla, Quale38, Quisnmith, RJFJR, Raajj81, RadicalBender, RainbowKix, Radon210, Raelx, Ragib, Rahulv11, RainR, Rajkiran.singh, RexNL, Riasmaja77, Rich Farmbrough, Rich Janis, Rjwilmsi, Rmky87, Robert K S, RobertG, Robinh, RockMFR, Rockethot, Rodii, Rogdov, Ronsard, Ronz, Rouier, Roux-HG, Rray, Rrjanbiah, Rthrasher, Rtmyers, Ruhrfisch, Rumschlagm, Ryukong, S0crates9, S3000, SDSandecki, Sachinairan, Saddiqq, Saebjorn, Sagam1, Saisatha, Salamurai, SallyForth123, Sam, Sam Blacketer, Samorvil, Samuel horse, SandyGeorgia, Sarlancaster, Saroger, Scarian, SchuminWeb, Schwnj, SEbmarmallo, Seahorsy, Search Engine Optimization Basic, Search Engines Web, Search-Engines-Optimization, Searchbliss, Searchdoctor, Semexpertindia, Semnews, Semnews, Sengkang, Seoadr, Seocompany, Seoguy, Seolinks4u, Seopositions, Seotactics, Seotraf, Seowiki, Seowizz, Seoz87, Sepguy, Serps, Sesu Prime, Sfacets, Sgodion12, Shabda, Shadowjams, Shahrukh, Shandaman, Sharanyan, Sharewarepro, SheffieldSteel, Sheley, Sherwoodseo, Shierra, Sonny82, Sorcerak, Soonyasch, Sowmyaram1985, SpaceFlight89, Spartan-James, Spectre2473, SpuriousQ, Spyrit safe, SqueakBox, Srikanth8000, Smec, Ssipseki2, Stabz, Starlionblue, Stateful, Suhalbansal, Superbeecat, Supercoop, Supplements, Surania, Sushilover boy, Sutcliff, Sweetspicelife, Sycthos, SyedHasan.Mahmood82, Synlighet, TJLoop, TNLNYC, Tangotango, Tariqabjotu, Thivierr, Thizz, Thomasdk98, Thuresson, Tiddly Tom, TimBentley, Timl2k4, Timmim, TimothyDWagner, Timstaines, Titanske, TommyKiwi, Tomtraff, ToninMaep, Tony1, Tougar, Tqbf, Urlofus, Uriah923, Vary, Vedmanrya, Veinor, Verbal, Versageek, Versus22, Viagra, Viajero, Vicarious, Vijay1403, Vikasamrohi, Vinetrajput, ViperSnake151, Vipsem, Visor, Vistadivine.com, Vkstudios, Voyagerfan5761, WATP, Wabam, Wavelength, Web2mayhem1, Web4uckdesigns, Webhamd, Webyes, Whatley, Whomp, WikHead, Wiki navid, Wikien2009, Wikiindian123, William Avery, WilliamH, Willyboy104, Winchelsea, Wit, Wlk6568, Wmahan, Woohookitty, Wookipedian, Work permit, Wox2, Wrockca, Wuhwuzdat, Xaosflux, Xerocs, Xobxela, Xponse, Xxhopingtearsxx, Y.pramod, YAM, Yardandgarden, Ybbor, Yellow7, Yerpo, Yonidebest, Youngboy2003, Zacheos, Zefrog, Zigger, ZimZalaBim, Zntrip, Zojj, Zzuuzz, 1886 anonymous edits

Strategy Source: http://en.wikipedia.org/w/index.php?title=Strategy Contributors: Addshore, Aff123a, Ahoerstemeier, Alansohn, Alberta74, Allen Moore, Alynna Kasmira, Ancheta Wis, Andreas Kaufmann, Andrewpmk, AndriuZ, Antandrus, AntiWhilst, Apoctacharlask, Aree, Arjuna909, AshriAardvark, Avalin Aardvark, Avalon, Avmanzo, AxelBoldt, Boatearth, Bongwarrior, Borgx, Brick Davejblair, Doppelgangland, Dorit, Dreadstar, ElixirofLife, Elkadi, Elkadio1, EnSamulili, Enirac Sum, Exemplar sententia, Exeunt, Extar, Fbooth, Filos96, Firebird2k6, Freeklefoot, Frisco21, Jayhands, Jaysweet, Jeff3000, Jim62sch, Jkhanfer, Johnwaterman, Joong-gun14, KeithD, Kevyn, Khalid hassani, Kirill Lokshin, Kl4m, Krator, Kuru, Lachambre, Ladii Kiima, LeaveSleaves, Monishasarkar, Monkey Bounce, Mormegil, Mr. Billion, Muchness, Mydogategodshat, Namtiota, NawlinWiki, Old Moonraker, Omegapowers, Ooga Booga, Paradigm68, Passandid, PatrickFlaherty, Pearle, Prof 7, Prupito69, RHaworth, RN, Ralfipedia, Richard@fbrc.org, Richphil, Rinconsoleao, Rockfang, Ronz, Royote, S0crates9, Sandstein, Sjö, SmallHalkman, Smmurphy, Spitfire, Stefano, Stevenwagner, Stevertigo, SueHay, SummerWithMorons, SvenAERTS, Swaq, Szazmaniacs, The Rambling Man, TheGrza, Thseamon, Tide rolls, Timo Laine, Tobycat,

TreasuryTag, Trident13, Truman Burbank, Ulflarsen, Van helsing, Veinor, Versageek, VictorAnyakin, Vivek.raja22, West81, William Avery, Wortafad, WpZurp, Yerpo, Zhenqinli, Zyaar, Александр, 251 anonymous edits

Web page *Source*: http://en.wikipedia.org/w/index.php?title=Web_page *Contributors*: 16x9, ABF, AM346, Aboutmovies, Acaca1, Agendum, Ahoerstemeier, Alex43223, Amaraiel, Andre Engels, Andrejj, Andrevan, Angela, Antandrus, Antonio Lopez, Appraiser, Artie p, B4hand, BW, Babedacus, Babyburns, Berend de Boer, Bkonrad, Blackcanoflysol, Blindwaves, Bobblehead, Bomac, Bonadea, Brave37 Inmates Advocate, Bryan Derksen, CL, Cadaeib, CanadianLinuxUser, Capricorn42, Carl Caputo, Catgut, Cdc, Chamal N, Chicken Wing, Chinnceb, ChiragPatnaik, Chorltonmeateater, Claygate, Closedmouth, Coalcarbon, Conversion script, DMacks, DaCropduster, DanielSmith1840, Dark Lord of the Sith, Darrenhusted, DarthShrine, DaveTheRed, David Biddulph, Dbadman, Deadbarnacle, Den fjättrade ankan, DerHexer, Diberri, Discospinster, Dissident, Dlewis3, Dppowell, Dreadstar, Dreftymac, DylanW, Elfmage, Emre D., Epbr123, Eurleif, Evercat, Everyking, Excirial, Fan-1967, Ferat, Filemon, Fragglet, Fudoreaper, Funkiemunkey, Gaia Octavia Agrippa, Gail, Gardar Rurak, Gardenhoser!, Gioto, Gobozo, Gogo Dodo, Goobergunch, Gpanterov, Gökhan, HartzR, Hkpawn, ITurtle, Iamanerd2215, Iamtheari, IanBailey, ImageObserver, Iranway, Ithicar11, J.delanoy, J04n, JFreeman, JLaTondre, JRSP, JaGa, Janejellyroll, Japlay, Jhessela, Jimmy, Jni, Jojit fb, Jon chapman, JoseGonzalez66, Jusjih, Kateshortforbob, Kbdank71, Kiergray, KnowBuddy, Kraupu, Krauss, Kwekubo, LOL, LaMenta3, Larry wall, LeaveSleaves, Levineps, Lfh, Lhademmor, Lightdarkness, Lineface, Litefantastic, Loul, Luna Santin, MER-C, MacTed, MadDoc, Mark Renier, MarkHab, Maser Fletcher, Mboverload, Mdbest, Mditto, Meamemg, Mindmatrix, Minghong, Mrdj204, Mxn, Mzajac, Nanshu, NawlinWiki, Neutrality, Nigelj, NoPetrol, NuclearWarfare, Nufy8, OCNative, Octane, Ohnoitsjamie, Oicumayberight, Orioane, PapaWhitman, Patrick, Peruvianllama, Pi, Pip2andahalf, Porqin, Possum, Qirex, RJaguar3, Rajenderk, Rasmus Faber, Reisio, Remember the dot, RobJ1981, Robocoder, RockMFR, Ronz, Rrburke, Rror, Rzelnik, SMC, Sade, Scarian, Schapel, Schulte, Seth Ilys, Shades176, SkyWalker, Someone else 90, Sonjaaa, SpaceFlight89, Speck-Made, SqueakBox, Stan Shebs, Ste900R, Stephen B Streater, Steve Smith, Stevietheman, Suleyman Habeeb, Superwad, Swollib, TechPurism, Thatguyflint, The Giant Puffin, The Rambling Man, Thingg, Tinus, Tiuks, Tobogganoggin, Tslocum, UBeR, Umapathy, Unisouth, Untchbl, Unyoyega, Utcursch, Ventusa, Versageek, Versus22, Vishav0175, Vjanoschka, Wapcaplet, Webdesigningeasy, Webzero, Weyes, Wiki alf, WikipedianMarlith, Willking1979, Willsoncomputers, Wimt, Wizzerman2, Xelgen, Yamamoto Ichiro, Yarnalgo, Yonghokim, Zaharous, Zznuzz, Zzyzx11, Ævar Arnfjörð Bjarmason, 447 anonymous edits

Image Sources, Licenses and Contributors

LaVergne, TN USA
17 December 2010
209153LV00002B/153/P